ONE NATION, UNDER SURVEILLANCE

Privacy From The Watchful Eye

by

Boston T. Party

Published by

JAVELIN PRESS

(Without any 4 USC §§ 105-110 *"Federal area"* or *"State."*)

www.javelinpress.com

ACKNOWLEDGMENTS

I am very grateful to all my distributors and readers who so enthusiastically have supported my other eleven books. Thank you for the very satisfying career mission.

It has been my honor to serve you.

DEDICATION

I dedicate *One Nation, Under Surveillance* to the Liberty-strangling officials of our Federal Government and their hidden masters. Your actions are quickly awakening that sleeping giant — the American spirit — and for that, I thank you.

By all means, continue to *"sow the wind"* so that you may *"reap the whirlwind."* I realize that you scoff at any judgment for your actions because Americans are rubes. Good. I'm glad that you're haughty — please don't change.

I urge Congress, the President, the courts, and federal agents to *escalate your oppression*, so that America becomes *so* nauseous of tyranny that she finally vomits you out. You have much to accomplish soon, so get on with it. (*"A police state is the price we pay to enjoy a free country"*, eh?) The sooner Americans see you for what you are, the better.

You will soon overstep yourselves. Tyrants always do. You're confident that you've got it all worked out, that you see where Nero and Hitler and Stalin failed, that modern technology is unassailable. I'm delighted that you believe your "New World Order" plan to be infallible. It's not infallible — for either of two reasons.

❶ Popular resistance will defeat you, or . . .

❷ Even if you *do* get your NWO, you'll rot from boredom by having such utter control. The "fun" of tyranny isn't in *being* the conqueror, but in the *conquering itself.* (Just ask Alexander the Great.) Lose or "win" — *you've already lost.*

In the long run, you really aren't all that smart, are you?

by Boston T. Party (Kenneth W. Royce)

You & The Police! (revised for 2009!)

The definitive guide to your rights and tactics during police confrontations. When can you *refuse* to answer questions or consent to searches? Don't lose your liberty through ignorance! This 2009 edition covers the *USA PATRIOT Act* and much more.

168 pp. softcover (2009) $16 + $5 s&h (cash, please)

One Nation, Under Surveillance
Privacy From the Watchful Eye   (new for 2009!)

Explains precisely how to lay low from snoops of all types. Extremely thorough on computers, data, Internet, VoIP, digital gold, and prepaid cellphones. This is the huge replacement of his *Bulletproof Privacy*. Boston retired in 2009; this is his last title.

480 pp. softcover (2009) $27 + $7 s&h (cash, please)

Hologram of Liberty
The Constitution's Shocking Alliance
with Big Government

The Convention of 1787 was the most brilliant and subtle *coup d'état* in history. The nationalist framers *designed* a strong government, guaranteed through purposely ambiguous verbiage. Many readers say this is Boston's best book. A jaw-dropper.

262 pp. softcover (1997) $24 + $6 s&h (cash, please)

Boston on Surviving Y2K
And Other Lovely Disasters

Even though Y2K was Y2¿Qué? this title remains highly useful for all preparedness planning. **Now on sale for 50% off!** (It's the same book as The Military Book Club's *Surviving Doomsday*.)

352 pp. softcover (1998) only $11 + $6 s&h (cash, please)

Boston's Gun Bible (new text for 2009)

A rousing how-to/*why*-to on our modern gun ownership. Firearms are *"liberty's teeth"*. No other general gun book is more thorough or useful! Indispensable! Covers the *D.C v. Heller* case.

848 pp. softcover (2002-2009) $33 + $7 s&h (cash, please)

Molôn Labé! (a novel)

If you liked *Unintended Consequences* by John Ross and Ayn Rand's *Atlas Shrugged*, then Boston's novel will be a favorite. It dramatically outlines an innovative recipe for Liberty which could actually work! A thinking book for people of action; an action book for people of thought. It's getting people moving to Wyoming!

454 pp. softcover (2004) $27 + $7 s&h (cash, please)
limited edition hardcover $44 + $7 (while supplies last)

Safari Dreams (new for 2008)
A Practical Guide To Your Hunt In Africa

Possibly the most useful "one book" for making your first safari. Thoroughly covers: rifles, calibers, bullets, insurance, health, packing and planning, trip prep, airlines, choosing your PH, shot placement, and being in the bush. Don't go to Africa without it!

352 pp. softcover, 100 color photos (Jan 2008) $30 + $7

www.javelinpress.com
www.freestatewyoming.org

TABLE OF CONTENTS

Introduction by Boston T. Party

INTRODUCTION

Quotations are in this form. Any original emphasis is under-lined. **Any added emphasis of mine is in boldface.** *Omit-ted text is always replaced by ellipsis (. . .).*

When I supplement a quote, my nonitalicized comments are within ( ) or [ ] — (like this, for example).

MY GOAL FOR YOU

The modern socialist State is premised on this presupposi-tion: that all things belong to the State, but a portion of this State-owned capital is temporarily leased to private individu-als and organizations. This view of the State has influenced much of modern democratic theory.

The free-market-constitutional view of the State is that it is under legal restraints, that the citizen is the sovereign of the legal order, and that whatever authority which citizens have not formally delegated to the State belongs to them.

The battle over the rights of privacy should be seen in light of these two incompatible views of man and the State. *It is a battle over the definition of what constitutes criminal behavior.*

— Dr. Gary North; foreword to Mark Nestmann's *How To Achieve Personal and Financial Privacy In A Public Age*

What I *can* do for you is fill in the cracks between existing privacy books written by opportunists, dabblers, and some guy who once hid out in the 1950s Spanish mountains from Franco. I've used at least some variants of privacy measures since junior high school. My experience is real, current, and on-going as an active political dissident, author, and speaker for 20 years. There probably aren't many Americans (other than actual fugitives) who have lived privacy as much and for long as I have. In fact, I intentionally *overdid* my own privacy to learn how far you can take matters before they begin to work against you.

Because of the general nature of *One Nation, Under Surveillance*, I cannot very deeply discuss certain topics which deserve their own books, such as trusts and complex financial tactics. Some components are also highly dynamic given the changing technology (computers and the Internet) and legal climate. This book gives you a head start, but do stay up to date.

At the risk to some of my own privacy, I have decided to share much of this knowledge and experience with you. I can't divulge *all* of my tricks, but much is here to be of good value to you. There is a shockingly short half-life to this kind of information, so use it *quickly.*

"Why bother? There's no privacy any more!"

If that were true, then mega-corporations and governments wouldn't still be trying to collect more information about you, merge databases, increasingly track your movements, and plant RFID chips in everything. **They do this only because there still remains lots of available privacy.** If they've "won" already, then why do they continue to fight? The *"privacy's dead!"* argument is just a modern example of Sun Tzu's "defeat the enemy without fighting by convincing him that resistance is futile". We've not yet lost, but easily could:

> [T]*he* [Nazi] *revolution arrived not with a rush but covertly and, at times, even comically. There were no battles to fight, no bastilles to storm.* **Men and women fell into the arms of the new Reich like ripe fruit from a tree . . . .** [it] *was orderly and disciplined. But the reason lies not so much within the Nazis themselves as in the lack of an effective opposition . . . .* [M]*illions watched passively, not deeply committed to resistance.*
> — George Mosse, *The Nazi Culture*

Granted, the ID requirements and databases and cameras do make privacy more inconvenient and difficult, but real privacy can still be enjoyed if you work at it.

Perhaps we will one day have a society less larded by laziness, envy, greed and vociferous government. This won't be for quite a while. Much will have to occur before that's even remotely possible. Until then, keep your assets hidden and your principles cautiously visible. As they used to say in the Balkans, *"Tell the truth and run."* Run and hide so that you may speak the truth another day — *until backed into a corner.*

ONUS IS MY LAST BTP BOOK

. . . I am tired to death of caring deeply about matters over which I have no control. It is a waste of time, a waste of life and it quickly becomes boring. It may be the case that I cannot help caring but I can decide not to dwell upon miserable matters over which I have no influence.

. . . I guess I've concluded that the best way to make sure liberty recovers this time around is for me to stay healthy, keep writing, stay standing upright and to otherwise go about the business of living. That way, when liberty is ready to return, I'll be here to embrace and nudge it along.

— Wendy McElroy

www.wendymcelroy.com/news.php?extend.2259

After 20 years of my BTP writing career, I feel very strongly that *One Nation, Under Surveillance* is my last title. This "business" is consuming, and, if allowed, all-consuming. I will not allow that for me, and by now all this feels poised to become all-consuming if it continued for even a few more years. I've written (as BTP) all that I imagined I ever could, anyway.

In fact, I've come to believe that further absorption in these subjects will come to interfere with my ease of living a life unfettered of overly deep concerns about the Government, the economy, etc. I've "rowed my oar" long and hard, and it's time for me to sail other seas. Much of what I've written originally was for auto-diadactical satisfaction, with book sales financing each module of education if I thought my material was worthy of wider consideration. I've generally learned what I set out to learn, and have taught what I've set out to teach.

To be accurate, I'm not quitting but reducing drastically how much I think and write about what I have since 1989. I'll occasionally make my point with a new essay here and there, and in other books (for a more mainstream market).

ONUS was very difficult to muster up the energy to write. Even though I'd begun it in 2006, I had mentally retired by 2007, inclined to neither finish it nor write the sequel to *Molôn Labé!* However, I could not in good conscience leave you with my outdated 1997 *Bulletproof Privacy*. Not after the past 12 years of vast growth in computers, the Internet, VoIP, digital gold, and prepaid products — and laws meant to stifle privacy.

On those subjects I devote half of *ONUS* — more pages than in all of *Bulletproof Privacy*.

I am very pleased with the outcome, especially regarding all the computer topics. What I could not well cover I at least gave the right direction for your own Internet research. While I can almost guarantee no revision of *ONUS*, I will may have an addendum page (though very irregularly refreshed) on www.javelinpress.com for new privacy information and links. I should also do so for *Boston's Gun Bible* and *You & The Police!*, but do keep in mind that I am trying to retire from all this.

The truth of America's situation is by now clear enough to the moderately concerned. Nobody likely needs me to clarify anything anymore — not at this late stage. What we are facing is, in effect, an environmental issue regarding tyranny's pervasiveness. It's as though the toxic gas of oppression is everywhere. I'm tired of describing that gas. We cannot reduce the national toxicity; we've missed *that* bus. Obama's election proved that conclusively (as would have McCain's).

Don a gas mask, folks, and make your way to the West and Wyoming's fresher air. (Learn of like-minded folks of the FSW at www.freestatewyoming.org) Once there, fill your new lives with cooperation, friendship, love, joy, and accomplishment. This is what I am doing, after 20 years of writing to describe the toxic fumes. I now understand the socio/eco-political environment well enough to avoid it killing me. Beyond that, however, it's up to me to thereafter live a life.

Thank you all very much for supporting me and my books all this time. It's been a fascinating journey, and I've met the most amazing people along the way. I am deeply humbled and grateful that my work has had an impact on your lives.

> *It does not take a majority to prevail . . . but rather an irate, tireless minority, keen on setting brushfires of freedom in the minds of men.*
> — Samuel Adams

Continue to fight for what you know is right, and always remember: *We are the good guys!* We are making a difference!

Boston T. Party

Wyoming, Spring 2009

❖ 1

WHY PRIVACY?

Far from the madding crowd's ignoble strife.
— Thomas Gray

Here are the Top Six Reasons why individuals want to preserve their privacy:

    ❻   **high-pressure salesmen and "legal fraud"**
    ❺   **the increasing threat of burglary and violent crime**
    ❹   **divorce, family disputes, and lawsuits**
    ❸   **gossip and false information**
    ❷   **political, religious, and racial persecution**

And the Number One Reason?

oppressive government, high taxes, and war

[The] *"disappearing" of individuals is obviously discomforting to institutions and governments determined to control personal activities in the Land of the Free. To them it appears downright seditious, since in reality their power depends directly on the number of people they can control . . .*
— *100 Ways to Disappear and Live Free;* Eden Press, p. 3

To stop terrorism and organized crime, the American people must give up some of their personal freedom and privacy.
— Janet "For-The-Kids" Reno

Janet Reno asking us to give up *"some"* of our personal freedom and privacy is like a child molester asking a young girl to give up *"some"* of her virginity. (And this wasn't just Reno talking; all

AGs spout the same pap.) The federal camel is never satisfied with just his *nose* under the tent — he wants to climb in bed, too.

> *There are countless reasons why someone may need the reassurance of anonymity. The most obvious is as a protection against an over-bearing Government. Many people reside in countries where human rights are dubious and they need anonymity to raise public awareness and publish these abuses to the world at large.*
> *Privacy and anonymity are very important principles associated with both freedom of speech and democracy.*
> — www.privacy.li/security_faq.htm

To those who think there's no need for quality privacy — that I'm being wholly ridiculous — just stay home in your sheep pen and wait for the rude knock on your door when you at last bleat that the shearing is too close for comfort. By then, it'll be too late to do anything but sit still and take it.

LET ME SPELL IT OUT FOR YOU

> *The ultimate cause of evil lies in the interaction of two human factors: 1) normal human ignorance and weakness and 2) the existence and action of a statistically small (4-8% of the general population) but extremely active group of psychologically deviant individuals.* **The ignorance of the existence of such psychological differences is the first criterion of ponerogenesis.** *That is, such ignorance creates an opening whereby such individuals can act undetected.*
> *The presence of such "disease" on the individual level is described in the Almost Human section of this website. However, depending on the type of activity of psychopathic and characteropathic individuals,* **evil can manifest on any societal level.** *The greater the scope of the psychopath's influence, the greater harm done. Thus any group of humans can be infected or "ponerized" by their influence. From families, clubs, churches, businesses, and corporations, to entire nations. The most extreme form of such macrosocial evil is called "pathocracy".*
> — www.ponerology.com

In a real good lather, I originally wrote most of the following years ago, in 1997. I'm saddened by how accurate it still reads, but will keep it along with a few modern additions.

the "DemoPublican" party

The National parties and their presidential candidates, with the Eastern Establishment assiduously fostering the process behind the scenes, moved closer together and nearly met in the center with almost identical candidates and platforms, although the process was concealed as much as possible, by the revival of obsolescent or meaningless war cries and slogans (often going back to the Civil War). The argument that the two parties should represent opposed ideals and policies, one, perhaps, of the Right and the other of the Left, is a foolish idea acceptable only to the doctrinaire and academic thinkers. Instead, the two parties should be almost identical, so that the American people can throw the rascals out at any election without leading to any profound or extreme shifts in policy. Either party in office becomes in time corrupt, tired, unenterprising, and vigorless. Then it should be possible to replace it, every four years if necessary, by the other party, which will be none of these things but will still pursue, with new vigor, approximately the same basic policies.
    — Carroll Quigley, Council on Foreign Relations member, from his book *Tragedy & Hope* (1966), pp. 1247-1248

The secondary ponerogenic associations are **groups founded with an independent and attractive social ideal, but which later succumb to moral degeneration.** *This degeneration leaves an opening for "infection and activation of the pathological factors within, and later to a ponerization of the group as a whole, or often its fraction" (Lobaczewski, 160). Governments, ideologies, and religions are institutions founded by people whose lack of awareness of specific psychological realities and other moral failings leave them open to covert infection and subsequent take-over by those without conscience. The fact that these institutions have been in existence and have a long-standing tradition has allowed them to acquire a much greater membership and notoriety. When such an organization, working towards some social or political goal, is already accepted by a large number of normal people (e.g. American Republicanism or Evangelical*

Christianity), ponerization of the group provides the widespread influence that primary ponerogenic unions lack.
*After its takeover by psychopathic elements within (e.g. the Neoconservative takeover of American Republicanism), **the ponerogenic group is protected by a "mask" of the group's traditional values.** This will happen in spite of the fact that these values are obviously distorted and disregarded. For example, such a group will pass legislation and behave solely to benefit those in control, often becoming violent and starting wars of aggression. Normal members of such a group naively protect such deviant behavior, not realizing it is the work of deviants. **Its pathology remains hidden by those who do not wish to see it objectively.** Justifications and prepared ideologies are promulgated; subconscious selection and substitution take place, and the pathology is effectively cloaked behind a mask of sanity. Those who belong to "the party" will label the opposition as pacifists, socialists, liberals or terrorists, or whichever label is most effective in order to invalidate their criticism. Unfortunately the government will only become more pathological in its behavior and egotistical toward other nations until the deviant psychological aspects are either purged or destroy themselves.*
— www.ponerology.com

If your former Democratic or Republican party seems to have gone crazy, now you can understand why. Both mainstream parties have become "ponerized":

When [pathological] *individuals are treated as normal, more perceptive individuals will leave the group. When the group has become sufficiently pathological, [remaining] members will either perceive its new direction in moral terms (e.g., "We must kill them all on the principle of justice and democracy"), or as a form of psychological terror. As more healthy people leave the group, taking on more counter-revolutionary positions, individuals with psychological anomalies join, removing their masks of sanity ever more often.*
*. . . New members are psychologically screened. No one with too much independence or psychological normality is allowed in the group. (Such screening should have taken place to root out psychological deviants in the first place.) **Detractors are treated with paramoral condemnation. In short, the patients have overtaken the asylum.***

> *. . . The initial stage of ponerization, where membership is increasingly pathological, requires specific psychological and factual knowledge in order to recognize. The second, more stable and overtly pathological stage, is readily apparent to most normal people, but is interpreted in moral or sociological terms (i.e., without knowledge of psychological differences).*
>
> *Over time, as the group becomes more heavily ponerized, the spellbinders who originally led such a group are relegated to the task of repackaging the ideology for propaganda purposes. The leadership roles become saturated with more psychopathic individuals, while the "normal" group acquires more characteropathic individuals.*
>
> — www.ponerology.com

If the following isn't pathological arrogance, then I don't know what is:

> *Barack Obama will require you to work. He is going to demand that you shed your cynicism. That you put down your divisions. That you come out of your isolation, that you move out of your comfort zones. That you push yourselves to be better. And that you engage. Barack will never allow you to go back to your lives as usual, uninvolved, uninformed.*
>
> — Michelle Obama

Hey, Michelle! The best way that I can work for America is to pull my own weight and not need your husband's "help". I remain cynical about his obvious motives for control. I *could* push myself to be even better *if* he and his oppressive system were not on my neck. Thus, I remain unengaged, isolated from, and uninvolved with his plan of government. We are forever divided. That will continue to be my "comfort zone". Readjust *yours,* if you don't like it.

gun ownership

> *As long as gun owners and other pro-Second Amendment citizens stay politically active, the next 15, 30, and 45 years can produce much more progress, and the role of the judiciary in protecting Second Amendment rights will continue to grow.*
>
> — Dave Kopel, 26 June 2008, *Reason* Magazine
> www.reason.com/news/show/127201.html

45 years? As if the 2nd Amendment has that kind of time! At the current Orwellian rate, in just 15 years — and certainly within 30 years — most Americans will have GPSed RFID chips in their bodies. (The 2008 *Heller* ruling was just a *Nice doggie!* to an abused populace now beginning to growl.) In *45* years the Government will be renditioning dissenters to the *Moon*.

Gun ownership will soon come under renewed federal assault, regardless of the *Heller* decision. First will be .50BMG target rifles and semi-auto battle rifles (probably for the phony rationale that we're arming the Mexicans). Scoped, bolt-action rifles will become the next bogeyman of the liberals: *"We gotta ban them 'sniper' rifles!"* Ammo will gradually be taxed or regulated out of retail existence (unless microstamped with serial numbers). Handloading will require a special permit.

Got a concealed handgun permit? Goody for you, but don't expect to roll back tyranny with your Walther PPK or Glock. Liberty requires brave men with rifles. It always has.

homeschooling

This and spanking your own children will be attacked by the *U.N. Convention on the Rights of the Child*. Children tattle on their parents. (Recall the daughter who turned in her pot-smoking parents.) Read or watch George Orwell's *1984*.

Meanwhile, the national mandatory testing criteria (focusing on unimportant or diluted goals) will attempt to undo much of the fine work of homeschooling.

Globe, Inc.

They have given us into the hands of the new unhappy lords,
Lords without anger and honour, who dare not carry their swords.
They fight by shuffling papers; they have bright dead alien eyes;
They look at our labour and laughter as a tired man looks at flies.
And the load of their loveless pity is worse than the ancient wrongs,
Their doors are shut in the evenings; and they know no songs.
— G.K. Chesterton, "The Secret People"

The big corporations are international whores, looking to bed with slave labor wherever it may be found. And who *pays* for the trick? Well, the *slaves* can't afford it, so *we* do—as simpering economic voyeurs. We ghoulishly preside over own destruction. Today, corporations are like station-wagon sized carp — they no longer have any natural enemies (since they now run the government) and they're practically immortal. Watch these movies in this order sometime: *Network, Michael Clayton, Rollerball, Gattaca, 1984, THX1138,* and *The Matrix.*

food   (GIGO — Garbage In, Garbage Out)

A handful of corporations (Monsanto, Cargill, ADM, General Foods, etc.) enjoy near total vertical integration of what the public consumes as "food". From fertilizer-poisoned dead soil, to genetically modified seeds (with terminator genes), to obscene chemical processing, to your supermarket. And, revealingly, these same agribusiness corps are also big pharma. They first sell you their poison to hook you into their "antidote".

Start learning about raw, whole, organic, local, seasonal food! It is full of nutrients (but not toxins), is delicious, and will set you back on the road to lifelong good health. Join your local food co-op before it gets raided by SWAT (as did the Manna Storehouse in Ohio in 2008). Stock up on heirloom seeds. Learn to garden, and cook. There's nothing private about the hospital!

television — the visual brain cancer

Regardless of content, the very act of watching TV lowers IQs. Studies have by known proven that the act of watching TV and playing video games changes the *physical* structure of your brain. And not for the better, either. TV engenders many specific traits of sociopathy: short attention span, easily bored, need for instant gratification, and insensitivity to suffering.

Every wonder *why* they call it TV *"programming"*? Put a boot through your TV before it mentally, morally plunders your family. Our nation now has the approximate literacy rate of Guatemala. Language missionaries from Nigeria and Pakistan come *here* to teach *English.* Half of adult Americans believe that criminal suspects are guilty until proven innocent, and only one-third can correctly identify the Bill of Rights. One-fifth of Americans don't know who won WWII!

If you're spending more time with TV than books, then you're part of the problem because your "information" comes from self-interested conglomerates and you probably can no longer think your way out of their consumer paradigm.

rampant consumerism

The privacy aspects of this are huge, with the inevitable data collection, manipulation, and customer tracking. What the corporations would love to be able to is track your every move in order to sell you something as you pass by whatever stores match your consumer profile. (A great scene on this very thing was in *The Minority Report*.)

Before buying any new product, ask yourself if its purpose is to replace or negate some worthy skill. Then ask yourself if you really *need* it, and can buy it right now with *cash*. Finally, are there less expensive alternatives? These four questions will save you a lot of money throughout your lifetime.

dollar-based income and savings

Dump that Olde Maid before you lose the *other* half of your retirement. The dollar is being torpedoed on purpose to move us into a global depression (for the "solution" of a regional and then international currency).

Get into usable things, and precious metals. Do it now, and do it discreetly. (My *Boston on Surviving Y2K* has many tips.) This is inherently more private because of the lack of reporting. Buy with cash, and trade, or sell for cash.

human integrity

When an honest but mistaken man learns of his error, he either ceases to be mistaken, or ceases to be honest.
— Peter E. Hendrickson

In a sort of ghastly simplicity we remove the organ and demand the function. We make men without chests and expect of them virtue and enterprise. **We laugh at honor and are shocked to find traitors in our midst.**
— C.S. Lewis

the Age of America is gone

Men without chests. Children without morals. And women who put up with both. A country without honor, probably without a future. And we've allowed it to happen. Thinking it cute to fingerpaint with a turd, we're now drowning in a cesspool—a cosmic payback if I've ever seen one. America was a brilliant rocket of a nation which launched from a wilderness and illuminated the globe with a colorful explosion of accomplishment. She's now falling to earth, just a fizzle of smoking ashes and cardboard.

The show's over, the enchantment gone, and the world is laughing. Not politely snickering, but *laughing*. We are fat and soft and whining and stupid, and everyone knows it but *us*.

The first phase of macrosocial disease, i.e. social hysterization, is the opening through which pathocracy manifests. **Such a period of societal spiritual crisis is associated with the exhausting of the ideational, moral, and religious values heretofore nourishing the society in question.** *Individuals and groups grow increasingly self-serving, and the links of moral duty and social networks loosen. People become concerned with trifling things, ignoring more important issues such as commitment to the future, or involvement in public matters.*

The hysterical patterns finally get passed from the ruling class to the less privileged classes. This characteristic contempt for factual criticism, for normal thought patterns and nations, obviates the need for media censorship. **A pathologically hypersensitive censor lives within each citizen.** *This has been repeatedly demonstrated by the American media in relation to the omissions and distortions of the Kean-Zelikow 911 Commission Report, the propaganda leading to the Iraq war, the death toll of Iraqi citizens, the reality in Palestine.*
— www.ponerology.com

our modern savagery

The concomitant blood sports are just arriving (*i.e.*, *The Ultimate Fighting Championship*). Read *The Report from Iron Mountain* and its proposed revival of brutal sports to quench the mass blood lust.

America is right on the verge of a savage race war. The inner cities have become sprawling factories of thugs meaner than July rattlesnakes, but without their morals. Acoustic flatulence oozes from every stereo, incessantly urging teenage *gangstas* to *"kill that pig."*

To understand just how far we've regressed, watch one of the 1950's grade-school "Mr. Courteous" films where, *"Thomas knows to say 'Please' and 'Thank you!' and to wait his turn in line."* Or, watch any episode of *Dragnet*, whose toughest criminal laughably seems today a wimp. (I remember one show which, in utter seriousness, dramatized the shoplifting of 26¢ of gum!) Yeah, the 1950s were repressed, but I'll take their manners and clean-cut faces any day over our modern wolf-packs of teenagers with the immorality to blush a sailor. And now we're truly *befuddled* at 9 year olds dousing their sleeping parents with gasoline, or crack-house first-graders shooting their classmates? I just read of an 11 year old *girl* arrested for multiple rapes. (What will it take to shock a decade from now?)

the Freedom Movement

Oh, so you *believe* the Freedom Movement will save America? Larded with New Age opportunists, magicians, dolts, high-pressure profiteers, and phony "Christians" — not to mention being heavily infiltrated by the feds — *I don't think so.*

What the Freedom Movement needs is a healthy dose of real-world practicality, not the self-righteous, self-gratifying intellectual masturbation of endless legal study. **The law is becoming increasingly** *irrelevant.* And I do mean *all* law: common, statutory, equity, constitutional and maritime. As so wisely observed by Patrick Henry, petitions and legal supplications have never forced a committed, oppressive government to set free the people.

Even my own 2009-revised *You & The Police!* has a narrowing window of applicability. Get it and use it while you *can*. Soon, the entire Supreme Court will pack up and go home, leaving a note for Congress and the President saying, *"Do whatever you think is fair. We trust you! XOX, The Justices."*

The law no longer works because America has spun off her legal axis. We are entering the classic final stages of a civilization's cycle. To work, the law requires a decent society made up of literate, responsible individuals who respect the property rights of others. That society no longer exists. Today, *half* the country gets a government check, and half of *them* cannot read.

Relying on the law today is like expecting iodine to stop gangrene. It's too late for topical remedies and we're too wimpy to cut off the leg. Apparently, we'll go down with the putrefying, black stump of our "Land of the Free, Home of the Brave" Mythology. **Freedom requires bravery.** We'll rather die clutching our illusions than bravely face the truth. Oh, well. Every nation since past went through the same thing. We merely completed the cycle at our typical blur.

America is the only nation in history which miraculously has gone directly from barbarism to degeneration without the usual interval of civilization.
    — Georges Clemenceau (1841-1929)

So it is that much more important to speak up; to tell the truth; to defend the freedoms of all people to speak, live in peace, pursue happiness in a world of liberty, so long as they do not commit aggression against their fellow man. For defending this vision of a free and peaceful world, for sticking up for the rights of others no matter who they are or what they believe, we at the Campaign for Liberty and those of like mind have been wrongly targeted by an overbearing government. But we who love liberty have the right ideas and the passion to stand by our principles. In the end, the national police, state governments, Homeland Security and all the SWAT Teams and spying powers in the world cannot defeat a idea that is true and whose time has come. And it is this idea — this idea at root of Ron Paul's Love Revolution — the dream of peace and freedom for all Americans — that truly frightens those who favor the total state, intimidation and fear directed abroad and toward peaceful dissent at home. It is the idea of liberty, not militias or terrorists, that most threatens the establishment, even as it offers nothing but hope and promise for the American people and the people of the world.
    — Anthony Gregory, "Peaceful Dissent and Government Witch Hunts"   www.campaignforliberty.com

It is far too late now to tackle sub-issues head on, especially through presidential elections. America had her last chance in 2008 with Ron Paul, and blew it. The only possible "Freedom Movement" left is a widely backed and peaceful *secessionist* movement. Failing that, a civil war seems all but assured.

the American public
A Pragmatic Perspective On The Tax And The Rule Of Law

Hey, don't bother me with that "morality" argument, and all that stuff about "upholding the rule of law". I'm a pragmatist. I'm just interested in looking out for "numero uno", and living my life without any hassle!

Really! I don't care if the government

    * takes 45% of my earnings;

* habituates itself to the conveniences of "creativity" in the writing of laws and the behavior of its officers in courtrooms in order to do so with an appearance of legitimacy;

* uses my money to mess with foreigners on behalf of special interests, engendering hatred and contempt of all Americans— including me;

* uses my money to finance my own surveillance, regulation, supervision and dictation to suit the purposes of those who control the government apparatus;

* uses my money to pay for an army of lawyers who will sue me or prosecute me if I make my own choices about who works for me and on what terms; about what I say— and when, and how; about what I do with my own property; about whether I'm equipped to defend myself and those I love; and about how I raise and educate my children;

— *just as long as I'm left alone!**
— www.losthorizons.com

Most civilization is based on cowardice. It's so easy to civilize by teaching cowardice. You water down the standards which lead to bravery. You restrain the will. You regulate the appetites. You fence in the horizons. You make a law for every movement. You deny the existence of chaos. You teach even the children to breathe slowly. You tame.
— Frank Herbert, *Dune*

You know what the problem is. The fences aren't just 'round the farm. They're up here — in your heads.
—Ginger, in the movie *Chicken Run*

here comes our Brave New World — from *Microsoft!*
The overriding obsession of Bill Gates is biotechnology — how genetic code is similar to binary code, how in the future humans would be downloaded onto chips, and the human spirit burned into silicon to replace the carbon-based host:

*The most interesting thing to me is not sequencing the data. **It's understanding the [genetic] program.** How does it work?*

Well, someday they're gonna unravel this (DNA code) and we'll actually be able to put people onto

chips. And the rest is a software (control of the hardware) *problem.* (quoting Bill Gates)
    — Stephen Manes and Paul Andrews; *Gates,* p.456

What technology *can* be misused, *will* be. We're in for control measures that will make Nazi Germany look pastoral. We're in for a vicious persecution of *anybody* unaccepting of that control.

If you want a picture of the future, imagine a boot stamping on a human face — forever.
    — George Orwell; *1984*

WE HAVE LOST OUR COUNTRY

Mankind is entering into an era of social control that is increasingly castrating the liberty of conscience. The rhetoric preserves the illusion of freedom while the policy debilitates it. One can think like he is free, he is just not permitted to act like he is.
    — Trenton Fervor

The first step in the ponerization (making evil) *of a group often appears as a moral distortion of the group's original ideology.* **The existence of simplistic concepts (e.g., whether moral or legal) blocks any ability for critical thought in relation to the existence of psychopaths or their possible influence on the initial warping of the group's ideology.** *Such doctrinaire concepts are prevalent in the neoconservative ideology. For example, "You're either with us or against us (in the War on Terror)" and the completely arbitrary use of the labels "terrorist", "terrorist sympathizer", and "suspected terrorist."*
    — www.ponerology.com

the paranoid U.S. Government

It is not merely the antiwar movement the feds and the military are spying on. During the Tea Party antitax protests held last month, a number of people reported the presence of DHS Federal Protective Service at the rallies. "The Department of Homeland Security has an important public safety mission," says spokesman Russ Knocke. "In a post 9/11 world, I think the public would be comforted to know that part of our mission is to maintain situational awareness of possible vulnerabilities to public safety or even security, such as, for instance, at large public gatherings. The department will, as a routine matter, maintain situational awareness of large public gatherings and share that with state and local partners."

Most recently, military police have patrolled civilian events such as the Kentucky Derby and the Boston Marathon. DHS, federal agencies, and military police have participated in illegal (under Posse Comitatus) checkpoints in Tennessee, California, Texas, and elsewhere. These operations are designed primarily to acclimate the populace to the presence of uniformed and armed soldiers in our midst — in essence, a standing army — a notion completely antithetical to the sensibilities of the founders.

— www.progressive.org/mag_mc071806a

I've found it very helpful to analyze the psychopathology the US Government as if a person. Dr. Millon's theory fits too well. Our dear old "Uncle Sam" is a very sick guy:

Cognitive Style — Mistrustful

(e.g., is unwarrantedly skeptical, and cynical of the motives of others, including relatives, friends, and associates, construing innocuous events as signifying hidden or conspiratorial intent; reveals tendency to read hidden meanings into benign matters and to magnify tangential or minor difficulties into proofs of duplicity and treachery, especially regarding the fidelity and trustworthiness of a spouse or intimate friend).

— traits of the paranoid, from Dr. Theodore Millon's evolutionary theory of personality as a multifunctional and multistructural construct

When government officials call people like me "conspiracy nuts" I have to laugh because of their own historical spinning of conspiracies. Very rarely in American history has there been a full decade without some overblown fear being foisted upon us. In the 20th Century alone it was: immigrant hordes, the Hun, the (artificially created) Depression, the Nazis, the West Coast Japanese-Americans, the Soviets, domestic "fifth column" Communists, drug dealers, the militias, global warming, and *Al Qaeda*. In nearly every case either the Government had covertly supported these threats (to enlarge their danger), lied about them being threats when they weren't, or aggravated the situation without ever intending to actually solve it.

"No-fly lists" and patting down grannies at airports is outright *paranoia*. The NSA listening in to our phone calls is paranoia. Sneak and peak warrants? Paranoia. Laptop confiscations at the border? Paranoia. SWAT team raids on peaceable farming families for civil matters? *Paranoia*.

April 2009 DHS assessment of "rightwing extremism"

This very illuminating report was called "Current Economic and Political Climate Fueling Resurgence in Radicalization and Recruitment". In it there were over sixteen condescending and minimalizing references to the concerns of millions of Americans. Here are some examples:

> playing on their fears
> perceived threat
> if economy is perceived to worsen
> perceived government infringement on civil liberties
> to intensify fear and paranoia
> with the perception
> frustration over a perceived lack of
> perceive recent gun control legislation as a threat to their RKBA
> extremist paranoia has the potential
> exacerbating rightwing extremist paranoia
> share a belief
> rightwing extremist paranoia
> "New World Order" conspiracy theories
> part of a subversion strategy

How is an economy *"perceived to worsen"*? By objective fact, it either worsens or it does not. OK, now how did the DHS term their *own* beliefs?

> currently planning acts of violence
> could create a fertile recruiting environment
> they have not yet turned to attack planning
> could lead to the potential emergence
> likely would attract new members
> has the potential to turn violent
> will attempt to recruit
> have the potential to boost the capabilities
> learning the art of warfare

dangers of rightwing extremists
indicates the emergence
may be invigorating
likely to grow in strength
potentially making

"Could / may   be / likely / potential / danger / indicates / not   yet"?
If that's not breathless paranoia, then it doesn't exist at all.

Morphologic Organization — Inelastic
(e.g., systemic constriction and inflexibility of undergirding morphologic structures, as well as rigidly fixed channels of defensive coping, conflict mediation and need gratification, create an overstrung and taut frame that is so uncompromising in its accommodation to changing circumstances that unanticipated stressors are likely to precipitate either explosive outbursts or inner shatterings).

Their own language makes Alex Jones seem anxiety free! Even if an objective party called both sides of the language even, which has actually suffered more from the other? Thus, which group rationally feels more pressed upon? Not the US Government, but yet they ramp up their own hysteria, which only fuels the people's concerns, as this fine essay explains:

It is one thing when unreasoning panic strikes the popular imagination of a portion of the common people.

It is quite another and much more dangerous thing when it seizes the minds of national security government bureaucrats and law enforcement agents with guns.

When THEY react without thinking and falsely label the portion of the populace who in all other times are their most steadfast friends, they force upon us the worst of all worlds — a landscape of frightened power without reason. And people die as a result. People most surely die.

History proves this beyond argument. The prospect of a politicized national security hierarchy leaping at shadows is for me the most ominous event in an administration which has thus far made a cottage industry of ominous events.

What will this country look like in three more months? Six more months? Another year?

The collective unreason embodied in the MIAC Report and the DHS screed on so-called "right wing extremists" would be hysterically funny were it not deadly dangerous.
*. . . **Thus these panicked partisans fulfill their own prophecy. They take law-abiding people who are already suspicious of the government's competence and motives and provide evidence that convinces the citizenry that their suspicions are fully justified.***
. . . If the national security apparatus of the United States of America wants to know the philosophical and operational underpinnings of the constitutionalist movement, they need only read a book by the historian Robert Churchill, To Shake Their Guns in the Tyrant's Face and the extensive end notes in the documentation at the back of the work.
Yet why do they not take this simple step? Because they fear that what they will find is that the historical legitimacy of the constitutional militia paradigm of armed and active citizenship as the guarantor of individual liberty would challenge every prejudice and pre-conception they had and would shake them to the very core.
It is exactly this question of legitimacy that is at the heart of the issue here. It is why they lie. It is why they feign ignorance, why they slander and why they attack.
*. . . **These are not innocent lies. They are what is known in military parlance as intelligence preparation of the battlespace.** The conflation in the public mind of veterans, political speechmakers and constitutional militia men with mad dog neoNazi terrorists is not just to make us ignorable or to discredit us in the court of public opinion but to kill all of us for what they perceive as a good cause.*
— Mike Vanderboegh, "Hysteria"
http://sipseystreetirregulars.blogspot.com/2009/04/hysteria.htm

Projection — Regulatory Mechanism *(Functional domain) (e.g., actively disowns undesirable personal traits and motives, and attributes them to others; remains blind to one's own unattractive behaviors and characteristics, yet is overalert to, and hypercritical of, similar features in others).*

If the US Government were *truly* so concerned about reducing "extremist paranoia" then they could begin to de-energize the reasons for it. Repeal the Federal Reserve Act, the National Firearms Act, the Gun Control Act, and the "USA PATRIOT"

Act for starters. Then there would no longer be anything for the "extremists" *to* protest. Ah, but to cure the patient would kill the federal doctor. To a paranoid government, anything not under its control is "out of control."

the latest threat *d'jour* is "terrorism"

But liberty, as we all know, cannot flourish in a country that is permanently on a war footing, or even a near-war footing. Permanent crisis justifies permanent control of everybody and everything by the agencies of the central government.
    — Aldous Huxley, *Brave New World Revisited*

It means the potential of a weapon of mass destruction and a terrorist, massive casualty-producing event somewhere in the western world — it may be in the United States of America that causes our population to question our own Constitution and to begin to militarize our country in order to avoid a repeat of another mass-casualty-producing event. Which, in fact, then begins to potentially unravel the fabric of our Constitution.
    — General Tommy Franks, *Cigar Aficionado*, Dec. 2003
      www.infowars.com/print/ps/franks.htm

To those who scare peace-loving people with phantoms of lost liberty, my message is this. Your tactics only aid terrorists, for they erode our national unity and diminish our resolve. They give ammunition to America's enemies, and pause to America's friends. They encourage people of good will to remain silent in the face of evil.
    — Attorney General John Ashcroft, December 2001

Object Representations — Unalterable
(e.g., internalized representations of significant early relationships are a fixed and implacable configuration of deeply held beliefs and attitudes, as well as driven by unyielding convictions which, in turn, are aligned in an idiosyncratic manner with a fixed hierarchy of tenaciously-held, but unwarranted assumptions, fears and conjectures).

"Phantoms of lost liberty", **Mr. Ashcroft?** Hmmmm, gosh — maybe those extremists are just imagining things! Let's see:

East German "*Yourpapers!*" travel environment and checkpoints
hiring former East German Stasi spy boss Markus Wolf for the DHS
hiring of former KGB General Yevgeni Primakov for the DHS
police profiling based on political bumper stickers (thanks, DHS!)
secret "No Fly" list with unknown criteria and no appeal for removal
near total lack of financial privacy
a 50+% government burden of taxes, regulation, and inflation
inflationary theft of savings, pensions, and investments
the intentional destruction of the dollar for eventual global currency
the purposeful fermentation of a national depression
the so-called "*USA PATRIOT*" Act
warrantless "National Security Letters" in violation of the 4th Amd.
refusing the writ of *habeas corpus* to American "*enemy combatants*"
electronic eavesdropping with illegal help of the telecoms
infiltration and disruption of nonviolent street protests
diluting protest impact with faraway "Free Speech Zones"
surveillance of anti-war Quakers in Florida as "extremists"
notoriously corrupt voting machines known for ballot deletions
near total transparency of our medical history
states selling private drivers license data to marketing firms
demonization of peaceable gunowners and their gunshows
outrageous intervention in health supplements and organic foods
NAIS numbering of all livestock, even such not commercially raised
the property threat of "civil forfeiture" and "eminent domain"
an increasingly federalized and militarized police
military troops on our streets *as* police (bye-bye Posse Comitatus)
the imminent conscription (slavery) of our youth in "national service"
the likely return of a military draft for endless foreign interventions

Phantoms of lost liberty? **Can he truly *believe* that?** In today's police state, what real liberties have we *left*? Ashcroft should heed the wise words of that federal judge who ruled against the government in the "Lackawanna Six" case:

> *We must never adopt an "end justifies the means" philosophy by claiming that our Constitutional and democratic principles must be temporarily furloughed or put on hold in cases involving alleged terrorism in order to preserve our democracy. To do so would result in victory for the terrorists.*

> *If Tyranny and Oppression come to this land, it will be in the guise of fighting a foreign enemy.*
> — James Madison

Just because you control the regime now does not mean it cannot turn on you and devour you. The Founders understood this, especially those who lived long enough to survive the crisis posed by the Alien and Sedition Acts. Never pass a law that you wouldn't be willing to see your own worst political enemy enforce upon you.
— Mike Vanderboegh

The "Concept of Operations for Police Intelligence Operations" document is another indication that the military is in the process of incrementally imposing a military dictatorship by stealth in the United States under cover of the bogus GWOT . . . .

*The next terrorist attack will be pulled off by the same people as the first one — not a distant organization of patsies and dupes created by the CIA and hiding out in caves, but forces within the shadow government. **Before this can happen, however, the military and police state apparatus must be in order.** "Concept of Operations for Police Intelligence Operations" provides us with another glimpse of the operational plans now underway.*
—http://archive.newsmax.com/archives/articles/2003/11/20/185048.shtml

*According to a view that is widely held (although it has been challenged by the Nuremberg principles), the state itself is an entity that is not subject to the moral law; it is free to do anything it deems necessary to protect or promote it national interests. The central authorities, in acting for the state, are similarly not subject to moral restraints that might operative in their personal lives . . . According to this view, the freedom from all restraint devolves on the central decision maker [e.g. Hitler] from a higher authority, the state, of which he is merely the servant. . . . He too claims that he had no choice in that he was responding to authoritative demands. . . . **The whole doctrine is, of course, extremely dangerous because of its total circularity.***
— Herbert C. Kelman, psychologist
"Violence Without Moral Restraint: Reflections on the Dehumanization of Victims and Victimizers"
Journal of Social Issues 29(4):pp.45-46 (1973)

No one can point to a single incident where national security was impaired because someone insisted on their right to free speech or their right to privacy or their right to due process.
— Judge Andrew Napolitano, *Constitution in Exile*

evidence that terrorism is just an excuse to rule us

[S]*ince the State Department began counting terrorist deaths in the late 1960's, even including the deaths from the attack on the World Trade Center towers on September 11, 2001, **the number of deaths from terrorism has been about the same as the number of people who have died from severe allergic reaction to peanut butter* . . . *the most effective response to terrorism is the one most likely to frustrate terrorists and least likely to become public policy —ignore it.*

. . . by the twenty-first century, the United States had already reached an advanced stage of empire — and an aging empire needs a little more than banal reality. **It needs delusion to keep it going.** *It desperately needs an enemy to justify defense budgets and military spending. What else can you expect?* *Americans need to believe* [through incessant propaganda] *that they are confronted by a vast army of terrorists ready to "destroy our civilization."*
— Bill Bonner and Lila Rajiva, *Mobs, Messiahs, and Markets*

Besides, the government doesn't really *believe* their whole terrorism bogeyman, anyway:

In June 2004, the Court held in an eight to one decision that Hamdi was entitled to have the government file and prove charges against him. The Court also said that Hamdi [as an American citizen] *was entitled to the assistance of counsel for his defense.*

Regarding Hamdi's case, Justice Sandra Day O'Connor wrote that "a state of war is not a blank check for the President when it comes to the rights of the Nation's citizens." **Rather than try him for a crime, the government summarily released Hamdi, just days after arguing that he was so dangerous to American national security that he could not be permitted even to speak to a lawyer and had to stay in solitary confinement.** (p. 228)
— Judge Andrew P. Napolitano, *The Constitution in Exile*

hypersensitivity a trait of the paranoid
Mood/Temperament — Irascible
(e.g., displays a cold, sullen, churlish and humorless demeanor; attempts to appear unemotional and objective, but is edgy, envious, jealous, quick to take personal offense and react angrily).

The gravest crimes in the State's lexicon are almost invariably not invasions of person and property, but dangers to its own contentment: for example, treason, desertion of a soldier to the enemy, failure to register for the draft, conspiracy to overthrow the government. Murder is pursued haphazardly unless the victim be a policeman, or Gott soll hüten, an assassinated Chief of State; failure to pay a private debt is, if anything, almost encouraged, but income tax evasion is punished with utmost severity; counterfeiting the State's money is pursued far more relentlessly than forging private checks, etc. All this evidence demonstrates that the State is far more interested in preserving its own power than in defending the rights of private citizens.
   — Murray Rothbard

Self-Image — Inviolable
(e.g., has persistent ideas of self-importance and self-reference, perceiving attacks on one's character not apparent to others, asserting as personally derogatory and scurrilous, if not libelous, entirely innocuous actions and events; is pridefully independent, reluctant to confide in others, highly insular, experiencing intense fears, however, of losing identity, status and powers of self-determination).

Notice, that if you ever resist bureaucratic 'law,' you are not prosecuted for resisting an inane and unconstitutional law, but for `defying the court' or `resisting arrest.' Separating the act of resistance from the initial law which motivated the act is one of the slickest ways to bring a populace into line with bureaucratic law.
   — Joel Skousen, *The Survival Home Manual*

Expressive Behavior — Defensive
(e.g., is vigilantly guarded, alert to anticipate and ward off expected derogation, malice, and deception; is tenacious and firmly resistant to sources of external influence and control).

"Either you're with us, or with the terrorists." — G.W. Bush
Interpersonal Conduct — Provocative
(e.g., not only bears grudges and is unforgiving of those of the past, but displays a quarrelsome, fractious and abrasive attitude with recent acquaintances; precipitates exasperation and anger by a testing of loyalties and an intrusive and searching preoccupation with hidden motives).

was 9/11 "*a new Pearl Harbor*"?

Many Americans are now wondering, especially after reading leadership quotes like these:

*Moreover, as America becomes an increasingly multi-cultural society, it may find it more difficult to fashion a consensus on foreign policy issues, **except in the circumstance of a truly massive and widely perceived direct external threat.***
— Zbigniew Brzezinski, *The Grand Chessboard*

*[T]he process of transformation, even if it brings revolutionary change, is likely to be a long one, absent some catastrophic and catalyzing event — **like a new Pearl Harbor.***
— co-author Rabbi Dov Zakheim, "Rebuilding America's Defenses: Strategy, Forces and Resources for a New Century" (September 2000, page 51) published by The Project for a New American Century

Zakheim was formerly CEO of System Planning Corporation, International Division (www.sysplan.com — check out their remote piloting systems for airliners), Undersecretary of Defense and Comptroller of the Pentagon (who couldn't account for missing *billions* of dollars), and a VP at the Booz Allen Hamilton consultancy firm. Interesting guy...

Strength Through Unity. Unity Through Faith.
— totalitarian motto in *V For Vendetta*

The 10 Habits of Highly Effective Dictators
by Naomi Wolfe

❶   Invoke an external and internal threat

❷   Develop a paramilitary force

❸   Create a secret prison system - use torture to intimidate

❹   Spy on citizens

❺   Arbitrarily detain and release them

❻   Harass citizen dissenters and their organizations

❼   Target high profile writers and other key individuals for dissent

❽   Intimidate the press

❾   Recast dissent as "treason" and criticism as "espionage"

❿   Subvert the rule of law

in the grip of psychopathological control

As nightfall does not come at once, neither does oppression. In both instances, there is a twilight when everything remains seemingly unchanged. And it is in such twilight that we all must be most aware of change in the air — however slight — lest we become unwitting victims of the darkness.
    — Supreme Court Justice, William O. Douglas

Everything within the State, nothing outside the State, nothing against the State.
    — Mussolini

An unchallengeable government cannot resist over time becoming a tyrannical government, as Lord Action observed:

Power corrupts, and absolute power corrupts absolutely.

However, by the time the people begin to think of rising up for their rights, they will realize far too late that they had allowed it to become unchallengeable. We are very nearly there.

We are fast approaching the stage of the ultimate inversion: the stage where the government is free to do anything it pleases, while the citizens may act only by permission; which is the stage of the darkest periods of human history, the stage of rule by brute force.
    — www.libertysprice.com

Given a healthy society, the perversion of character in individuals can be contained. But the perversion of justice, with its reaction upon all a country's institutions, has historically placed nations and even civilizations beyond recall.
    — J. Evetts Haley, *A Texan Looks At Lyndon* (1964), p.53

An "unchallengeable" government is one which approaches:

omnipotence   (laws + universal police/military might)

omniscience   (laws + interlinked databanks)

omnipresence (laws + universal surveillance cameras + snitches)

There is *always* the next "reason" to further increase government powers. Even though nearly half of the 9/11 terrorists had used credit cards to buy their tickets (and thus could have been intercepted at the airports), the government howled that the 4th Amendment too severely hampered police powers. (This was wholly untrue.)

The government fails to prevent terrorist acts with the sweeping powers it does have, yet always seeks more in order to prevent the next act: *"Our problem today is that there is not enough government."* Truly, government is a disease masquerading as its own "cure". Here's likely why:

> *Moreover, we should consider that the state not only acts like a recruitment center for psychopaths, but that psychopaths probably invented the state to take advantage of the rest of us. I can give you no better explanation for the existence of an organization that fails in every ethical dimension and invokes psychopathic thinking at every turn than this.*
>
> *Our battle for liberty appears not just as a conflict between those who want freedom versus those who want control, but instead as the battle between normal people and the psychopaths. I have found incredible explanatory power of our world within the psychopathic hypothesis:* **The world feels wrong because psychopaths run it.** *. . . Without understanding physical laws, we would never have gained the massive improvements in our quality of life from technological developments. Similarly, without understanding our social systems, we will never escape from the tyranny unleashed on us by psychopaths. We should spread the word and explore this rich vein of thought with vigor.*
> — Will Groves, "Why Does the World Feel Wrong?"
>   www.strike-the-root.com/archive/groves.html

I didn't say it would be easy, I just said it would be the truth.
— Morpheus

PRIVACY IS NOT SHAMEFUL

The right of privacy . . . is essentially the right not to participate in the collective life — the right to shut out the community.
    — Thomas I. Emerson, *The System of Freedom of Expressions*

The Constitution . . . conferred, as against the government, the right to be let alone — the most comprehensive of rights and the right most valued by civilized men.
    — Justice Louis Brandeis

Without anonymity there can never be true freedom of speech.
    — www.freenetproject.org

Too often, privacy is mistakenly equated with concealing something shameful or evil — thus, the old *"if you've got nothing to hide, then . . ."* rationale parroted by the clueless.

Society involves a great deal of friction and we are constantly clashing with each other. Part of what makes a society a good place in which to live is the extent to which it allows people freedom from the intrusiveness of others. A society without privacy protection would be suffocation, and it might not be a place in which most would want to live.
    — Prof. Daniel J. Solove, "'I've Got Nothing to Hide' and Other Misunderstandings of Privacy"
    http://ssrn.com/abstract=998565

Too many wrongly characterize the debate as "security versus privacy." **The real choice is liberty versus control.** *Tyranny, whether it arises under threat of foreign physical attack or under constant domestic authoritative scrutiny, is still tyranny. Liberty requires security without intrusion, security plus privacy. Widespread police surveillance is the very definition of a police state.* **And that's why we should champion privacy even when we have nothing to hide.**
    — Bruce Schneier, "The Eternal Value of Privacy"
    www.schneier.com/essay-114.html

Prof. Daniel J. Solove's *A Taxonomy of Privacy*

The concept of "privacy" is a large and complicated one, and its meaning and relevance is often person-dependent. Solove's excellent contribution here is most helpful to expand the *"shorthand umbrella for a related web of things"*.

Information Collection
Surveillance (chills even lawful activity)
Interrogation

Information Processing
Aggregation (gleaning the whole from the parts)
Indentification
Insecurity (increasing vulnerability to potential abuse)
Secondary Use (*e.g.,* DL and Census data)
Exclusion (your inability to access and correct errors)

Information Dissemination
Breach of Confidentiality
Disclosure
Exposure
Increased Accessibility
Blackmail
Appropriation
Distortion

Invasion
Intrusion
Decisional Interference

In many instances, privacy is threatened not by singular egregious acts, but by a slow series of relatively minor acts which gradually begin to add up. In this way, privacy problems resemble certain environmental harms which occur over time through a series of small acts by different actors.

The law frequently struggles with recognizing harms that do not result in embarrassment, humiliation, or physical or psychological injury.

— Prof. Daniel J. Solove (op. cit.)

privacy from the government

It's probably true that ordinary citizens uninvolved in political activism have little reason to fear being spied on, just as most Americans seldom need to invoke their 1st Amendment right to freedom of speech. But we understand that the 1st Amendment serves a dual role: It protects the private right to speak your mind, but it serves an even more important structural function, ensuring open debate about matters of public importance. You might not care about that first function if you don't plan to say anything controversial. But anyone who lives in a democracy, who is subject to its laws and affected by its policies, ought to care about the second.

Harvard University legal scholar William Stuntz has argued that the framers of the Constitution viewed the 4th Amendment as a mechanism for protecting political dissent. In England, agents of the crown had ransacked the homes of pamphleteers critical of the king — something the founders resolved that the American system would not countenance.

In that light, the security-versus-privacy framing of the contemporary FISA debate seems oddly incomplete. Your personal phone calls and e-mails may be of limited interest to the spymasters of Langley and Ft. Meade. **But if you think an executive branch unchecked by courts won't turn its "national security" surveillance powers to political ends — well, it would be a first.**
— Reason magazine contributing editor Julian Sanchez
www.latimes.com/news/opinion/la-op-sanchez16mar16,0,4039194.story

Anonymity is a shield from the tyranny of the majority . . . It thus exemplifies the purpose behind the Bill of Rights, and of the First Amendment in particular: to protect unpopular individuals from retaliation — and their ideas from suppression — at the hand of an intolerant society.
— Justice Stevens, *McIntyre v. Ohio Elections Commission,* 1996

Even if most Americans do not (yet) feel the need to be private from the government, it is paramount to retain that right of privacy for possible future need. A pillar of any free society is that the government *not know* too much about what the honest citizenry are doing. As the Godfather advised, "*Keep your friends close, and your enemies even closer.*" The government (which its paranoid pathology) sees the American people as its enemy, and whittling away our privacy is what keeps us "close". (For Census 2010, everyone will get the intrusive "long form".)

When the target is leftists, antiwar activists, or "un-American" radicals, statist conservatives have tended to look the other way. When the target is cultural conservatives, gunowners and American patriots who love the Constitution, it is statist liberals who tend to downplay the danger.

In truth, all such fear-mongering, when capitalized upon by unchecked national police powers in an atmosphere of hysteria, poses a severe threat to American liberty, and must be taken very seriously by any culture that respects freedom and the very foundations of civilization. The right to peacefully dissent and oppose government deprivations of life, liberty and property, is an inalienable right as fundamental as any other.

*The right to question the government, even from a mistaken point of view, is at the heart of America's proud heritage. When America relinquishes this understanding, it comes to adopt the features of the supposed enemy. In the name of rooting out Communists, America became just a bit more communistic. In an effort to keep an eye on violent extremists, the government resorts to violence and extremism. **All the labor agitators, Muslim sympathizers and militia groups put together can never threaten American freedom and security as much as an unleashed police state in a climate of fear.***

— Anthony Gregory, "Peaceful Dissent and Government Witch Hunts"   www.campaignforliberty.com

Privacy is an insurance policy against oppression. Privacy allows a tyrannized citizenry to think independently, freely, and clearly. (Imagine if bookstores were regulated as gun stores!) To speak out, network, and organize against unruly government — all of this in perfect accord with your natural rights, and in tradition with our American history and Constitution. We did not form the servile institution of government for the goal of limitless obedience to that servant. Neither did the States federate themselves under the Constitution for the utter dissolution of their own autonomy and prerogatives.

*The issue, however, often is not whether the NSA or other government agencies should be allowed to engage in particular forms of information gathering; **rather, it is what kinds of oversight and accountability we want in place***

when the government engages in searches and seizures. *The government can employ nearly any kind of investigatory activity with a warrant supported by probable cause.*

Therefore, the security interest should not get weighed in its totality against the privacy interest. **Rather, what should get weighed is the extent of marginal limitation on the effectiveness of a government information gathering or data mining program by imposing judicial oversight and minimization procedures.** *Only in case where such procedures will completely impair the government program should the security interest be weighed in total, rather than in the marginal difference between an unencumbered program versus a limited one.*

Far too often, the balancing of privacy interests against security interests takes place in a manner that severely shortchanges the privacy interest while inflating the security interests. Such is the logic of the nothing to hide argument.

. . . The nothing to hide argument speaks to some problems, but not to others. It represents a singular and narrow way of conceiving of privacy, and it wins by excluding consideration of the other problems often raised in government surveillance and data mining programs. When engaged with directly, the nothing to hide argument can ensnare, for it forces the debate to focus on is narrow understanding of privacy. But when confronted with the plurality of privacy problems implicated by government data collection and use beyond surveillance and disclosure, the nothing to hide argument, in the end, has nothing to say.

— Prof. Daniel J. Solove (op. cit.)

A government which knows everything about its people is an *unassailable* government, for the people can no longer safely congregate nor precipitate. In an Orwellian state in which all your communications, transactions, and associations are monitored/approved, from whence comes any possible readjustment — much less a successful *revolution* from it?

Even in today's "teenaged" police state, the government has excellent knowledge of the dissenters' "community of interest", residence locations, spending habits, and gun ownership. (Imagine the impossibility of a modern-day Lexington and Concord with *4,000* militiamen in the field!)

When privacy goes, the people have in a sense "thrown away the key" to their shackles. Think of your decreasing privacy as being measured for a tailored straightjacket.

What do you have to hide? Today, perhaps nothing. Next year, maybe a lot depending on new information and revised priorities. Privacy is a comprehensive insurance policy. Keep up on the premiums, even if you're not quite sure why.

the coming Dark Age . . . if we allow it . . .

The rise of state capitalism in the 19th century was the rise of "free-range serfdom." Additional liberties were granted to the human livestock not with the goal of setting them free, but rather with the goal of increasing their productivity.
— www.youtube.com/watch?v=P772Eb63qIY
True News 13: Statism is Dead - Part 3 - The Matrix

We're now entering the final chapter in the peaceful struggle for Liberty. Parroting legal arguments won't cut it. Democratic action is largely futile, and certainly only temporary. What's become important is what actually *works.*

*Our aim is nothing less than to create a world system of finan-cial control in private hands to dominate the political system of each country and the world economy as a whole . . . . **But in general his freedom and choice will be controlled within very narrow alternatives by the fact that** [every man] **will be numbered from birth, and followed, as a number,** through his educational training, his required military or other public service, his tax contributions (sic), his health and medi-cal requirements, and his final retirement and death benefits.* (p. 866)
— Carroll Quigley; *Tragedy and Hope* (1966)

*As a teenager, I heard John Kennedy's summons to citizen-ship. And then, as a [draft-dodging] student at Georgetown, I heard that call clarified **by a professor I had named Carroll Quigley.***
— Bill Clinton, 16 July 1992

Let no more be heard about the New World Order being a para-noid myth of the Patriot Movement. The NWO has been a coor-dinated, energetic plan for decades. So confident were the

Insiders in *1933* (with the election of their man, FDR), that they bragged about it on the $1 bill — *"Annuit Coeptis Novus Ordo Seclorum"* — Announcing the Birth of the New World Order. These words frame a 13-level pyramid with the capstone Masonic Eye. More revealing still is that this "announcement" was not placed on the (then) uncommon $100 bill, but on the proletarians' $1 bill for *all* to see.

So what does this all have to do with *privacy?* I'll *tell* you what: **privacy *works.*** Privacy means *insulation* from our curdling society. It means a respite from the growing insanity of our culture. Those of you who want to be grist for the New World Order mill, go right ahead. Give this book to somebody else, and save yourself the read. But to those of a less sacrificial bent, use this book while you *can*. Privacy *works*.

go from this	to *this!*
Windows	Puppy Linux
online directly	online only through proxies
credit-based cell	prepaid cell phone
local ISP email	offshore and encrypted email
checks	cash, M.O.s, and digital gold
credit cards	prepaid debit cards
mail at home	home is never a mailing address
bank accounts	digital gold accounts
grocery store "food"	health food stores, farm co-ops
living in town	living in the country
frequent air travel	drive instead if within 1000 miles
gas on credit card	pay with cash, always
FFL guns	buy with cash at gun shows and ads

I sincerely hope that *One Nation, Under Surveillance* is helpful to you and many thousands like us. Batten down the hatches, for a real storm is imminent.

PRIVACY VS. PARANOIA

A psychiatrist once had a patient who was utterly convinced that he was to be eaten by a giant chicken who thought him a kernel of corn. Years of therapy were required to realign the patient with the reality that he was safe from giant chickens. On the afternoon of the breakthrough, he confidently declared that "I am a man — not a kernel of corn!", thanked the doctor profusely and left with a profound sense of personal triumph. Minutes later he rushed back inside, panicking because there might be a giant chicken in the parking lot.

The doctor reminded him that he was not a kernel of corn.

"Yes, but does the chicken know?"

The concept of privacy is not universally poignant to all. A large percentage of people really do not care if the government and corporations know about their spending habits, travel patterns, or social networks. Comedian Bill Maher once mocked the notion of personal privacy given how unprivate Americans are with their Facebook, MySpace, blogs and webcams.

Other people, however, see the world as a dangerous place, and strive to insulate themselves from it. I'm certainly one of them, and likely you are, too. There are evil people and institutions who seek to gain unlawful and unethical control of our lives. But, that is no excuse for indirectly relinquishing your life to them out of fearful isolation.

As soon as there is life, there is danger.
— Ralph Waldo Emerson

While there is danger in the world, you must keep your perspective of that in balance. Paranoia is a delusion that there is relentless and personal danger from without, and the truly paranoid always feel directly at risk from such. A paranoid person will feed his delusions of persecution. A classic case was that of Ernest Hemingway. By the time he took his own life to escape his own self-made prison of paranoia, Hemingway had grown to believe that his friends were spying on him, his phone was tapped, and government agents were closing in on him for any one of several offenses. None of it was true.

The purpose of a privacy plan is for peace of mind. It is actually a form of insurance. A good friend of mine in Johannesburg enjoys his beautifully tricked-out Land Rovers. As we tooled around the city, I asked him if he was concerned about theft (which was rampant). *"No, not at all. That's what I pay insurance for. If this ever gets stolen, it's not my problem, it's the insurance company's problem. Why should I worry about theft when it's no longer my problem? They are the ones who should be worried."*

For your own privacy, pay only as much as what gives you general peace of mind. You can achieve 80% of all possible privacy with about 20% of the expense and hassle. Please, please, *please*: decide right now that 80% of the privacy pie will have to be enough for you.

But what about that remaining 20% of possible privacy? **It will consume too much of your time, joy, and money.** Unless you're a fugitive from justice, it's just not worth it. And, even then, it still probably would not be worth it as the fugitive is not free just because he's not in prison. There are many examples of fugitives having turned themselves in after decades only because the anxiety grew too much to bear. For them, it was relief to go to prison!

Fugitive-level of anxiety aside, if you act pursued long enough it will probably engender others to pursue you. Speaking of wild animals in his classic *Meditations on Hunting*, Ortega y Gasset had this thought-provoking comment:

> *The only adequate response to a being that lives obsessed with avoiding capture is to try to catch it.*

Too much privacy will ironically draw attention to yourself, and the most basic of scrutiny will uncover for what they are your measures of IP proxies, maildrops, and e-voice mail. Not that your personal information behind that is vulnerable, but you will be "marked" as a privacy nut and others will wonder *why*. Are you a drug-dealer? Running from the law? Skipping out on a large debt? None of this scrutiny is helpful, and can ironically more harm your privacy than had you lived out in the open.

As a form of insurance, you can go overboard with privacy. The paranoid private person pays far too much for his insurance — so much that it becomes a paralyzing expense. Imagine that you owned a $100,000 car. Would it make much sense to pay $100,000 for the fullest possible comprehensive zero deductible policy (including a Lloyd's of London rider for acts of terrorism, meteoroid damage, nuclear disasters, etc.)? No, because you've in effect already stolen the car from yourself with such excessive insurance.

Do not seek total peace of mind through privacy measures, because that snake will eat its own tail. Although crafting an existence 99% immune to the snooping of others is possible, it would not be a life. Such a barren existence would be a terrifying and confining hertimage, far worse than whatever magnified danger it had been created to protect against. I've experimented significantly in that direction, so I know what I'm talking about. The purpose of privacy is peace of mind and freedom.

If you practice, for long enough, extreme measures of privacy, it will eventually show in your face and body language. A perceptive person will instantly spot it. This happened to me, in an embarrassing and angering moment. Several years ago I happened to speak at a conference along with a very famous author and psychologist, a man I had long admired as legendary in his field of self-esteem and philosophy. I was excited to meet him finally. He had just arrived at the hotel to check in and I spotted him in the lobby chatting with a friend of mine. I walked up to say hello, and my friend said to him, "*Oh, do you know Ken Royce?*" This famous doctor gave me a disapproving look and replied, "*He looks like a fugitive.*" My first thought was "*Well, you look like some old queen from Brentwood!* " but I was too stunned to say so. (The best retort came to me later: "*Shouldn't we all be fugitives from . . . injustice?*") Naturally, this first encounter dashed my admiration for such a pompous ass, however, it got me thinking about the cost I had been levying on myself for privacy. I probably did look like a fugitive, as I used to intensely dislike making long-in-advance scheduled public appearances. Dr. Nathaniel Branden had indeed an insight to me, but I nevertheless still resent his astonishingly unprofessional and unkind remark. (The episode often reminds me to prefer loving people over intelligent people.)

Few people I've met are more private than I, but one in particular makes me look positively public. "Ron" is probably by now truly paranoid about the government. (If he could listen to Alex Jones 25/8, he would.) His extreme measures of building a fully stocked bunker home (including an escape tunnel!) in the country and his haunted skulking-around demeanor have ironically made him widely recognized figure. Having blown his local privacy (in part from a dispute with a construction subcontractor), he felt forced to sell his place and relocate to another state. (This took several years and tens of thousands of miles in property shopping.) I consider Ron a friend who has been very kind and helpful to me, so I don't write this to embarrass him (assuming he recognizes himself). However, I am deeply concerned for his emotional health. Many times I've said, "*Ron, you're all set! You're ready for the Apocalypse and Armageddon. You've covered all the bases. Let's say that Alex Jones is right about the upcoming PATRIOT ACT 3. What would you being doing differently? How else could you possibly prepare? Ron, you're done! You've paid for this insurance policy, and now it's high time to go out and live a life. Meet a nice woman at the grocery store and ask her out to dinner!*"

The wisest use of insurance is to cover only that portion of loss that you otherwise could not afford to lose. Meaning, you must always be willing to "self-insure" for the other portion. To go through life with a "zero deductible" philosophy (as Ron does) is to avoid having to self-insure; to avoid dealing directly with your fears. Always ask yourself: "*Even if _____ was known about me, what's the worst that could happen? Might happen? What is it that I am truly afraid of?*" Chances are, you could live through it, including seizure of your assets and a prison term. (If anything, you could use any misfortune as a place to rebound from. Many people less intelligent or gifted than you have.)

If this 20% of self-insured privacy still makes you nervous (as it often does me), I offer this idea. Have an extremely private fall-back location you can go to if your 80% privacy level ever fails you. Set it up totally with cash, do not link *anything* to it (*e.g.*, mail, internet, phone, etc.), stock it well for self-sufficiency, and tell nobody. You won't live there, but only use it as a last resort if ever compelled to. That accomplished, you've now a duty to relax and enjoy life as you constantly overcome your fears. Sure, continue to use prepaid cell phones and mail drops for your privacy, but resist the temptation to seal yourself off hermetically and thus amputate your spirit.

If your privacy is never compromised, you'll wish that you'd more lived a life. If, however, your privacy is ever compromised — you'll wish that you'd more lived a life! **Privacy is a means to an end, and not the end itself.** It is always at least marginally isolating. When your privacy measures begin to significantly limit your freedom of action, your goals, and your relationships, and your personal growth — then you'll know that you're taking privacy too seriously and you should instantly evaluate what exactly it is that you're still afraid of. I've had my privacy intentionally blown by "friends", and it was oddly liberating. In a way, they did me more good than harm.

If you do not conquer your fears, then your fears will conquer you.

Learn to catch your obsessions before they cement into delusions. Hemingway did not, and his own mind killed himself via shotgun. That's a much more tragic end than from enemy action. Paranoia is an "auto-immune" disease of the mind, beginning from worry:

> *Worry is the misuse of the imagination.*
>   —Dan Zadra

Use your imagination for joyful and beautiful things, and not for endless scenarios of persecution. **If you are truly to be persecuted, it will probably come regardless of your trying to avoid it.** And when it does finally catch up with you, you will profoundly lament all those wasted opportunities to swim in oceans, pick flowers, try new things, inspire others, make love, and nap in a meadow. Yes, evil people and institutions do exist, but they are losers of the first order who don't deserve your daily focus. *"The best revenge is living well."*

> *Work like you don't need the money, love like you've never been hurt, and dance like you do when nobody's watching.*

Create only as much privacy as you can safely handle, and then forget about life's dangers. None of us will get out of this alive, and you can't take your stuff with you.

On your tombstone there are two dates: birth and death.
That hyphen between them . . . was your life.

Did you spend it living and loving fully . . . or hiding in fear?

THE RULES

To be successfully private requires the observance of several crucial rules. Extrapolate from these, and you'll do fine.

don't draw attention to yourself

Don't be overtly covert. Privacy is about being covertly overt — *seeming* like normal folks at the surface level. If you behave mysteriously or suspiciously, you've already lost, in the long run, your *war* for privacy. The general public and the government shouldn't have any idea that you're a private person, because they'll resent you for it.

privacy is always *complicated* — think it through

Even the most *basic* privacy stance (without the use of aliases and ID) is still fairly complicated. For example, you wouldn't want the bill from your secret voice mail sent to the mailing address reserved for government and generic commercial correspondence.

Therefore, you must draw out the linkages of who-knows-what with an electronic-style schematic. You simply will *not* be able to conjure and manage all this in your mind — *trust me on this*. Without a schematic you'll miss some hidden crossovers, and if you're ever *really* scrutinized, the investigator will most assuredly draw out a schematic and discover them.

privacy is *expensive* — don't be greedy

I have a friend who is wonderfully prepared to ditch his city life and relocate to his well-stocked farm retreat three hours away. Having visited his retreat, I'm almost envious. Set on 50 acres in a quiet valley, he's got food (stored and growing), a small cabin, spare vehicles, fuel, and all the supplies he and his wife are likely to need. He's cultivated good relations with his neighbors and is already trading with them to mutual advantage. In a word, he's *set*. At the drop of any ominous hat (martial law, economic collapse, etc.), he's there.

One small problem: he's already *blown* his privacy. How? Not by arranging the property purchase over his home phone (unless his line was monitored). No, what blew his privacy (and he's yet to appreciate this) is that he operates his "Omega Man" retreat as a commercial farm — *and declares it on his tax forms!* By wanting that tax deduction, by loving the money more than the privacy, his retreat is all for naught. If the feds ever become interested in him, all they'll have to do is simply pull up his 1040s. He might as well have gotten a listed phone number.

Privacy is expensive. Even the most basic stance will cost about $40 per month. Don't be greedy. Recognize the costs (emotional, social, and financial) and pay them without grousing about it. Don't try privacy if it's too costly, because you'll get cheap on yourself and ruin the whole game.

privacy is *inconvenient* — don't be lazy.

The best laid-out plan with all the expensive frills can be — no, *will* be — devastated by just *one* lazy slip. *Laziness* will be most tempting in the use of telephones. It's highly inconvenient to have to leave your house to make an alias pay phone call across town. (This is why I strongly discourage your having a home phone. It's just too *easy* to misuse.) Yet if you succumb to laziness that *one* time, and your line has a pen register or trap, that one phone call *will* unravel your tightly wrapped scheme.

Just *one* good loose end is *all* an investigator needs. **Loose ends are created by poor planning and lazy tradecraft.** I've read several hundred true-crime accounts and detective novels to understand this well. In a multi-million dollar insurance fraud, the allegedly deceased husband (from a small plane crash in the ocean) kept in touch with his wife by calling her at the same pay phone at the same time. His supposed death was brilliantly planned and executed. He went to ground without error. Calling *her* was clever (no long-distance records on her line), but using the *same* pay phone was *lazy*. The PI, having followed her, became suspicious since it's not normal to be called *at* a pay phone. He simply bugged the pay phone, and discovered his location in San Juan. Had they used *several* pay phones, they would have pulled it off.

privacy is *private* — don't be glib
A convicted drug dealer posted a $1,000,000 presentence bond and bolted with his wife and children. Having planned his run for months, he was in perfect shape to succeed with another $1,500,000 salted away.

His first mistake, after several months, was to contact his family and friends. During a skip trace, if nothing is uncovered within a few weeks, a good investigator will put the case on a shelf for a few months and work on other things. He knows that everyone slips up — if not immediately, then after a few months of being on the run (which is tedious and nerve-racking). So, after a few months, he began to miss his family and friends.

Using several mail forwardings in series to hide his location, he wrote his mother and sent pictures of his children. One photo, taken outdoors, clued the feds that he was in Virginia. What clinched it was his bragging in a letter that he, a convicted felon on the run, had befriended a retired FBI agent.

The feds simply wrote to all Virginia-area retired FBI agents. The befriended agent read it and, of course, turned in his new buddy. Don't be glib.

be *consistent* — be *thorough*
If bulletproof privacy is important to you, then think it through ahead of time, be consistent, and fight the urge of convenience. Nothing else will do — trust me on this. Privacy measures add up to a *lifestyle* which rewards you with the tranquility you've dreamed about. The privacy life-style is an indispensable *means* to that end. You cannot enjoy *that* end without *those* means. Know this in advance and make a quality commitment. Don't fool yourself into thinking half-assed measures will accomplish your goals. They *won't*. As Hans and Franz would say, *"Believe me now, or hear me later."*

work your story out in advance
Don't allow yourself to be surprised. Know beforehand what is required of a transaction and be prepared for it. Don't be too pat with your recitation, however. Yarns are *weaved*.

always have a benign, logical explanation
When asked for your phone number, reply that it's unlisted, or that you've just moved and haven't had one

connected yet, or that you're staying with friends and can't give out their number, or that you're just passing through town.

privacy requires the spinning of yarns

Though, I'll discuss this more fully in a few pages, know in advance that you will most likely have to "lie." Would you tell a mugger about your money belt, or would you "lie"? Similarly, our system and society is bent on stealing your quiet joy. You will have to "lie" to protect your privacy.

be friendly — be relaxed — be unremembered

Surly people are not only remembered — they're talked about. *"This guy came in today —geez, what an *sshole!"* The *last* thing you want is to be talked about. Keep your cool and avoid making poor impressions.

Nervous behavior will strike people as odd. It makes them curious, if not outright suspicious. Nervousness is quenched by confidence — confidence is gained by success — success comes from experience, and experience comes from, well, *experience.* This isn't armchair stuff. You'll have to actually go out and *do* it. After a while, it'll be second nature.

privacy requires your alertness

This is especially true if you're due for any official scrutiny. You must develop sensitive antennae and keep them up at all times. Before being moved on, you *will* have *some* advance warning: frequent airplane overflights, vehicle drive-bys, a noticeable change in the attitude of bank and postal clerks, a sudden increase in hang up calls, new acquaintances who ask too many questions or too readily agree with your views, your friends and family being quietly sniffed out, etc.

You will likely have warning signs. In *The Silent Brotherhood*, FBI agents were often spooking their neoNazi targets (who usually lost their tail, and even escaped capture on several dramatic occasions). Had the suspected Unabomber not been *so* successful a hermit, he'd have heard about the swarm of feds in Suburbans milling about his lonely county for weeks. (Understand that I've no sympathy with "The Order" and the Unabomber was a malignant coward. I'm simply sharing an observation from their cases.)

Stay alert and you'll probably avoid being surprised. **Alertness, however, is *not* paranoia.** Paranoia is a mental disorder of delusional grandeur and persecution so acute as to be paralyzing. You probably aren't so deserving of persecution, so don't whip yourself into a frenzy. Do as much as you can for yourself, relax and try to *enjoy* life.

"WHAT IF I HAVE TO *LIE?*"

To answer this requires a philosophical aside. First of all, it is not illegal to use an alias so long as there is no fraudulent intent. For example, it's pretty obvious that "Boston T. Party" is not my given name. I use this *nom de plum* to afford myself a bit of privacy and to evoke a fun, patriotic flavor. There is no intent to defraud anyone.

Now, let's take the "innocent alias" concept a bit further. Many privacy measures require representations which are untrue. Remember, all of my books are written, not for bonafide criminals, but for peaceable folk who just want to increase their personal freedom. Thieves, con-men, those who initiate violence, etc. *should* be caught and punished. Such crimes are called *mala in se* — "evil in themselves."

However, *mala prohibitum* ("wrongs prohibited," or rules and regulations concerning victimless offenses) are simply degradations of our Liberty. Emerson once said, *"Good men must not obey the laws* (rules) *too well."* As long as you don't hurt or rip off people — as long as there is no fraudulent intent — these techniques can be used with a clear conscience.

By "fraud" I mean intentionally deceiving somebody into acting to their detriment. Throughout my many years of privacy living I have *never* defrauded another. I have established many forms of commercial service under some kind of alias, purely for my own privacy. The bills were always paid. **The moral: Do not hurt others.**

THE PUBLIC FACE OF PRIVACY

When in public, *act* like the public. Never draw attention to yourself. At home, you can skulk about all you want, but in public, do not be overtly covert.

This is absolutely vital when you are establishing your voice mail service, buying plane tickets, getting ID, etc. The clerk must feel perfectly comfortable with the transaction. Don't blow it by being nervous, sarcastic, impatient or rude. Be polite, smile and practice an agreeable banter. Such an attitude is *oil* to the transaction. Do not, however, be *too* polite or officious — do not try *too* hard.

Know in advance the documentary requirements for the transaction and have your "legend" well buttressed and rehearsed. Do not be caught off guard, or else you'll probably stammer and ruin the deal. RELAX! To the clerk, you're just another public face. Be fairly cheerful, yet nonchalant.

Do not make a fuss about: the long wait in line, the bureaucratic pointlessness of the thing, and ID or SSN requirements. You're there to complete the transaction, and so is the clerk. **Give her what she needs, and she'll return the favor.** Do what it takes to accomplish your goal. Regarding the SSN, you either don't have one or you don't know it, or give her a fake one (research the proper birthplace 3 digit sequence and have the fake number done on a metal card). Don't start fulminating about the SSN being some Mark of the Beast prequel (even though we all know it that probably *is*).

Once you've got your paperwork, ID, tickets, etc. you should politely and smoothly bid the clerk a *"Good day!"* and leave. Don't gush relief at the counter — have your party later.

It just takes a bit of practice. The first few times you'll understandably be nervous. That's why you should start with the small stuff first (a mail drop, etc.). Then, when it comes time for bigger transactions, you'll be ready.

❖ 4

HOW TO MESS UP

An adventure is usually the penalty for lousy planning.
— Shorty Jenkins, miner & prospector, 1943

Let me show you how poor privacy techniques will work *against* you. In *The Manhunter*, U.S. Marshal fugitive catcher John Pascucci outlined how he caught the escaped Nazi war criminal Bodhan Koziy from an original nine month time line (the amount of lead time a wanted person has on his pursuers).

First, Koziy mentioned to various neighbors that he was going to Albuquerque or Toronto or Costa Rica. His neighbors also told Pascucci that Koziy had sold his fridge, which meant that he'd probably left (at least) the state. Calling the newspaper, Pascucci traced the 12 September classified ad. He then called every moving company and found the one which had moved the Koziys on the 20th. Talking to a mover, he learned that the stuff went to a warehouse for a couple of days and then was shipped to Albuquerque. Koziy's son lived there.

The son was totally uncooperative. Yes, he knew where his dad was, but he wasn't talking. (Since Koziy was wanted only for a civil matter, his son couldn't be compelled to talk.)

Pascucci then leaned on a Jewish surnamed exec at American Express to get Koziy's charge records. Scanning the sheets for "triggers" (pieces of info which lead to even more pertinent pieces) he noticed a travel agency charge. Plane tickets had been purchased to Albuquerque, Toronto, and Costa Rica. A Waldenbooks charge was quickly identified as *Fodor's Guide to Costa Rica*. But even this didn't break the case:

> I know that for fictional detectives, A leads to B, which leads to C, and breaks the case. **But in real life, A leads to B,**

> **which leads to dick, and then the information that
> breaks the case waltzes in from left field.**
> *But that's not because of luck; it's because you're working
> in several directions at once.*

Koziy's "driver's abstract" (a DMV record more detailed than the standard profile) said that he'd been in a minor traffic accident with a G. Morelli, which turned out to be his married daughter. Pascucci weaseled Gina's phone records from S.E. Bell, which showed three calls to Costa Rica. He flew there.

The calls had been made to pay phones in lobbies of three different San José hotels. In one of the hotels, Pascucci noticed a car rental agency and learned that Koziy had rented a car, driven it for 90km. and returned it on 16 April. The time line had shrunk to less than a month, and Koziy was probably living within a 45km. radius.

A routine airport surveillance photo of incoming nonresidents confirmed that Koziy *was* in Costa Rica. An old address of Koziy's was found, but he had moved 15 days prior. In that time 120 new phone lines had been connected, 95 of which were residences.

Pascucci then had a real-time record of Gina's calls started. Once accomplished, a U.S. Marshal visited her with a sham "no prosecution" deal for her father. As predicted, she immediately called Costa Rica, and the number was one of the new 95 residential numbers. From there, it was easy.

Learning from a Nazi's mistakes

The lesson in all this is that even a very *light* trail leading to you will work as well for an investigator as a very heavy trail. A trail is a trail, and good investigators will pick up the light trails. Leave no trail whatsoever. Besides being a creep who wiped out dozens of Jewish families, Koziy's mistakes were:

❶   mentioning to *anyone* his destination of Costa Rica
His first basic mistake. It made Pascucci think internationally. The Toronto misinfo was great, and Albuquerque was credible as his son lived there, but mentioning Costa Rica blew it.

❷   selling his stuff from his *own* place
He should have taken it directly to a buyer, or had his daughter
sell it for him later. The neighbors shouldn't have known of its
disposition so they couldn't have then updated the time line.

❸   placing a classified ad in his *own* name and number
Plain stupid, unless done for misinfo. He could have gotten a
temporary voice mail number posing as somebody just briefly in
town. The ad clarified the time line enough for Pascucci to
phone all the movers with a general date of Koziy's move.

❹   having a listed mover transport his stuff
Really stupid. He should have moved it himself, or with the
help of some college kids — off the record. Use *bona fide* movers
only for misinfo. At least move your stuff to another city, and
have the mover pick it up from there to break up the trail.

❺   his son *admitting* that he knew where his father was
There was *no* reason to admit this. His son should have
expressed strong dislike for his father. Although this mistake
didn't materially help Pascucci, it *could* have.

❻   charging travel-related items on a credit card
Unbelievably stupid. Use your credit card *only* for utterly
neutral and bland charges, or for misinformation. Besides one's
phone records, credit card charges are the biggest triggers.

❼   his daughter making calls from *her* phone to Costa Rica
Catastrophically stupid. It broke the case. He should have
called *her*. It is *far* more difficult to trace the *origin* of an
international call, especially long after the fact.

❽   renting a car in a the same hotel where he was called
An easy error to make. If you're receiving a call somewhere,
make sure that no person or camera is around to identify you.
Also, *never* transact business nearby, much less in the same
building. Travel good distances to make/receive your calls.

❾   not having a *2nd* safe house/phone *already* established
Also an easy error to make. If you think you might have to bolt,
you should set up your next place, phone and vehicle in advance
so that old and new records don't relay to each other.

It may seem like I'm confusing hindsight with wisdom. **Much of wisdom is using the *hindsight* of others as your *foresight*.** Remember, all the mistakes in Life have *already* been made by the 100 billion dead *before* you. Wisdom actually consists of *not* reinventing the *square* wheel. Learn from others' mistakes because there is not enough *time* to learn the Lesson from purely your *own* mistakes — that's lesson #1.

Take note of the mistakes *others* made which compromised Koziy. As tight as one's system is, it is still vulnerable to others. The more hermetic you are, the more likely it will be that friends or family will blow your privacy for you (usually unintentionally) vs. you blowing it yourself. For that reason it is important that you screen and limit what you divulge to even normally trustworthy. What isn't known cannot be divulged.

That's what my book will show you — not to be *redundantly* stupid. You'll probably get found out by some common gaff; you're unlikely to be found out through some truly unprecedented error.

However, if you *are,* write me so we all can *learn* from it.

PRIVACY & YOUR DATA

YOUR DATA SHADOW

You go through life dropping little bits of data about yourself everywhere. Following right after are big vacuum cleaners sucking them up.
— Evan Hendricks, editor of *Privacy Times*

In the information age, we all have a data shadow.

We leave data everywhere we go. It's not just our bank accounts and stock portfolios, or our itemized bills, listing every credit card purchase and telephone call we make. It's automatic road-toll collection systems, supermarket affinity cards, ATMs and so on.

It's also our lives. Our love letters and friendly chat. Our personal e-mails and SMS messages. Our business plans, strategies and offhand conversations. Our political leanings and positions. And this is just the data we interact with. We all have shadow selves living in the data banks of hundreds of corporations' information brokers — information about us that is both surprisingly personal and uncannily complete — except for the errors that you can neither see nor correct.

What happens to our data happens to ourselves.

This shadow self doesn't just sit there: It's constantly touched. It's examined and judged. When we apply for a bank loan, it's our data that determines whether or not we get it. When we try to board an airplane, it's our data that determines how thoroughly we get searched — or whether we get to board at all. If the government wants to investigate us, they're more likely to go through our data than they are to search our homes; for a lot of that data, they don't even need a warrant.

Who controls our data controls our lives.

It's true. Whoever controls our data can decide whether we can get a bank loan, on an airplane or into a country. Or what sort of discount we get from a merchant, or even how we're treated by customer support. A potential employer can, illegally in the U.S., examine our medical data and decide whether or not to offer us a job. The police can mine our data and decide whether or not we're a terrorist risk. If a criminal can get hold of enough of our data, he can open credit cards in our names, siphon money out of our investment accounts, even sell our property. Identity theft is the ultimate proof that control of our data means control of our life.

We need to take back our data.

Our data is a part of us. It's intimate and personal, and we have basic rights to it. It should be protected from unwanted touch.

We need a comprehensive data privacy law. This law should protect all information about us, and not be limited merely to financial or health information. It should limit others' ability to buy and sell our information without our knowledge and consent. It should allow us to see information about us held by others, and correct any inaccuracies we find. It should prevent the government from going after our information without judicial oversight. It should enforce data deletion, and limit data collection, where necessary. And we need more than token penalties for deliberate violations.

This is a tall order, and it will take years for us to get there. It's easy to do nothing and let the market take over. But as we see with things like grocery store club cards and click-through privacy policies on websites, most people either don't realize the extent their privacy is being violated or don't have any real choice. And businesses, of course, are more than happy to collect, buy, and sell our most intimate information. But the long-term effects of this on society are toxic; we give up control of ourselves.

— Bruce Schneier, "Our Data, Ourselves", May 2008
www.wired.com/commentary/securitymatters

Computer databanks are awesome, but they're also vulnerable. They rely on *input* and are therefore *lazy*. You can use the system against itself to create a false confidence. If you insist that utterly *no* records exist on you, then you'll quickly attract the attention of some flesh-and-blood investigators, as a blank file is highly unusual and suspicious. So, have a fat file, but *you* are the one who feeds it with good-looking, dead-end data.

credit information

The trillion dollar credit reporting industry is dominated by the Big Three: TRW, Equifax, and Trans Union. Other than the feds themselves, these companies are the largest repositories of information about us — nearly 450 million files on 160 million people. Just about anybody with an allegedly relevant business purpose can learn your credit transactions, SSNs, birthdates, mortgage records, employment and salary histories, telephone numbers (even if nonpublished), email accounts, and information on legal matters, family makeup, bankruptcies, tax liens and your current as well as previous addresses.

The comforting side to all this is that *you* are usually responsible for disclosing all this data — they get it passively. Thus, *you* can misinfo the system to your desire, and it will be reported as fact. With my help, a mail drop will show as your physical address and a voice mail as your telephone number — not to mention other diversions.

Employment Information Service (EIS)

If you've ever filed for workman's compensation or sued an employer, you're likely to be blacklisted by this Gretna, Louisiana databank. Founded in 1966 as a nonprofit corporation by oil and gas bigwigs (including George Bush's Zapata Oil), it maintains nearly a million files.

Then, there are databankers specializing in pre-employment criminal background checks, such as the Information Resource Service Company (IRSC) which tells whether a person has been arrested — even if no conviction resulted.

Medical Information Bureau (MIB)

This nongovernment databank contains summaries of health conditions on more than 15,000,000 Americans and Canadians (who regularly flee their own socialized health care). The data comes from insurance applications, physicians' files and hospital records. Hospital gossip and miskeyed entries end up as file "gospel" which is nearly impossible to retort or remove. The MIB distributes over 30,000,000 reports a year.

These files are not all private. Clerks, salesmen and investigators access them regularly. The DoJ recently gutted HIPAA, the 1996 medical privacy act:

> *An authoritative new ruling by the Justice Department sharply limits the government's ability to prosecute people for criminal violations of the law that protects the privacy of medical records.*
>
> *The criminal penalties, the department said, apply to insurers, doctors, hospitals and other providers — but not necessarily their employees or outsiders who steal personal health data.*
>
> *In short, the department said, **people who work for an entity covered by the federal privacy law are not automatically covered by that law and may not be subject to its criminal penalties . . .***
>
> *As Schneier put it: "This kind of thing is bigger than the security of the healthcare data of Americans. Our administration is trying to collect more data in its attempt to fight terrorism. Part of that is convincing people — both Americans and foreigners — that this data will be protected. When we gut privacy protections because they might inconvenience business, we're telling the world that privacy isn't one of our core concerns."*
>
> — NYT article "Ruling Limits Prosecutions of People Who Violate Law on Privacy of Medical Records"

And these people can be trusted to keep our health and biometric data secure? Oh, and once the federal Human Genome Project is complete, nobody with "defective" genes will likely qualify for health insurance. We're on the brink of a vast, computerized eugenics program envious of Nazi concentration camp "doctors." Watch *Gattaca* for a glimpse of our future.

government databases

I can't list every one, but here are the big ones. Many of them were rolled into DHS, or are now accessible by DHS (such as CIS, NIIS, STSC, NAILS, IBIS, NLETS/NCIC, EPIC, and OASIS).

DARPA's Information Awareness Network

On this book's front cover, notice the IAO emblem which I placed into the highway CCTV camera. The IAO's motto (visibly readable in the image) is *Scientia Est Potentia* ("Knowledge Is Power") with the $1 Masonic Eye. When I first saw the IAO emblem I thought it a sick joke, however, IAO is a division of DARPA of the Department of Defense.

> *Information Awareness Office is to gather as much information as possible about everyone in a centralized location for easy perusal by the United States government.*
> *Including but not limited to: internet activity, credit card purchase history, airline ticket purchases, car rentals, medical records, educational transcripts, drivers license, utility bills, tax returns and any other available data.*

DARPA runs a program called "Human ID at a Distance", which is *apropos* of the cover's highway camera.

National Crime Information Computer (NCIC)

> *It's a fast-moving brokerage of criminal data over which information is exchanged by sixty-four thousand law enforcement agencies throughout the United States and Canada. NCIC responds to more than one million inquiries every day, or about 11.5 per second.*
> *If NCIC only bartered in records of convicted criminals, it would be hard to complain about...* **But NCIC goes much deeper.** *. . . [I]t also supplies files on individuals in trouble* (whatever that is) *with local authorities for any number or reasons: people arrested but not convicted of crimes, people with radical* (whatever that is) *political leanings, and people whom law enforcement authorities consider worth watching more closely because they're suspected of real crimes* **or because their behavior is erratic or eccentric.**
> — Jeffrey Rothfeder; *Privacy For Sale,* (1992) p.130

Even *this* isn't "good" enough; the FBI wanted to reshape and expand it to "NCIC 2000" with free, unquestioned access to databanks at airline reservation systems, car rental companies, banks, retailers, credit bureaus, insurance and phone companies — not to mention IRS, SSA and INS records. Never mind that NCIC records are woefully inaccurate and stale.

On a chilling note, the FBI has spent *billions* since 1988 to create a national DNA databank. Ostensibly for only known offenders, parents of missing children and individuals who cannot be positively identified, this will eventually extend to all

Americans. (The feds would like all newborns to get a heel stick-before leaving the hospital.)

Treasury Enforcement Communications System (TECS II)

Located in Newington, Virginia, TECS II determines if somebody entering the USA has committed previous customs violations or is wanted by other government agencies. TECS contains over a billion records in 700 tables to identify and keep track of federally suspect people, businesses, vehicles, boats, and aircraft. Acts as a portal to NCIC.

Worse than its quasi-omniscience is its gross *inaccuracy*. A secret 1990 study by the GAO found errors in **59%** of the sampled records. This means dirtbags can enter undetected while you and I are erroneously detained and inspected.

Interagency Border Inspections System (IBIS)

Initiated in 1989 as part of TECS, and it interfaces with the NCIC and also the 50 states through NLETS. Centralized records of aliens, their visas, and I-94 Arrival Records are also stored here. Portable IBIS devices (replacing the CD-ROM based PALS) are now issued to agents for use in primary inspections.

All license plates of border-crossing vehicles are read and entered into IBIS, as well as any interagency "lookout" information. When you and your license plate number is entered at one of nearly 300 ports of entry, the system searches through its own records, plus those of the DEA, FBI, the DoD, etc. Any person flagged will be at least detained. Lookout records can be temporary (90 days or less) or permanent (called the "A-File"), and IBIS records are accessible by some 20 other federal agencies and Interpol. NAILS and PALS are often used as a backup to IBIS.

When you enter Customs, the CBP agent knows information extremely varied and detailed — including which hospital your child was born in! I'd get your international traveling done with quickly, before it becomes even more intrusive.

If you are ever questioned at length during a secondary inspection, it may due to some "lookout information" about you being in NAILS or IBIS. Have your attorney write a letter to CBP inquiring the reason for the questioning. 31.7 of the CBP Inspector's Manual is illuminating here:

If an individual was questioned as part of the normal inspection process (i.e., without any lookout information), the response should be drafted accordingly.

However, in those case when lookout information was the reason for the referral to secondary inspection . . . the CBP response to the inquiring party will be limited to stating that the inquiry is being taken under consideration.

They won't tell you anything about the lookout information or which agency provided it to CBP, but the response is still informative.

Financial Crimes Enforcement Network (FinCEN)

This is the Treasury Department's sophisticated network using "artificial intelligence" to investigate complex financial dealings among disparate individuals and institutions. FinCEN has 200 employees from the IRS, FBI, Secret Service and the FDIC and works closely with the BATF, NSA, INS, FDIC, DEA, CIA and DIA. It can access over 135 financial databases, including land and real estate records, and credit reports.

Created in 1990 ostensibly to catch drug-related money-laundering operations, FinCEN was *really* formed to centralize financial information on honest Americans. According to Congressman Ron Paul, the feds admit that FinCEN is a trial run for a world system and they also admit that they want all bank employees to function as spies for the government. Its director bragged that FinCEN *"is a lot like Big Brother."*

FinCEN heavily relies upon Forms 4789 (Currency Transaction Report, or CTRs) and 8300 (the retailers' equivalent). More on all this in the chapter *Money.*

FBI'S Terrorist Watch List

The FBI has retained almost 24,000 names on the nation's terrorist watch list without current or proper justification, while failing to include people who are subjects of terrorist investigations, according to a Justice Department report issued yesterday.

The FBI's lapses "create a risk to national security," Justice Department Inspector General Glenn A. Fine said in the report. In addition, he said, keeping people on the list improperly can lead to unnecessary delays for travelers at airports, along highways and elsewhere.

Of the 68,000 submissions that the FBI has made to the watch list since 2004, almost 24,000, or 35 percent, were sourced to old or non-terrorism investigations, the report found.

At least 35 terrorism suspects who should have been on the list were not included, or their names were submitted after lengthy delays — in two cases, three years after investigations were opened. Of these, 12 traveled into or out of the country during the period in which they were not on the list.

— "FBI's Lapses on Terrorist Watch List Put Nation at Risk, Report Warns"

www.washingtonpost.com/wp-dyn/content/nation/natio nalsecurity/index.html

CAPPS-II (now to be called "Secure Flight")

CAPPS-II, the government's vast computerized system for probing the backgrounds of all passengers boarding flights, will be fielded this year. Total Information Awareness, a program that would link diverse databases and allow the FBI to collate information on all Americans, was halted at the federal level after a huge public outcry, but is continuing at a state level with federal funding. Over New Year's, the FBI collected the names of 260,000 people staying at Las Vegas hotels.

Instead, the Department of Justice, fueled by a strong police mentality inside the administration, is directing our nation's political changes in response to Sept. 11. And it's making trade-offs from its own subjective perspective — trade-offs that benefit it even if they are to the detriment of others.

— Bruce Schneier, "Slouching Towards Big Brother", January 30, 2004

http://news.com.com/2010-1028-5150325.html?tag=nefd_acpro

DMV and vehicle registration

Again, they only know what you *tell* them. It's plain foolish to register your car in your own name and address — especially if you're an attractive single woman. At the minimum, form a private LLC (or Nevada or Wyoming corporation) with a P.O. box address to own your public assets.

In Chapter 7 I'll show you how to create a seemingly valid *street* address which is completely bogus. Such serves as your "official" address for all licensing and registration.

telephone records

The Congress retroactively immunized the telecoms from lawsuits for betraying their customers' private data, not that any future lawsuit has any chance of ever proceeding:

From Rooms 4315 and 4944 of the FBIHQ came 700+ illegal requests for telephone subscribers' records and "community of interest", when no subpoenas existed. This rogue unit treated AT&T and Verizon/MCI as dumb terminals:

Due to exigent circumstances, it is requested that records for the attached list of telephone numbers from the date of inception to the present time be provided. A subpoena or NSL requesting this information has been submitted to the United States Attorney's Office (USAO) who will process and serve them formally to _____ as expeditiously as possible.

Additionally, please provide a community of interest for the telephone numbers in the attached list.

— FBI Unit Chief, Communication Analysis Unit

The Electronic Frontier Foundation (www.eff.org) should be financially supported for uncovering this gross and illegal invasion of privacy. The FBI office is under criminal investigation.

Facebook, MySpace, etc.

Any privacy-conscious person would be *foolish* to download any personal material about himself there. Read Facebook's "Privacy Policy" about data dissemination:

By posting Member Content to any part of the website, you automatically grant, and you represent and warrant that you have the right to grant, to Facebook an irrevocable, perpetual, non-exclusive, transferable, fully paid, worldwide license to use, copy, perform, display, reformat, translate, excerpt and distribute such information and content and to prepare derivative works of, or incorporate into other works, such information and content, and to grant and authorise sublicenses of the foregoing . . .

There is strong evidence linking Facebook to the Government:

*FACEBOOK was initially conceived by Mark Zuckerberg but the venture was first funded with $500,000.00 in capital from PayPal founder Peter Thiel. **With millions more to come***

**from sources with close ties to D.A.R.P.A, the Central
Intelligence Agency and the Department of Defense.**
Another $12.7 million came from James Breyer he is
closely associated with a venture capital company called
InQtel established by the CIA in 1999 and he served on the
board of BBN. InQtel deals in information technology and . . .
most notably "nurturing data mining technologies".
Dr. Anita Jones former Director of Defense Research and
Engineering for the U.S. Department of Defense. While with
D.A.R.P.A. her responsibilities included serving as an adviser
to the Secretary of Defense. Dr. Jones was also served on the
board of directors for InQtel and is now employed by BBN.
D.A.R.P.A. runs the Information Awareness Office whose
task it is to collect data on as many people as possible. Their
website is full of references to the war on terror, terrorism and
terrorist. The IAO claims its programs are for identifying and
responding to threats of terrorism.
— www.spiked-online.com/index.php?/site/article/4482/

INTERNATIONAL DATA-SHARING

According to a June 28, 2008 New York Times article, US and
European officials are nearly agreed upon a "binding
international agreement" which would allow "European
governments and companies to transfer personal information
to the United States, and vice versa." Under the cloak of
terrorism prevention, European governments could request
"private information - like credit card transactions, travel
histories, and Internet browsing habits" about American
citizens.

Envision an RFID-chipped consumer tomorrow, and full
content-recording by the NSA of your every phone call and
email — and all of this shared with foreign governments!

SURVEILLANCE CCTV CAMERAS

For a glimpse of our future, look to England:

In our ever-growing surveillance society, the average Briton is
being recorded 3,000 times a week

An investigation by The Sunday Telegraph has now uncovered just how much personal data is being collected about individuals by the Government, law enforcement agencies and private companies each day.

In one week, the average person living in Britain has 3,254 pieces of personal information stored about him or her, most of which is kept in databases for years and in some cases indefinitely.

The data include details about shopping habits, mobile phone use, emails, locations during the day, journeys and internet searches.

Every day the average person makes three mobile phone calls and sends at least two text messages. Each time the network provider logs information about who was called as well as the caller's location and direction of travel, worked out by triangulation from phone masts. Phone companies already retain data about their customers and give it to 650 public bodies on request.

An average of 50 websites are visited and 32 emails sent per person in Britain every day. Google receives around 68 searches from the average person each day and stores this data for 18 months.

A total of 520,000 requests were made by public officials for telephone and internet details last year, an increase from around 350,000 (or 49%) the previous year.

Every number plate picked up by the system is stored in a database with date, time and location for two years.

Britain now has more CCTV cameras in public spaces than any other country in the world. A study in 2002 estimated that there were around 4.2 million cameras, but that number is likely to now be far higher.

On the London Underground network, Transport for London (TfL) keeps footage for a minimum of 14 days. TfL operates more than 8,500 CCTV cameras in its underground stations, 1,550 cameras on tube trains and up to 60,000 cameras on buses.

— "How Big Brother watches your every move"

A poignant reader comment to the above:

We are all part of a system carefully designed from the very beginning. This all goes back before everything.

The more it became, the harder it was to tell it existed. Now only the few know the world they are born into is a prison, an enforced way of life.

Its not easy to see the obvious because we don't have the facts at the beginning, but when you stop and look around you see its all artificial, no one can live freely, everyone has to make a living by earning money to eat, and live with a roof over their heads.

The only way to get out of this mess is to finally accept we must not be governed whatsoever, we have to go back to the old ways, to live independently and only by ourselves.

But people are scared of that, because no one knows how to do that now thanks to the dark ones.

RADIO FREQUENCY ID CHIPS

If you can't identify things, you can't count them, you can't work out whether or not you can eat them, you can't work out whether or not they are friends or foe.
— Kevin Ashton, of Proctor & Gamble

The Auto-ID Center has a clear vision — to create a world where every object — from jumbo jets to sewing needles — is linked to the internet. Compelling as this vision is, it is only achievable if the center's system is adopted by everyone everywhere.   Success will be nothing less than global adoption.
— Helen Duce, an Auto-ID Center associate director

RFID chips are passive battery-free devices which, when subjected to radio energy, broadcast their unique serial number. They cost only pennies, and can be less than half a millimeter square and as thin as this page. There are serious plans afoot to create an "Internet of things" whereby every single item produced will have its own RFID tag. The potentiality of tracking control is enormous, a level of new omniscience never before contemplated. RFID chips:

can be read without your knowledge
can be read at great distances with a high-gain antenna
are difficult to remove
can cause disruptions if maliciously jammed

could be linked to your credit card number
have potential for counterfeit
can mark you for crime (burglars inventorying your house from afar)
can mark you for violence

Some examples of new technology such as atomic weapons, genetic cloning, nanotechnology, and RFID chips should have never been invented because mankind hasn't the responsibility or wisdom to avoid their abuse.

The really ominous thing about RFID is that chips can be passively read at considerable distance, and you'd never know it. That data would not only inventory your possessions, but your associations (even with strangers).

Depending on your politics and interests, imagine you're attending a gun show, a peace rally, a union meeting, a religious service, or a talk by a prominent Muslim cleric. Your right to attend any one of these events is protected by the First Amendment, which guarantees you free assembly with others, so it would be inappropriate for government agents to storm such an event and demand to see ID.

In the spychipped future, however, they could figure out who was there without having to ask. *With portable RFID readers in their backpacks, agents could mill around such events, pick up all the RFID tags* [from EDLs] *associated with the people in attendance, cross-reference them in commercial databases, and create a fairly thorough list of who was there.*

Not only would that information identify those people, but it could identify their extended web of contact as well. *For example, if Katherine were scanned while wearing her husband's winter scarf, the watch her mother bought her for graduation, and a pen she borrowed from a journalist, the government would know whom to begin questioning about her for more information.*

Even if the government could not determine who purchased the objects detected at the event, the unique RFID numbers the objects contain could still pose a threat to their owners' civil liberties. After the agents skimmed the numbers from the items associated with a peace rally, for example, they could put the objects themselves on a watch list. Even without conveying the identity of the individuals carrying them, the objects could communicate a "peace rally association" (or

a gun show association, etc.) that government agents could use later.
That way if a pair of shoes detected at a controversial event later showed up at an airport checkpoint, the wearer could be singled out for further questioning — or even be prevented from boarding the aircraft at all. (pp. 196-197)
— Katherine Albrecht & Liz McIntyre,
Spychips: How Major Corporations and Government Plan to Track Your Every Move with RFID (2005)

The above is a perfectly plausible scenario, and one cooked up by a couple of housewives! (In *The I.D.* chapter I quoted that true story of mobile passport reading.) It is difficult to imagine the true greater potential for Orwellian abuse.

Technology . . . is a queer thing. It brings you great gifts with one hand, and it stabs you in the back with the other.
— C.P. Snow, New York Times, 1971

corporations leading the way to an RFID nightmare

They are licking their chops at the marketing potential of instantly assessing any customer's personal goods and thus how to sell him more of the same. (Don't you already get enough junk mail, spam, and telemarketer calls?) Consumer data is already inappropriately shared, so imagine the evil committed from an RFID database!

It is wrong to spy on people through the products and services they buy.
— CASPIAN statement

RFID companies incestuous with government officials

Former Secretary of the Department of Homeland Security Tom Ridge joined the board of Savi Technology, the primary RFID technology provider for the Department of Defense, just four months after resigning from his cabinet post. Following in his footsteps, Former Secretary of Health and Human Services Tommy Thompson joined the board of VeriChip Corporation, makers of the human RFID implant. (p. 236)
— Katherine Albrecht & Liz McIntyre, *Spychips*

UNCHALLENGEABLE GOVERNMENT

From the point of view of the Justice Department, judicial oversight is unnecessary and unwarranted; doing away with it is a better trade-off. They think collecting information on everyone is a good idea because they are less concerned with the loss of privacy and liberty. Expensive surveillance and data-mining systems are a good trade-off for them because more budget means even more power. And from their perspective, secrecy is better than openness; if the police are absolutely trustworthy, then there's nothing to be gained from a public process.

When you put the police in charge of security, the trade-offs they make result in measures that resemble a police state.

This is wrong. The trade-offs are larger than the FBI or the Justice Department. Just as a company would never put a single department in charge of its own budget, someone above the narrow perspective of the Justice Department needs to be balancing the country's needs and making decisions about these security trade-offs.

The laws limiting police power were put in place to protect us from police abuse. Privacy protects us from threats by government, corporations and individuals. And the greatest strength of our nation comes from our freedoms, our openness, our liberties and our system of justice. Ben Franklin once said: "Those who would give up essential liberty for temporary safety deserve neither liberty nor safety." **Since the events of Sept. 11 Americans have squandered an enormous amount of liberty, and we didn't even get any temporary safety in return.**

— Bruce Schneier, "Slouching Towards Big Brother", January 30, 2004

http://news.com.com/2010-1028-5150325.html?tag=nefd_acpro

Now, there will no longer be any judicial oversight or remedy, if Obama's DoJ legal motion for dismissal is granted:

[I]ndeed none of plaintiffs' claims could proceed against any defendant (the NSA, the President, the DNI) — *because, at every stage, litigation plaintiffs' claims would require or risk the disclosure of information that is properly subject to the state secrets privilege and related statutory privileges.*

> *. . . While the dismissal of private claims is a significant step, long-standing authority holds that "the greater good" is the protection of the national security interests of the United States.* (p. 11-12)
> — Case 3:08-cv-04373-VRW, filed 04/03/2009
> www.eff.org/files/filenode/jewel/jewelmtdobama.pdf

Basically, where state secrets must be disclosed to litigate plaintiffs' claims, the case cannot proceed. Standing cannot be established or refuted without the disclosure of state secrets and harm to national security. The disclosure of privileged information would also be required to adjudicate plaintiffs' claims on the merits.

> *The sole basis for this* ["dragnet"] *allegation remains media reports concerning activities allegedly authorized in 2001, and the Government's acknowledgment of the Terrorist Surveillance Program in 2005. The TSP ended in 2007, and plaintiff's allegation as to any ongoing "dragnet" authorized by the President* **is sheer speculation** *that could not be addressed in further litigation without the disclosure of classified intelligence sources and methods.* (p. 34)
> — Case 3:08-cv-04373-VRW, filed 04/03/2009

Translation: since the Government will not provide you any proof of illegal spying, you have no evidence to sue them. Wow.

> *In other words, beyond even the outrageously broad "state secrets" privilege invented by the Bush administration and now embraced fully by the Obama administration, the Obama DOJ has now invented a brand new claim of government immunity, one which literally asserts that the U.S. Government is free to intercept all of your communications (calls, emails and the like) and — even if what they're doing is blatantly illegal and they know it's illegal — you are barred from suing them unless they "willfully disclose" to the public what they have learned.*
> *This is the first time* [the DOJ] *claimed sovereign immunity against Wiretap Act and Stored Communications Act claims. In other words, the administration is arguing that the U.S. can never be sued for spying that violates federal surveillance statutes, whether FISA, the Wiretap Act or the SCA.*

Thus: how the U.S. government eavesdrops on its citizens is too secret to allow a court to determine its legality. We must just blindly accept the claims from the President's DNI that we will all be endangered if we allow courts to determine the legality of the President's actions. Even confirming or denying already publicly known facts — such as the involvement of the telecoms and the massive data-mining programs — would be too damaging to national security. Why? Because the DNI says so. It is not merely specific documents, but entire lawsuits, that must be dismissed in advance as soon as the privilege is asserted because "its very subject matter would inherently risk or require the disclosure of state secrets."

President Obama promised the American people a new era of transparency, accountability, and respect for civil liberties. But with the Obama Justice Department continuing the Bush administration's cover-up of the National Security Agency's dragnet surveillance of millions of Americans, and insisting that the much-publicized warrantless wiretapping program is still a "secret" that cannot be reviewed by the courts, it feels like deja vu all over again.

— "New and worse secrecy and immunity claims from the Obama DOJ", Glenn Greenwald, April 6, 2009
www.salon.com/opinion/greenwald/2009/04/06/obama/index.html

Folks, we are now seeing the final chapter of our rights. There is no accountability of the Government to The People.

PAPERS

There are companies that offer a reconstruction service for documents that have been conventionally strip-shredded into thin segments using software that analyzes the graphical patterns that go to the edge of each piece. First, workers paste the random shreds onto standard sheets of paper, which takes three to seven minutes per page. The pages are scanned, and software analyzes the pieces for possible matches. **Up to 70 percent of a document's content can be recovered.** A company in Houston offers this service and charges about $2,000 to reconstruct a cubic foot — less than 100 pages — of shredded strips. According to the Times, the *company will soon offer a service to reconstruct cross-shredded documents for $8,000 to $10,000 per cubic foot.*

Here is some simple advice: If you don't *absolutely* need it, don't keep it! Paper records form a wake for others to follow. For example, I do not keep handwriting samples, travel schedules, non-vital receipts, routine letters, magazine labels, old catalogs (don't forget the inside order form, often with your address preprinted), previous working drafts of my writing, etc.

And how do I "not keep" them? Only one method of disposal meets my standard: **shredding *and* burning**. You should thoroughly burn the bits of your own paper trail at *least* monthly, if not weekly. Leave a short wake behind you. You'd be amazed at how many people have been arrested and convicted by evidence found in their car or trash. Don't throw it away, *burn* it! (*Extreme tip:* soak the ashes, too.)

For those of you still paying income taxes, store your receipts and diskettes *away* from your house or business. These records should be available only at *your* disposal, not the IRS. during some raid (which happens more often than you'd think).

Never carry around with you revealing paperwork. (I cover this in my *You & The Police!*) Right now, go through your own wallet or purse and imagine what all those bits of paper would tell about you to a complete stranger or the police. Would your home address or phone number be found? A sensitive "To-Do" list? Travel plans? Private correspondence?

If you must *temporarily* have such paperwork with you on the road, then keep it in a combination-lock briefcase in the trunk. This offers a firm, legal barrier to all general searches.

PRIVACY & TECHNOLOGY

Soon it will be possible to assert almost continuous surveillance over every citizen and maintain up-to-date complete files containing even the most personal information about citizens. **These files will be subject to instantaneous retrieval by the authorities.**

— Zbigniew Brzezinski; *Between Two Ages* (1970)

Sometimes, the very measures that are put in place to safeguard our liberty, threaten liberty itself.
— from the movie *Eagle Eye*

Databanks are manifestations of computer technology. But what *is* technology? It is merely the multiplication of human effort by artificial means. It is not magic, it is only *leverage*. As leverage, it multiplies the *effect and scope* of the operator.

Technology is vital to oppressive governments as they simply *cannot afford* man-on-man surveillance. East Germany tried it and went bankrupt. (Watch the excellent movie about just this, *The Lives of Others*.) In Romania, one citizen in *five* was a paid government informant. (Romania never *went* bankrupt — it never *escaped* bankruptcy.)

Governments rely upon technological leverage to be nearly omnipresent, and omnipresence is the prerequisite to omnipotence. Any leverage, however, requires a *fulcrum*. That fulcrum is knowing on *whom* to focus. By being a public agitator, you've given government the necessary fulcrum to use its techno-leverage against you. Neutralize that fulcrum and the lever itself is rendered useless. By being private, we force on government an inefficient, costly, and ineffective system of Romanian man-on-man surveillance. The government *cannot* win without its techno-leverage and its broad-based social conditioning through the media megaphones.

While we are working to counter the social conditioning, not enough is being done to counter government's techno-leverage. There are a few ways to do this:

even the playing field by matching technology

This is difficult, expensive and time-consuming. Americans simply don't have the required time and money. While we do need some really well-equipped people, we just can't afford it *systemically*. (However, if you've the money, you can equip yourself *nearly* as well as the black bag boys.)

The battle between the rulers and the ruled is (for now) primarily one of *information*. For example, the putative collapse of Soviet communism was greatly assisted by the mass influx of computers and fax machines. Similarly, the Federal Government has grown panicky over the explosion of talk radio, desktop publishing, digital gold, encryption, and VoIP.

Especially the Internet. No wonder the feds are pushing for an "Information Highway" (singular). *One* superhighway would be easiest to control. (They'd rather prohibit the thing altogether, but they're too late. That particular cat is already out of the bag. That's why they're working on Internet2, for themselves, so they can shut down ours when desired. I forecast that to occur by 2015.) What we need, and what we'll probably succeed in getting, are *several* highways and hundreds of smaller roads.

Information, however, is merely *one* key — it is not *the* key to our eventual Liberty. Once governments realize that they've lost the information battle, they'll see no choice but to resort to the blackmail of *food.* Food is leverage, especially over the urbanites. Hungry people, regardless of their informational capabilities or libertarian politics, will "see the light":

> *Food is power. We use it to change behavior. Some may call that bribery. We do not apologize.*
> — Catherine Bertini, Exec. Dir. U.N. World Food Program
> U.N. 4th World Conference on Women, Sept. 1995

We're winning the information battle, but at the same time let's also enhance our physical self-sufficiency and preparedness. Move to the country, till the soil, homeschool your children, and train with the firearms you *should* have by now *already* acquired. The privacy measures I outline *are* important, but do not ignore the *physical* measures.

low-cost countermeasures

A private life is an example of this. The NVA's method of warfare against us in Vietnam is another. **The finer the net, the more *slowly* it must be trolled.** As long as you remain a bright, quick, little fish — the net won't catch you. Sure, the net *will* catch millions of human shrimp, but you and I will not be one of them.

We *want* government to stay top-heavy and rely mostly upon its expensive techno-leverage. We want them to be vulnerable to the weather, quirky satellites, bad cameras, and an unexpected shortage of AA cell batteries. Folks, night vision devices and laser range-finding gear is neat stuff, but first learn to live and fight without it. Never rely upon the "gravy."

rendering oppressive technology moot

Technology has always been a double-edged sword. Who gets cut by it largely depends upon who wields it from the *higher* position. If you can't gain elevation on your opponent because he controls the high ground, don't just stand there. Leave the room and make his sword *irrelevant*. The government is stronger and taller than us. Did David slog it out with Goliath? No. David kept his distance and calmly put a rock in Goliath's temple. He made Goliath's strength and height irrelevant.

Similarly, we cannot beat the government in a slugging match. Fine; one should never fight the enemy's game — make him fight *yours*. My view is that we should concentrate on using the tools we have *today* to *circumvent* the system and force a paradigm shift. Freedom-loving individuals should have their *own* private communications net and their *own* economic system (preferably in encrypted digital form backed by warehoused gold). Let the government swat at *air*.

So, FinCEN will have real-time access to our credit card and banking transactions. *So what?* We'll quit using them in favor of cash and digital gold. Try to paint us into a corner and we'll jump to another *building*.

Personally and systemically, we need to transform into *ghosts*. This book is about the *personal* transformation. An upcoming book will address the *systemic* transformation, but we'll need many more individual ghosts before our vaporish world can be possible. **We must first neutralize the government's leverage and force to them to go "man-on-man."** *Then* it will be a personal battle which no American can *ignore*. *Then* it will be the personal battle which no government has ever *won*.

We *can* make the oppressive "real-world" irrelevant. The tyrants first made freedom inconvenient and then out of reach. We will wield that *back* edge of the technological sword.

We will swing that sword and win back our country.

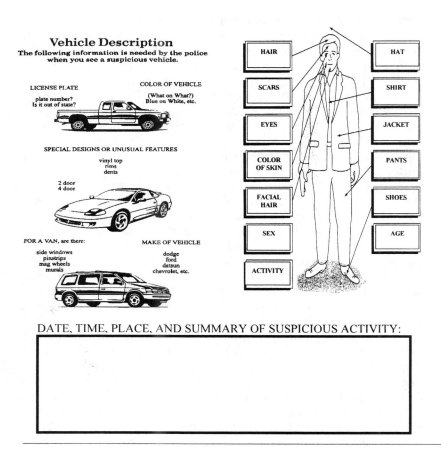

DATE, TIME, PLACE, AND SUMMARY OF SUSPICIOUS ACTIVITY:

For additional information on reporting suspicious activities go to the website of the Pennsylvania Office of Homeland Security at:

http://www.homelandsecurity.state.pa.us/

PRIVACY & PEOPLE

We live in a human world. While no man is an island, and I wouldn't want to be an utter hermit, being a peninsula suits *me* just fine. Although everybody needs people, a minor link to humanity is enough for me. I prefer to define that link's quality and quantity as much as *reasonably* possible. This is a weighty goal by itself, but when one adds stringent privacy measures the task can become quite formidable.

Since we do live in a human world, you must at least occasionally rub elbows with people. To do so, yet retain privacy, requires a certain kind of person; one who plans ahead, thinks quickly on his feet, has the easy capability to spin yarns, and a *good memory*. Above all, one must have a good memory.

LEVELS OF INTIMACY

You should have concentric levels of trust. The better you know somebody, the more intimate you allow them to become.

Americans are notorious for their immediate "friendships" and first-name/arm-on-shoulder relationships. Though I love our sense of easy rapport, it's often at the cost of incredible shallowness and fickleness. Having lived abroad, I prefer the European *time-based* approach to establishing friendships. There, it generally takes at least a *year* to be considered one's friend. In the Germanic countries, when an elder accepts a youth as a friend it's commemorated by the **Du**zenshaft—an evening of drinks whereby the youth is officially invited to call the elder by the informal *Du* instead of the formal *Sie*.

There is no such equivalent rite of passage in America. We've completely erased any former distinction between acquaintances and friends. We've cheapened our friendships, and though as an insular sociological phenomenon it has escaped our *own* notice, foreigners are painfully aware of it. **My fellow Americans, heed this advice:** if you befriend a foreigner, do not voice invitations to write letters or visit your home unless you will damn well *keep* your promise. When a Dutchman hears that he is welcome in your home when visiting Memphis, he is relying upon your word. Put him up without fail. If his visit's timing doesn't mesh, then put him up at a friend's or at a hotel. Make your word mean something.

I have visited the homes of dozens of foreign friends and never once was an invitation extended to me withdrawn when I was due. When a European invites you as a guest, he *means* it and it is a great honor. (Be a *good* guest. Take his family out to a nice dinner, or leave them a nice gift from America.) Americans, on the other hand, invite frivolously and are shocked when Gunter from Stuttgart actually calls. Our country has bad enough of a reputation. Don't sour it further. If you meet a foreigner traveling through your town and you two hit it off, invite him/her to your home, if for nothing but a coffee. Let's undo decades of damage. O.K., enough on that.

Understanding the progression of public, acquaintance, friend, good friend, and best friend, let's start.

privacy with the public

The "public" means clerks, passersby and the like. These people need to know very little about you — only enough to accomplish your goal. They're not generally entitled to your voice mail number and P.O. box, unless absolutely necessary (*i.e.*, during a classified ad sale). Be polite, keep your word, do your deal, and leave. If you like somebody in particular, then he gets to become an acquaintance.

privacy with your acquaintances

An acquaintance is neither fish nor fowl — neither public nor friend. It is a difficult relationship in America. We are by nature a friendly people, and it's only natural that your acquaintances will want to become your friends. This is not necessarily a bad thing (some of your acquaintances *should* become friends), however, the lesson here is *not* to allow the transformation to be *routine*. In my estimation, of all the people one knows by name, 80% should remain merely acquaintances.

Acquaintances are such because of a basic common interest and affinity. Thus, they will usually deserve to have your voice mail number and mail-drop address, but nothing more. Only friends (and perhaps only *good* friends) should know where you live (or your real name if using an alias). Whatever the common interest, let acquaintanceships remain there until you feel *very* comfortable in befriending them.

Do not significantly avail upon your acquaintances, nor allow them to significantly avail upon you. Such is done only amongst *friends*. Do not ask him to take you to the airport or use his mower. Never lend to or borrow from an acquaintance.

If the acquaintance comes to realize that you're intentionally stunting the growth of the relationship (and most won't), he can become hurt or even pushy. You must handle this very adroitly. Even though the issue *is* a personal one, you cannot be unfeeling and coarse about it. Explain that you've been badly hurt in the past and that you've grown to prefer taking longer time in making friends. Most folks will be satisfied with this, and will value a future friendship with you all the more. The rest you should quietly drop as acquaintances. Learn earlier, rather than later.

the acquaintance neighbor

Although he's not a friend, he knows: where you live, many of your habits, and who many of your friends are. **He must be *very* carefully managed.** He is in a position to cause you great grief and inconvenience. (Randy Weaver's problems were much exacerbated by his poor relations with a neighbor.) **The main things to avoid cultivating in your neighbors are: *annoyance, curiosity, suspicion and envy*.** Do not flaunt your wealth or share your business with them. Do not get into hassles with them. Keep contact to a minimum, though not suspiciously so. Be cheerful, polite, respectful, moderately helpful — this is the cost of living in town and having neighbors. If you're unwilling or unable to pay this modest fee, then buy hundreds of acres in the country.

Befriending a neighbor acquaintance is not recommended. A neighbor friend is like a marriage. Besides, if you move and he is questioned — can you trust him to not divulge your new location? As wonderful as most of my neighbors have been, I personally have preferred *not* to befriend them and thus be free to relocate without trace.

privacy and your friends

Every friendship is a sort of secession, even a rebellion. It may be a rebellion of serious thinkers against accepted claptrap or of faddists against accepted good sense; of real artists against popular ugliness or of charlatans against civilized taste; of good men against the badness of society...

Whatever it is, it will be unwelcome to Top People. In each knot of friends, there is a section which fortifies its members against the public opinion of the community in general. Each is therefore a pocket of potential resistance. Men who have real friends are less easy to manage or "get at"; harder for bad authorities to corrupt. Hence, if our masters, by force or by propaganda about "togetherness" or by unobtrusively making privacy impossible, ever succeed in producing a world in which all are companions and none are friends, they will have removed certain dangers, and will also have taken from us what is almost our strongest safeguard against complete servitude.
— C.S. Lewis; *The Four Loves*

You may have the same problem that I *used* to have — *too many friends*. A million rhinestones cannot make wealth, but a handful of diamonds do. I was a Rhinestone Baron, wondering why I was continually disappointed with my friends.

I used to make friends the American way — *profusely*. My PDA once contained over 1,100 people. It was ridiculous. I didn't need so many "friends," but what to do? As the waggish quote goes, *"It's easy to make a friend. What's hard is to make a stranger."* Obviously, I couldn't call up 900 people and tell them they've been to demoted to Acquaintance First Class.

So, I allowed a natural attrition based on an important criterion of mine. Those who kept in regular touch with me *by letter* stayed onboard. I wanted to keep those friends who were letter writers, and who would write to me. Generally, the letter-writing friends have been better friends than the phone-calling ones. There's just something special about writing a letter, and stamping the envelope. Email just can't compare.

best friends

To me, there are friends, good friends, and *best* friends. A *best* friend is one for whom I'd die defending, and vice versa. A *best* friend understands your need for privacy, and could be trusted with just about all of your secrets. This book's measures will largely be moot for best friends. While one can't have too many best friends, they are so rare and so time-consuming in development that I doubt one could make more than one a year. In the times ahead, we will desperately need all the best friends we can make. A man ending up with as many as *six* best friends is wealthy beyond words.

good friends

A *good* friend is an extremely solid person. He knows many, but not all, of your secrets. He knows your real name and where you live. Hopefully, he is enroute to becoming a *best* friend, but this is not always possible or advisable. You'll know if that's the case. Good friends can easily become jealous of your best friends if they sense a dichotomy. Therefore, friends shouldn't know there are *good* friends and good friends shouldn't know there are *best* friends. Tell them when they've *been* "promoted" but don't warn them of any possible upgrades.

friends

A "mere" friend is one you trust about a third of the way. You constantly test his strength, reliability and discretion. Is he a whiner, a braggart, or a bully? Find out ASAP. Making a new friend is exciting, but keep things toned down. He's much more than an acquaintance, but much less than a best friend. Remember, he's a *candidate* for bigger things.

from friend to good friend to best friend

In general, friends should make up only *20%* of who you know. "Mere" friends will make up 80% of your friends; good friends 18%; best friends 2%. For example, if you know 1,000 people (and most of you do), 800 should be acquaintances, 160 friends, 36 good friends, and only 4 best friends. I'm being silly, of course, but these figures seem in the ballpark.

A good timetable is at least a *year* between levels. Acquaintance, year one. Friend, year two. Good friend, year three. *Best* friend, year four. Folks, I'm not kidding about this! Make friendship *stand* for something. Make people *earn* it.

Would you throw a house together in a month and expect it to shelter you in a storm? Friends are roofs over our heads. Take the time to build a *quality* human shelter.

girlfriends

More guys have unnecessarily confided sensitive matters to their girlfriends, only to their detriment. Many men in prison today are pondering Shakespeare's wisdom, *"Hell hath no fury like a woman scorned."* **You never know a woman until you break up with her.** If a woman feels mistreated, then all bets are off. Most guys dumb enough to own unregistered full-autos were caught because their ex snitched.

Therefore, if she absolutely doesn't *need* to know something, and you're not defrauding her by your silence — *be quiet.* This takes some diligent compartmentalization. That doesn't make it "bad" — that just makes it *real. Nothing personal.*

relatives

Do not relax your standards with relatives. Just because a random human is your cousin or sister by complete accident of birth, don't divulge your life secrets unless they've gone through the filtering process.

Be very careful about what phone number and address you give to relatives, even to your own parents. Not so much that they'll purposely betray you, but *inadvertently.* One's relatives are much more easily discovered than one's friends. Relatives will absorb the initial questioning and will be watched the longest. Train them well, or leave them out of the loop.

One P.I. told the story about a skip trace who was close to his out-of-state mother. So the P.I. calls his mother, *"Mrs. Jones, this is Dr. Malcolm at Cleveland General Hospital. Your son, Brian, has been in a severe car accident and we need you to fly out and to identify him and sign some papers."* (or something like that). Mrs. Jones, caught totally off-guard and now in a panic, calls her son's number given to her only for emergencies. The P.I. later got her long-distance records. Clever, huh?

Relatives should be trained not to believe every "old friend" or "emergency" call. Have them say only, *"Give me your name and number. If we hear from him, we'll tell him you called."* They should use a prepaid calling card from a payphone to reach you, and *never* dial your home from theirs. Analyzing their MUDs is an easy way to find a skip trace.

your spouse

If you're *contemplating* marriage, accept nothing less than a best friend. If your spouse is not at least a *good* friend, then you've got problems. Ideally, your spouse should be not only *a* best friend, but *the* best friend you have.

If you're *already* married, making a best friend of your spouse should be your Number One earthly priority. Most men are morons, slaving at a job and thinking that their wives get all turned on by the Good Provider thing. Yes, husbands *should* support their families — but families need *more* than that. Men, take *time* to be *with* your wife and children. Share *yourself*, not just your paycheck. Or, you can hear *Cats and the Cradle* over the radio, and cry enroute to the office in your Mercedes, suddenly realizing how empty your entire life became, why your wife is sleeping with the tennis coach and your children never come to visit. Guys, catch a clue.

That aside, back to privacy. You should develop code gestures, words and phrases, mutually plant caches and test each other's privacy measures. You are a *team*. Perform as one.

your children

They are *yours*, not the State's. The State, however, wants their minds and souls and bodies — so you will have to *fight* to keep them. This is difficult, especially with threats such as the *U.N. Convention on the Rights of The Child*.

Maintain *perfect* relations with your neighbors, or else some do-gooder will inform "social services" that your children are undernourished, neglected, abused, etc. Once a case file is started, every local bureaucrat will be hypersensitive to anything regarding your family. You might as well move.

Regarding social behavior, your children should be polite and respectful without volunteering information or answering personal questions. Train them to *never* repeat your actual address to anybody, nor discuss family matters. If ever strenuously questioned by authorities, they should know to reply, *"I don't know. You'll have to ask my parents that."*

Do not divulge to them anything that they do not absolutely *need* to know — especially sensitive activities. As with anybody, trust them only as far as you must. They shouldn't be burdened with heavy family secrets, anyway.

how to not register your children

First rule: "Social Security Numbers" are not mandatory. (www.ssa.gov/pubs/10023.html   www.ssa.gov/pubs/10023.pdf) Hospitals will insist on parents filling out the SSN application before mother and baby check out — *absolutely refuse!* For those of you still filing unrequired Form 1040s, an SSN is asked (though not required) for all claimed dependents — **but you're *not required* to claim *any* dependents**. Keep them off the tax rolls, even if it costs you the tax deduction.

You might want to home birth with a midwife, for privacy and to avoid getting a "Birth Certificate" which registers your child with the Commerce Department as a *"national resource."* Create your own "Record of Birth" with signed witnesses.

protecting your children's minds

Whatever you do, do *not* send them to public schools. The "education" is worse than poor; it is designed to sap their independence and ruin their critical thinking. (Read the books by former public school teacher John Taylor Gatto.) The State wants "world citizens" — that is, androids with no American allegiance or strong family ties. Send them to a quality *private* school (which refuses federal funding and the attached strings).

If a private school is too expensive or unavailable, then consider home-schooling. You can even join local families to pool resources and expertise. Some states allegedly "require" that you register as home-schoolers, but you could easily avoid that by saying that you're just passing through from Mississippi, Virginia or South Carolina (which have repealed compulsory attendance laws). Stay low key.

protecting your children's bodies

Be very suspicious of "compulsory" vaccines. You have a parental right to refuse vaccinations on medical, legal, and religious grounds. Find out (if you can) exactly *what* is in those flu shots, etc. — before subjecting your children to some mystery vaccine. Gulf War Syndrome has been decisively linked to the U.S. military's anthrax vaccine according one tireless researcher (www.Vaccine-A.com). SIDS is believed to be a delayed vaccine-induced injury. In Japan, children aren't vaccinated before 6 years of age and SIDS is nearly unheard of. You can refuse vaccinations C visit www.mercola.com and www.vaclib.org. Also fascinating is the probability that Baxter deliberately weaponized in 2009 their H3N2 flu shot with deadly H5N1 avian flu. (Baxter claims it was an "accident", which is *impossible* under BSL3 standards.) The full story is at: www.prisonplanet.com/accidental-contamination-of-vaccine-with-live-avian-flu-virus-virtually-impossible.html

I am personally suspicious of fluoridated water. Sodium fluoride (not the same as naturally occurring calcium fluoride) is a by-product of making aluminum and is listed as a *poison* by the CDC. (What do you think *rat* poison is made of? Check the label.) Fluoridated water does *nothing* to enhance teeth hardness as claimed (studies have now proven this) and European countries have outlawed it since the 1970s — so what's *really* the point? What do the French and the Swiss know that we don't? Drink well water or distilled water.

ON TRUSTING PEOPLE

For example, fully 90% of all FBI arrests are directly due to the *"helpful cooperation"* of neighbors and relatives. Keep your mouth shut. Never get chatty with government officials. Don't talk to the State. Only silence *can't* be used against you.

"Trust only if you can, and then only if you have to."
It's the *second* part of this maxim which will protect you, as trusting is easier than qualifying the absolute *necessity* of trusting particularly. Let me express my aphorism another way: If you believe a person trustworthy on an issue, but can *wait* to find out, then wait. From my own experience, I cannot recall a *single* incident where I *should* have trusted, but did not, or waited too long. I can, however, think of dozens of times where I trusted too early (and sometimes *far* too early).

Trust only at the last minute, so to speak. Why trust too early? There's no advantage, and much potential risk. This is true because of immutable human nature: **People are *verbs*.** Fewer than 5 in 100 you'll ever meet are solid, dependable, and thoroughly trustworthy souls.

The other 95% exhibit merely varying *degrees* of reliability, and some of them *seem* totally trustworthy for quite a while, until a real crunch arrives. Take your time to trust.

putting friendships to the test

I am retrospectively a big believer in this. Something is reliable only if it's been *proven* to be reliable. If you haven't tested your friendships by important (though not utterly crucial) matters, then you've no idea how strong they really are.

I once knew a couple my age for many years who seemed to be high-quality people. We had spent lots of time together and knew each other well. Then, one day, I needed an urgent favor. It was a big favor to me, but a small one to them (which required no risk or expense and only 5 minutes of inconvenience). They hemmed and hawed and finally declined. (I went to another friend, who immediately and cheerfully agreed.) A few days later, they told me that they'd been *"stupid"* and were profoundly sorry, and now would gladly help. I replied that, while I appreciated their change of heart, tests of friendship often come in sudden moments and that I could never trust them as I once had. (To their credit, they took it well.)

intentional tests

Trust is like a muscle, and it must be at least sporadically exercised. For example, I make a point of occasionally (say, yearly) lending and borrowing small amounts of money. (Such is collected/paid back within days.) A friend who is not good for $50 is a very weak friend.

A similar kind of test is entrusting a secret. In all of my friends I've confided one interesting item, unique to their ears alone. (None of them are earth-shattering, but they are juicy enough to tempt any gossiper.) Each friend is a vault for a particular secret, and if one of them gets out, I know the source.

Yes, I realize that all this may sound cold and inhuman, but I'd rather learn of any weakness or betrayal earlier (and in a smaller context), rather than later (and in a crucial matter).

when trust is betrayed

In the past few years I've lost two good friends and even a best friend. Two of those three actually turned on me with their betrayals of trust. One was a blatant Narcissist. The other, was also a narcissist, but much worse. You'll meet him next.

THE SOCIOPATH

It ain't what ya don't know that hurts ya. What really puts a hurtin' on ya is what ya knows for sure, that just ain't so.
— Uncle Remus

A sociopath (or "psychopath") is an intraspecies predator:

Imagine — if you can — not having a conscience, none at all, no feelings of guilt or remorse no matter what you do, no limiting sense of concern for the well-being of strangers, friends, or even family members. Imagine no struggles with shame, not a single one in your whole life, no matter what kind of selfish, lazy, harmful, or immoral action you had taken. And pretend that the concept of responsibility is unknown to you, except as a burden others seem to accept without question, like gullible fools. Now add to this strange fantasy the ability to conceal from other people that your psychological makeup is radically different from your theirs. Since everyone simply assumes that conscience is universal among human beings, hiding the fact that you are conscience-free is nearly effortless. You are not held back from any of your desires by guilt or shame, and you are never confronted by others for your cold-bloodedness. The ice water in your veins is so bizarre, so completely outside of their personal experience, that they seldom even guess at your condition.

In other words, you are completely free of internal restraints, and your unhampered liberty to do just as you please, with no pangs of conscience, is conveniently invisible to the world. You can do anything at all, and still your strange advantage over the majority of people, who are kept in line by their consciences, will most likely remain undiscovered. (p.2)
— Martha Stout, Ph.D., *The Sociopath Next Door*

A sociopath is somebody who, through a combination of heritable condition, genetic predisposition and upbringing, has no sense of interconnectedness (bonding) with living beings and thus no foundation for an active conscience (like the 96% rest of us who do have one). Studies indicate that sociopathy involves an altered processing of emotional stimuli at the level of the cerebral cortex, and thus sociopaths simply cannot process emotional experience, such as love and caring.

For those of us who have been successfully socialized, imagining the world as the psychopath experiences it is close to impossible.
— Dr. Robert D. Hare, *Without Conscience: The Disturbing World of the Psychopaths Among Us*, p. 78

sociopathy is a *noncorrectable* disfigurement of character

It cannot be cured by therapy.   Sociopaths are wired wrong, and not only do they not know it, their disorder (in contrast to narcissism) causes them no anxiety:

Sociopathy stands alone as a "disease" that causes no disease for the person who has it, no subjective discomfort. Sociopaths are often quite satisfied with their lives, and perhaps for this very reason there is no effective treatment. (Stout, p.12)

Psychopaths don't feel they have psychological or emotional problems, and they see no reason to change their behavior to conform to societal standards with which they do not agree.
To elaborate, psychopaths are generally well satisfied with themselves and with their inner landscape, bleak as it may seem to outside observers. They see nothing wrong with themselves, experience little personal distress, and find their behavior rational, rewarding, and satisfying; they never look back with regret or forward with concern.   They perceive themselves as superior beings in a hostile, dog-eat-dog world in which others in order to obtain their 'rights,' and their social interactions are planned to outmaneuver the malevolence they see in others.   Given these attitudes, it is not surprising that the purpose of most psychotherapeutic approaches is lost on sociopaths. (Hare, p.195)

Morals, ethics, etc. are foreign concepts never having been internalized as personal boundaries:

About one in twenty-five individuals are sociopathic . . . . It is not that this group fails to grasp the difference between good and bad; it is that the distinction fails to limit their behavior. (Stout, p.9)

These "people" are fairly rare, yet still common enough at 4% of adults.   (It is generally believed by experts that 3% of men and 1% of women are sociopaths.)

If privacy is important to you, a sociopath will know it and use it against you. In the case of a former best friend, I was shocked to learn that he was a full-blown sociopath (*e.g.*, a pathological liar, serial thief, and shameless war vet fraud). Covetous of anybody with actual experience and reputation exceeding his own, "Jack" tried to destroy what he couldn't have. Extremely dangerous to your finances and emotional health, sociopaths cannot be even occasionally trusted. What drives them is power over other people, and they achieve this through very clever manipulation

sociopaths and morality

Dr. F. Scott Peck's seminal book *The People of The Lie* contains the best definition of evil I've yet read. To paraphrase:

- The evil hide their motives with lies.

- Evil people want to appear to be good.

- When confronted by evil, the wisest and most secure adult will usually experience confusion. (This is guaranteed if he doesn't understand sociopathy.)

- Evil seeks to discourage self-thinking (fosters dependency).

- We must have an ongoing dedication to reality at all cost.

Guiltlessness was in fact the first personality disorder to be recognized by psychiatry, and terms that have been used at times the past century include *manie sans d'lire*, psychopathic inferiority, moral insanity, and moral imbecility.

According to the current bible of psychiatric labels, the *Diagnostic and Statistical Manual of Mental Disorders IV* of the APA, the clinical diagnosis of "antisocial personality disorder" should be considered when an individual possesses at least three of the following seven characteristics:

❶ failure to conform to social norms
❷ deceitfulness, manipulativeness
❸ impulsivity, failure to plan ahead
❹ irritability, aggressiveness
❺ reckless disregard for the safety or self of others
❻ consistent irresponsibility
❼ lack of remorse after having hurt or stolen from another person

They understand the difference between right and wrong, but are not emotionally constrained by it. This is outlandish to moral people. Just so you aren't tempted to believe that I'm exaggerating things, read an illuminating forum exchange between three sociopaths. (Typos/misspellings are theirs.)

I have a craving for all things anti-social. I love perversity, I love violent or hardcore pornography, and I love anything anti-social that gives me a cathartic release or stimulates my mind. I cannot sate this craving. What should I do? I cannot relent in my pursuit for hedonism, and my lack fo any sex life has resulted in me becoming more sex-starved than ever. The fantasies keep getting more violent, and the urge stronger. I've had to live transgressively through my visual scenarios which involve violent fantasies, but even this is starting to fail. Also, the speaking of anything vulgar titillates me.

*It sickens me the whole way criminals are treated in this country. **Nobody is able to grasp the idea that there's no objective evil in the world, and that evil actions are caused by imbalance**...that sociopathy is imbalance and is no more or less of a sickness than someone with depression.*
— sociopath A

If there is no objective evil, then there can be no objective good, either. Sociopaths truly believe that morality is just a construct, used to hinder them. They believe that nobody is actually moral, and those who claim to be are just hypocrites. The sociopath sees himself the superior being because he does not voluntarily restrain himself to such shackles.

Now read the ghoulish responses that post received:

i think i understand where you're coming from because i've been experiencing similar things for a while now. i personally have come to terms with the fact that im a "horrible" human being and i think that's fine. might as well embrace it, right?

***my cravings . . . involve extreme violence and inflicting as much physical and psychological suffering as possible.** i haven't acted on them, so they're just really detailed thoughts/dreams for me also.*

personally, i feel society should be punished as thoroughly and frequently as possible.** no amount of tears would ever be enough. **people should live in a permanent state of terror. they have marginalized people like me

*(and i guess people like you, if you feel the same) because of arbitrary decisions over what's "right" and "wrong." **who put them in such a position and who is to say we must follow them?** i think society is way behind where it should be and the people who are criminals now will be regular citizens in the future.*
     — sociopath B

*Society has a lot of weird, arbitrary standards set in place - and the norm has never been consistent with what I like, and there's nothing set in stone that says we have to follow these arbitrary rules. It's freeing once you cut God out of your life, as you don't live your life according to this moral code. **I can be a scumbag, with little to no compunction or remorse.** Society's irrational, it's headed down a slippery slope, and I see no reason to accomodate it, other than when I absolutely have to for my own self-gain. **I get a sort of sadistic glee anytime I circumvent the conventions or do something deemed 'immoral', and the more I do such a thing, the better.***
     — sociopath A

Society tries to punish the sociopath with its fake morals, hence the sociopath is justified in fighting back as a scumbag. At this point, sociopath C can't resist joining in:

*I don't belive humans should live in a "constant state of terror", I pretty much like the way occidental society lives: in this constant state of hedonism and stupidity. **The moral thing is so oblivious that It doesn't even comes to my mind when I do something that could be seen as "bad".** I wouldn't be surprised if morals and norms were establish by people like you who simply wanted to manipulate the mass to exploit it. Now, we're stuck with those norms and morals and "good and bad".*

. . . The "thrill" you get when doing something that is seen as "bad" woudn't be that amusing if it were seen as "good".

*I don't get the point of whining about how society is. I, off course, would like to live far away from humans, from thier laws, morals and money. But since it ain't easy, **I prefer seeing this society as a big playground. I assure you that because people are hedonist, delusional, "good", idiot and happy... they are much more "enjoyable". By***

this I'm talking about the manipulation and all those games you would probably "enjoy".
— sociopath C

Notice their use of quotation marks for "good" and "bad"? Again, morality does not exist; there's no objective evil. They honestly believe this, and trying to explain morality to them is like describing colors to a blind man. Only selfishness exists:

We're all selfish. I'm selfish, and anyone who fails to see their own selfishness is clearly blind - it's an unfortunate part of humanity. We all want our needs fulfilled and those that are at the top of the chain - those that know which societal targets to hate, those who know how to manipulate better in conversation, will obviously fulfilled more of their needs. And to eliminate suffering or any kind of selfishness would be ideal, but it's not going to happen. **I prefer just to take that selfishness to the extreme, because I can and it's pleasurable.**

Many of us get a thrill from picking on this target to no end - I don't claim to know everyone, but I can tell you based on my own experience and comparing with others, that **the feeling of superiority one derives from ganging up on societal targets is nice.**

I just want let our generation know that anyone who isn't blessed into the genetic lottery is essentially screwed over. Life's a game of chance right now, and if you've lost it, you've lost. . . . I wish the human race would be trimmed back anyways. The genetically superior are set in place to succeed, as much as I can tell. Some people are given this innate stroke of genetic luck, given more of an aptitude for a skill or a trait, or just physically superior. It's fucked. I hate it. **The inevitable cycle of society angers me to no end, so I refuse to play nicely.**
— sociopath A

So, to recap this demented ethos:

sociopathy is a genetic error, not a personal choice
the sociopath is not bound by rules which penalize him
anything goes to achieve selfish desires
whoever gets manipulated and burned is at fault for weakness

In 2008 the University of Chicago tested young sociopaths with fMRI scans and discovered that their brains light up with pleasure at the suffering of others. Their empathy pathways showed no abnormality, which suggests that sociopaths are indeed empathic . . . but in a *sadistic* sense. (They enjoy hurting because it confirms they are achieving power.) This confirmed Heilburn's "warped empathy" theory of 1982:

> *One way to interpret these results would be in terms of a sadistic, effective-processing psychopathic model of violence in which inflicting pain or distress upon another is arousing and reinforcing (pleasurable). Such a model would assume that acts inflicting pain are more intentional than impulsive and that empathic skills promote arousal and sadistic reinforcement (pleasure) by enhancing the psychopath's awareness of the pain and distress being experienced by the victim.*

Coleridge called Shakespeare's Iago a "*motiveless malignancy.*" This is why sociopaths are so hard for most people to understand . . . at first. They are completely counterintuitive to basic human decency. Being evil for the sheer sake of evil is a foreign idea us. However, once you've "wrapped your mind" around their nature (and it's a predictable one, too), sociopaths are easy to understand. They'll do what they can get away with.

the sociopath's characteristic exploitiveness
It is a high level of exploitiveness that most singularly exposes the sociopath.
> -- Steve Becker, LCSW

I also believe this. Sociopaths are all about manipulation and exploitation. I recall a most illuminating anecdote of "Jack" regarding a family photo. His three brothers all had goofy faces, while he was only smug. Just before the shutter clicked, he whispered the idea that they all should "*look like retards*". They went along with it — he didn't, of course. Even at just 10 years old, he was already an accomplished manipulator of his family.

mimicry of appropriate emotions and morality
*The psychopath is like a color-blind person who sees the world in shades of gray but who has learned how to function in a colored world. He has learned that the light signal for 'stop' is at the top of the traffic signal. **When the color-blind***

> *person tells you he stopped at the red light, he really*
> *means he stopped at the top light.* He has difficulty in
> discussing the color of things but may have learned all sorts
> of ways to compensate for this problem, and in some cases
> even those who know him well may not know that he cannot
> see colors. (p.129)
>   Like a tourist using high-school French to ask directions
> in Paris, psychopaths have trouble putting into words
> emotional ideas because they are vague and poorly
> understood. In this sense, emotion is like a second language
> to the psychopath. (Hare, p.136)

This emotional mimicry can often come across as forced or fake.
I saw this myself many times with "Jack" but discounted it to
his foreign origin and background, *i.e.*, the difficulty outsiders
can have expressing themselves in other languages and
cultures. It so happened that he was a *moral* outsider.

Recall from the movie *Bladerunner* the detailed test given
to suspected androids to pierce through their artificial
emotional landscape. A superior "Replicant" required over 100
questions, the last being *"The entrée consisted of boiled dog."*
Accomplished sociopaths are like that. Sometimes it takes
months or even years to unmask them, and even when you do
many of your mutual friends won't easily believe it.

do sociopaths feel love or hate?

Apparently not. fMRI scans show that sociopaths respond
to the linguistic brain section but not the feeling section.

do sociopaths feel fear?

Not really, as this has been linked to dysfunctions of the
amygdala in the brain, another emotion processing center.
High risk situations do not much affect sociopaths, as they focus
on the reward and not the likely consequences.

do sociopaths feel guilt?

Generally not, and if they somehow do it is blocked out by
disassociation and compartmentalization. (*I.e.,* their victims
somehow deserved being hurt.) They also are very good at
focusing on their source of reward while ignoring punishment.

the sociopath *always* lies, and *how* he does it

To feel powerful and superior to normal decent folk, the sociopath must manipulate them as his puppeteer. He feels something like a sexual thrill from this:

> . . . this is power, especially when the people you manipulate are superior to you in some way. Most invigorating of all is to bring down people who are smarter or more accomplished than you, or perhaps classier, more attractive or popular or morally admirable. **This is not only good fun; it is existential vengeance.** (p.4)
>
> . . . the game is the thing. The prize to be won can run the gamut from world domination to a free lunch, but it is always the same game — **controlling, making others jump, "winning."** Evidently, winning in this fashion is all that remains of interpersonal meaning when attachment and conscience are absent. (Stout, p.49)

No manipulation is possible without lying. Lies are core to all sociopaths. They will lie even when they don't *have* to, just for the thrill of being believed.

how the sociopath succeeds in lying, and lying BIG

> The size of the lie is a definite factor in causing it to be believed, because the vast masses of a nation are, in the depths of their hearts, more easily deceived than they are consciously and intentionally bad.
>
> The primitive simplicity of their minds renders them more easy victims of a big lie than a small one, because they themselves often tell little lies **but would be ashamed to tell big ones. Such a form of lying would never enter their heads.** They would never credit others with the possibility of such great impudence as the complete reversal of facts.
>
> Even explanations would long leave them in doubt and hesitation, and any trifling reason would dispose them to accept a thing as true. **Something therefore always remains and sticks from the most imprudent of lies**, a fact which all bodies and individuals concerned in the art of lying in this world know only too well, and therefore they stop at nothing to achieve this end.
>
> — Adolph Hitler, *Mein Kampf*

Everybody is subject to something called "egocentrism" where you believe that other people are basically like you. If you are honest, a sociopath will know it and use it against you. (Sociopaths are also egocentric, believing everybody else is also depraved and a liar — though too weak to slough off their phony morality.)

In my case, "Jack" had set up such an outlandish scam on me, that it didn't seem like a scam. Couldn't be a scam because friends don't scam friends. (My egocentrism working against me.) However, it was such a huge and ridiculous story that it quickly unraveled after my first suspicion. The hard part was not disproving his tale, but trying to understand *why* he had done it (and in such a risky manner). Having stolen over $10,000 in guns and gear from me in a landlord/tenant scam, he miscalculated that I valued my privacy over my stuff. (To his surprise, I filed a criminal complaint despite the detriment to my privacy. I also persistently informed his friends and business partners of his years of theft and fraud.)

My classic mistake was trying to understand it from a morally sane perspective, and it took a while to get past that. Only by later learning about sociopathy did any (and all) of it make sense. All the classic clues had been there over the three years of "friendship", had I known what to look for.

a sociopath's always lies, and always without shame

After I graduated I went on to Harvard and received PHd in psychology. Next I went on to Yale where I received my law degree(tops in class of course). Unfortunatly, the Gulf War broke out and I was off to do my patriotic duty. As a commander of an F117 squadron flying penetration raids to knock out Iraqi military communication structures, I was shot down behind enemy lines. Using standard evasion and escape techniques I managed to return to my unit where I was awarded the congessional medal of honor. I met my current wife(Nikki Taylor) during my ticker tape parade in New York. I will be unable to attend the reunion due to my wifes hospitalization as a result of her recent accident.

— classmates.com entry of a really flagrant sociopath

Normal people are embarrassed when caught in a lie. This is wholly untrue with a sociopath. Since they cannot feel shame (though sometimes humiliation), catching them in a lie will not garner you an apology. Rather, he usually will attack you for your lack of trust in him. If not that, then he will oddly and smoothly move on to the next lie.

It doesn't matter to him if he's caught in a lie — only that the lie no longer works with *you*. He'll just go to another lie. It's very weird when you experience it, and you'll begin to wonder if you're dealing with an alien. (In a way, you *are*.)

the sociopath's algorithm of reversal

To lie believably, the sociopath understands that nothing lies like the truth. His trick, however, is tell to co-opt the flattering truth about others as his own, and to conversely lay his putrid traits on others.

For example, sociopath "Jack" claimed many skills and experiences of others never his own:

800+ hours of fighter jet combat, with dozens of aerial kills
shot down, yet (dramatically) escaped as a POW
a subsequent career in "Special Forces"
Arabic translator for a U.S. Ambassador, and the FBI
the saving of life with his EMT skills
a B.S. degree in Aeronautical Engineering
the heroic shooting of a charging elephant in Tanzania

What he projected of himself on others included:

drunkenness, lying, thievery
racist and anti-Semetic remarks
horribly bad credit with looming home foreclosure

In both reversals "Jack" was able to initially sound very credible because he had the basic facts straight — he just changed the names. When word got out, he just moved on to other lies.

their too-pat and incredible life story

From several sociopaths I've known, one thing they all had in common was the early insistence to program others with their fanciful story. (I call it "setting the stage".) They do this to weed out the suspicious and identify the trusting, and it's very effective. You'll tend to believe them if you have no specific reason not to. Beware the set-stage life history.

the indispensable pity ploy

What I like better than anything else is when people feel sorry for me. The thing I really want more than anything else out of life is people's pity.
    — a convicted swindler who used elaborate investment
    scams, quoted by Dr. Martha Stout

Pity? Why would a sociopath want *pity*? Because it deactivates your B.S. detector. **You cannot pity somebody and simultaneously be *suspicious* of them.** If you learn anything about sociopaths, learn that. "Jack" was notorious about the pity ploy. Whenever he was late, he'd claim a massive plumbing leak on a jobsite. His most blatant pity ploy (none of it true, of course) was emailed to me by a friend:

> *Some months ago "Jack" called me and told me that he had been diagnosed with stomach cancer. He went on to describe in intricate detail the radiation treatment he was getting and how this was creating a great financial strain on him because he was also paying for all of his girlfriends medical bills. Of course this information was told to me with the usual caveat of swearing not to tell another soul that he had cancer, especially his girlfriend.*

protecting yourself from a possible sociopath
    How can we recognize them? It's difficult because the very good ones have learned to mask themselves well. However, they cannot perfectly emulate healthy human beings:

> *When deciding whom to trust, bear in mind that the combination of consistently bad or egregiously inadequate behavior with frequent plays for your pity **is as close to a warning mark on a conscienceless person's forehead as you will ever be given.*** [Though rarely violent, such a person is] *probably not someone you should closely befriend, take on as your business partner, ask to take care of your children, or marry.* (p.109)
> — Dr. Martha Stout, *The Sociopath Next Door*

Stout recommends ceasing all contact after experiencing a total of just three: lies, no-shows, or irresponsible acts. This is excellent advice which will drastically limit the damage:

When considering a new relationship of any kind, practice the Rule of Threes regarding the claims and promises a person makes, and the responsibilities he or she has. Make the Rule of Threes your personal policy.

*One lie, one broken promise, or a single neglected responsibility may be a misunderstanding instead. Two may involve a serious mistake. **But three lies says you're dealing with a liar,** and deceit is the linchpin of conscienceless behavior. Cut your losses and get out as soon as you can. Leaving, though it may be hard, will be easier now than later, and less costly.*

Do not give your money, your work, your secrets, or your affection to a three-timer. Your valuable gifts will be wasted. (p.157)

I'd recommend that you *quietly* keep count, and not confront the suspect along the way. Once you've reached your three, simply cease all contact without any explanation. This will deny the sociopath a valuable feedback loop, and force him to thereafter wonder where he went wrong.

BTP tips for discerning the sociopath

The major red flags are grandiosity, shameless lies, unreliability, lack of empathy, and a flair for manipulation. Here some multiple signs of sociopaths which I gleaned from books, and from bitterly earned personal experience:

● have a narcissistic and grossly inflated view of their self-worth and importance, a truly astounding egocentricity and sense of entitlement

● unusually magnetic charm or charisma, excellent at impression management

● polished acting skills, immediately presentable when needed

● often try to overwhelm others with flattery, feigned concern, kindness, or generosity

● make excellent use of social/professional roles and titles to dissuade dissent, scrutiny, or confrontation

● uncanny ability to spot decent and trusting people, the fertile soil of a sociopathic weed

● will invariably find and exploit the psychological weaknesses of others

- require our regular pity (especially with claims of being over-worked, cheated, or victimized) to keep our blinders on regarding their behavior (*i.e.*, one cannot pity a person and simultaneously suspect them of deceit)

- tell grandiose/unlikely-yet-convincing stories, usually putting themselves in the best light (this is especially common with new acquaintances). Known for "too incredible to believe" tales about themselves of luck, courage, stamina, wit, quick-thinking, etc. These stories often have great width and color, but very little depth if you scratch the surface (and can usually be disproven in 10 minutes on the Net).

- are deceitful to an incredible extreme ("*I lie like I breathe, one as much as the other.*"). They will baldly lie and deny with great colorfulness and detail, even when the truth is obvious to all and/or when lying serves no clear benefit.

- their lies, while convincing on the surface, often contain contradictory or logically inconsistent statements (which unfortunately escape initial detection because truthful people have no conception of such casual, regular, and thoughtless deceit)

- quite prone to regular and seemingly mindless or risky thievery, especially in the case of "covetous psychopaths" (who will steal mostly for the denying vs. the having)

- when challenged/confronted, will either deny everything, rationalize their behavior, or counter "*Why would I do something like that? What would be the reason?*"

- are notorious for not answering the question posed at them, or being evasive and unresponsive. They are masters at circumventing discussion of their own behavior.

- are masters of misdirection; shifting focus/blame on accusers

- known for "*if you throw enough shit, some of it will stick*" behavior

- will minimize or deny consequences of their actions to others ("*They have insurance, and probably made money on the loss!*")

- frequently successful in talking their way out of trouble, even during confrontations with the criminal justice system

- seldom embarrassed at their own financial, legal, or personal problems -- they haven't the basic humanity to even be ashamed

* smooth lack of concern if found out (BIG red flag to sociopathy!), because shame or guilt is not only an emotion, but one linked to conscience. ("*The psychopath's indifference to being identified as a liar is truly extraordinary; it causes the listener to wonder about the speaker's sanity. More often, though, the listener is taken in.*" Hare, p.48)

* known for their impulsiveness to achieve immediate satisfaction, pleasure, or relief

* known for "consistent irresponsibility" extending to every part of their lives. They do not honor formal or implied commitments to people, organizations, or principles.

* usually with horrendously bad credit histories

* often late (and usually with unassailable and/or dramatic excuses). They don't care about other people's schedules, and resent having to conform to social rules of punctuality.

* often fail to conform to social norms, sometimes to the degree of recklessness

* inability to tolerate routine or monotony, as they are easily bored

* exhibit a profound general lack of empathy (the ability to "walk in another's shoes" by constructing a mental and emotional facsimile of others)

* cannot genuinely bond with others, and their relationships are invariably loveless, one-sided, and short-term

* see children as an inconvenience, and will scar their own

* often described as "deceitful" and "manipulative" and "spooky"

* "*tend to see any social exchange as a 'feeding' opportunity, a contest, or a test of wills, in which there can be only one winner. Their motives are to manipulate and take, ruthlessly and without remorse.*" (Hare, p.145)

* able to tailor stories about the same event or person to others, and usually under the guise of "confidence" so that those deceived do not readily speak with each other and piece things together

* are masters at social compartmentalization, keeping their victims mutually unaware of each other, or even mutually antagonistic by slyly pitting them against each other without their knowledge--all the while considering the psychopath as their "friend"

- just as they often try to evoke pity for themselves, they create or further poor impressions of others in a sort of pre-emptive self-protection for when others eventually discover the psychopath friend to be a liar, thief, and manipulator.

- see life as one big chess board, with people as pieces to move about. (*"Whoever is weak is also a sucker; that is, someone who demands to be exploited."*)

- sometimes able to fool elaborate psychological tests, such as the MMPI, and appear normal

- exhibit shallow "paint-by-the-numbers" emotions (they know the words, but not the music, of emotional life)

- usually lack the physiological responses normally associated with fear or anxiety, and are known for preternatural calm and composure during intense situations (*e.g.*, police stops with a dead body in the trunk)

- have a greater need for stimulation (in order to feel alive at all), and thus assume greater risks/dangers

- incapable of actual remorse, and they rarely even try to fake it

- do not know that they are evil (it's an alien concept to them), and thus feel fine about themselves.

- avoid other sociopaths (because they cannot be easily fooled), and the last thing an egocentric, selfish, demanding, callous person wants is someone just like himself

- are often suspected by police officers (*"I never did like that guy!"*) who deal with sociopaths every day

- once finally outted, are known to blithely move on to new people (*i.e.*, chess pieces), hobbies, and places

- are generally immune to psychotherapy because they see nothing wrong with themselves and thus have no problem to be addressed.

Over time, we can recognize their lives for their careening emptiness and hollowness (and often by their remarkably dead eyes), marked by innumerable deceits and irresponsibilities. While they cannot be cured or fixed, knowing who they are by the trail of human wreckage is sufficient warning for the curious, who then wisely shun such "people."

the sociopath's M.O.
Imagine the ocean is full of dolphins. And [the main character] *Profit is a new kind of shark that looks just like a dolphin. He could maneuver among the dolphins and the dolphins would say 'Welcome!' in dolphin talk. And then, one night, he'd start eating them.*
— PROFIT co-creator John McNamara

PROFIT follows the corporate skullduggery of junior V.P. Jim Profit, a full-blown sociopath. In his labyrinthine predation, he breaks up marriages, sets up a senior exec for a felony arrest and prison term, and even compromises the psychiatrist of his archenemy (a woman head of corporate security who sees Profit for what he is) to get inside her head during hypnosis. (And all that is post-childhood, after he set afire his father.) Teaming up with Profit is his also-sociopathic stepmother, as if one perfect sociopath weren't enough. The actor who played this sociopath thought it all rather cute:

I don't see him as an amoral or immoral individual. I think he had a superior set of moral values that enabled him to act with relative impunity.
— Adrian Pasdar, "Jim Profit"

The (deservedly) cancelled series PROFIT is a fine educational tool for discerning sociopathy, especially for those who don't grasp how sociopaths operate — and who won't believe your descriptions, either. (They could read *Othello* for the sociopath Iago, but that's probably expecting too much these days.) The sociopath's M.O. is very competently dramatized in this series (with helpful voice-overs), offering many key lessons:

❶ sociopaths scheme further ahead than moral people can usually anticipate

❷ they audio/video record their victims much more often than vice versa

❸ if victims tip off their plans for justice or revenge, sociopaths make it backfire

❹ sociopaths see sudden adversity as a challenge; they thrive on it

❺ they always act behind the scenes, which is difficult to discern

❻ they are masters of manipulation through compartmentalization

❼   most people are clueless (or in denial) about local sociopaths

❽   those who warning others are often ignored as Cassandras

dealing with a confirmed sociopath

What is so damnably frustrating to moral folks is that sociopaths seem to be coated in Teflon, rarely caught and punished for any significant percentage of their abuses. They can apparently talk and connive their way out of any scrape. This will remain true until moral folks begin to network together and expose their local sociopaths.

Reverse-engineering the sociopathic M.O. learned from PROFIT, here are some tips on how to protect yourself:

❶   record every conversation you have with known sociopaths

❷   get co-victims talking to each other and "comparing notes"

❸   NEVER tip your hand as to how you plan to expose the sociopath

❹   avoid appearing "obsessed" about warning others and/or getting justice — it will greatly weaken your cause

❺   create opportunities for others to correctly discern being manipulated

❻   form alliances, and foment action by others — *i.e.*, don't do it all alone

❼   trust only those who have also been damaged by the same sociopath

❽   take your time in gathering evidence from all angles, anticipating his oiliness

❾   honestly evaluate your own weaknesses and how they've been exploited

❿   don't drop one ball at a time on his head; drop several at once

Sociopaths swim throughout the human sea, and the sooner you begin to recognize their hidden shark-fin, the less damage they can do. But, it's up to you to act, because:

All that is necessary for the triumph of evil is that good men do nothing.
— Edmund Burke

optical illusions: sociopath autostereograms

Below is reprinted an essay I wrote for the excellent website www.lovefraud.com which informs about sociopaths.

www.lovefraud.com/blog/2007/05/20/optical-illusions-autostereograms -and-sociopaths/

> *Autostereograms produce an illusion of depth using only a single image. The image is usually generated by computer by repeating a narrow pattern from left to right. By decoupling eye convergence from focusing operations, a viewer is able to trick the brain into seeing a 3D scene.*
> — http://en.wikipedia.org/wiki/Stereogram

how to see an autostereogram

With your face about 6" from the image, look through it as though it were a window (and your trying to see something beyond it) and then move slowly back (keep the same beyond focus). You will see a 3D image come into view. This is called "parallel viewing" because your eyes are unfocusing slightly (*i.e.*, diverging towards parallel) as if seeing something beyond the 2D image. The muscles inside your eye that control the focusing lens relax. www.vision3d.com/3views.html is a helpful webpage with viewing tips. Various autostereograms are at: www.vision3d.com/sghidden.html

the sociopath's autostereogram

Sociopaths train the unsuspecting to see differently. They train us to see the autostereogram image of their story.

Of their *lie.*

The mind muscle that controls mental focus is coaxed into relaxing. In the hands of an experienced sociopath, we do this unknowingly. Their goal is for us to transpose reality (the flat 2D nature of their shallow lives) for a mirage (their fictitious 3D image of accomplishment, success, bravery, generosity, integrity, etc.).

We are taught to not only see their mirage, but transpose it for reality — and keep transposing it until we forget what the reality ever was. The more relaxed your focus, the more intense and real the mirage will become.

Another helpful parallel is that once you've seen a particular autostereogram several times, it is *much* quicker to see that image than any new autostereogram. You've conditioned your mind to expect what it has already seen, and you will almost instantly bypass the 2D for the 3D.

You now *seek* the lie.

Over time, and without conscious effort, you will routinely forsake reality for a mirage.

You can blink, or even close your eyes for several seconds, and not lose the mirage *because you've retained it in your mind*. Your focus has become so casually relaxed that you've lost focus altogether.

To act within this mirage as if it were reality will confuse your friends and family, and they will question your judgment, loyalty, and even sanity. At that point, you are operating fully within the sociopath's construct, a dreamworld created solely for his enjoyment and benefit. He controls the rules and pace of the game, and thus the outcome.

He takes. You give. He wins. You lose. That is the probable outcome, and you won't grasp that until afterwards you've even lost. It may take months or even years to fully realize the hugeness of the lie you lived in. Once you do, you will be ashamed at your own foolish trust.

how can I avoid the sociopath's mirage?

By knowing how it feels when your mind's focus is being relaxed. It's a brief odd sensation, like putting on somebody else's glasses. If you comport yourself past that sensation, you will lose your own focus. Remember, "*decoupling eye convergence from focusing operations*" is the 3D trick.

This odd sensation is your B.S. Detector, especially when they are acting. The "*Hey, wait a minute!*" reaction is your subconscious trying to get your active attention that something is wrong, untruthful, contradictory, dangerous, or even evil. Whenever "something doesn't add up" ... trust it!

Whenever you feel it, immediately stop listening to the speaker, mentally step back and regain perspective. Instantly challenge the prima facie untruthful and exaggerated. Don't be shy — cry *Bullshit!* Seek independent corroboration. Consult with his/her former friends, lovers, business partners, etc. (Sociopaths usually have extremely bad credit.)

Keep your eyes open. It is possible to spot them before they strike. Selective distrust is the parent of security.

Once you've confidently identified a likely sociopath, coolly disengage *all* contact, and quietly warn others to beware.

getting out of the sociopath's mirage if already in

The sociopath's 3D lie can only be seen from only one vantage point — the one you've been slyly placed *at* (through trust and gullibility) and subsequently anchored *to* (through familiarity and loyalty).   If you shift (even slightly) your perspective . . . the image will vanish.

Usually, somebody will say that one thing that finally jolts the return of your mental focus — if only momentarily. The mirage will then vanish, if only momentarily, and *that* is your chance to regain focus by piecing together the lies told to you.

These mirages are fragile things. They require constant vigilance by the sociopath to maintain the viewer's limited perspective and relaxed focus. (This is the purpose of frequent pity-ploys. It is emotionally impossible to *simultaneously* pity yet suspect deceit. Your mind can do only one or the other.)

Escaping from the sociopath's mirage and returning to reality is an uncomfortable process. It will take much time for your mind to reorient itself. This often engenders considerable confusion.

Time away from the sociopath can allow your mind to regain its focus, but usually that isn't enough. You will need the surrogate clear focus of your friends and family who haven't been fooled by the mirage. Give what they say (no matter how painful or embarrassing) a chance, and hear them out.

Contact others who have been conned by the same sociopath; you will validate each other and this is incredibly relieving and comforting. Soon, the mirage will no longer have any influence over you, and you'll wonder how you ever believed it at all.

sociopaths elsewhere (the "*kunlangeta*")

That is what the Yupi Eskimo call a man who repeatedly lies, cheats, steals, and sexually takes advantage of women. When anthropologist Jane Murphy inquired what was done about these *kunlangeta*, one Eskimo man replied,

> *Somebody would have pushed him off the ice when nobody else was looking.*

That so, it seems highly unlikely that their *kunlangeta* ever amount to our 3% of men in society!

final thoughts on sociopaths

I expounded for these past 20 pages because sociopaths are the *one* class of people which you absolutely *cannot* trust. Good character development requires these three things: the ability to love, impulse control, and moral reasoning. Sociopaths have *none* of them. (The rest of us have at least one!)

Most normal folks you *can* trust with certain information, or during particular moments, and they respond naturally over time and friendship. You understand their self-interest and ethical bounds. As long as you do not mistake a sociopath for a person of character, your privacy is generally safe from those whom you rightfully consider your friends.

THE I.D.

First of all, do understand that I am not urging you to commit fraud or break any laws. This is only a discussion, which I hope will engender great caution. As I mentioned earlier, I won't get into much detail on alias IDs (manufacture or procurement). I recommend that you peruse the alternative book catalogers (Paladin, Eden, Delta, etc.) as the subject of IDs is too large for this book. Meanwhile, I will discuss IDs in general terms to acquaint you with the subject.

Alias ID is very risky business. You should carefully consider *who* might be looking for you and how *far* they'll go to find you. Don't *under* construct ID for your situation. There are three kinds of "cooperative" ID: using somebody else's ID; procuring *bona fide* ID through fake paperwork; and manufacturing what *looks* to be *bona fide* ID. The first two are government issued, and the third you "issue" to yourself. Each has their uses and limitations.

USING ANOTHER'S ID

Assuming that you can procure ID from somebody whom you sufficiently resemble, *and* that you don't get him into trouble, this method may indeed work as a supporting role.

a near "twin" friend as willing donor

Very seldom do two friends sufficiently resemble each other for this to work, and even when they do it is all the more rare that one would lend out his ID to the other.

The only real value to this I can yet envision is a one-time use of a friend's passport to leave the country permanently (with the passport being couriered back to him by DHL or FedEx). Once the lendee was overseas, he could then use his US passport to travel thereafter. Even that is risky for the lender because he would have to somehow "return" to the USA to keep the CBP records in sync. (Appearing at a marina CBP office allegedly from a sailing trip across the ocean could work. Even easier would be having the lendee go to Canada, and the lender later sneaking across to "return" from Canada.)

do not use another's ID without consent

You might see an ID left behind at a bar, liquor store or nightclub. Do not use it! It is *wrong,* and it won't even be very useful. Be aware that a lost ID is noted on the state computer when the holder goes to replace it. A *stolen* ID is listed in the NCIC. Any significant computer check (accomplished by any cop with a radio) would reveal that you're not "Charlie."

Finally, if your "donor" got into trouble himself, your alias could be a ticking bomb. Have fun explaining that you're *not* "Charlie" and were "only" using his driver's license.

USING FAKE PAPERWORK

This is the best option for long-term use, but it is becoming increasingly more difficult with such new proposed standards (such as the REAL ID).. You'll encounter most of your risk during application, but once received you'll be fine as long as you keep a fairly low profile. (I wouldn't, however, try to then get a security clearance with the NSA.) Any serious background check will quickly bring down your tent, especially if any fingerprint, facial biometric, or DNA data of your old self exists in the records.

the application

The younger you are, the easier it is to explain why you're only *now* getting your first driver's license, SSN, or passport.

the birth certificate (BC)

The BC (or its equivalent—church birth record, family Bible record, or newspaper announcement) is the father of all

IDs, fake or not. Years ago, people successfully simply used the BC of a deceased infant who would have been their age. The feds have pretty much cataloged the nation's death certificates into a database to prevent that method (especially for passports). Don't use the "dead baby" scam.

Being dead and being *declared* dead are two different things. Only when one is declared dead is a death certificate filed. A BC from a person who became missing *without being declared dead* might work — as long as he *stayed* missing. The research to learn of such a person would be difficult, but I offer the idea, nonetheless.

After much thought, I think that the best way is to simply *create* your personality and its own BC.

What the government *doesn't* know and *can't* know is the name of everybody who has been *born*. Many people join the "system" for the first time as adults. They could have been sailing around the world or been children of missionaries. Absent conflicting information or firm suspicion, the government must accept that you are who you *say* you are.

Never forget that. All "knowledge" ultimately derives from a foundational *belief.* **For example, do you have *personal, firsthand knowledge* of your own birthday?** No, you can't — you were a newborn infant without a calender. We must all take our parents' word for it. Similarly, if you concoct a totally fictitious personality and present a concocted BC (or equivalent), the government must take *you* at *your* word.

A believable BC and cover story will get you a driver's license. With a driver's license, you can get *everything* else. Eden Press seems to be the most ID oriented of the alternative book sellers, and I would start there. There are even companies which sell blank BC's (and equivalents).

at the desk, applying for it — you big phony

Remember, this is *routine* for the clerk. Keep it that way. Getting a driver's license for the first time at 43 years of age will seem suspicious. The DL is the hardest to get late in life because *everyone* in America learns drives in high school. But relax; once you have your license the hard part is over. SSN's, credit cards and passports are often originally applied for in one's later years. So, what to tell the driver's license clerk?

Moral: have a plausible story to allay her doubts in under 30 words. Anything longer will *sound* like a story. Tell her that you grew up in NYC and never learned how to drive because you took the subway. Tell her that you were blind from childhood until recently when you had the latest laser surgery. Make it short and sweet, where she goes, *"Oh!"*

You should also have any necessary supporting documentation, such as NYC paperwork (letters addressed to you, club memberships, etc.) or a newspaper article on the miraculous eye surgery you had. Don't make it obvious that you're trying to prove your case. Don't try *too* hard, because that's not routine for applicants.

For your address, *never, never* give your real address. Don't even give out a *friend's* address, however willing he seems to cover for you. (People are *verbs*, not nouns. He would probably roll over on you with enough carrot or stick.)

If the clerk asks for your phone number, have an Internet voice mail number handy (*i.e.*, faultlessly recallable, as would be the case if it were somebody's home number).

If the clerk seems hinky about the whole thing and excuses herself to *"check on something"* — calmly and politely leave (*"While you're doing that, I'll go get my money. It's in my friend's car."*) Not *your* car, because you don't have a driver's license yet, remember? Moral: *leave* before chancing an arrest. You can try again elsewhere under another name.

using this alias and its ID

So, you fooled them all and got your alias ID. Great, but you're not invincible. Don't get all cocky and think you can get away with anything. Don't piss off some government agency or skip out on your new credit card debt. Don't give anybody *any* reason to start digging in your past — a past which doesn't exist. If you blow this alias, the next one will be harder to create. They'll already be looking for you, and the screening procedure will be tougher (*e.g.*, requiring biometric data) the next time.

TOTAL ID CREATION

Technology is the classic double-edged sword here. Publishing software, color laser printers and high resolution scanners make it possible to create quality documents in your own home. Ragnar Benson's book, *Acquiring New ID —How to Easily Use the Latest Computer Technology to Drop Out, Start Over, and Get On With Your Life* (www.paladin-press.com)

covers exactly this (though dated by 2009). For example, one can actually produce a visually near-perfect driver's license.

The flip side is that government records are well networked by computer and accessible by any diligent cop. There are a myriad of available databases: TECS II (Treasury), EPIC and MIRAC (immigration databanks), NADDIS (the DEA's databank), IBIS, state DMVs, and all the new ones of DHS. A fake ID being *visually* persuasive is no longer sufficient; it must now convince the *computers*.

Well-crafted ID will work only *until* you're subject to some investigation. (Create a totally fake DL from Iowa and your L.A. cop will be real curious why the Iowa DMV has no record of issuing it.) Spoof ID has its place, but think it through. Most routine computer checks are within databanks listing wanted criminals. Honest folks, clean aliases, and extraterrestrials won't be in there. As long as the computer check is simply looking for positive hits and not utter verification of the document and its owner, you should be fine.

The future of fake ID is bleak. Databanks are becoming more sophisticated and better linked. And, hordes of Americans (not to mention illegal aliens) are now using alias IDs to escape bureaucracies and regulations. The feds will soon use this to justify new forms of "unforgeable" documents, such as the REAL ID or "Enhanced DL".

the foreign ID

This is undoubtedly the most useful class of created ID. Links to foreign databanks are very slow and spotty. Best of all, nobody here knows what a French DL *looks* like. (When I say "foreign" I mean *really* foreign, not Canada or Mexico.) Don't create French ID unless you can converse fluently in French, because you'll someday encounter a cop who can *parlais*.

When asked to show your U.S. visa, reply that you're only *half* French, that your father is American, and that as a dual national you don't *need* a U.S. visa. This half-and-half story is surprisingly versatile: it explains why you don't have a SSN or state DL. And, as an apparent tourist, you'll be treated with more courtesy and leniency for the small stuff.

creating foreign ID yourself

If you have a foreign friend, ask him to send a photocopy (preferably in color) of his DL and personal ID card. Scan this in your computer and doctor it to your needs. (Some color printers encode their own serial number through nearly invisible yellow dots. A savvy person would be aware of this "banding".)

Be very thorough in your use of foreign materials (paper and staples, which are quite different than domestic supplies). Age your document convincingly with scratches, spots, bent corners and the occasional stain (tea works well).

Have supporting ID in business cards (which are usually oversized), club cards, tram tickets, stamps and currency exchange receipts (your foreign friend can get these for you), etc. The supporting paper is just as important as the DL. Read up on the fantastic job the OSS did in WWII for our spies dropped into Axis territory.

buying foreign ID

A company called RTA (303-727-7962) manufactures Nicaraguan International Driving Permits (IDPs). "Valid" for four years, they cost $200. With supporting ID, this might work pretty well, especially if you speak Spanish.

Or, you can buy a passport, driver's license and vehicle registration from the "Washitaw Nation" — apparently an American Indian nation. Rightway Travel at 303-629-9599.

Some of these foreign DLs are pretty silly (such as the Adwal Free Port driving permit from Somalia) and are rarely recognized as legitimate during the average traffic stop.

getting valid foreign ID by going overseas yourself

This is surprisingly easy to do, either officially or not (as some foreign DMV clerks are bribable). You could even foreign-flag your vehicle there, too. All this has the great advantage of being legitimate, and withstanding a computer check.

Occasionally naturalization, citizenship and therefore access to another legitimate passport can be bought if enough money lubricates certain unofficial channels. This process can range from several years to several months depending on the amount of money and level of contacts involved.

— www.powerprivacy.com (now defunct)

a valid foreign passport

Possible, but usually expensive. Residency and/or capital investment are often required. (Those of you with a full-blooded Irish grandparent can get a Irish passport, last I heard.)

Eden Press sells *The Second Passport Report 2009* :

   * *Second Citizenships in the World Post 9/11 and Financial Collapse*
   * *Nine Important Questions to Consider When Obtaining a Second Foreign Passport*
   * *Different Types of Second Passport Programs*
   * *Six Wide Open Back Doors to European Passports*
   * *Banking and Camouflage Passports Explained*
   * *Fast Track or Instant Economic Citizenship Programs - and How they Work*
   * *How the Grey Market, Discretion and Corruption Work in the Third World*
   * *Passport Programs Past and Present from A to Z*
   * *Passports Through Marriages of Convenience*
   * *How to Deal with Fixers, Escrow Services and Avoid Scams*
   * *Little-known documents You Can Use in Lieu of Passports*
   * *How to Obtain Diplomatic and Service Passports*
   * *How to Avoid Criminal Methods of Identity Theft and False Passports*
   * *How to Deal with Immigration and Customs Officials at Border Crossings*

Mexican *Matricula Consular de Alta Seguridad* (MACS)

The MCAS is an identification card issued to foreign nationals living in the U.S. by the Mexican government via their 47 consulates. The National Council of La Raza estimates that more than 350 financial institutions currently accept them. Customers with the IDs — including illegal aliens — are able to open checking and savings accounts, order check cards, safe deposit boxes, cashier's checks and wire billions of dollars to Mexico.

If these were legal aliens, they'd simply use their passport. So, obviously, the MACS cater to illegal aliens. The Mexican government has no centralized database, and no intra-consular communication for verification. MACS are issued to anyone who can produce a Mexican birth certificate and one other form of identity, including documents of very low reliability. Some consulates will issue MACS without any documents, based solely on a *questionnaire*.

American banks love the MACS, so that they can continue tap into handling fees of the $18 billion/year wired to Mexico.

the nonvalid "camouflage passport" (CP)

Or, you can buy a nonvalid CP, designed to shield your American nationality from hijackers. These are excellent re-productions of passports from now defunct or renamed nations, such as: British Honduras, Dutch Guiana, New Hebrides, Burma, Rhodesia, Ceylon, and Zanzibar. CPs are currently legal here if not used for fraudulent purposes, but not often legal in other countries (especially for financial transactions).

While these will *not* get you into foreign countries, they will probably suffice for intra-U.S.A. documentation. How many cops will know that British Honduras is now Belize? Besides, a *real* British Honduras passport would be valid until it expires — even if Belize was formed later. (I met a guy who has established a pretty complete new life under one, with a mail drop, rented apartment, utilities, and banking.)

Don't use your real name. Pick a foreign mail drop as your ID's address. You might even use a disguise for the photos.

A passport (no choice of country), driver's license and two supporting IDs (insurance card, club membership, etc.) sell for $399. Write Scope International Ltd., Forestside House, Rowlands Castle, Hants, PO9 6EE, England, UK. I've also seen these passports advertised by other companies, though I cannot personally vouch for any CP seller. *Caveat emptor*, especially of Internet companies hawking CPs.

take a new set of passport photos every other year

That way, one could make their new documents appear to have been issued years ago.

on *being* a foreigner

Wear foreign clothes—especially shoes. Funky shoes and a Grand Canyon T-shirt says *"tourist"*—which is exactly the idea. Your local youth hostel will have foreign kids passing through. Stop by to learn some foreign color.

Learn the foreign mannerisms. Russians, for example, peel their bananas from the bottom, not from the stem. In a cinema, most foreigners will pass through a row *facing* those already seated, unlike us. Europeans count 1 to 5 from thumb to pinky. (Only Americans save the thumb for last.) The 🖐 hand sign means "*sshole" in most countries, so foreigners wouldn't use it here to signal "O.K." (When Dan Quayle visited South America as our Vice President, he often flashed an insultingly obscene 🖐 to the crowd, to the horror of his hosts.) Do some research on how "you" are supposed to act.

Know about your foreign country and home town. Know the history, and keep up on current events. If you claim to be from Paris, know who your mayor is, what color the buses are, how much the Metro costs, and the hot nightspots.

Speak with a *slight* accent — don't overdo it. A *moderate* clumsiness in cadence and syntax is enough. (Most foreigners speak very good English, and you'll be sincerely complimented on yours. Modestly thank them.) The trick to the clothes, accent and mannerisms is to *suggest* foreign status. Let the cop or clerk make the ancillary links himself.

REAL ID

Per the REAL ID Act, . . . citizens of states that are not REAL ID compliant may not use their driver's licenses or identification cards for official federal purposes such as boarding federally regulated commercial aircraft or accessing federal or nuclear facilities. If these citizens do not have other acceptable forms of identification (e.g., a U.S. passport), they may suffer delays due to the requirement for enhanced security screening.
— DHS website

The DHS is 180,000 person agency out of 22 separate agencies.

This requirement goes into effect December 1, 2014, for those who will be under 50 years of age on that date. Those who are 50 or older on December 1, 2014, will have until December 1, 2017 to comply. If you are not able to provide the proper documents to obtain a Real ID DL/ID, the DMV will issue you a license or ID card under the existing state requirements that will permit you to operate a motor vehicle

*and provide identification documentation for purposes outside
of the Real ID Act.*
— www.dmvnv.com

Rammed through Congress with unanimous Senate approval,
the REAL ID Act was bundled with emergency Iraq war
funding and tsunami relief.

*The Real ID Act says applicants will have to supply DMV
offices with documentation of their date of birth, proof of their
Social Security number or a document showing they are a
legal resident not eligible for Social Security, and a utility bill
or other documentation of their residency. People who move
will be prohibited from getting a license in their new state of
residency until their license in the previous state is canceled.*

However, public and state resistance has delayed
implementation. Over 20 state legislatures have variously
opposed the REAL ID scheme, 11 of whom have actually
prohibited their own compliance with it. The whole $28 billion
unfunded mandate complaint of the states will be mollified by
federal funding, just as the government has forced you to cough
up billions to allow telecoms to monitor phone calls and emails.

The initial purpose of the REAL ID seems reasonable (for
the feds), but can and will expand over time:

*Section 201(3) of the Act provides that the term "official
purpose" includes but is not limited to accessing Federal
facilities, boarding Federally-regulated commercial aircraft,
entering nuclear power plants, **and any other purposes that
the Secretary shall determine.** DHS proposes to limit the
regulatory definition of "official purpose," **at this time,** to
those purposes expressly stated in the Act. DHS, under
discretionary authority granted to the Secretary of Homeland
Security under the Act, **may expand this definition** in the
future. DHS seeks comment on the proposed scope of
"official purpose," and how DHS could expand this definition
to other federal activities.* (p. 17)
> — DHS Minimum Standards for Driver's licenses and
> Identification Cards Acceptable Federal Government
> for Official Purposes
> www.dhs.gov/xlibrary/assets/nprm_realid.pdf

Notice that the Congress has no say-so on the required display of the REAL ID — only the DHS Secretary does. (*"What would Himmler do?"*) Next would be other federally controlled trains, national parks, federal courthouses and other places. It could easily be required for all mass transit, voting, gun and ammo purchases, collecting a government check, and transacting with *"financial institutions"*:

> *In December, a provision slipped into an appropriations bill allowing the FBI to obtain personal financial information from banks, insurance companies, travel agencies, real estate agents, stockbrokers, the U.S. Postal Service, jewelry stores, casinos and car dealerships without a warrant — **because they're all construed as financial institutions.***

REAL ID is going international, which was always the plan

> *Furthering the American Association of Motor Vehicle Administrators (AAMVA)'s control strategy here in North America, implementation of REAL ID is "de facto" enrollment of each state into AAMVA's Driver's License Agreement (DLA). AAMVA has pushed the DLA, which meets REAL ID specifications, for nearly ten years. The implementation of this DLA is crucially important to the global effort because it mandates the sharing of all U.S. drivers' license information with Mexico and Canada. This egregious step places U.S. citizen's data at the mercy of Canadian and Mexican privacy controls, further exacerbating the identity theft problem, and violating Constitutional law and national sovereignty by essentially having states form a treaty with a foreign nation.*
> *— www.govtech.net/magazine/story.php?id=94105*

This all helps explains why the North Carolina DL now has a hologram of the "North American Union" on the back, which harkens back to the whole Western Hemisphere Travel Initiative.

the *"Oh, don't worry!"* excuses

The REAL ID has been touted a "merely" or "simply" an "improvement" on DL integrity. Here are some fatuous claims:

"It will save us from identity theft."

> *Identity theft solutions focus much too much on authenticating the person. Whether it's two-factor authentication—ID cards,*

> *biometrics, or whatever—there's a widespread myth that authenticating the person is the way to prevent these crimes.*
>
> *But once you understand that the problem is fraudulent transactions, you quickly realize that authenticating the transaction, not the person, is the way to proceed.*
>
> *To mitigate that risk, we need to concentrate on detecting and preventing fraudulent transactions. We need to make the entity, which is in the best position to mitigate the risk, responsible for that risk. And that means making the financial institutions liable for fraudulent transactions.*
>
> *Doing anything less simply won't work.*
>
> — Bruce Schneier, "Solving Identity Theft"

Any national ID card with such centralized data means that successful identity thieves would become much more effective. (Have you noticed that the more technological ID systems have become, the more they are criminally abused?)

Besides, identity theft is only an issue regarding credit transactions. For those of us who live and work and shop only by cash, what threat is there of any identity theft?   Bank accounts and credit cards have no leverage over such people.

"*It will save us from terrorists.*"

> *"It's going to have some expense,"* [DHS Secretary] *Chertoff said. "It's going to be somewhat inconvenient. **But if we don't get it done now, someone's going to be sitting around in three or four years explaining to the next 9/11 commission why we didn't do it.**"*

What utter dreck. Most of the 9/11 hijackers had state-issued drivers licenses, and a lot of safety *that* gave us then. Authenticating a traveler's identity can neither predict nor prevent future actions:

> *No, the government didn't have this stuff in place, precisely because it had been working on it and knew its limitations and didn't find any value for the costs involved. It's going to be hard to know how these technologies can be applied to increase national security. We're not just going to turn these machines on and start catching terrorists.*
>
> — Jim Wayman, former head of the US Biometrics Center

Of the 25 countries that have been most adversely affected by terrorism since 1986, eighty percent have national identity cards, one third of which incorporate biometrics. This research was unable to uncover any instance where the presence of an identity card system in those countries was seen as a significant deterrent to terrorist activity.
— Privacy International Study conducted in 2004

Do we really believe a terrorist bent on murder is going to dutifully obtain a federal ID card? Do we believe that people who openly flout our immigration laws will nonetheless respect our ID requirements? Any ID card can be forged; any federal agency or state DMV is susceptible to corruption. Criminals can and will obtain national ID cards, or operate without them. **National ID cards will be used to track the law-abiding masses, not criminals.**
— Congressman Ron Paul, May 2005

"The data is protected."

What a laugh. No, it's not. Your SSN is not. Your DL is not. All is sold, shared, or hacked — routinely, every day. The REAL ID Act has no data protection provisions at all! Oh, and:

[DHS] *appointed a senior Microsoft Corp. executive to head a section charged with protecting the federal government's computer networks from cyber attacks.*

Phil Reitinger, currently "chief trustworthy infrastructure strategist" at Microsoft, will become deputy undersecretary of DHS's National Protections Program division.
—http://law.du.edu/index.php/privacy-foundation/privacy-homeland-security

A *Microsoft* wonk in charge of DHS computer security? M$ has never once written a generally bug-free OS. Why not appoint Reinhard Heydrich as head of the ADL?

"REAL ID is voluntary — so what's the fuss?"

Yes, it is voluntary and the states can still go on producing their own federally noncompliant DL/ID cards, but in an increasing environment of federally-controlled places and institutions (and occupations!), not having a REAL ID would further place millions of Americans in a corner. They would not be able to fly out of the country (maybe not even from Canada or

Mexico, if those governments adopt TSA-style airport screening which demands REAL ID).

Finally, since the feds have threatened to withhold federal funding (that old trick) if states don't implement REAL ID, this is hardly a "voluntary" act by the states.

"*REAL ID is not a national ID card.*"

Jim Harper, Cato's director of information policy studies and author of "Identity Crisis: How Identification is Overused and Misunderstood," is arguably the staunchest critic of Real ID on privacy grounds.

"The average person does not see the privacy consequence," Harper said. "The one that I prioritize the most is the likelihood that Real ID will be used for tracking and surveillance. That's not an immediate concern but down the line you can be sure it will used that way."

With national standards and the full sharing of DL info amongst the states, the federal government, Mexico, Canada, soon Europe, and later Asia . . . what would be the *difference* between REAL ID and a national ID card?

*Digimarc IDVS enables the detection of falsified identity credentials at critical points of inspection such as a Department of Motor Vehicle (DMV) offices, in a police cruiser, **transportation access points, retail point of sale or any other environment** where there is a need to ensure the authenticity of documents presented to establish one's identity.*

— Digimarc's Real ID Act information page

*The Real ID Act, then, is about more than a driver's license. It puts in place a set of standards for Identity Management (IdM) **that can be leveraged across an entire government organization to create an integrated citizen identity** security program.*

— Electronic Data Systems, the very company likely to
    maintain AAMVA's driver's license database

A Powerpoint presentation from L-1 Identity Solutions, the major biometrics company in the U.S. today, bolsters this claim. A slide in that presentation includes a graph which charts future likely applications for biometrics.

> *Phase 1 of this "blueprint" for biometric implementation utilizes the authority of Federal agencies to impose such requirements as REAL ID.*
>
> *Phase 2 utilizes bureaucratic leveraging on regulated industries to implement biometrics.*
>
> ***Phase 3 anticipates mass implementation on the citizens at large for such everyday activities as buying and selling.** As an example, under Phase 2 DHS is attempting to force airlines to pick up the costs of collecting biometrics from foreigners at airports. **In Texas under Phase 3, a company is experimenting with using the driver's license as a debit card.***
>
> — Rep. Sam E. Rohrer, "REAL ID: Connecting the Dots to an International ID, www.newswithviews.com"

"*REAL ID does not use biometrics.*"

"*It's only a digital photograph, which all states already require.*" This is a half truth. The REAL ID digital photo standard is an extremely high one, and is effectively biometric with appropriate software. As Rep. Rohrer explained:

> *The global body setting this format, the International Civil Aviation Organization (ICAO), is a specialized agency created under the United Nations. Biometric data can be produced from a simple digital photograph of this quality by running the picture of a person's face through a software program which measures and analyzes the unique, personally identifiable characteristics of that face. **The process results in a unique numeric code which identifies a person according to facial measurements.** You read that correctly. A unique number or "code" is developed from an algorithmic formula which converts a digital biometric sample to biometric "face print" data. Under REAL ID biometric facial recognition technology, you become a number literally worn on your face - a number which is read by computer, tracked by surveillance camera, and distributed worldwide. Clearly, this international standard provides global compatibility of American citizens' biometric data collected through REAL ID.*
>
> *No sufficiently compelling need exists to warrant government mass collection and storage of such sensitive information about its citizens. Concern heightens even further when private corporations control the databases being set up to house this information. As an example, L-1 Identity Solutions houses a database of U.S. driver's license*

information. This company, which has consolidated a virtual monopoly on the driver's license issuing market in the U.S., will handle all private information collected during the license issuing process.

Read the footnote from page 68 of the DHS's proposed standards:

*DHS is proposing that digital photographs comply with current ICAO standards. (The relevant ICAO standard is ICAO 9303 Part 1 Vol 2, specifically ISO/IEC 19794-5 - Information technology - **Biometric data interchange formats** - Part 5: Face image data, which is incorporated into ICAO 9303.)*

Finally, DHS proposes that states use "biometric information" to verify identity of REAL ID renewals.

"REAL ID does not require RFID technology."
True, technically, but the DHS proposals do suggest it.

now, something worse than even REAL ID
The feds are currently trying to scuttle their REAL ID scheme for an RFID replacement — the EDL.

Homeland Security Secretary Janet Napolitano this week said she is working with governors to repeal the Real ID Act, which was passed in 2005 and went into effect last year.

The bill is popular in Washington, but is scorned by many governors who bear the responsibility and cost of validating that holders of driver's licenses are citizens or legal residents of the United States.

*Napolitano, former governor of Arizona, said she has met with governors of both parties recently "to look at a way to repeal Real ID." She said she wants to substitute the federal law **with "something else that pivots off of the driver's license** but accomplishes some of the same goals. And we hope to be able to announce something on that fairly soon."*

The EDL will be touted as more secure than REAL ID (which used a commonly readable 2D barcode, which even some cell phones could interpret as PDF417 image). You must admire the cleverness of use a weaker ID to sell a *stronger* one!

The Europeans are also on the EDL path, beginning in 2013 with their chipped credit-card license.

National governments have a choice of whether to issue the new forgery-proof licences for 10 or 15 years.

To prevent "driving licence tourism" a European licence database will be created.

Some EU countries currently issue driving licences for life. Germany and Austria were reluctant to agree to a licence that had to be regularly renewed, but dropped their objections in March.

The phasing in of the new licence will be completed by 2032.

The European Union's 300 million drivers currently use a total of 110 different paper and plastic licences.

— http://news.bbc.co.uk/1/hi/world/europe/6180617.stm

brought to you by Big Brother, Inc.

Infineon, Gemalto, Smart Card Alliance, BlueBear Network, L-1 Identity Solutions, VisionSphere Technologies, Hewlett-Packard and Microsoft are several of the many corporations drooling over the national identity programs.

The tech giants have been working on a code base that will allow them to offer a set of technology components for functions such as online and offline demographic and biometric data capture, regional verification and registration, and document lifecycle management.

— www.infoworld.com/article/05/05/27/HNmshpidsystems_1.html

boycott and shun the REAL ID enablers!

In my recent article, Shunning the Real ID Enablers, I laid out my reasons for launching my personal boycott against the two American behemoth corporations that are colluding to create the software (Microsoft) and hardware (Hewlett-Packard) that will form the backbone of a federally imposed national ID card. Libertarians, perhaps more so than most other people, understand that we can never depend on politicians to take up the cause of individual freedom unless it happens to coincide with their personal interests. By necessity then, the fight against nationwide human branding will almost certainly come down to grassroots resistance.

*1] **By not supporting these companies, they have fewer profits to plow into the R&D,** advertising, and other pushing of their spying stuff onto us (letting them know why you won't buy their products — with a polite letter, as Kirsten suggests — is a very good idea too);*

2] Your shopping will be consistent with your principles — no supporting companies whose actions are stealing this country's liberty; and perhaps most important —

*3] **As the NID progresses, it will be increasingly important to have networks of individuals outside the system to do business with.** This can take many forms, and I'm not going to address them now. Thinking now of goods and services that you can offer, that will not feed into the NID enablers or their spy networks, is an excellent idea.*

If Americans really wanted Real ID, why did the powercrats have to sneak it past us, buried in a "patriotic" war-fighting and "charitable" tsunami relief spending bill? No, our control freak federalcrats have thrust this down our throats.

*It's time to barf it back into the bald-faced lying faces of the Beltway Bolsheviks. **If freedom is to be the philosophy of the future, the future starts now.***

— Garry Reed, www.freecannon.com/ShunIDEnablers.htm

support anti-REAL ID organizations!

The grass roots opposition to REAL ID is huge:

www.realidrebellion.com/
http://epic.org/privacy/id_cards/
/www.katherinealbrecht.com/
www.antichips.com/
www.spychips.com/
http://blog.identitytheftsecrets.com/news

Also, I highly recommend the groundbreaking book *Spychips — How major corporations and government plan to track your every move with RFID.*

THE USA PASSPORT

A USA passport is held by only 1 in 4 Americans. While up from 1:6 last decade, it nonethesless astonishes me that 3 in 4 Americans are content with their own border as a locked fence! Even if you have no plans to travel, get a passport this year. If you waited past 2006, then you waited too long to avoid RFID. The next phase will probably be some biometric fingerprint data (as required for US Visas), so get your passport this year.

since 2007, all passports have an RFID chip

I will cover RFID chips in other/more detail elsewhere, but include the below information regarding the passport chips. We were originally to get these chipped passports in 2005, but for an embarrassing revelation from some privacy experts:

> *To his credit, UnderSecretary of state Frank Moss came to the International Conference on Computers, Freedom, and Privacy last sporing to face the critics of the US RFID passport scheme. During his panel, the ACLU's Barry Steinhart demonstrated a reader effective at 10 inches.*
>
> *Afterwards, in the hallway, EFF's John Gilmore explained how the range could be extended to 10 feet. **Travel writer Ed Hasbrouck then laid out a scenario in which terrorists used an off the shelf RFID reader to detect the presence of a US Passport holder on a bus in Beirut, triggering a pre-installed bomb.***
>
> *This apparently impressed Moss, who delayed introduction of the chipped passports originally scheduled for last June, so that they could be made with wire mesh shielding to prevent them from being read when closed. He also directed the data be encrypted, bringing us to the flaw identified in the diary.*
>
> — www.dailykos.com/story/2006/2/3/162911/3140

Before I describe the problem, some context on the surrounding controversy may be helpful. RFID chips are passive, and broadcast information to any reader that queries the chip. So critics, myself included, were worried that the new passports would reveal your identity without your consent or even your knowledge. Thieves could collect the personal data of people as they walk down a street, criminals could scan passports looking for Westerners to kidnap or rob and terrorists could rig bombs to explode only when four Americans are nearby. The police could use the chips to conduct surveillance on an individual; stores could use the technology to identify customers without their knowledge.

RFID privacy problems are larger than passports and identity cards. The RFID industry envisions these chips embedded everywhere: in the items we buy, for example. But even a chip that only contains a unique serial number could be used for surveillance. And it's easy to link the serial number with an identity — when you buy the item using a credit card, for example — and from then on it can identify you. Data brokers like ChoicePoint will certainly maintain databases of RFID numbers and associated people; they'd do a disservice to their stockholders if they didn't.

*The State Department downplayed these risks by insisting that the RFID chips only work at short distances. In fact, last week's publication claims: "The proximity chip technology utilized in the electronic passport is designed to be read with chip readers at ports of entry only when the document is placed within inches of such readers." The issue is that they're confusing three things: the designed range at which the chip is specified to be read, the maximum range at which the chip could be read and the eavesdropping range or the maximum range the chip could be read with specialized equipment. **The first is indeed inches, but the second was demonstrated earlier this year to be 69 feet. The third is significantly longer.***

And remember, technology always gets better — it never gets worse. It's simply folly to believe that these ranges won't get longer over time.

— Bruce Schneier, "The ID Chip You Don't Want in Your Passport"

I wouldn't want *my* passport read by strangers, but that is now easily possible, and from a moving car on the street!

Think of it this way: Chris Paget just did you a service by hacking your passport and stealing your identity. Using a $250 Motorola RFID reader and antenna connected to his laptop, Chris recently drove around San Francisco reading RFID tags from passports, driver licenses, and other identity documents. In just 20 minutes, he found and cloned the passports of two very unaware US citizens. Fortunately, Chris wears a white hat; his video demonstration is meant to raise

awareness to what he calls the unsuitability of RFID for tagging people. Specifically, he's hoping to help get the Western Hemisphere Travel Initiative — a homeland security project — scrapped.
   — Hacker war drives San Fran, cloning RFID passports
   www.engadget.com/2009/02/02/video-hacker-war-drives-san-francisc
   o-cloning-rfid-passports?icid=sphere_blogsmith_inpage_engadget

The State Department *pooh-pooh*s such concerns, alleging that the passport must first be opened and scanned before its data can be read. Oh, *really?*

Those security blunders were initially corrected by adding metal shielding to the passport cover to minimize its readability when closed, dialing back the range of the electronics and adding a special electronic protocol called Basic Access Control (or BAC). This scheme required the passport to be opened and scanned before its data could have been properly interpreted by an RFID receiver.
   — www.powerprivacy.com (now defunct)

A Dutch television program "Nieuwslicht" recently worked with local security firm Riscure to successfully crack and decrypt a Dutch-prototype RFID passport. In this case, the data exchange between the RFID reader and passport was intercepted, stored, and then the password was cracked later in just 2 hours on a PC giving full access to the digitized fingerprint, photograph, and all other encrypted and plain text data on the RFID tag — just perfect for slapping together a cloned passport, eh?
   — www.theregister.co.uk/2006/01/30/dutch_biometric_passport_crack/

(US passports use the same ISO 14443 RFID tag and Basic Access Control encryption scheme. Great.)

The University of Amsterdam's Jeroen van Beek was reportedly able to clone and manipulate a pair of British passports in about the time it takes you to sip down your first cup of joe in the morning, and worse still, they were accepted as genuine by the software "recommended for use at international airports." The tests point out a number of vulnerabilities, including the fact that the microchips could be susceptible to having falsified biometrics inserted for use. As expected, talking heads at the Home Office still insist that any

chip manipulation would be immediately recognized by the electronic readers, so we'll leave it up to you to decide who's telling the truth here.
> — More e-passports hacked within minutes, security questions abound, by Darren Murph, Aug 7th 2008
> www.engadget.com/2008/08/07/more-e-passports-hac ked-within-minutes-security-questions-aboun/

The other security mechanisms are also vulnerable, and several security researchers have already discovered flaws. One found that he could identify individual chips via unique characteristics of the radio transmissions. Another successfully cloned a chip. The State Department called this a "meaningless stunt," pointing out that the researcher could not read or change the data. But the researcher spent only two weeks trying; the security of your passport has to be strong enough to last 10 years.

This is perhaps the greatest risk. The security mechanisms on your passport chip have to last the lifetime of your passport. *It is as ridiculous to think that passport security will remain secure for that long as it would be to think that you won't see another security update for Microsoft Windows in that time. Improvements in antenna technology will certainly increase the distance at which they can be read and might even allow unauthorized readers to penetrate the shielding.*
> —www.washingtonpost.com/wp-dyn/content/article/2006/09/15/AR200 6091500923.html

is the SSN required to get a USA passport?

No. Here is my layman's understanding of the matter:

you cannot be required to get an SSN for a USA passport

That is very well established. 26 USC 6039E(b)(1) clearly states *"if any"* regarding the TIN (taxpayer identification number) on the passport application.

Here is the form letter the SSA has sent out for years regarding the general question whether the SSN is required:

> *This is in response to your recent letter about the Social Security Number (SSN).*
>
> **The Social Security Act does not require a person to have an SSN to live and work in the United States, nor**

does it require an SSN simply for the purpose of having one. However, if someone works without an SSN, we cannot properly credit the earnings for the work performed.

. . . The Privacy Act regulates the use of SSNs by government agencies. They may require an SSN only if a law or regulation either orders or authorizes them to do so. Agencies are required to disclose the authorizing law or regulation. **If the request has no legal basis, the person may refuse to provide the number and still receive the agency's services.**
— www.cjmciver.org/sapf

Even state DMVs admit that no SSN is required for their DLs:

"If I don't have a Social Security Number, can I get a driver's license or identification card?"

Yes, you would be eligible for a non-compliant DL/ID under the existing Nevada requirements.
— www.dmvnv.com/dlresidency.htm

Because of the requirements for the issuance **of commercial driver's licenses,** *the majority of State DMVs already have access to the SSA database for verification of SSNs.* (p. 57)
— DHS Minimum Standards for Driver's licenses and Identification Cards Acceptable Federal Government for Official Purposes

If you don't have an SSN, and don't want one, then don't get one!

what if I already have an SSN?

However, if you were assigned an SSN, must you include it in your passport application? No. The application for an SSN Form SS-5. The Office of Management and Budget (OMB), pursuant to the Paperwork Reduction Act of 1980, has indicated that the filing of the SS-5 is *"required to obtain or retain a benefit"* when given that choice and the choices *"voluntary"* and *"mandatory"*. A passport is not a benefit, it is a right derived from your constitutional right to travel.

The legal section referred to by the Passport Office to demand your SSN is 31 USC 7701(c)(1), because paying them for your passport you are *"considered doing business with the government"*. This is easily disproven by reading the section, which refers to federal lenders, contractors, etc.

My thanks to the indefatigable Peter Hendrickson at www.losthorizons.com/comment/Etc/YourPapersPlease.htm for the clarification. Another great researcher who "walks the talk" is Neil McIver at www.cjmciver.org. (Neil got his passport without an SSN, and tells you how he did it.)

US passport vs. REAL ID

I've read very carefully the DHS proposals for REAL ID, and every applicant must either provide their SSN or proof of SSN eligibility (*i.e.,* "non-work authorized non-immigrant status.") Curiously, however, is that the US passport (which may or may not, depending on the applicant's awareness, have an SSN linked to it) is accepted at Federal facilities for "official purposes" and for boarding commercial aircraft.

can the passport RFID chip be deactivated?

Sure, but microwaving your passport may cause it to burst in flames. Hammering it may work, but this hasn't been confirmed to my satisfaction. Your safest bet is to shield it more effectively than its wire-mesh cover. (Scroogle "passport wallet materials".)

a damaged RFID chipped passport *may* not be reissued

This is the case in Germany and elsewhere, from what I've read. Seems very plausible. Big Brother has no sense of humor.

some misc. passport tips
consider avoid disclosing your SSN

"Not for Identification", remember?

request the 48 page passport

It's got twice the number of pages, and costs nothing extra. You'll be glad you did if you travel frequently and don't want the thing to fill up with stamps before the 10 year expiry.

keep your *expired* passport with you on travels

If you lose your current passport when overseas, having the expired one as a backup could be very helpful. Although it won't likely get you into other countries, the CBP admits that Americans can return home on an expired passport:

12.4 United States Passports.

*(a) General. A United States passport **(even if expired)** may be accepted as evidence of* [U.S.] *citizenship in the absence of information showing that the holder has expatriated.*
— U.S. Customs and Border Protection,
Inspector's Field Manual (2006) p. 19

I would keep it in your ankle wallet that has your traveler's checks receipts and spare credit card.

THE "ENHANCED DL"

Enhanced driver's licenses have built-in radio chips providing an identifying number or information that can be accessed by a remote reading unit while the license is inside a wallet or purse.

The technology already had been implemented in Washington state, where it is promoted as an alternative to a passport for traveling to Canada. So far, the program is optional. [BTP Note: Add New York to the RFID EDL list.]

But there are other agreements already approved with Michigan, Vermont, New York and Arizona, and plans are under way in other states, including Texas, she said.

But Opsommer said Big Brother concerns certainly have some foundation.

"So if EDLs are the new direction for secure licenses in all states, it just reinforces what many have been telling me that DHS wants to expand this program and turn it into a wireless national ID with a different name," he said. "We'll wake up one day and without a vote in Congress DHS will just pass a rule and say something like 'starting next month you will need an EDL to fly on a plane, or to buy a gun, or whatever.'"

The goal is to incorporate a passport RFID chip within the EDL. The Canadian province British Columbia has issued their new EDL which they say is "*an acceptable document for entry from Canada into the United States by land and water.*"

The EDL is the last step to a genuine NID here in "Amerika". Current DHS Secretary Janet Napolitano is now trying to get REAL ID repealed, in order to replace it with the

RFID EDL. Once the interlinked databases and high-tech cards are in place, the EDL will be read (overtly or without your knowledge) by local readers for nearly everything, *especially* for such privacy-oriented transactions as gas pumps, prepaid cell phones, and Internet cafe use. Any cash purchase over $100 would likely require a card swipe. If any of this seems farfetched, you only need to look to the example of England.

THE NATIONAL ID IN BRITAIN

While I don't often quote at such length, the below synopsis of what is about to become law in the U.K. is highly instructional for what is in store for a compliant USSA within 10 years.

You may have heard that legislation creating compulsory ID Cards passed a crucial stage in the House of Commons. You may feel that ID cards are not something to worry about, since we already have Photo ID for our Passport and Driving License and an ID Card will be.no different to that. What you have not been told is the full scope of this proposed ID Card, and what it will mean to you personally.

*The proposed ID Card will be different from any card you now hold. **It will be connected to a database called the NIR, (National Identity Register)**, where all of your personal details will be stored. This will include the unique number that will be issued to you, your fingerprints, a scan of the back of your eye, and your photograph. Your name, address and date of birth will also obviously be stored there.*

*There will be spaces on this database for your religion, residence status, and many other private and personal facts about you. There is unlimited space for every other details of your life on the NIR database, which can be expanded by the Government **with or without further Acts of Parliament.***

By itself, you might think that this register is harmless, but you would be wrong to come to this conclusion. This new card will be used to check your identity against your entry in the register in real time, whenever you present it to 'prove who you are'.

Every place that sells alcohol or cigarettes, every post office, every pharmacy, and every Bank will have an NIR Card Terminal, (very much like the Chip and Pin Readers that are everywhere now), into which your card can be 'swiped' to check your identity. **Each time this happens, a record is made at the NIR of the time and place that the Card was presented.** *This means for example, that there will be a government record of every time you withdraw more than £99 at your branch of Nat West, who now demand ID for these transactions. Every time you have to prove that you are over 18, your card will be swiped, and a record made at the NIR. Restaurants and off licenses will demand that your card is swiped so that each receipt shows that they sold alcohol to someone over 18, and that this was proved by the access to the NIR, indemnifying them from prosecution.*

Private businesses are going to be given access to the NIR Database. If you want to apply for a job, you will have to present your card for a swipe. If you want to apply for a London Underground Oyster Card, or a supermarket loyalty card, or a driving license you will have to present your ID Card for a swipe. **The same goes for getting a telephone line or a mobile phone or an internet account.**

Oyster, DVLA, BT and Nectar (for example) all run very detailed databases of their own. They will be allowed access to the NIR, just as every other business will be. This means that each of these entities will be able to store your unique number in their database, and place all your travel, phone records, driving activities and detailed shopping habits under your unique NIR number. These databases, which can easily fit on a storage device the size of your hand, will be sold to third parties either legally or illegally. **It will then be possible for a non governmental entity to create a detailed dossier of all your activities.** *Certainly, the government will have clandestine access to all of them, meaning that they will have a complete record of all your movements, from how much and when you withdraw from your bank account to what medications you are taking, down to the level of what sort of bread you eat - all accessible via a single unique number in a central database.*

This is quite a significant leap from a simple ID Card that shows your name and face.

Most people do not know that this is the true character and scope of the proposed ID Card. Whenever the details of how it will work are explained to them, they quickly change from being ambivalent towards it.

The Government is going to COMPEL you to enter your details into the NIR and to carry this card. *If you and* *your children want to obtain or renew your passports, you will be forced to have your fingerprints taken and your eyes scanned for the NIR, and an ID Card will be issued to you whether you want one or not. If you refuse to be fingerprinted and eye scanned, you will not be able to get a passport.* **Your ID Card will, just like your passport, not be your property. The Home Secretary will have the right to revoke or suspend your ID at any time, meaning that you will not be able to withdraw money from your Bank Account, for example, or do anything that requires you to present your government issued ID Card.**

The arguments that have been put forwarded in favour of ID Cards can be easily disproved. ID Cards WILL NOT stop terrorists; every Spaniard has a compulsory ID Card as did the Madrid Bombers. ID Cards will not 'eliminate benefit fraud', which in comparison, is small compared to the astronomical cost of this proposal, which will be measured in billions according to the LSE (London School of Economics). **This scheme exists solely to exert total surveillance and control over the ordinary free British Citizen,** *and it will line the pockets of the companies that will create the computer systems at the expense of your freedom, privacy and money.*

If you did not know the full scope of the proposed ID Card Scheme before and you are as unsettled as I am at what it really means to you, to this country and its way of life, I urge you to email or photocopy this and give it to your friends and colleagues and everyone else you think should know and who cares. **The Bill has proceeded to this stage due to the lack of accurate and complete information on this proposal being made public.** *Together & Hand to hand, we can inform the entire nation if everyone who receives this passes it on.*
— Frances Stonor Saunders, Mar 2, 2007
http://blog.wired.com/27bstroke6/2007/03/national_id_car.htm l#comment-62060972

BIOMETRIC ID

This is real "mark of the beast" stuff, and it's nearly here. Such an ID would digitize your body's characteristics (iris, DNA, fingerprint, voiceprint, Human Leukocyte Antigen, etc.). Your number would become "Your Number" on your new ID.

branding our American soldiers like cattle

The U.S. military already uses such an evil control device for called the *Multi-Technology Automated Reader Card*, or MARC. Several soldiers have been court-martialed for refusing to give blood and saliva samples for the DNA registry.

"Your DNA identification number, please?"

Other DNA registrants include babies and criminals. Soon, DNA or some other form of biometric ID will be demanded of us all in the guise of either driver's licenses, health cards, worker citizen cards.

Project L.U.C.I.D.

Read Ira Levin's *This Perfect Day* to understand what could be in store for us if the Project L.U.C.I.D. goes on-line. Once the human sheep have been branded with the *"Universal Biometrics Card"* (containing 5 *giga*bytes of personal data) they will be tracked by the **Logical Universal Communication Interactive Databank** (L.U.C.I.D.). We are to be tagged like fish, and globally watched like suspected terrorists. *All* of us.

> [L.U.C.I.D. designer] *Dr. Jean-Paul Creusat, M.D., who works on the staff of* Interpol, *a European-based international police agency, and who is also somehow affiliated with the United Nations, involved with two little-known U.S. corporations, Advanced Technology Group and Birkmayer Software,* [is] *designing a system for a worldwide, criminal justice computer tracking . . . and control network, to be used by the CIA, FBI,* et al. ***All of this he does while claiming to be independent, with funds . . . being "privately generated."***
> — Texe Marrs; *Project L.U.C.I.D.,* (1996) p. 36

Today, even *secular* journalists and authors are recognizing the modern parallels to St. John's description of the Beast system.

AT&T's equipment corporation **Lucent** Technologies boasts of its operating system **Inferno**, written in language **Limbo** with protocols called **Styx**. (*Three* synonyms for hell is just a *coincidence*...) The *Inferno* network system is designed to make TVs, phones, etc. *interactive* and tied to L.U.C.I.D. Orwell's *1984* spying telescreen from Hell — I mean *Inferno*.

THE FINAL ID: IMPLANTED CHIPS

The basic system consists of an implantable biochip transponder and an external scanning device. The transponders come in various sizes, the smallest of which (at this time — but remember, everything is getting smaller) is about the size of an uncooked grain of rice (11mm). The transponder is a glass tube made of soda lime glass which is known for biocompatibility.

This type of transponder is a passive device, meaning it has no batteries and never can wear out. It is energized by a low-frequency radio wave from the scanner. Once the scanner is activated, it digitally displays the decoded ID number on a liquid crystal screen. . . .

Each transponder comes prepackaged inside a sterilized needle, which is discarded after use. ...In order to prevent the biochip from moving around, one end is sheathed in a polypropylene shell. This coating offers a surface with which fibrous connective tissue begins to bond within 24 hours after injection. **In other words, once the biochip is implanted, it becomes part of you with an "unlimited lifespan" (Trovan).**

— *The Mark of the New World Order*, p. 316-7

Whatever the excuse, know that smart cards are merely a temporary expedient in the goal of mass implantation of digital transponder chips. Don't laugh — L.A. County already requires them for all pets. Hundreds of human beings have already been "chipped", most notably top officials in Mexican government.

Are these implants to be the *"mark of the beast"*?

There's little difference between a MARC *held* in your hand and a mark *implanted* there (Revelation 13:11-18). The really eerie thing about Rev. 13:16 is the **subtopical,** not topical, nature of the mark of the beast: *"And he causeth all, both*

small and great, rich and poor, free and bond, to receive a mark **in** *their right hand, or* **in** *their foreheads:"*
    The word *"mark"* (*Strong's Exhaustive Concordance of the Bible*, No. 5480) is from the Greek word *charagma* which is connected by *The Expanded Vine's Expository Dictionary of New Testament Words* to **stigma** (*Strong's* 4742), in which *Strong's* references *stigma* back to the Greek **stizo**, which means "*. . . to* **prick, stick, incise, or punch for recognition of ownership.** *Scar of service:* **a mark.**" Beasts of the Beast.

RFID implants deep inside the body

    If the below were not fully verifiable, I'd have thought the notion was purely in the realm of science-fiction:

> *A patent application (# 20044174258) titled Method and Apparatus for Locating and Tracking Persons lays out Persephone Inc.'s nightmarish idea: the surgical implantation of their tracking device deep in the body. They've targeted the head, the torso, the deep muscle of limbs, and the lumen of organs like the GI tract and the uterus as ideal locations for implantation. There they'd be next to impossible to remove without major surgery.*
>
>   *"Removal of the implanted device by a runaway juvenile would likely be impossible." When not tracking runaways and kidnapping victims, the deep organ implants could have "secondary uses" to track "incarcerated individuals, military personnel, business travelers, [and] mentally impaired individuals . . . ." Someday, they may even include GPS-type implants, so that people could be hunted down "when an activation signal is sent to the implantable device to begin locating and tracking the person."*
>
>   *The device could do more than just track — it could also vibrate, electroshock the implantee, broadcast a message, or serve as a microphone to transmit his or her words to a remote location.* **"Because the device is implanted in the person, it can also provide a shock, vibration, or other warning . . . [that] may be progressive, such that a person is subjected to a shock of increasing magnitude as he leaves a zone of confinement or enters a forbidden zone."** *(pp. 186-188)*
>
>   *There's little doubt in our minds that were the Holocaust to happen today, the Nazi predators would have done more than issue yellow stars to mark their victims. They would*

almost certainly have tagged every Jew with a mandatory RFID implant, preferably deep in the body where it would be impossible to remove.

When the low-tech world goes bad as it did in Nazi Germany [with only IBM punch cards], *it's a nightmare, but when the RFID world goes bad, the nightmare could permeate every aspect of the victims' lives, making camouflage and escape all but impossible. RFID could fulfill dictators' wildest dreams, providing near total omniscience and control over every aspect of society.* **When RFID goes bad, it will be unlike anything we've ever seen before.** (p. 211)

— *Spychips: How Major Corporations and Government Plan to Track Your Every Move with RFID* (2005)

YOUR LINE IN THE SAND

Future IDs are not really about positive identification. They are really about *control*. Control is a right of *ownership*. Since the Social Security Number was created in 1935, Americans have been herded onto the federal ranch. Those voluntarily branded with an SSN are property of the U.S. government. (Try to *act* like a free person today and you will be judicially thrown back into the cowpen by the scruff of your neck.)

How have we arrived at our putrid state? How have Americans come to be utterly *owned*? How did we accept the haughty demand of government to be licensed for marriage, driving, owning a pet, and conducting a business? Why didn't we *revolt* when government was still hesitant and timid?

Will we take the *"mark"*? Will we be the perfect chattel of the global socialists? If the biometric branding goes forward, then America will obey and suffer without end. Many Americans simply will *not* tolerate this gross invasion of privacy. I predict that the push for a biometric national ID card will be the final straw for fencesitters. **That scheme should be *everybody's* line in the sand.**

If there is one lesson about this that the Holocaust taught us, it's that the Jews should have refused to wear their identifying yellow star of David. The ones who did refuse had a chance to evade capture, and many of them did — some living in 1945 Berlin right through the end of the war.

FINANCIAL PRIVACY

Anything which stores value, is a unit of measure, and replaces direct barter is "money." Really, what makes something truly money is that somebody else (ideally a complete stranger in a foreign land) readily *accepts* it in trade.

	long-distance?	possible alias, anonymous?	location, no record?	details, no record?
cash	?	✔	✔	✔
M.O.	✔	✔	?	?
3rd party check	✔	?	?	✗
personal check	✔	✗	?	✗
prepaid debit	✔	✔	✔	✗
digital gold	✔	?	✔	✗
PayPal	✔	✗	✔	✗
credit card	✔	✗	✔	✗
eCache	✔	✔	✔	✔
LIberty Reserve	✔	✔	✔	✗
Hawala	(not evaluated by press time)			
Loom	(not evaluated by press time)			

CASH

This will be a big shock to you, but I highly recommend using cash wherever possible. Credit cards and checks, though convenient, create records. Privacy is never convenient.

While cash is not preferred for long-distance transactions with strangers, this is solved by using M.O.s.

The real downside with cash, however, is that it is a poor long-term store of wealth. It's not that too much cash is being printed, but banking credits in the form of dollars — and cash is therefore being indirectly debased. If you keep cash, then you're still beholden to the economic policies of that nation. Nevertheless, it is wise to hold 3-6 months of expenses in cash.

always pay for these with cash:

Use cash and concoct a one-time transaction alias if a name if needed. While this list cannot be all-inclusive, it's a good place to start. Think of other items on your own.

- **guns, ammo and shooting supplies**

Go to gun shows for anonymous purchases. Have utterly *no* records of gun-related items tied to your name.

- **books and magazines**

One's reading list speaks volumes of one's interests, tastes and habits. Be careful of which books you check out at the library. Frequent used bookstores, but don't get chummy. It's preferable to buy gun magazines at the newsstand rather than to subscribe. Isn't privacy worth an extra few dollars a year?

Extreme Tip: If you don't have an alias with separate address for mail-ordering, then don't order books directly from controversial booksellers in your own name. Go to a local bookstore and prepay your alias order in cash through them. (Know the title, author and ISBN of your book.) When they ask for your phone number, reply that you're just visiting and that you'll call *them*.

- **airline tickets**

I'll qualify this with the warning that cash-purchased tickets can red-flag you for secondary screening at the airport. One way around this to is buy a prepaid debit card with cash and then use it online to book your flight.

- **auto parts**

No use having your make and model of car easily traceable through credit cards or microfilmed checks.

- **tires and shoes**

Both leave identifying tracks. You never know what weird situation may arise in which not leaving traceable tracks is advantageous.

Extreme Tip: Since your car's license plate will often be noted on the tire invoice, you might use an old plate from another car and throw some mud on the expired sticker.

- **grocery store purchases**

Their inventories are wonderfully computerized these days. Look at your next receipt and you'll be amazed at the detail recorded. *Exactly* what, where and when is there for checking. Your diet, house cleaning habits and contraceptive usage could be analyzed by sicko government types. (This isn't much of an issue *now*, but the Thought Police are growing. Read *This Perfect Day* by Ira Levin to see where we're probably headed.)

Cash should certainly be used for any "value" card purchase, as this shopping history is retained by the store for their greedy marketing purposes.

- **any item which might be returned for a refund**

If you pay cash, you'll be refunded in cash instead of by check. Keep your receipt.

- **pets and supplies**

You don't want vet records of "Whiskers" the cat to be traced to you, so they shouldn't have your address or phone number. For the rabies tag, concoct an address or give out an email address.

MONEY ORDERS

M.O.s are lovely. Buy them with cash and no ID is required. They're available practically everywhere. They only cost 25¢ to 99¢. Use them whenever you must mail payment, or when you don't want to be seen.

Granted, a paper trail *is* created, but records are not sorted by the purchaser's name. The issuer will have the cashed original, the payee's bank will have a microfilmed copy, and you might even have the receipt. Unless, however, one knew *where* to start (with the M.O. company, the payee, or your records), there's no picking up the trail. Most often, the payee (who got paid) is the point of investigatory origin.

Mail order houses will record their customers' names and shipping addresses. If you used an alias and had your UPS package sent to a private mail receiving service—*so what?*

address-related M.O. payments

If, however, you M.O. paid rent, storage space, utilities or home phone service, then an address *could* be discovered. Even so, how would they know to check your *landlord's* banking records unless they already knew where you lived? (It's easy to catch birds by sprinkling salt on their tails.)

For *each* address, buy your M.O.s from the *same* place to avoid comingling information (domicile with storage unit, for example). Never buy consecutive M.O.s from any one store, and don't use the same store more than once every six months.

what about the receipts?

Keep them *only* if you might need to later prove payment. Address-oriented receipts (i.e., utilities, rent, home phone, etc.) should be kept *at that address* and not in your car or on your person. When you buy an addressed-oriented M.O., put the receipt in a locked briefcase as soon as you get to your car. **Don't leave them in your wallet or purse.** You might get arrested for some old traffic ticket and your address get discovered. Once home, transfer the receipt inside. Be thorough and stay sharp.

Receipts for sensitive mail order products should not be kept at home, in your car or on your person. Scan them (or take a digital photo) and store in an encrypted volume on flash drive (which offers more plausible deniability than a hard drive). Burn the receipts after archiving them. After you no longer need a digital copy, shred the files.

Yeah, I know, all this is a *pain*. Well, privacy *is* a pain. If you're not up to it, then just go get a checking account. Fishbowl *"Yes, Sir!"* living is *easy*—that's why so many people don't *mind* it. But hey, only *learning* to live privately is difficult. Once learned, it's merely tedious and somewhat inconvenient.

watch out for "structuring"

Since any cash transaction exceeding $3,000 in a single day is reportable on a *Currency Transaction Report* (CTR), some simply spread out large purchases over several days or purchase orders. **It is a crime (called "structuring") to intentionally avoid the reporting requirement.** Structuring works like this: let's say a "Peeping Tom" law was passed which prohibited looking in somebody's window for more than 10 consecutive seconds per minute. Anyone who innocently looked in a window for 9 seconds one minute, and 9 seconds another could be charged with "structuring" by splitting up 18 seconds of looking into more than one minute —

thus circumventing the "Peeping Tom" statute.   Only a government lawyer could have thought *that* up.

PRE-PAID DEBIT CARDS

Fairly new products, these are a *huge* boon to privacy, especially on the Internet. Even for those not highly sensitive about privacy, prepaid debit cards should be used for most online purchases to protect one's actual credit card. Save your real VISA for what prepaid debit cards cannot do: renting cars, automatically reoccurring subscriptions, casios, etc.

That bank/nonbank link is the key to the problem, because the ["open system"] cards have ATM privileges but are not linked to personal bank accounts, which are closely monitored.

reloadable cards are not private!

Reloadable prepaid cards create a "formal banking business relationship" require compliance with Customer Identification Program (CIP) procedures:

Obtaining A Card: The USA PATRIOT Act is a federal law that requires all financial institutions to obtain, verify and record information that identifies each person who opens a Card Account. What this means for you: When a consumer opens a Card Account, BankFirst will ask for the consumer's name, address, date of birth and other information that will identify the consumer. The consumer will need to provide his/her Social Security number if a U.S. citizen or personal Tax ID or passport number if a non-U.S. citizen. BankFirst may also ask to see your driver's license or other identifying documents.

Reloadable debit cards are registered only with extensive personal information, including your SSN. They may offer a slight privacy advantage over credit cards, but not much.

nonreloadable cards offer great privacy

*Bank Secrecy Act - MSB Regulations (31 CFR Part 103)
Requires issuers, sellers and redeemers of "stored value' to have an effective Anti-Money Laundering Program. However, they are not required to register as Money Services Businesses (MSBs). Nor are they required to file Suspicious*

Activity Reports (though they would have to file CTRs for transactions of more than $10,000.)

Nonreloadable cards, however, do not (yet) require all this, but some are valid up to $500 (these are curiously hard to find).

If used online, they require only a very basic registration of address, email, and sometimes phone (and none of this seems to be confirmed, anyway). Your IP address *will* be logged, so be careful to protect your privacy there.

limitations of debit cards

They will not work in casinos, ATMs, gas pumps, car rentals, "open purchases" (such as hotel room deposit), or for reoccurring monthly/annual purchases. (Some are valid only in the USA, so avoid these.)

Several states (most of them back East, of course) forbid registration and use of nonreloadable (*i.e.*, private) debit cards.

cost of debit cards

Purchase fees run about $6, which for a $500 card is pretty cheap (1.2%) considering the privacy (and not risking your real credit card with fraud and ID theft).

Monthly service fees begin only after a year, and then are only $1-2/month. Most cards would be used up before then. Besides, they are valid for less than two years, anyway.

criteria for choosing a prepaid debit card:

up to $500?   minimal registration?   valid internationally?

Sometimes you'll have to scrutinize the package text to make sure that the card doesn't require an SSN. (It will, if it proudly brags about FDIC protection.) Since the cards are preprinted with an expiration date (just like milk cartons), choose the latest expiration date (often 2-3 years ahead).

how to register online

Before you register your card, think through very carefully all the details. (This includes mapping out which IP proxies you will use to register which cards.) If you use a foreign proxy, a USA address/phone may redflag the merchant depending on the vigor of their card clearing service. Thus, you may have to sync your registration IP with your address/phone so that they're both at least from the same state (if not city).

Have a free throwaway email account set up in Yahoo, Gmail, etc. If you don't have an alias address/phone already arranged, a quick workaround is to use the number of a realtor and the address of one of their listed homes. Easily found online, both are valid in the sense that they do exist but nothing ties them to you.

extreme tip: to confuse original location of purchase

If you have friends around the country, you all could trade cards with each other. That way, your card's purchase location not only gives nothing away, it also provides an important level of disinformation about where you may reside. Or, you should buy them when you're out-of-state. (Registration address should be in the same state as the IP address.)

most extreme tip: delay card activation

Try to avoid activating them within 30 days of store purchase, *i.e.*, within the time window that store video footage is generally kept.

avoid American Express debit cards

They are not accepted as widely as VISA and MC.

make sure the card is valid worldwide

Since many online privacy products are sold by foreign companies (such as proxy tunnels) or their payments are cleared by foreign banks, be sure that your nonreloadable debit card is valid internationally. (This rules out WalMart's cards!)

VISA has a nice debit card (*"The Ideal Gift"*) that works around the world, one-time loadable up to $500.

use different cards for different purposes and aliases

You should have different cards not only for different persona, of course, but also perhaps for different uses. Whatever you pay for with the same card is now linked forever together, and helps form a basic trail. (If you buy multiple products on the same card, be absolutely sure that provide each company *exactly* the name, email address, and phone. They are understandably nervous about the fraud potential of cards.)

All this is easy to keep track of in simple Notepad files, encrypted within a TrueCrypt volume. Once a card is used up, shred that file. Also, unless you really need to use the card in person, don't carry it with you. (After I enter the card info into my computer, I physically shred the card and burn the bits.)

how to spend the small remaining balance of $4.38?

You can either use it physically in a store (if you haven't destroyed the card, and don't mind being tied to that location with a likely security camera record), or

transfer it into another card (not permitted by all issuers),

donate it to some deserving shareware firm (if they don't use the privacy-invasive PayPal to accept card charges), or just eat the $4.38 and consider it merely another cost of privacy. I heartily recommend:

www.eff.org	(Electronic Frontier Foundation)
www.puppylinux.com/bkauler	(Barry Kauler's labor of love)
www.truecrypt.com	(awesome encryption software)
www.xp-Antispy.org	(excellent tool)

PAYPAL

I do not recommend PayPal for anything. Somebody once bought 10 *Holograms of Liberty* and created an account for me. I've not been able to get that money from the Javelin Press account. Many PayPal excuses and user agreement changes (to which I never consented) have locked up those funds.

PayPal is U.S.-only, expensive, extremely unprivate, and prides itself on revocable transactions.

If you must use them for merchant processing, use dedicated and empty bank accounts with no overdraft, and a dedicated credit card with no credit line and a balance as close to zero as possible.

If you read the many thousands of scam complaints against them, you will find among them many cases where Paypal has initiated fraudulent direct debit requests on customer's banks, and in many cases been wired significant sums with no approval from the customer. If I steal a credit card and use it to buy something from you, YOUR account can be shut down, and they will attempt to recover the chargeback from your bank account and credit cards attached to your account. They will also shut down any account you

*have spent to since the original fraud. It doesn't matter if you
have 5 years of squeeky clean high volume . . .*
— www.privacy.li/digitalcurrency.htm

For other info on the sins and omissions of PayPal:

www.paypalsucks.com
www.paypalpetition.com
www.ripoffreport.com
www.aboutpaypal.org
www.paypalwarning.com

DIGITAL GOLD CURRENCIES

*What we need now is a Free Money Movement comparable
to the Free Trade Movement of the 19th century,
demonstrating not merely the harm caused by acute
inflation...but the deeper effects of producing periods of
stagnation that are indeed inherent in the present monetary
arrangements. I still believe that, so long as the management
of money is in the hands of government, the gold standard,
with all its imperfections, is the only tolerably safe system but
it is better to take money completely out of the control of
government. The only way to save civilization will be to
deprive governments of the power over the supply of money.*
— von Hayek, *The Denationalization of Money* (1976)

This is the most promising and exciting development in the
ongoing monetary revolution. A digital gold currency (DGC) is
physical gold in digital warehouse receipt form, tradeable on
the Internet amongst thousands of people and firms. Each year
many billions of dollars do so. A DGC account balance may also
be fully redeemed in bullion or in a national currency.

DGC advantages
- ✔ wealth is stored in actual gold, not evaporating currencies
- ✔ physical gold is stored in offshore vaults — continually audited
- ✔ no fractional reserve banking — 100% gold assets
- ✔ an actual economy of growing global network of DGC users
- ✔ very inexpensive transacation fees (from 0.1% to 2%)
- ✔ person-to-person payments
- ✔ micropayments of <$2 no problem, and cost-effective

✔ irreversible transactions, like cash or bullion
✔ immediate payment (what email is to snailmail)
✔ ideal for multiple "pass-through" transfers
✔ digital certificates (safer than credit cards)
✔ funds can be accessed by ATM debit card
✔ contractually valid, and free of government price-fixing schemes
✔ enhances your financial privacy through offshore data havens
✔ brings gold into the 21st century with fresh usefulness
✔ noninflationary (*i.e.,* you're no longer part of the M3 problem)
✔ a parallel financial system that weakens the banksters

DGC cons

☞ technologically dependent upon computers and Internet
☞ your gold is held overseas by strangers
☞ outright theft has occurred (OSgold was a classic scam)
☞ theft by fraudulent transaction very difficult to recover
☞ account setup not very private (almost as bad as a bank)
☞ diminishing privacy with U.S. exchange providers
☞ DGC transactional history kept on file, handed over by decree
☞ account value fluctuates with spot price of gold
☞ some DGCs charge a storage fee for the gold warehousing
☞ under severe government scrutiny

Although there are clearly some privacy concerns, a quality DGC provider is still much more private and secure than your bank or credit card. Your wealth is stored in gold, and your account history can be gleaned only through a valid court order of appropriate jurisdiction to that offshore DGC.

Point being, anything you are currently comfortable doing by check and credit card (*i.e.,* with such low privacy) can and should be done instead through DGCs.

exchange providers

You can only receive DGC if somebody spends some to your account. The exchange provider transforms national currency (in whatever form) into DGC by accepting your check, etc. and then crediting your DGC account with the prevailing amount of gold. Their fee for this service is about 2-4%.

why don't the DGC providers accept customers' funds?

Because this would immediately subject them to all the banking regulations. e-gold used to fight from high ground on this very issue, until July 2008 when they caved to prosecution. (Perhaps this plea bargain was a clever way to delay the issue's adjudication, as it is not yet settled as a point of law. Maybe Dr. Jackson threw himself on top of the DoJ's grenade and bought time for his DGC squadmates. Just theorizing . . .)

funds generally accepted by exchange providers

Subject to each firm's policies, but pretty much anything: check, wire transfer, cash, money and postal orders, credit cards, Western Union, Moneygram, domestic internet bank transfers, etc.

U.S. vs. offshore exchange providers

(1) the term "unlicensed money transmitting business" means a money transmitting business which affects interstate or foreign commerce in any manner or degree and--

(A) is operated without an appropriate money transmitting license in a State where such operation is punishable as a misdemeanor or a felony under State law, whether or not the defendant knew that the operation was required to be licensed or that the operation was so punishable.

— 18 U.S.C. § 1960

U.S. exchange providers are considered "money transfer" businesses and thus are required to obtain ID on clients for most transactions. It's also a federal crime to break a state money laundering law . . . even without *mens rea*.

Offshore exchange providers are often not subject to similar laws in their home countries, but nonetheless must be sure you're not an internet fraudster or credit card scammer. (By the way, "offshore" means any country not your own.)

thoroughly research before trusting exchange providers

This industry is naturally vulnerable to fraudsters, so beware of whom you choose. Settle only for those with years of spotless reputation.

Power Privacy says that GoldThrift are fast and reliable.

privately sending funds to an offshore exchange provider

For privacy (yet some degree of security over cash) use M.O.s which are negotiable outside the U.S. (This eliminates our postal M.O.s.) WalMart sells $500 M.O.s with no ID required. Your location of purchase and mailing are knowable to the exchanger, and his bank might microfilm his deposits. Nonetheless, M.O.s are still pretty private. International FedEx is an option if speed/reliability are paramount.

Another way to send funds is through a prepaid debit card, such as international VISA. The nonreloadable (*i.e.*, private) cards max out at $500, and your card fee is 1-2%. This is an expensive way to move money, but it is faster (typically same day) and more secure than snailmailing M.O.s. (It also keeps your vulnerable credit card out of the Internet loop.) You could reuse the card's registration name/email/phone for successive cards, but keep track of the running total before it hits $10,000 and thus triggering possible reporting requirements.

One used to be able to send a bank wire without having a local account, but I've found this impossible today, and, besides, such is the furthest thing from being private.

DGC providers

To break up the banking cycle and thus legally avoid banking regs, they are funded solely through the exchange providers, who credit the DGC account you designate. The main DGC providers have solid reputations for fiscal honesty. (Truly, your main risk is through the exchange providers.)

If the lessons of e-gold and e-bullion teach us anything, it is that your DGC must not have *any* ties to the U.S. Thus, the vital criteria are:

100% offshore situs (legal incorporation and domicile)
100% offshore servers
100% offshore gold storage
100% reserve ratio

	100% offshore?	audit trail?	fed free?	good rep?	strong privacy?
eCache	✔		✔	✔	✔
GoldMoney	✔	✔	✔	✔	✘
Pecunix	✔		✔	✔	+/-
e-bullion	(avoid! — see related text)				
e-gold	✘	✘	✘	+/-	✘

eCache   https://ffij33ewbnoeqnup.onion.meshmx.com/

A very interesting alternate to account-based DGCs. Instead, you purchase and circulate anonymous "digital bearer certificates". Digital gold coins which cannot be tracked any more than cash and coins. No account need ever be opened, which solves most of the privacy issues of ID and proof of residency. eCache cannot even keep track of customer IP history because eCache is accessible only through TOR (which naturally limits its client base to sophisticated Netizens, a small pool indeed).

A fascinating DGC twist, well worth exploring to satisfy yourself that the certificates are backed by real gold, held by trustworthy people, and spendable in sufficient scope.

www.goldmoney.com

Founded by a man I like and respect, Jim Turk, who is very well educated and experienced in international banking, finance, and investments. His *Freemarket Gold & Money Report* investment newsletter has been published since 1987. GoldMoney is highly regarded as a most professional firm, with third party secure storage (with ViaMat), a transparent audit trail (by Deloitte and Touche) and good customer service. A *much* better company than e-gold (and nearly as large) without any history of rolling over for the DoJ.

Up to a certain limit, no ID is required. Above that, and you must email/fax them a scanned photo ID and utility bill. (They have recently tightened up their policies considerably, so this seems to have changed.)

www.pecunix.com

A small but well-regarded DGC founded by entrepreneurial maverick Simon "Sidd" Davis. Rhodesian by birth, Davis had a very successful construction company providing low-cost housing in South Africa. Pecunix is very security minded, and uses automated PGP/GPG encryption. (They have reportedly never suffered any kind of security breach.) Their interface is most innovative and efficient, such as the merchant shopping cart accepting 4 DGCs (http://gold-cart.com/).

A growing company with a very big future!

www.1stdigibank.com

For advanced users who would like to combine the digital gold world with traditional offshore banking services there is a bank called First Digital International Bank (www.1stdigibank.com) which piggy-backs on the e-gold and goldmoney system. It is run by privacy oriented PT's and has its servers offshore. Effectively, it's a way of spending and storing e-gold or goldmoney without themselves being aware of it. On top they don't charge storage fees AND even pay interest on gold holdings - a very progressive approach! It is something you should explore by yourself when you are comfortable with the first two.

1mdc pioneered the "piggybacking" (on U.S.-based e-gold, which was a fatal error). I've no experience with them, but if there is an option of piggybacking, certainly choose GoldMoney.

e-bullion

Now under a dark cloud of disrepute as founder Jim Fayed was indicted in July 2008 for operating an "unlicensed money transmitting business". (A concurrent attack on e-gold, by the way.) Since e-bullion provided its *own* in-house currency exchange service, the feds may have had a theoretical case.

Fayed was also charged for complicity in murdering his wife who was about to divorce him and break up his financial empire (by cooperating with the authorities). A car fleeing the murder scene had been rented days prior with Fayed's AmEx card — a card found in his wallet during a search.

I'd seek another DGC.

SupraGold

A Lichtenstein DGC which I consider a "too good to be true". (They also tout an offshore check-cashing service for 7% fee.) Large and reputable DGCs avoid hawking anonymity (as it attracts criminals and thus government scrutiny), but not SupraGold:

SupraGold is anonymous, you can open a FREE account under any name, corporation name or moniker!

Through a well diversified group of independent market makers it is possible to negotiate in- and out-exchanges to an acceptable level of costs. We know one market maker who even pays you a premium when you want to sell your SuparGold.

You can receive and send wire transfers which never put a trace back to you (if correctly structured and with the help of exchangers)
There are at least 3 options to obtain an ATM-card based and drawn on your SuparaGold holdings, thus allowing you to easily cash your gold and spend it in a real world scenario.
SupraGold is not a start-up! They have been starting to offer their service in early 2005 to some private and elite users. Since the demise of e-gold, LibertyDollar, 1mdc (others will follow!) they now have streamlined the SupraGold-system to be usable worldwide and in masses. The monthly growth rate is a whopping 5% as of this writing!
— www.privacy.li/digitalcurrency.htm

Gee, how could it be sexier than *that*? SupraGold is the equivalent of a 23 y/o model hitting on a fat, balding accountant. Investigate and use at your own risk! Their PGP key is at:

www.privacy.li/pgp_key.htm

e-gold (avoid, avoid, avoid!)

I had high hopes for DGC customer privacy, until 2008 when the first and largest digital gold organization rolled over. First, in May 2007, they handed over $11,000,000 in others' assets to the feds (with no evidence of any criminal activity).

The next year, even though the Government had previously admitted that banking laws did not have jurisdiction over DGCs, e-gold founder/director Dr. Douglas Jackson cravenly pleaded guilty to conspiracy to engage in money laundering (18 USC 1956 — 20 years and a fine of $500,000) and conspiracy to operate an unlicensed money transmitting business (18 USC 1960 — 5 years and a fine of $250,000). e-gold was hit for millions in fines and forfeitures.

So much for Jackson's pre-indictment offer to the feds in tracking down child porn transactions and credit card fraudsters. (Some gratitude from the DoJ!) The U.S. Secret Service has had it in for the DGCs and e-gold from the start, and refused to accept Jackson's offer of assistance.

Worse still was Jackson's toadying announcement that his prosecution and plea agreement were somehow good things:

The resolution of the criminal case however provides for a second chance, an opportunity to address the flaws embedded in the e-gold system and to transform the "e-gold

Operation" into the institutions I, the other directors, and our longsuffering employees and contractors have always envisioned, one that serves to advance the material welfare of mankind.

In harmony with this transformation, we acknowledge that e-gold is indeed a Financial Institution or Agency as defined in US law and should be regulated as a Financial Institution. E-gold Ltd. has submitted an application to FinCEN to be registered as a Money Services Business and will be seeking licensure in all states that require it. Most importantly, working in conjunction with US government agencies, we will be exerting every effort to bring e-gold into compliance with US law and regulation as quickly as possible.

— http://blog.e-gold.com/2008/07/a-new-beginning.html

"embedded flaws"? "transformation"? "should be regulated"? "advance the material welfare of mankind"? Just disgusting.

Just because a *very* small portion of e-gold's volume was misused by actual criminals (*i.e.*, related to fraud, terrorism, or child porn) was no valid reason to roll over to the DoJ. **Anonymity of transactions is not inherently evil.** Jackson, for the sake of his honest customers, should have gone all the way to trial. In fact, he should have stood up for his clients in 2007 and refused to allow the seizure of $11.3 million of gold belonging to 1mdc and others.

That he caved was a tragic thing for the DGC industry, which must now fight an uphill battle to offer customer privacy. The feds, naturally, could not contain their glee:

Also as part of the plea agreement, the businesses will create a comprehensive money laundering detection program that will require verified customer identification, suspicious activity reporting and regular supervision by the Internal Revenue Services' (IRS) Bank Secrecy Act Division, to which the Financial Crimes Enforcement Network delegated authority according to federal regulations.

"By failing to comply with money laundering laws and regulations, the E-Gold operation created an environment ripe for exploitation by criminals seeking anonymity in conducting online transactions," said Acting Assistant Attorney General Matthew Friedrich. "This case demonstrates that online payment systems must operate according to the applicable rules and regulations created to ensure lawful monetary transactions."

activating a new DGC account

When setting up an account, you will likely be asked for:

    name
    mailing address
    email address
    phone number
    birthdate
    Social Security Number (SSN), or,
        number from another country
    scanned in photo ID
    utility bill, or something linking you to that address
    username for the Netspend system
    password restoration question

think your IP address through very carefully

Do not open or access your account over an IP browsing proxy. Banks have gotten very good about noting when logins are being performed from known proxies, and restricting access as a result or quietly flagging the account for further investigation. When applying for or otherwise accessing your account, be sure to do it from an IP address not associated with your real identity, ideally from a laptop on somebody else's wireless network.

    — Power Privacy e-newsletter

I would open the account from a public wifi IP address in the town of your stated address. After a few months of "normal" account access and usage, I think it would be OK to use proxies.

Some offshore DGCs may even go so far as to prohibit the opening of accounts through American IP addresses. With an offshore proxy (or activating the account while in Europe) this is not insurmountable. Where there's a will . . .

have a well-tested mailing address

The DGC may insist on posting something to you as part of the activation process. Make sure that it doesn't get returned as "no such address" or "undeliverable".

low-profile account activity

Transactions under $5,000 and balances under $100,000 shouldn't attract much attention.

GOLD & SILVER COINS

This is *real* money with perfect intrinsic value, and it is not held by strangers in a foreign country. Buy *bullion* coins because when gold and silver coins are again outlawed, few will pay any numismatic premium for your contraband $20 St. Gaudens, and no hick will have *heard* of PCGS. (And even if he *had*, he'll bicker over grading, *"Looks lahk MS62 tuh me!"*) I also dislike old $20 gold pieces is that the Government may forcibly trade you out of them for $20 FRNs. (This theoretical risk also applies to the modern gold American Eagles in $5, $10, $25, and $50 face values.) See chapter 11 of my *Boston on Surviving Y2K* for a full discussion on gold and silver coins, numismatic and bullion. Buy with cash at gun and coin shows. Split up your stock. Visit www.the-moneychanger.com.

CREDIT CARDS

Protesting too loudly about [the power of credit card companies] *isn't going to help either,* **because the disturbance you kick up is going to end up in one of your files.** *And on that come and get it day when you're totally and completely dependent on our card . . .* **you might be left alone without one.**

— Terry Galanoy, former Director of Communications of VISA International

Distinct from prepaid debit cards, credit cards are almost a must today, especially to rent cars or reserve hotel rooms. If you already have your VISA or AmExp, don't dump them. Feed them address and phone disinfo. Your credit cards should have little or no activity, and certainly *none* at gun stores, travel agencies, favorite bars, or other illuminating places.

If you have no cards, but want some, get them *before* you quit your job and start a cash economy business. Getting cards can be tough, though keeping them is easy if you'll just pay your bills. Perhaps a friend might get a supplement card for you on his account. Avoid the photo credit cards.

get a foreign credit card

Many foreign banks offer debit VISAs with your "credit" being commensurate with your account balance. Typically, these account cards require an opening balance of at least

US$10,000. (Only stipulates the opposite, that your balance can never *exceed* $9,500. www.escapeartist.com)

Foreign VISAs are great because you're not listed in the domestic databanks, and the records are harder (though not impossible) for the feds to acquire. You can repatriate $3-500 per day at ATM's. (ATM's have cameras. *Extreme tip:* wear a full-face motorcycle helmet with sunglasses during the transaction, and approach from the side.)

CHECKS

Your canceled checks record the names of your doctors and hospitals, the publications you read, the relatives you help, the religious and charitable activities you support, the volume of business you give your liquor store and the amount you spend on transportation. **The information in canceled checks can be a mirror of your life, a reflection that you do not want seen by the wrong set of eyes.**

— Robert Ellis Smith; editor of the *Privacy Journal*

First, the banks think it's *their* money. Reconciling the account monthly and arguing with Bookkeeping is great fun. Lastly, your privacy goes out the window. Since 1970, banks have been required to microfilm *both* sides of any checks over $100. Since sorting those out is too labor-intensive, they simply microfilm them *all* and will turn them over to the government on demand.

While businesses must often use checks, you personally don't have to. Insist on cash, or cash the check at the payor's bank. (Now, many banks are insisting that noncustomers have their *fingerprint* digitally read before cashing a check.) If that bank is far away, endorse it through a friend's account. **Quit using checks!** It's the banks' way of creating credit "money" out of nothing. Use cash and M.O.'s — starve them out! Besides, checks bounce and banks are constantly going bust. Use cash for extra safety (as long as the cash is readily accepted, and someday it *won't* be, so be prepared with gold and silver).

LOANS & MORTGAGES

Try to avoid them. Investment capital is one thing, but to pay interest on *depreciating* goods is a financial sin. (Even a home can be a depreciating asset. Ask around.) Worse still is all the information you'll have to divulge on the application. Save up and buy it outright. *Earn* more money—don't borrow it.

IRAs, 401Ks & KEOGHs

These tax-deferred savings plans are congressionally created corrals to lure in private pensions. One day soon, Congress will mandate that a portion (ever to increase, of course) must be "invested" in Treasury securities—for your "protection," you see. Therefore, you should plan to drop out at some point, even if it means taking the 10% early withdrawal penalty. Until then, you can *truly* invest your capital in gold coins which are stored for you by a trustee. While the IRS won't let you keep them yourself, it beats having your life's savings left at risk in the stock market.

TIPS ON PREVENTING ID THEFT

❶   Never sign backs of credit cards. Put "PHOTO ID REQUIRED."

❷   When you are writing checks to pay on your credit card accounts, DO NOT put the complete account number on the "For" line. Instead, just put the last four numbers.

❸   Never print home/work phone numbers, or your SSN on checks.

❹   Place the contents of your wallet on a photocopy machine. Do both sides of each license, credit card, etc. You will know what you had in your wallet and all of the account numbers and phone numbers to call and cancel. Keep the photocopy in a safe place, and encrypt the scan.

❺   Have the toll free numbers and your card numbers handy so you know whom to call. Keep those where you can find them.

❻   File a police report immediately in the jurisdiction where your credit cards were stolen. This proves diligence to the card companies.

❼   Call the 3 national credit reporting organizations immediately to place a fraud alert on your name and also call the Social Security fraud line number. The alert means any company that checks your credit knows your information was stolen, and they have to contact you by phone to authorize new credit.

Equifax 800-525- 6285	**Experian** 888-397-3742
Trans Union 800-680-7289	**SSA** (fraud) 800-269-0271

YOUR MAIL

In June 2004, subscribers to Reason magazine received a personalized issue that had their name, and a satellite photo of their home or workplace on the cover.

Now, if *that* doesn't creep you out, then just skip this chapter.

RECEIVING YOUR MAIL

How you set up your mail is as important as your phone. The primary rules are: ❶ Have your senders omit their return address and use yours instead, and ❷, *never* receive mail at your house. *Ever!* To receive mail there first requires that you give out your home address (and don't have a number on your house) — something you never want to do. Well, then, what are the alternatives to getting mail at the end of your driveway?

how to create a red herring address

Sometimes a P.O. box will *not* be accepted — they (DMV, P.O., library, credit cards, cell phone provider, etc.) want a *street* address. You want to provide a *prima facie* legitimate address which doesn't lead anywhere. Don't be a smartass and say *"1060 W. Addison"* in Chicago, which is Wrigley Field. You want to cost the investigator precious time. A good red herring is something that *can't* be discounted with a simple phone call.

the country road ploy (while it lasts!)

Here's an original Boston tip, but its usefulness is shrinking as country properties are getting addressed. Use some fictitious box number on a very remote rural route, preferably way down some dirt road. Pick an RR which is *really* far flung (see the map in your phone book). Buy a mailbox, affix some decals for your number and nail it to a 4x4 post when you are certain the mail carrier won't drive by. Wipe off all finger-prints. Don't use it for a mail drop, and never return. Most rural route mail carriers are contracted help and not actual U.S.P.S. employees (quasi-feds). They'll likely stuff your phony mailbox without asking why it just appeared on their route.

This address *looks* bonafide, yet *really* wastes an investi-gator's time because it *is* "bonafide." An RR box number is time-consuming to check out, much less *stake* out. Imagine all the fun he'll have living in his car, waiting for you to pick up your mail. Have some junk mail sent there, and some postcards from Gunter in Vienna asking when you're coming over. Every minute spent on false leads means a minute lost on real leads.

"Which number, please?"

If the RR box is too much trouble, almost as good is the address of a large apartment complex (omitting any room number). Check the Yellow Pages or a collective brochure on the city's apartments. This address can't be easily discounted as false, even by interviewing the manager and the tenants.

General Delivery (G.D.)

This is a free service. Smaller post offices provide quicker and more personal attention than big city stations. Your mail will be returned to the sender after 30 days, so be diligent about picking it up. Usually, some form of ID will be required, though not always (especially if you're a known regular). If you make a several month habit of general delivery, some clerks will try to make you get a P.O. box. Though I haven't researched the Do-mestic Mail Manual (D.M.M.) for any time limits on G.D., you might check it out.

The main disadvantage to G.D. is that you can only pick up your mail in person during lobby hours. This is inconvenient and demands excessive transactional exposure. Therefore, use G.D. for infrequent tasks, and vary the P.O.s.

If you're overseas, you can receive mail c/o any American Express office. If you've an AmEx card or traveler's checks, the service is free — otherwise it's a buck or two. Get the AmEx listing of all their offices and let your people know where you'll be and when. I've used this service often, and it's a great way to keep your foreign address private. AmEx is also quite helpful with other traveling needs (language barriers, directions, etc.). They'll also cash a cardmember's U.S.A. check! Such takes at least two weeks to clear, giving you that much more locational privacy over the real-time ATMs.

the P.O. box

I like small town P.O. boxes. They're fairly private and dirt cheap. The yearly box fee is as little as $24. Outside large cities, a P.O. will leave the front door open so you can pick up your mail 24/7. Choose a P.O. which has after hours lock boxes for oversized parcels (the greatest postal innovation in years, besides self-adhesive stamps). Since there's no national registry, you could have many boxes across the country.

For the application procedure, minimal ID and a local address are required. Do *not* conjure up an address, because it'll likely be noticed as such. Use my RR box or apartment complex ploy. Stick a new address label on a canceled envelope to "prove" receipt of mail at your spoof address.

helpful previous boxholders

You will undoubtedly receive a bit of mail for previous boxholders. Why not receive a thing or two in *their* name? Even though it arrived in *your* box, you can easily disavow it as a stranger's mail. *Do not* get them into trouble, however.

the private mailbox

These are commercially operated alternatives to the U.S.P.S. The yearly box fees start at $100 — at least twice than a comparable P.O. box. For this extra expense, you get to call in and check for mail, plus have the convenience of a fax number and UPS shipping/receiving. Since you *never* want UPS packages delivered to your house, having them sent to a private receiver is a great service (though you don't have to be a boxholder and can simply pay $1-3 per package instead).

Postal form 1583 (*Application for Delivery of Mail through Agent*) now requires ID, and these companies are more stringent about it than the P.O. Some even photocopy the applicant's ID, or expressly warn that no warrant shall be deemed necessary for cops to obtain information. (Mail Boxes Etc., now The UPS Store, is notorious for this.) Visit your available services and choose wisely. If run by elderly people or immigrants, *beware* — they'll typically bend over for any badge that walks in the door. Find an independent *nonchain* store. The best staff are funky-type college kids. They dislike authority and will rarely give out private info to the law (unless strongly threatened or well-paid for it).

mail forwarding services

Most private mailbox services also forward mail, and not just for their boxholders. Some companies are purely forwarders. For postage and $1 fee per piece, they'll send on your mail. Simply address and stamp your letter and nest it inside a larger envelope with a $1 bill. No fuss, no muss.

To *receive* mail from a forwarder, you must obviously give them some address. You can forward through other forwarders, but don't use too many (3+) or else your mail takes much longer, is at more risk to loss or theft, and looks like hell when it finally arrives. Get a copy of Budd's Remailing List from Eden Press.

a word or two of caution

Some basic rules: Pick up your mail at infrequent and varied times. Never sign for certified or registered mail unless you expect it. Any mail not for you, throw it away — don't re-mail it. If you've reason to believe that your P.O. is being watched, pickup only during business lunch hours, have your mail forwarded, or picked up by a friend, or let it sit for a while until they give up and quit the stakeout.

If you're ever *really* sought after, and they can't find you, they have some clever tricks. Assuming you've rented a box and they've staked out the application's bogus RR box or apartment address to no avail, the only alternative is to try and catch you at the mail drop itself.

There are two general methods. The first is to have a clerk tip them off the next time you visit the lobby. If this happens, the chances are good that you'll notice the clerk's change in attitude towards you. They're clerks, not actors. If he has to *"check something in back"* and leaves his window, *get out.*

If the clerk route is not deemed reliable (or isn't possible because a private investigator has no official capacity to arrange it), then they'll have to hang out across the street and wait for you. If you never check your mail more than once a week at varied times, the stakeout will be a *real* drag.

If your description is vague or unknown, they'll send a distinctive package to you which must be picked up at the window (i.e., a long, yellow mailing tube which won't even fit in the parcel lockboxes). If you ever receive such a surprise, *don't take it outside* — somebody is probably waiting for you to generously ID yourself. You should refuse it, which is sound policy with unexpected parcels from unknown people.

the self-addressed, stamped envelope (SASE)

Frequently, readers will send me letters asking for my reply and helpfully enclose a SASE. (I answer these first.) While I happily use their SASE, I *never* lick the envelope. I use a foam moistener instead. Although I trust my readers, some nasty character could spike the glue with some unpleasantness and I wouldn't know it until it was too late. Such caution is not paranoia, but simply studied prudence.

be alert to unusual patterns or delays in receiving mail.

In a "mail cover" operation, officials will photocopy your received envelopes for return addresses and meter ID's. In the 1960s, the feds caught many people with undeclared foreign bank accounts simply by tracing the metered mail to Swiss banks. No mail on Saturday and a big batch on Monday can signal a mail cover, as nonpostal feds don't work on Saturdays.

SENDING YOUR MAIL

How you send your mail is also important. Speed of service and the postmark are sometimes vital criteria.

how to send from "A" and get a "B" postmark

You can have somebody (friend or company) forward it on as described above. Or, in some areas a big city P.O. will send a truck out to pick up rural *outside* dropboxes. Although I lived an hour away from Austin, I used a box serviced by an Austin P.O. truck. The way to check this for sure is to buy some prestamped, blank postcards from any P.O. and send them to yourself, having notated each card with which dropbox it was sent from. Remember, this distant postmarking is only for *outside* dropboxes, not those inside a P.O.

low exposure mailing

Sensitive letters or cash should be wrapped in foil, as certain sprays (*e.g.*, Freon) will make the envelope temporarily opaque. Tape all flaps and sides with your initial or code underneath (so the receiver will know *you* taped it). Don't get funky on how you address your mail. Sovereign style addresses are of marginal legal value (at best), and will only draw attention to the letter. Use block letters in black pen on plain envelopes. Use the *recipient's* address (if you're *sure* of it) as the "return" address. Some people have a P.O. *and* a street address. Use one as the sendee and the other as the sender — that way, even if you forget to affix postage, they'll still get it.

Avoid leaving saliva DNA with self-adhesive stamps and envelopes. If you've no choice but glued flaps, moisten with water. All P.O.s have them.

I prefer stamping my own mail (under 13 ounces) to avoid visiting a clerk's window. You'll need a rate sheet, a scale and many assorted stamps. Avoid using postage meters unless absolutely necessary. Each meter has an ID number, tied to the renter.

Also, I think it's wise to send mail from a P.O. other than where you receive. If this isn't convenient, then send your mail from a dropbox. (Be sure to note the pickup times so that you don't needlessly cost your mail an extra day.) I never drop off mail at a private mailbox company. Use U.S.P.S. boxes only.

Outgoing mail requiring postal clerk attention should be carefully thought through. Plan ahead where that return receipt should arrive, what the contents are, etc. Sometimes you can't avoid having to visit a clerk. Most are very nice, however, some are quite nosey. If you don't want them to inspect your mail after you've stepped away, simply ask for appropriate *stamp* postage (as opposed to metered, which cannot be handed back to you). Since this is a little uncommon, use the excuse that the piece isn't *quite* ready to go yet as you have to first verify the address, *blah, blah, blah.* Walk out with it and send from a dropbox.

TELECOMMUNICATIONS

When telephones were newly invented, a budding futurist was laughed at because he envisioned the day when every *town* would have one. Today, multiple phone lines per *household* is quite common, hence the clunky new area codes. The 1990s proliferation of cellular phones was only the first wave in personalized telecommunication. Next came satphones (no matter where you are on the *planet,* your location will be always known while your satphone is on). Now, we've got Internet telephony called VoIP (Voice over Internet Protocol), and this fascinating technology is only just beginning. If set up properly, VoIP provides *superb* privacy features.

It is my view that, besides your own tongue, the telephone is the instrument second most potentially compromising of your privacy. (Your online activity is now first.) If you will learn to govern how, when, and to whom your calls are made, the difficult task of privacy will then largely be accomplished. For Americans, however, this is an exceedingly inconvenient habit to perform over many years.

Frankly, it's just not *practical* to be without voice comm Besides, to be without one seems odd and suspicious. So, it's vital to have a phone number for expediency's sake and not to draw attention to yourself. This can be accomplished with surprisingly little sacrifice in privacy, as I'll explain shortly.

METHODS OF COMPROMISE

I'll list them in increasing order of severity.

your landline phone number
Gee, now the whole *world* knows where you live and how to call you at anytime. Sadly, a nonpublished number is no stumbling block for the resourceful, though it will hamper the random public. Your number has already been sold to the Census Bureau who will happily pester you with dozens of calls to badger you into answering their 70 intrusive questions.

With prepaid cell phones and VoIP, there is no longer any financial or privacy incentive to keeping a landline.

your cell phone service address
Using your home address for billing purposes is just plain foolish — you might as well have a landline for all the privacy given up. However, even if you use another mailing address or have an anonymous prepaid cell phone, using it from home will beacon your block area (within 500' radius) to the system.

your phone records
Records of all calls (made and received, local and long-distance) are easily obtainable by officials and private investigators. Also, and not widely known, your *local* calling records (Message Unit Details, or MUDs) are kept for at least 6 months *and will be analyzed* during any serious investigation. *Many* criminals have been convicted because of their MUDs.

the "pen register" to learn of your network
This is like a mail-cover for telephones. It notates the time, date, number dialed and duration of your outgoing calls. More sophisticated units work with Caller ID and notate your *incoming* calls as well. Pen registers are often, though not always, operated directly from the phone company. The feds, however, enjoy dedicated lines to their buildings.

the "trap" to record the conversation
In the analog days, placing a trap on a line required the assistance of AT&T. Today, digital switching centers and touch-tone phones are in use for the entire American system. This modernization has brought benefits to the public, as well as to government snoops.

The feds can now activate *online* a phone trap. Since 9-11 the process is supremely automated, and doesn't require warrants from multiple jurisdictions. Authorities have computers with voice recognition which transcribe conversations.

the "trace"

In the days of mechanical switching and rotary dial phones it required 30-90 seconds to complete a trace, but not any more. With digital equipment, a trace is *instantaneous*. (Caller ID is merely a commercially available trace.) Whenever you call 800 #s, 911, the police, the operator, or high-level officials, your number is immediately displayed—unless you're "phreaking" the system (as in the movie *Ransom*).

misc. telephone privacy tips

buy all phones and calling cards with cash or debit card

This should go without saying, but I mention it for those who aren't naturally privacy conscious.

encrypt calling card info and destroy card and its receipt

The card is just the conduit for the number, which is info you should encrypt somewhere, such as a convenient PDA.

beware of your background noise

Airports, highway gas stations, and PA announcements are noisy, and will inform the listener of your whereabouts.

Caller ID now works even through calling cards

I discovered this the surprising way at a friend's house when I used a favorite brand of calling card to phone somebody. I left a message, and hung up. A few minutes later he called me back directly at my friend's! My prepaid long-distance card had suddenly become transparent to Caller ID! Wow. This is today the norm, and probably because of legislation.

Test your card for this before relying on its privacy.

avoid payphone surcharge by using courtesy phones

Hotels, copy chain stores, etc. often have courtesy phones which will allow the dialing of toll-free numbers.

INTERNET VOICE MAIL & FAX

These are excellent for many uses, particularly when you need a phone number for classified ads or Internet transactions. Basically, if you can *imagine* some variant of service, it likely already exists and it's just a matter of finding it. I won't list any here as they come and go and change hands, but do a Scroogle search and you'll discover many.

internet voice mail

Many are free for 30 days, and have no registration info requirement beyond a name and email address. Some even offer free call forwarding (use a prepaid cellphone to receive live calls), Caller ID, and will email you the .wav file of messages (which keeps your location private, if you use a proxy tunnel). One former example was www.craigsnumber.com.

You could theoretically daisy-chain a few of these for added layer of privacy, requiring snoops to interact every link in the chain. This will at least delay your identification.

Several companies will rent you your own toll-free number which can forward calls or simply act as voice mail. You can either collect messages online, or call in from any phone, which is the height of convenience. Your prepaid debit card will be billed the few cents/minute for the calls. One good thing about toll-free numbers is that its ANI (automatic number identifier, a sort of Caller ID) is very effective in piercing through calling cards, payphones, and blocked calls. (Something to keep in mind for the reverse when you call them!)

internet fax

There are even services which will send a free fax to a landline from your emailed text or photo. Very cool! This came in very handy when I was in Africa one summer and had to send a timely fax for a legal matter. I had wifi, but was nowhere near a fax machine. I found an e-fax service through Scroogle search, used my digital camera as a scanner to make a .jpg of the signed document, and e-faxed it in. Worked perfectly! It saved me an entire morning of going into town.

VoIP TELEPHONY

Voice-over-Internet-Protocol is a marvelous technology, and (*if* well understood and used properly) a real boon for privacy seekers. It reportedly has our NSA and Britain's GCHQ in knots because VoIP bypasses the entire telecom backbone.

> *They are really afraid of this - Voice over IP (VoIP) - which is harder, much harder, to monitor.*
>
> *Think about this, though. If they get a warrant to monitor a specific person's phone calls, they can still do it, no matter this technology. They just have to put a tap in the target's house.*
>
> *But, what they actually want, is to be able, by remote control/flipping a switch, start tapping anyone (which is what they can do with modern telephone switching equipment, today). Oh, and since they have control over that, without any real monitoring [by the courts], they only bother with warrants when they want to use the surveillance in court. The rest of the time (most of the time?), they just listen at their leisure.*
>
> ***That's what they are afraid of losing.*** *If more people adopt this new technology, and they aren't given the technical power to monitor at will. That's what this is about.*
>
> *Time for many more people to sign up for these services!*
>
> — "DeepChip" to the author

VoIP uses the Internet to send compressed voice streams as data packets to the recipient computer (which decodes the data) or even to a regular PSTN phone (land or cell). All this happens on-the-fly and it sound just like a real phone call in your mike/speaker headset.

Calls are very cheap, and often free. It is *the* way to stay in phone contact with folks in other countries. The VoIP provider will instantly show you who on your network is currently available to receive a real-time call. Pretty amazing stuff. VoIP is the wave of the future, and expect IP-based cellphone networks soon. There are two types of VoIP, and only the second one if of real use for privacy:

broadband VoIP

> *For Vonage and 8x8, you add a box to your broadband internet (cable modem or DSL), they assign a phone number (you pick the area code), and you can get rid of your "tapable"*

landline. Cheaper than landlines too. Some minor disadvantages, truly minor. From then on, when you call or get calls, the sound is digitized, and sent as little packets over the internet. If your counterpart is also using VoIP, the phone call never gets on the telephone company networks. If your counterpart has a standard phone, the phone call gets on the telephone network, close to your counterpart.
     — "DeepChip" to the author

computer software VoIP

This turns your computer into a so-called "softphone" allowing voice comm with other such computers, and even real telephones (land and cell) in the existing telecom network. This is huge growth industry, and the first to incorporate the encrypted Zfone package (more soon) will emerge the winner.

privacy advantages of VoIP
generally no central storage points

Except for Vonage, most VoIP providers have no central gateways for the media data packets to pass through. VoIP is P2P (peer-to-peer) software, and it is difficult to patch in to make copies of the data. Thus, the lack of 4th Amendment protection for third party "stored records" is not an issue (as with email, credit card receipts, and phone records).

on-the-fly encryption is available and free (Zfone)

Because IP networks are much more open than land/cell phone PSTN networks, VoIP interception is easy. (View the demo at www.siptap.voipcode.org) Unencrypted VoIP is at great risk from organized crime, hackers, jobsites, and governments. Thus, VoIP *must* be encrypted. While Skype does proprietary encryption, it is closed-source and reportedly hacked. PGP inventor Phil Zimmermann has once again saved the day with his Zfone software (which does not require PKI, public key infrastructure). It remains outside the regulatory realm of *CALEA* because Zfone is neither a PSTN phone company (*e.g.*, Sprint) nor VoIP provider (*e.g.*, Vonage). *CALEA* does not apply to end users, and only end users handshake the encryption key.

VoIP can be used with wifi and broadband

This greatly enhances your geographical privacy, especially if you're using large cloud broadband.

VoIP can be used with SSH and VPN tunnels

This almost guarantees your geographical privacy, as well as keeping the local ISP deaf to your telephony. Their logs cannot reveal whom you called or (with Zfone) what you said. However, many tunnel providers use NAT (which Zfone can't penetrate), so inquire before you sign up.

VoIP can spoof a desired geographical area

Have a U.K.-based VoIP phone number if you wish, yet make/receive calls from Kentucky.

VoIP can help satisfy nearly ALL privacy requirements

your location	foreign IP tunnel, via random public wifi = 0!
your identity	whoever your foreign IP believes you to be
whom you call	see above, if they are also private
what is said	with Zfone, known only to you and the caller

The only possible logs are from your foreign proxy (which will have your local IP), and the VoIP provider's call data between two accounts (though without any call content) — but that is actually very little usable information (especially if your called party also has a vigorous privacy protocol). Traffic analysis (TA) of your single proxy is possible because proxy chains such as TOR add too much latency (delay) in phone calls. (Besides, multiple proxies are not assured to thwart TA from a dedicated and resourceful attacker such as government.)

There has never in history been such corporate/government-class telephonic privacy available for the common man. (It's like have a STU-III, but even better.) VoIP is totally changing how we make "phone" calls.

general comparison: Skype, Magic Jack, and Vonage

Not that I recommend any of the three, but I quote the below to give you a product overview. VoIP differs widely.

> *Depending on what you need from a VOIP service, each of these services has their best points. If you are just mostly interested in chat and video chat with maybe a few cheap long distance international calls, **Skype** would probably be the best for you. You can chat free to another Skype user and international calls to Europe are as low as 2 cents per minute.*
>
> *Maybe replacing your current telephone service entirely is what you are looking for. In that case, I would go with*

Vonage. *But, I wouldn't cancel the current phone service until I had used Vonage for a few months. Also, if you have a lot of problems with your internet service going down, you would also be out of phone service during those times too. However, Vonage will relay any phone calls to another number for you, so if you use a cell phone also, that could work out for you.*

*If you're not really looking to replace your current phone service, but would like a way to make cheap long distance calls, give **Magic Jack** Internet Phone a try. I think in the future, Magic Jack may develop into a company to entirely replace your phone service, but a new company always has growing pains so I don't recommend getting Magic Jack and dumping your current phone service until they have more a track record behind them.*

-- www.voip2u.org

typical VoIP features

I don't have time or space for any kind of consumer report comparison of the below (visit www.vopi2u.org), and can only discuss the privacy aspects. Here's what to compare, however:

Free Calls to Landline Phones
Free Calls to Cell Phones
Free Calls to Other Computers
Free International Calling
Free Voice Mail
Free Caller ID
Free Call Waiting
Free Call Forwarding
Cost of Service
Reliability
911 Calling
Use ordinary Landline Phone with the Service?
Must Computer be turned on to use service?
Call Quality
Ability to Send & Receive Faxes

Skype

The current market leader, but the industry is still very young. There are better VoIP clients out there (from a privacy standpoint), and the first one which bundles Zfone with it will be the security leader. I have some severe issues with Skype.

is Skype inherently secure?

No, because of its VBR codec (more soon) and eerie ability to traverse NATs (often used by foreign proxy tunnel providers) and penetrate firewalls (and thus bypass your proxy tunnel). The sassy paper "Silver Needle in the Skype" (skype_BHEU06.handout.pdf) concludes several other damning security problems, such as:

hard to enforce a security policy with Skype
Skype traffic cannot be distinguished from data exfiltration
impossible to protect from attacks (which would be obfuscated)
totally nontransparent blackbox — no way to discern of backdoors
fully trusts any computer which speaks Skype

as a company, is Skype trustworthy?

I strongly doubt it. *Beware any free product which is not open source!* And, there are just too many reports of governmental access, likely with Skype's assistance:

Bavarian police searched the home of the spokesman for the German Pirate Party (Piratenpartei Deutschland) looking for **an informant who leaked information about a government Trojan used to eavesdrop on Skype conversations.** *There is a high probability that the Trojan is used illegally. A criminal law specialist said, 'The Bavarian authorities worked on the Trojan without a legitimate basis and now try to silence critics.' The Trojan is supposedly capable of eavesdropping on Skype conversations and obtaining technical details of the Skype client being used. It is deployed by e-mail or in place by the police. A Pirate Party spokesman said, '"Some . . . officials seem to want to install the Big Brother state without the knowledge of the public."*
— www.golem.de/0809/62474.html

Posting Anonymously to protect my job, **I have been working for a few months on software designed to extract skype calls from streams of captured packets.** *The software is highly distributed, and while I can't know the exact use, I'm guessing it will be installed near every network interconnect point. Interestingly, it has nowhere near the performance required to record every skype call on the internet, so it will probably only be used for certain targets.*

The good news is that the project is failing badly due to funding issues and poor management, and probably won't be deployed for years yet.
Note that this IS with the help of skype engineers - we haven't reverse engineered the encryption.
— from the Internet, but it seems fairly credible

A Canadian researcher has discovered that a Chinese version of eBay Inc.'s Skype communications software snoops on text chats that contain certain keywords, including "democracy." . . . privacy advocates and security experts are concerned that Skype, while presented by the company as a secure channel of communication, has some kind of "back door" that allows eavesdropping. Whether Skypetapping is already going on in the U.S. and Europe is a matter that the company has equivocated on for years.

"For a couple of years, maybe more, people have had the suspicion . . . that Skype pretends to be secure but actually isn't," said Bruce Schneier, the chief security technology officer of BT Group PLC, the British telecom carrier.

The software is distributed by Skype's Chinese partner, Tom Online Inc. Skype has acknowledged since 2006 that this version looks for certain sensitive words in text chats and blocks those messages from reaching their destination. The issue appears only to affect people using the Chinese software.

*What Villeneuve found was that **the Tom-Skype program also passes the messages caught by the filter to a cluster of servers on Tom's network.** Because of poor security on those servers, he was able to retrieve more than a million stored messages. The filter appears to look for words like "Tibet," "democracy" and "milk powder" — China is in the throes of a food scandal involving tainted milk.*

This directly contradicts a blog posting on Skype's Web site, which says that the software discards the filtered messages and neither displays nor transmits them anywhere.

Skype spokeswoman Jennifer Caukin said Thursday that "since its inception in 2003 Skype has never created a back door to the Skype software."

Yet both Schneier and Simson Garfinkel, an associate of the School of Engineering and Applied Sciences at Harvard University who has studied Skype's security, believe it would actually be trivial for the company to listen in on conversations.

"I can think of five or six different ways to eavesdrop on Skype. It's not that hard if you are the Skype company and want to provide legal access to law enforcement," Garfinkel said.

Peter Swire, a professor of law at Ohio State University, said that while he knows of no U.S. court ruling that has required Skype to comply with wiretapping requests, it's conceivable that the company is voluntarily cooperating with law enforcement. Swire served as the Clinton administration's privacy czar for two years.

Skype told News.com that it had not received a subpoena or court order to perform eavesdropping.

Yet German technology site Heise Online reported in July that Austrian officials claimed to be able to listen to Skype conversations. The relative quietness of the law enforcement community on the issue in recent years could be the result of such cooperation.

— www.cnn.com, "Questions arise on Skype snooping"

The below story seems more likely an attempt by Skype or the NSA to inject credibility into a blown communications channel:

Counter Terror Expo News of a possible viable business model for P2P VoIP network Skype emerged today, at the Counter Terror Expo in London. An industry source disclosed that America's supersecret National Security Agency (NSA) is offering "billions" to any firm which can offer reliable eavesdropping on Skype IM and voice traffic.

The spybiz exec, who preferred to remain anonymous, confirmed that Skype continues to be a major problem for government listening agencies, spooks and police. This was already thought to be the case, following requests from German authorities for special intercept/bugging powers to help them deal with Skype-loving malefactors.

— www.freedomfighterradio.net/?p=5416

What would make sense is for Skype to have accepted the NSA's offer of "billions" for access, as the parent company eBay has had to write down the market value of Skype by $1+b since the dot.com bust. If Skype were Zfone compatible, then maybe I'd take a chance on them. Instead, test other VoIP clients and find one of quality (*i.e.*, free, open-source, Zfone compatible).

Magic Jack   www.magicjack.com

Magic Jack Internet Phone is a VOIP phone service which allows you to make free local and long distance calls within the United States and Canada. You can also use Magic Jack phone service in Puerto Rico and the Virgin Islands. It consists of a device that is plugged into the computer's USB port and software that creates the ability to transmit voice over your high speed internet connection. Your computer must be on to use Magic Jack, although you will still receive voice mail. Magic Jack lets you use a standard telephone, including cordless telephones. Nothing special to buy, unless you want to. You may also use a headset or your computer's built in microphone and speakers, which would be easier to use when on the road instead of a bulky phone.

When traveling internationally, you may take your Magic Jack with you and call anywhere in the United States or Canada for free while you are away from home. Cheaper to use than Skype or Vonage, Magic Jack costs only $39.95 for the first year, and $19.95 each year after that.

In addition to Voice Mail, Magic Jack also provides Caller ID, Call Waiting, Call Forwarding, 3-Way Calling and free Directory Assistance — oh, and a free phone number.

Those of you in the countryside be aware that MJ does not connect through satellite internet.

MJ service interruption for undefined "excessive" use

If MagicJack sees excessive use or systematic or intentional misuse, it reserves the right, in our sole discretion, to terminate your use of the magicJack device and/or Software immediately, and you will not be entitled to get a refund of any licensing fee or any other fee you may have paid to us.

I've read of many online complaints about this. Apparently, even just one hour per day over time will trigger account termination even though MJ boasts of "unlimited" usage.

MJ's phone quality and customer service

MJ's customer service record (as of Nov 2008) has been abysmal. Florida's BBB gives them an F rating.

Phone quality is only fair to good.

VoIP clients to consider

Since I have not tested them all, assume no recommendation. Please study and compare them yourself.

XMeeting	http://xmeeting.sourceforge.net/pages/index.php
Apple iChat	www.apple.com/macosx/features/ichat/
Symbian	http://en.wikipedia.org/wiki/Symbian_OS
SIPphone	www.sipphone.com/
tpad	www.tpad.com
X-Lite	www.xten.com/index.php?menu=X-Series
VoIP Stunt	www.voipstunt.com
Free World Dialup	www.freeworlddialup.com/
	www.ipkall.com (for PSTN # routing)
	www.iptel.org/service

privacy tips for VoIP

avoid Skype!

I call Skype the *"Windows of VoIP"* — and that's no compliment. Although ubiquitous and functional, it's full of security holes — likely intentionally. Incompatible with Zfone.

Oh, and it's owned by eBay — *eeeeeeww!*

avoid Google Talk, Gizmo, and MS Office Communicator

They all use the easily hacked VBR (variable bit rate) compression, as does Skype. You have better alternatives!

avoid Vonage

Vonage can intercept data packets through central gateways. What can be intercepted can be stored. Also, Zfone is incompatible with Vonage.

is the VoIP provider outside the U.S.?

This could be important to you, to avoid U.S. jurisdiction and court orders. Tpad, for example, is registered in the offshore tax haven Isle of Man.

read the VoIP client Privacy Policy!

Understand before you install their software what data it collects and what their disclosure triggers are. Copy that page to your computer, for your own records (as PPs do change, and often without notice).

install your VoIP inside a large TrueCrypt volume

This will secure any call logs and records the VoIP software creates, especially your phone book. While all that is available from the VoIP provider, why make it easy by having this data on your computer in plaintext?

test thoroughly first from a nonsensitive IP

Visit a wifi cafe in another town during a road trip. Work out all the bugs before using from home. (This is also good advice for new proxy tunnel service.)

if using a tunnel, *ensure* that VoIP is running through it

Test! Your ZoneAlarm firewall will show you which IP it's using. If it's not going through 127.0.0.1, then it's connecting directly to your ISP! (Skype is notorious for this.) You might as well be using a landline for the same lack of privacy.

disable auto service with Internet connection restoration

You should manually turn on/off VoIP, and not let it turn on itself when sensing a wifi signal and logging on itself.

use multiple VoIP clients, each from their own foreign IP

Just as with email accounts and forums, don't access them through the same IP address. Diversity is vital component to privacy, including your VoIP usage.

pay for VoIP credit with cash or prepaid debit card

There is no privacy value to using check or credit card in your own name. Refer to the *Money* chapter for debit card info.

do not rely on VoIP for absolute comsec

There are simply too many intermediaries between you and your caller, and you can never discern who/where they are. Anything done on/over computers is inherently risky. The most secure form of comm is still face-to-face in a private setting.

ZFONE   www.zfoneproject.com

. . . FBI's wiretapping engineers are struggling with peer-to-peer telephony provider Skype, which offers no central location to wiretap, and with innovations like caller-ID spoofing and phone-number portability.

But DCSNet seems to have kept pace with at least some new technologies, such as cell-phone push-to-talk features and most VOIP internet telephony.

—www.wired.com/politics/security/news/2007/08/wiretap? currentPage=2

*I don't feel that the VoIP service providers can always be trusted to act with my interests in mind, so I don't want to involve their SIP servers in my encryption key negotiations. **If I want to speak Navajo with my friend on the phone, I shouldn't have to clear it first with the phone company.** It's just none of their business.*

   -- Phil Zimmermann, creator of PGP and Zfone

Zfone is such an important privacy development that it deserves its own subchapter here.

Unfortunately, phone calls from your computer are fundamentally different from phone calls from your telephone. Internet telephony's threat model is much closer to the threat model for IP-networked computers than the threat model for telephony.

And we already know the threat model for IP. Data packets can be eavesdropped on anywhere along the transmission path. Data packets can be intercepted in the corporate network, by the internet service provider and along the backbone. They can be eavesdropped on by the people or organizations that own those computers, and they can be eavesdropped on by anyone who has successfully hacked into those computers. They can be vacuumed up by nosy hackers, criminals, competitors and governments.

My greatest worry is the criminal attacks. We already have seen how clever criminals have become over the past several years at stealing account information and personal data. I can imagine them eavesdropping on attorneys, looking for information with which to blackmail people. I can imagine them eavesdropping on bankers, looking for inside information with which to make stock purchases. I can imagine them stealing account information, hijacking telephone calls, committing identity theft. On the business side, I can see them engaging in industrial espionage and stealing trade secrets. In short, I can imagine them doing all the things they could never have done with the traditional telephone network.

This is why encryption for VOIP is so important. VOIP calls are vulnerable to a variety of threats that traditional telephone calls are not.

   — Bruce Schneier, *Why VOIP Needs Crypto*, Wired News
    www.wired.com/news/columns/0,70591-0.html

Zfone is not a VoIP provider, but a software adapter of VoIP service you already have. It encrypts the call between those who have zfone. Basically, it takes care of negotiating STRP encryption session keys, requiring a second or two. No user codes to remember or exchange. Once a secure channel has been established, the zfone GUI says so.

Q: Why do we need Zfone? For that matter, why do we even need secure VoIP at all?

A: As VoIP grows into a replacement for the PSTN, we will absolutely need to protect it, or organized crime will be attacking it as intensively as they attack the rest of the Internet today. VoIP is far more vulnerable to interception than the PSTN. A PC on your office network can unknowingly host spyware that can intercept your corporate VoIP calls and store and organize them on a hard disk for convenient browsing by criminals half a world away, giving them trade secrets and insider trading opportunities.

The Internet is not a safe medium to carry our phone calls. But Zfone solves these problems. This technology has social benefits. It has the power to change our lives, enabling us to have a private conversation any time we want with anyone, anywhere - without buying a plane ticket.

Probably the best thing about Zfone is that it purposely does not require public key infrastructure (PKI) or key cumbersome certification. Also, it is not some proprietary closed-source client-bundled encryption scheme (as in Skype). Zfone works with nearly all VoIP clients (except Skype), and it's public beta test version is downloaded for free, now.

Even if your VoIP provider began to intercept and store your media traffic (which the Government is trying to force them to do, despite the current technical difficulty), Zfone's encryption of that traffic (with reset and disposed session keys) makes that a moot issue. Thus, the so-called *PATRIOT* Act's warrantless provision for "stored records" is foiled by Zfone. (It is also foiled by PGP for email, if you're using it!)

But make no mistake: to eavesdroppers, Zfone is anything but routine. The protocol is based on SRTP, a system that uses the 256-bit AES cipher and adds to that a 3,000-bit key exchange that produces the codes callers can read off to one another. It has been submitted to IETF for approval as an

internet standard, and by most accounts is strong enough to defy even the most sophisticated code-breaking technologies, from a hacker's packet sniffer to the acres of computers beneath Ft. Meade.
— A Pretty Good Way to Foil the NSA
www.wired.com/news/technology/1,70524-0.html

Zfone tech info

platforms   Mac OS X (10.4 or later)
Linux
Windows (XP and Vista, either 32-bit or 64-bit versions)

works with: X-Lite
Gizmo (audio, no video yet)
XMeeting
Google Talk VoIP client (but only when using RTP)
Yahoo Messenger's VoIP client (for audio)
Magic Jack
SJphone
Apple iChat calls on Mac OS X (Leopard)
Free World Dialup
iptel.org
SIPphone
(It does not work with Skype.)

architecture   ZRTP (media stream key negotiation)
SRTP (245-bit AES + 3,000 bit key exchange)
runs in the Internet protocol stack
ephemeral Diffie-Hellman with hash commitment
self-initiating cryptographic key agreement
filters/encrypts/decrypts media packets on the fly
session keys destroyed at end of each call

security   against MiTM (man in the middle), without PKI
SAS for users to verbally compare over phone
signaling protocol irrelevant
totally server independent — client side only
key negotiations are P2P through media stream
interoperates with any SIP/RTP phone
autodetects ZRTP encryption at other endpoint
available as a "plugin" for existing soft VoIP clients
available as an SDK for VoIP product developers

Zfone installation and use

Step 1: Getting your VoIP client software ready

Many things can go wrong with VoIP client software. There could be problems with your firewall, with getting VoIP calls to traverse your local network's NAT router, with your audio configuration choices (especially your microphone), with your VoIP service provider. For this reason, it is important that you get your VoIP client tested and working before you install Zfone. And get the other party to do the same.

First, you will need to get yourself a VoIP client, install it, sign up for a VoIP service provider, get a VoIP phone number (a SIP URI), and test your VoIP client to make sure it all works. Many VoIP service providers provide an echo server to make a test call, and it will echo your voice back to you. To call the echo server at Free World Dialup, enter this SIP URI in the "Call" text box: sip:613@fwd.pulver.com, then press the call button.

Step 2 : Downloading and installing Zfone

The Zfone public beta is available now for Mac OS X (10.4 or later), Linux, and Windows (both XP and Vista, either 32-bit or 64-bit versions). To download your copy right now, go to our Zfone Register-to-Download Page.

This new 22 Mar 2009 version implements the latest ZRTP Internet Draft protocol document (draft 15).

After you download it, run the install program and follow the installation instructions. Windows users should not interrupt the installation process, despite multiple warnings stating that the ZRTP Miniport driver is not Windows Logo certified. Just ignore the warnings and proceed with the install. It's dangerous to interrupt the installation of any device driver on Windows, including this one.

Before starting the installation process, Zfone for Windows creates the restore point, which stores your system information at the moment of installation. If you have any problems you can always restore your system state back to this restore point.

As usual, Mac OS X users will find the installation procedure self-explanatory. Linux users will actually have to compile the source code and build it, but we figured typical Linux geeks can handle that. Later, we will provide Linux binaries so you won't have to build it.

email registration for Zfone download no big deal

Since crypto software cannot be exported to certain countries (North Korea, Iran, etc.), the download must first get a ping back from your email account to verify your country. (A foreign proxy in Canada or Europe will work fine.)

The software itself is *not* in any way uniquely tied to your name or email address. There is no serial number, either, so you can make copies for your friends.

zfone tips

disable VBR codecs from zfone menu

Variable-bit rate codecs are not very secure because they change their bit rate based on the type of sound being compressed. Particular sounds can be inferred from this, regardless of crypto. Some phrases can be identified with an accuracy of 50% to 90%. That's quite a security issue!

VBR is used by Skype, Google Talk, Gizmo, and Microsoft Office Communicator. Avoid these VoIP products.

protocol tunneling (*i.e.,* packet filtering) will subvert Zfone

Until Zfone is integrated within a future VoIP client, it will be subverted by NAT router traversals. This is so because Zfone only recognizes RTP voice/video packets sent through UDP and not TCP. If your Zfone GUI shows "Idle" status during a call, move off your local network onto an external IP, or use two different VoIP clients (which often forces RTP onto UDP).

Ask your proxy tunnel provider about this, as PPTP, L2TP, SSH, SOCKS are all tunneling protocols. SSL, however, is *application* layer, and thus should work with Zfone.

always launch Zfone before VoIP, and run in background

Zfone must be running before any VoIP.

Zfone no replacement for good computer security

Savvy users can use an anonymizing or proxy service to conceal their location. Researchers discovered by embedding a unique, undetectable signature in [VoIP] packets, they can identify that signature when they reached their destination.

— www.evansthompson.com/2005/08/

Encryption for IP telephony is important, but it's not a panacea. Unfortunately, the biggest threat [is] eavesdropping at the end points. **No amount of IP telephony encryption can prevent a Trojan or worm on your computer** *— or just a hacker who managed to get access to your machine — from eavesdropping on your phone calls, just as no amount of SSL or e-mail encryption can prevent a Trojan on your computer from eavesdropping — or even modifying — your data.*

So, as always, it boils down to this: **We need secure computers and secure operating systems even more than we need secure transmission.**

— Bruce Schneier, *Why VOIP Needs Crypto,* Wired News

Make sure that your installation of Zfone does not create the file C:\Documents and Settings\All Users\Application Data\Zfone\zfone.log which contains much information (*e.g.*, the calculated shared secret). This seems to be a debug file only in earlier test versions, but I mention it nonethess. If it does exist, you can program your shredder to get rid of it before shutdown.

get your friends and family to use Zfone!

According to the FCC, you shouldn't be able to use VoIP and encryption that the FBI doesn't like:

. . . consumers are entitled to run [computer] *applications and use* [Internet] *services of their choice,* **subject to the needs of law enforcement.**

— http://hraunfoss.fcc.gov/edocs_public/attachmatch/FCC-05-151A1.pdf

Zfone is only effective if others are also using it. Get them off Skype and into another VoIP which is Zfone compatible. Burn copies of Zfone on CD with a simple setup tutorial of your own. Hurry, before Skype becomes too ubiquitous for the general public to do without!

Since The Powers That Be cannot breach the technological security that Zfone provides, they must instead hope that not enough of us ever use it to matter. This has so far been the case with PGP.

So as nice as it is, unless Zfone is adopted by mainstream VoIP providers, it will probably occupy the same limited market niche as the hyper-secure PGP program that ruffled so many government feathers over a decade ago.

— A Pretty Good Way to Foil the NSA
www.wired.com/news/technology/1,70524-0.html

CELL PHONE PRIVACY CONCERNS

The FBI has quietly built a sophisticated, point-and-click surveillance system that performs instant wiretaps on almost any communications device, according to nearly a thousand pages of restricted documents newly released under the Freedom of Information Act.

The surveillance system, called DCSNet, for Digital Collection System Network, connects FBI wiretapping rooms to switches controlled by traditional land-line operators, internet-telephony providers and cellular companies. It is far more intricately woven into the nation's telecom infrastructure than observers suspected.

It's a "comprehensive wiretap system that intercepts wire-line phones, cellular phones, SMS and push-to-talk systems," says Steven Bellovin, a Columbia University computer science professor and longtime surveillance expert.

The $10 million DCS-3000 client, also known as Red Hook, handles pen-registers and trap-and-traces, a type of surveillance that collects signaling information — primarily the numbers dialed from a telephone — but no communications content. (Pen registers record outgoing calls; trap-and-traces record incoming calls.)

DCS-6000, known as Digital Storm, captures and collects the content of phone calls and text messages for full wiretap orders.

Together, the surveillance systems let FBI agents play back recordings even as they are being captured (like TiVo), create master wiretap files, send digital recordings to translators, track the rough location of targets in real time using cell-tower information, and even stream intercepts outward to mobile surveillance vans.

FBI wiretapping rooms in field offices and undercover locations around the country are connected through a private, encrypted backbone that is separated from the internet. Sprint runs it on the government's behalf.

—www.wired.com/politics/security/news/2007/08/wiretap?
currentPage=2

Cell phones are the best example of the privacy price of convenience. They must be well understood and used very carefully. The legal hurdles of cellphone surveillance and tracking are constantly being lowered, so I won't get into the briefly current 4th Amendment warrant requirements under *CALEA*, etc. If you want to, a good overview is at:

Cell Phone Technology and Physical Surveillance
www.fbi.gov/publications/leb/2006/may2006/may2006leb.htm

Not that legal requirements any longer matter. Just assume that the telecoms and most companies providing "backhaul" connections (tower providers, third-party spam filters, gateway operators, outsourced customer-service centers, etc.) will spill whatever they have. (The telecoms are mewling for more congressional clarity about daisy-chain warrants, but that's only to protect themselves from liability.)

call records

The incoming and outgoing phone numbers, time, date, and call duration are all readily given out without a warrant. This level of surveillance requires only that investigators certify that the phone numbers are relevant to an investigation.

geographical location

Because of *CALEA*, cellphones must be able to be triangulated within a 500' radius (allegedly for 9-1-1 calls). That's within a city block. All cell phones (when turned on) transmit every 90 seconds a NAM (number assignment module) "*Here I am!* " signal so that the cell network know through which nearby towers to route your calls. The signal strength needed for triangulation is less than what's needed to support a call. *I.e.,* your phone could actually show no signal bars, but it is still likely pinging back and forth sufficiently for location.

Some cellphones (Sprint and Verizon) have GPS, which can be activated to track subscriber movement:

AccuTracking software turns your Motorola iDEN cell phones, RIM BlackBerry phones, Windows Mobile phones, Android phones carried by Nextel, Boost Mobile, AT&T(Cingular), T-Mobile, SouthernLINC or Telus MIKE (Canada) into a GPS tracking device. The AccuTracking online GPS cell phone tracking service lets you see real-time locations, speed, and headings of your children/family members or cars/vehicles, and receive email or SMS alerts when they move across the designated areas or exceeds speed limit.
    — www.accutracking.com

When Fletcher pulls out his phone and selects Mologogo, it displays a map of the streets around him while a dot shows his location. It also shows where Fletcher's friends are, if they have Mologogo running on their cell phones. The phones all transmit their locations to a Web site, so Fletcher also can log in from any computer and find his friends online.

"You can search for your friends. You can even set it up to track one friend," Fletcher says. "And if that's the person you are interested in today because they're doing something interesting, you might want to set it up just to watch them, to see where they are and what they're doing."

— www.npr.org/templates/story/story.php?storyId=6097216

Cell phone apps like Loopt and the new Google Latitude allow you to track your friends' physical locations, and be tracked in return . . .   But here's the kicker: As Kevin Bankston of the Electronic Frontier Foundation points out, the safeguards in place are only company policy, not a legal requirement. And policies can change.

— www.eff.org/press/mentions/2009/3/27

New Jersey's Montclair State University requires their students to carry $420/year GPS Sprint cellphones for tracking. "*For the children*", of course!

Generally, subscriber location information requires a warrant, but there are many ways to circumvent that, such as simply lying about an imminent subpoena:

These requests are coming out of a rogue FBI office as part of rogue records requests (in short, not only did the office not have the power to issue legitimate requests for records, they sent these requests, saying they'd already asked a U.S Attorney to start work on a proper subpoena, when they'd done no such thing.)

— http://blog.wired.com/27bstroke6/sunshine_and_secrec y/index.html

Also, telecom assistance may no longer be even necessary:

Documents obtained by the American Civil Liberties Union under a Freedom of Information Act request suggest that existing technology allows law enforcement to bypass wireless companies in locating individual cell phone users.

Using "triggerfish" technology, mobile phones are tricked into transmitting their serial numbers, phone numbers and other data by posing as a cellular phone tower. Until now, it's been believed that such technology could only be successfully employed with the help of the telecoms themselves, because the specific location of the phone couldn't be traced with enough accuracy.

But a document obtained by the ACLU and the Electronic Frontier Foundation from the Justice Department in a lawsuit and posted online last week says triggerfish can be deployed "without the user knowing about it and without involving the cell phone provider."

As Ars Technica explains, "That may be significant because the legal rulings requiring law enforcement to meet a high "probable cause" standard before acquiring cell location records have, thus far, pertained to requests for information from providers, pursuant to statutes such as the Communications Assistance for Law Enforcement Act (CALEA) and the Stored Communications Act."

"The Justice Department's electronic surveillance manual explicitly suggests that triggerfish may be used to avoid restrictions in statutes like CALEA . . . ," Ars Technica adds. "'By its very terms,' according to the manual, 'this prohibition applies only to information collected by a provider and not to information collected directly by law enforcement authorities."

Chttp://rawstory.com/email_story.php?sid=12918

the IMEI (International Mobile Equipment Identity)

Every US handset has its own embedded IMEI, which is *not* hidden by swapping out SIM cards (which contains only the cell phone number, phonebook data, text messages, etc.). Your handset's IMEI is embedded within all call data, making your call history and travel paths easily stored and analyzed.

Are there some phones without an IMEI? Only if you have a Chinese phone in India, but that closed in April 2009:

Connections will be terminated at the end of this month, immediately stripping out an estimated eight per cent of India's 375 million mobile phone users. India's mobile phone rolls are growing by around 12 million per month.

Unlike mainstream manufacturers, many cheap Chinese handsets on sale in India have no International Mobile Equipment Identity IMEI) code, which means neither ownership nor the user's position can be traced when it is switched on.

While mainstream mobiles leave a personal IMEI code on each call, and can be 'triangulated' between three mobile phone masts to identify the user's location, Chinese handsets simply show a set of zeroes.

> —www.wired.com/services/email/politics/security/news/2006/05/70829
> ?title=Cell-Phone%20Tracking:%20Laws%20Needed

caller profile ("community of interest")

[The government's Institute for Telecommunication Services http://its.bldrdoc.gov/ defines "community of interest" as a] *grouping of users who generate a majority of their traffic in calls to other members of the group. Note: The community of interest may be related to a geographic area or to an administrative organization. Synonym special interest group.*

Traffic is defined as a quantitative measurement of the total messages and their length, expressed in hundreds of call seconds during a specified period of time.

Never underestimate the power of computers for data mining and processing of your communications. By using statistical analysis engines, a target's normal behavior can be predicted and thus a profile compiled. Deviations from that profile will alert investigators to either a change of target behavior or the use by another of that phone.

While investigating the OKC Bomb(s) case, the feds analyzed *142 million* phone calls (and that was with 1995 technology). Did they believe that McVeigh and Nichols made millions (or even thousands) of calls? Certainly not, but that wasn't the point. The FBI evidently suspected some vast right-wing militia network (which didn't exist, and hadn't anything to do with OKC). The goal was to uncover interlinked networks of people. Everyone belongs to groups, and all groups communicate with other groups. Details of this can be learned, with several degrees of separation.

your cell phone can indirectly disclose other devices

If you say over the cell, *"OK, I'm online right now and will email you the file"*, your IP address can be accurately inferred by an investigator listening in. Within a 500' radius, there only just so many IP addresses, and if you've ever used it before that makes the inference even easier. (More on this later.)

call content

Cellular One used to routinely record all calls. Whether they or others do today is unknown, but likely.

Even if they go ahead and place an illegal, unwarranted tap on your phone, you're smart enough (I would hope) to avoid hanging yourself with your own tongue. Apparently, there are some 3,000 words which trigger automatic recording devices — words regarding crimes, terrorist acts, wanted criminals, etc. Also, there is voice pattern recognition software which will automatically record any conversation with a suspect's voice.

prepaid cellphones vs. payphones

Both have their uses, but prepaid cell phones (with multiple units, often changed) are more privacy enhancing.

prepaid cellphone advantages

imprecise geographical information (hampers camera surveillance)
no DNA left in public place (fingerprints, mouthpiece saliva, etc.)
convenience (pay phones are harder to find these days)
lower call cost
can be used in places without compromising ambient noise

payphone advantages

if used once/very infrequently, no call history to compile
strong anonymity (if used properly, by not calling illuminating #s)

The greatest disadvantage to using for any substantial length of time the same phone (whatever it is: cellphone, payphone, landline, or VoIP) is "community of interest" it provides.

the limited network approach

If you are in regular comm with a tight group which uses a dedicated prepaid cell phone to call only each other, this pattern can easily be discerned — *even if nobody blew it* by using their special phone to call a known number outside the group. A "cell" of three guys having unique phones to call only each others' unique phone will eventually stand out as an odd data pattern (called a "clique") to modern forensic tools.

Now, let's say these three guys understand all that, and seek to circumvent it. Easier wished for than accomplished. If they all drop their existing phone network for a batch of replacement phones — even those phones were purchased in different areas of the country, their odd "island" network would again show up over time. A small group of phones which call only each other, and nobody else calls them is suspicious.

Scroogle data-miner ThorpeGlenn's presentation paper "Identification of Nomadic Targets" and download a very interesting 11 page .pdf:

> *ThorpeGlen's vice president of global sales showed off the company's tools by mining a dataset of a single week's worth of call data from 50 million users in Indonesia, which it has crunched in order to try and discover small anti-social groups that only call each other.*

ThorpeGlenn crunched the CDRs (call data records) from over 8 *billion* events to discover numerous cliques ranging in size from 2 to 142 subscribers.

To avoid seeming like a clique, this 3-guy cell must add camouflaging data to their call history by using their phones to call other (nonincriminating) people and businesses. *I.e.,* they can still have their private network, but it must no longer *look* like one. Making (and receiving — important!) info-deadend calls to the barber, restaurants, random people of limited acquaintance (but not friends and family) in a nearby county or city will go far in disguising the actual purpose for that prepaid cell phone. (This is a lot of extra work, which is why disposable email accounts accessed via proxy with encrypted content is an easier way to go for a private comm network.)

And, the necessary network camouflage goes even further, to all the *rest* of their comm devices. Once a narrow physical area is known (often down to an actual address), a data-miner can track all communication devices used from there. A cell phone can indirectly point to an IP or MAC address or landline — and vice versa.

Another clique example is the classic hub-spoke topology, where the hub acts as command/control for members (who don't call each other, and may not even know of each other). Identify the hub, and the members can over time also be identified.

PREPAID CELLPHONES

No service contract or credit check is required, which means no name, address, or SSN. These are recent boon to privacy, though in today's (Forever) War on Terrorism they probably won't last forever. I expect their purchase to be soon legislatively tied to the buyer by credit card or DL. Meanwhile, however, they are about as anonymous as possible. The price for such privacy is a higher minute cost, though there are some prepaid plans (*e.g.,* Cricket) which are attractive for the gabby.

They work like this: you buy a phone (they're usually Nokias or LGs) from one of several prepaid cell phone providers (*e.g.,* Virgin, TracFone, Simple Freedom, AT&T, etc.) with cash. They're sold everywhere (*e.g.,* Target, WalMart, Office Depot, etc.). You fill them up with airtime (which expires usually in 60-90 days) as you need it. There is no monthly bill, no activation fee, no age limit, and no hidden costs. Service coverage can be is excellent, with great nationwide reception.

Airtime cards are bought with cash, and then you go to a nondescript phone (preferably a payphone) to recharge your cell. (All companies will allow you to recharge online by credit card, but this is hardly a privacy technique.)

Airtime on these cells is expensive, at least 10¢/minute in your home area (though this includes all domestic long-distance), and call time is rounded off to the next minute. (A 1:02 call will count as 2:00, which really adds up if you don't watch it.) Most phones have a call timer, and you should keep an eye on it. Train your friends not to gab, use your cell for more tactical vs. conversational purposes, and your monthly airtime costs should remain manageable.

If you're not some telephonic gadfly and can keep your airtime under $40/month, then a prepaid cellphone will likely be a good fit for you. Beyond their airtime expense and mild inconvenience to recharge, they are a great alternative for most users who value their privacy.

I think their highest and most logical use is to serve as an untraceable/disposable number for a limited circle of callers or for some singular purpose. A pair of discreet lovers, for example, would find them invaluable. So would a local unit of peaceable (though regularly training) militia. Somebody who frequently buys/sells through classifed ads would find their privacy useful. And, I've no doubt that police and government agents often use/discard them for their clandestine ops.

When these first became available, I wondered if their rarity would make them too easy to track. Today there are so many and used throughout society (*i.e.*, not just for the privacy conscious) that as a class of cell phone they aren't *quite* the magnet for surveillance they once were. (The same can be said for other prepaid products, such as debit cards. Prepaid has become a mass market concept.)

Now that you have a basic understanding of prepaid cells, let's discuss them in more detail. They will be similar, though with a bit of variance, in the following:

> phone features (*e.g.,* organizer, email, applications, games, etc.)
> phone cost
> service features (*e.g.,* voicemail, Caller ID, text msg., etc.)
> airtime cost
> home service area
> roaming cost
> setup privacy
> recharge privacy
> recharge hassle
> recharge fairness

cellphone features

Most prepaids will be Nokias, and with at least last year's features. Your phone will be packed with more internal gadgetry than you'll likely ever use, including cameras. But, if you're a tech hound, do compare before you buy.

cellphone cost

Generally between $20 and $60. The cheaper phones will suffice for most users. Some companies include 30-100 minutes of free airtime.

service features

Because of growing competition in this area (I mean, wouldn't *you* like to be routinely paid for service *before* you had to provide it, and thus totally dispense with account collection hassles?), all these phones will have voicemail, Caller ID (important for those who really value their privacy), call waiting, text messaging, etc. They are "real" cellphones with all the normal features.

I think voicemail is essential for most users. In fact, I think the inclusive voicemail of these phones is a very underappreciated feature. If used solely as a voicemail receiver, then it's even more private and elusive than going to payphones to retrieve messages (especially if calling long-distance), which can leave fingerprints and camera footage. Turn on the phone, retrieve your messages, and turn it off. Such a user would be *very* difficult to pinpoint in real-time. (Only a pager has more locational anonymity.)

airtime cost

From your Home area, about 10-20¢/minute, though this includes domestic long-distance charges (worth 5¢/minute). Since local payphone calls are all 50¢, any prepaid cell phone is like having a mobile payphone (if you keep your calls within 2 minutes). Payphone long-distance is 25-33¢/minute ($1.00 minimum), and calling card access fees there are $1.00, so prepaid cell long-distance make a lot sense for short calls.

Some companies (*e.g.,* Tracfone) give better deals on the larger the airtime card, other companies (*e.g.,* Simple Freedom, Virgin) do not. Some offer deals if you pay online by credit card, but that's just a ploy to gain more personal info about you. *"There's always free cheese in a mousetrap."*

Airtime cost has come down over the years, though I doubt it will ever drop much below 10¢/minute.

home service area

This is a very important consideration, because anywhere outside home/local constitutes "roaming" (which is double the local rate). Tracfone's home area (with 10¢/minute local airtime, the cheapest) can be changed up to 4x/year. Simple Freedom's home area is about 60% of the nation (though you'll pay 25¢/minute local).

On this point, where "home" is remains up to you. If you live in Kansas City but for some reason wanted a Philadelphia local number—no problem. Simply give the provider a Philly ZIP code or area code/exchange during setup, and they will program your phone with a Philly cell number. This (coupled with web-based email whose originating IP is provider's city vs. your local provider's) can go a very long way into spoofing others that you actually live in Philadelphia.

roaming cost

If you travel extensively, then roaming charges will become the major part of your airtime cost.

Simple Freedom is probably the best for nomads, with their *huge* home area. Unless you live/travel in west Texas, eastern Oregon, southern Washington, Nevada, Oklahoma, Maine, Kentucky, West Virginia, or Minnesota—their home network will likely include your area. So, your local friends back in Atlanta can dial your local # and reach you for just 25¢/minute even when you're skiing in Park City, Utah.

setup privacy

This varies tremendously by provider. AT&T asks way too many questions. Tracfone asks none. Simple Freedom (if you setup online, which is quicker — and use a *public* computer!) will activate with just name (pick an androgynous name, such as Terry, Pat, Chris, or Dana), and home address (use the Rural Route/Box or apartment complex trick I outlined earlier). Disclose no email address or telephone number.

When in doubt about each company's intrusiveness, simply visit each of their activation pages online *before* you buy. I recommend not setting up/recharging online, because it needlessly sacrifices a valuable foreign proxy tunnel IP.

recharge privacy

Never recharge your cell phone by credit card! This is a needless sacrifice of privacy, negating the whole purpose of these phones. Perhaps one day Congress will outlaw cash-purchased airtime cards, but meanwhile we still have them.

Buy them with locally with cash (or online by prepaid debit card), and preferably without any other purchases (especially those directly traceable to you, such as prescriptions and car maintenance). If that store has a payphone not under a camera, then you should use it (as your card's purchase point places you there *anyway* — using a different payphone just offers them more information about you).

Some airtime cards may be used from payphones (*e.g.*, TracFone), while some may *not* (Simple Freedom, and it's not on their brochure). While irksome, this is no big deal; simply use a courtesy phone found at hotels, copy centers, libraries, etc. These are not tagged as payphones, but as business lines (which do not compromise your privacy). *Never* recharge your cell phone from home, business, or places where you are known (your regular bar, hairstylist, etc.).

recharge hassle

Once you've purchased your airtime card with cash and have located a discreet phone, all you have to do now is walk through whatever steps your cell provider requires. Simple Freedom is easy: call their 800 number, enter your cell's 10-digit phone number, then your airtime card's PIN, and you're done. Tracfone's are easier still, as they will recharge themselves with a PIN (no payphone needed).

So, before you buy, ask owners of different phones how it works for them.

Curiously, airtime cards often cannot be used online, but only through phones. Not very good for privacy if you don't want to fire up your phone to recharge it.

recharge fairness

This refers to how often you must fill up your phone to keep your service active. If you let your airtime expire, you will lose your credit and they will reassign your number. Read the fine print *before* you buy.

Most providers offer a special airtime card that will secure your number for 6-12 months. While its airtime is quite high (up to $1/minute), you are in effect buying its voicemail service along with the talk time. For example, if you buy Tracfone's 12 month/100 minute card for $100, you're getting voicemail for just $8/month (plus 100 minutes of talk time). That's really not such a bad deal, as most local voice mail providers will charge at least that (plus ask for personal info).

So, if you plan on keeping your number for at least a year, but do not anticipate talking more than 200 minutes/month, locking up your service with a 12 month card is a good idea.

various prepaid cellphone providers
Tracfone

Probably the best out there, and certainly the one with the best national coverage. Airtime can be less than 10¢/minute if you have a DMFL (Double Minutes For Life) phone in conjunction with a promotional code (Scroogle for the current codes). Roaming charges are rare, and cost 2 credits/minute. Tracfone has an excellent selection of phones, and their customer service has greatly improved. Try a Tracfone first.

Net10 (10¢/minute, but customer service is mediocre)
Net 10 wireless is a division of Tracfone. All of the customer service is done by offshore South or Central American providers. If you are fluent in Spanish you will actually get better Net10 Customer Service by choosing the Spanish language option when you first get on the phone.
— www.compare-prepaid-cell-phones.com

Virgin
Aimed mostly at the youth market with monthly plans of $30-50 for airtime and another $15-20 for text messages. I find their registration policy to be privacy intrusive.

Cricket
If you live within a Cricket service area, and do a lot of talking, their various flat-rate monthly plans may ideal. For example, the most basic $35/month choice included unlimited local calls and texting, but no long-distance (you'll have to use a calling card, but this is no big deal). For $45/month you also get free 49-state long-distance, voice mail, Caller ID, Call Waiting, and 3-way calling. For heavy cellphone users who don't roam much, that's a good deal. You can buy online, but first have a way to discreetly receive their UPS.

cellphone privacy measures
Here are numerous tips; many of them will seem too extreme for most readers. That's fine; take your pick.

buy phone, airtime, and all accessories with cash
The phone and airtime are serial-numbered, and this data can easily be reconstructed against you if you were silly enough to have used a check or credit card.

Use a store that you *never* frequent, pay cash, and don't buy anything else there — then, or ever. Park down the street to avoid any store camera capturing your car or license plate. Have no other cellphone powered up at this time.

Extreme tip: Save this purchase for some distant out-of-town trip. (Same technique with buying prepaid debit cards.)

for Tracfone, go with the year plan and double minutes
This reduces your recharge exposure of having to buy an airtime card. (Obviously, for a specifically disposable phone, a year plan is probably excessive.)

carefully think through which area code is "yours"

Sometimes it's wise to hide your small town location with an area code of a metropolis. *E.g.*, get a Denver number even if you live in Glenwood Springs. Know in advance its ZIP code to provide for the registration.

avoid online purchase or setup

Why unnecessarily link the phone to an IP proxy, email address, or drop box? It's better to buy it in person with cash.

for voicemail setup, use the generic version

"Hello. No one is available to take your call" does not inform any caller that it's your phone. They'd have to hear you answer, which you may decide not to do for unknown numbers. Also, don't use the "record your name" option.

do not lose your voicemail PIN!

I did this once, and nobody could restore it for me.

never let your airtime expire during a service window

Tracfones can be "boot-strap" recharged with just the airtime PIN, but once you are late in doing so, you'll have to go to a payphone and spend about 10 minutes of tedium entering reactivation codes. Also, if you let the phone go past 60 days of its expiration date, you risk losing your original number. Stay on top of airtime renewals!

do not retain on your person airtime cards

Enter this data in passphrase-protected PDA.

never buy from same place airtime for multiple phones

This will easily link previously unconnected phones.

have a "public" prepaid cellphone knowable by govt

By "government" I also mean any business which acts as a near partner to government, such as banks, airlines, etc.

Whatever transaction is instantly knowable by government, such as your air travel, you might as well use the same cellphone for. To live this way betokens almost a split personality, with your public side and your private side. Never the two shall mix, including cellphone usage. So, give 'em a cellphone, because if you deny a number to the public sphere at large, that sphere will become *very* suspicious.

While you could use an Internet voice mail as your public number, I think a working prepaid cellphone where you can be called is better. Imagine the airline losing your luggage and the courier needs to call you. You want to be instantly accessible vs. playing telephone tag. (Besides, having a cell to call back really simplifies things, vs. using calling cards at payphones.) Sometimes, too private is conspicuous.

For this phone, tightly manage your call list and thus limit what "community of interest" is knowable from there. Talk to your parents and grandma, but not your private friends.

do not, if possible, use the phonebook feature

Why let your lost/stolen cellphone contain all that data? Even your call records are available from the provider, such takes a bit of time to access (assuming a proper warrant).

deactivate the constant locator "feature"

This will be in your Settings menu. (You cannot deactivate the 9-11 locator.)

delete dialed/received call records after each call

Do this before you leave the security of your car or building. Walking about in public with these records in your phone can be risky.

delete text messages ASAP

These are stored in your SIM card.

use the power up and keypad lock feature

These are not impregnable, but every little bit helps.

First, change the 3 digit lock/unlock code and the 6 digit security code (required for programming functions) and either remember those codes or store them in an encrypted file. Then, program your phone to power up always in the locked mode — requiring the 3 digit unlock code before use.

Don't lose your phone, however, because whoever finds it won't be able to power up and receive your call.

power up *before* you leave an area/place, *not* upon arrival

Thus, you reveal only what's in your locational past, and not in your locational present or future.

power up/down away from any informational location

Making calls from the WalMart you just shopped at can lead to purchase data (items you bought, and how paid), camera data (what you were wearing, whom you were with, and perhaps your vehicle), and human witnesses (who can relay any conversational and observational details).

Use your phone sparingly, and only from locations that can provide no ancillary information.

power up/down away from any directional node

The best place to power up/down is in the middle of town, or at a major crossroads. The worst place would near a highway on/off ramp.

Extreme tip: power up/down on a road and direction that provides only misinformation. You can make it seem that you've come from somewhere and/or are going elsewhere. For example, if you live north of town, loop in/out town from the east and power up/down from that direction.

power up and make calls while stationary, if possible

This avoids providing any vector of travel.

leave phone off/battery out — powering up as needed

This eliminates all data of your travel route and stops. Balance privacy with convenience.

being *too* cagey can indirectly be informative

Lets' say Bob has vowed to never use his cellphone from his private home area. That seems clever, but using it *only everywhere else* can draw a TA map that makes his hometown stand out as the deadzone he's made it to be. (This is an example of Sherlock Holmes's *"the dog that didn't bark"*.) Deadzones are unnatural. Where Bob lives can be inferred from where he so diligently tried to make appear that he was *not*.

A more obvious example would be to turn off your phone just before you arrive somewhere, and then power up just after you left. **What and how you *don't* communicate can often contain information.** Whatever you do *too* differently or leave out *too* often can draw attention to what you're hiding. (In the *Bourne Supremacy* a particular CIA agent was identified as having made a secret meeting because he turned off his cellphone during business hours — which is not normal. He should have just left it on in silent mode, but behind at the office.)

The more clever thing for our Bob to do is to use his private phone often enough in sensitive *general* areas to hide its importance amongst the nonsensitive areas. Spread out the data; hide a grain of sand on the beach. This will take some nuance, so start reading some spy novels. <wink>

code words and overt vagueness are suspicious

Another example of being too clever for your own good. Phrases such as *"Meet me at the house of the guy who has that big brown dog"* are silly. Nobody talks that way. Not that call content is usually listened to, but do work out a protocol much less obvious. Code first names for places are smart: *"Hey, meet me at 3 over at Charlie's"* could mean the target range. (Leaving your cell on while at the range, however, will clue a snooper what "Charlie" means.)

long-distance calling cards add another level of privacy

Your dialed call data shows only the 800 number. Not that the card company can't/won't reveal whom you really called, but every level you can add increases your protection. Besides, calling card companies are required to keep only three years of data.

If routinely using a calling card is too much hassle or expense, at least use it for calls which you don't want on your cellphone records. (*Really* sensitive calls shouldn't be made from your cellphone, anyway — not even through a calling card.)

imagine every # known, and every call being overheard

Do this, and you won't easily compromise yourself.

don't just power down — remove the battery

Kaplan's opinion said that the eavesdropping technique "functioned whether the phone was powered on or off." **Some handsets can't be fully powered down without removing the battery;** *for instance, some Nokia models will wake up when turned off if an alarm is set.*

Other mobile providers were reluctant to talk about this kind of surveillance. *Verizon Wireless said only that it "works closely with law enforcement and public safety officials. When presented with legally authorized orders, we assist law enforcement in every way possible."*

—www.thechicagosyndicate.com/2006/12/roving-bug-in-cell-phones-used-by-fbi.html

The authorities are also able (without your knowledge) to covertly power up cellphones to use as an open mike and track the owner's position. This is no internet rumor; it is confirmed. On that note, only charge your cellphone(s) in a nonsensitive area, and never while your other cellphone is charging or on. (Or, get a Faraday Bag from www.paraben.com.)

A helpful technique is to *carefully* cut out the phone's plastic tabs which prevent the battery from going in upside down. Adapt your phone this way, and you won't lose the batt.

if you have multiple cellphones, . . .

. . . never have them powered up at the same time.
. . . never power them up/down sequentially, on same day.
. . . never call each other, or any common number.
. . . never make joint airtime purchases.
. . . never transfer credit from one phone to another.
. . . often use multiple providers — don't stick with just one.
. . . always use them in separate and distant areas.

have a previously setup and fully charged backup cell

If an emergency forces you to ditch your regular phone, it will be comforting to have another one ready to go. (This also holds true regarding a spare laptop with backup data and settings.)

have a common privacy protocol with your friends

There's no point in all this if your friends keep their phones on (or off, but with batteries still in) as they meet you in some private location.

when disposing of a cellphone, remove the SIM and batt

The SIM you should crush and discard. The battery may be useful as a spare for another phone. The phone itself should be carefully discarded in random public trashcan, as it contains your prints and saliva DNA.

final thoughts

All this *will* go very far to increasing your cellphone privacy, but never believe that such is inviolable. Yes, you can make data collection and processing much more difficult for the snoops, but all bets are off if you're highly wanted. For example, Osama bin Laden's cell calls were routinely monitored (until his probable death by 2002; read the article "Osama bin Elvis" at www.spectator.org).

The best rule is if your location, call history, or call content is extremely sensitive — then do not then use a phone at all.

LANDLINES

home landline

I'll keep this simple: don't get one unless you *absolutely* need one in addition to a cell phone or VoIP.

your listing—if you *must* have a home phone

If you must list your number, at least have your address omitted.   Or, the phone company can list your number in another *name* — they don't care as long as they've got a viable billing name and address. I would list it in another name rather than getting a nonpublished listing in your own name, for two reasons: it's *free,* and a call to directory assistance won't have your real name in their records (thus, the caller won't learn that ❶ you're in such-and-such area, and ❷ you have a phone).

For ultra-privacy, have a friend establish the service in his name.   Understandably, he may want a cash deposit up front.   It's not so unusual for "A" to be on the rental agreement, and "B" to have the phone—especially in college towns.

If nobody is willing to establish service for you, use an alias.   Though increasingly difficult, it's still possible.   You'll have to pay a several hundred dollar deposit and explain why you don't have a social security number (*i.e.,* you're just starting college and have never had a job, you're from overseas, etc.).   Know beforehand that any new number so suspiciously established will be secretly listened in on by the phone company for several weeks. Keep it cool.

Regardless of how or by whom the service was established, you must always realize that those ten digits are physical locators for your house.   Once the number has been linked to you, you can be visited at *any* time.   Therefore, think long and hard before you get a home phone — then, think again.

Do *not* print your home number on checks, business cards, etc. Do *not* give it out to strangers, prospective dates, classified ad listings, shops, credit card companies, public officials, distant relatives, etc. The only people who should have it are *extremely* close friends and family members, *and even then* do not entrust it to them unless you really must (for emergency purposes, etc.).   They should call you from pay phones to avoid making MUDs.

Still, I can't stress this enough: **if you're into low-key living and invisible domiciles—*don't get a home phone*.**   Give the cell phone/voice mail/VoIP combination a fair, *first* try.

your calling records

Since anybody who *really* wants your records can get them, the only thing you can do is not *create* them. While this might seem to defeat the purpose of having a phone, such isn't too inconvenient with a bit of forethought and discipline.

local calls

There are certain local numbers you should *never* call from your home phone: your own voice mails, travel agencies, gun stores, doctors' offices, banks, credit card companies, and "sensitive" friends. Imagine which people and companies you don't want to be connected with by *your* MUDs, or through *their* Caller ID. Use a dedicated prepaid cellphone for the public.

toll-free calls

Just because they don't show up on your long-distance records doesn't mean that no records exist. For recordkeeping purposes, these are retained as MUDs. Also, a word of caution: all companies with toll-free numbers also have ANI (Automatic Number Identification), a sort of Caller ID. If you call them from your home they'll make an internal record of where you live. To be safe, use a pay phone for *all* toll-free calls.

long-distance calls

Since it looks suspicious to have utterly *no* long-distance calls on your bill, make a couple of harmless, generic ones each month. For ultra-privacy, never call family and friends.

And/or use prepaid calling cards.

pay phones

Just because it's a pay phone doesn't mean you can blab with complete abandon. First, consider the *brand* of pay phone. I would trust personally an off-brand over a Bell phone.

Then, there's *location*. Some suspect pay phone locations are: jails, airports and close proximity, bus and train stations, hotels, casinos, nightclubs with a notoriously criminal clientele, government buildings (including post offices), and any quasi-official institution.

If the brand and location do not ring any warning bells, be sure that you can speak in privacy with being overheard. Find *at least* a dozen more like pay phones and alternate their usage.

Never use the *same* phone for different calling-cards or personalities.

For ultra-privacy, never use a pay phone nearby your home, office, hotel, etc. This is an obvious hassle, but I'll be the first to tell you: privacy *ain't* convenient! For instance, *if they know the pay phone*, they'll scour that area's hotels, motels, restaurants, etc. *If they know your general location*, they'll get the records of all nearby pay phones and tap the ones they think you use regularly.

This is a common investigation procedure which has yielded much fruit. In *The Silent Brotherhood*, members of the "Order" bought cheap used cars for their getaway vehicles and dumped them. After an armored car robbery, the feds found one of the getaway cars and interviewed the prior owner. He recalled that the buyer asked directions from such-and-such motel. The feds then got the MUDs from every pay phone in that motel's area and found which one the car seller had been called *from*. Analyzing the rest of that phone's records, the FBI learned where the Order's out-of-state headquarters were. It all took a while, but time is *usually* on the side of the investigator.

The Order's mistakes (besides being a pack of neo-Nazis) were: *buying* their getaway cars and thus showing their face, calling the sellers from a nearby pay phone, asking for directions from their own motel, and using the same pay phone to call home. Loose ends always provide triggers, and enough triggers will crack *any* case.

Don't get *lazy*. Make your call just before you *leave* the area, not when you arrive. Don't use any nearby trashcans. *Never* use a pay phone at any frequented location where you are known or recognized (*e.g.*, bar, laundromat, car wash, store, etc.), or at locations which have security cameras (*e.g.*, gov't buildings, banks, liquor stores, etc.). Call your party (preferably at his pager) from one pay phone with coins, and have him call *you* at another pay phone in another town. Yeah, I *know* it's inconvenient, but that's the deal. Don't get lazy. Make *every* pay phone call a dead-end street which leads *nowhere*. Nobody *saw* you there, nobody *knows* you there, no successive calls were made, you left nothing at the scene, you *left* immediately after hanging up and wiping off prints—and you'll never *return* there.

the wise use of all other landlines

When using a home phone with a redial button, dial that phone's own number as your last call and hang up.   This prevents somebody from redialing your last party.   Avoid cordless phones—they are overheard without warrant by scanners.

If any phone is within 100 feet of a sensitive conversation, unplug the handset (not the phone itself).   Although the phone will still ring, this disconnects the mike and thwarts the "infinity" technique by covert types in which the mike is silently activated *without ringing* the phone.   (Infinity miking works even with cell phones, so remove the battery prior discussions.)   If you're *really* concerned, then unplug the phone itself.

Poor Mr. Pen Register!   Poor Mr. Tap!

If you've followed my techniques, your home phone will have no revealing calls made or received.   This will usually thwart the officials, as they rely on the pen register evidence to learn of one's associates and hopefully gain probable cause (PC) to obtain warrants (wiretap, search, or arrest).

red herring phone numbers

Many phone books today have reverse directories to look up a number or an address.   Missing numbers are either nonworking, nonpublished, or temporarily nonallocated.   Find one which rings but is never answered, even late at night.   That's "your" new number to give out, like the RR box number.

PREPAID CALLING CARDS

These are the greatest privacy innovation in years.   Long popular in Europe, they've finally hit our shores.   For $5-100 you can buy long-distance credit on a disposable card.   The higher the denomination, the lower the rate.   Calling 50 miles or 5,000 miles away costs the same.   (The cheapest rate I've so far seen is 2¢ per minute.)   Payphone access fees have gotten horrendous, up to $1.50/call.

Although different grocery and drug stores sell their own versions, they all work the same way.   To place a call, dial the company's master 800 number, then the card's PIN, and then the number you're calling. You'll be told how much credit the card has left and how many minutes remain. Depending on the company, it takes 35-50 seconds to connect your number. (Try several companies as the quality of service varies.) Usually, you'll get a *"One minute remaining!"* warning before being cut off. Once stored, *burn* the card. Do not "throw it away" and *never* recharge it with your credit card.

Many pay phones still display their number and allow incoming calls, but test them first by calling them yourself. (2009 Note: This may no longer be permitted since 9/11.)

how *private* are these services?

Good question. It would be an easy feat for the card company to use ANI and link where you're calling *from* with where you're calling to. However, if you make a perfect habit of using only payphones (and varied ones at that), then such will offer nothing but your general location.

Whether or not companies keep a record of a card's called numbers, you'll never know. I would suspect that they do, at least for a few months. For ultra-privacy, use separate cards for *each* frequently called sensitive number. Use different companies for each alias. Some calls are business and some are personal—each kind should have their *own* card from *different* companies. Such measures are tedious, but you'll get what you pay for. Half-assed measures will give you half-assed privacy.

One final thought: I wouldn't bet the ranch on these cards. They are at *least* a buffer to routine, low-level snooping—but that may be *all* they do. The feds and the telecoms are quite powerful and sophisticated, and if they get together against you, all bets are off. Be careful about whom you call from the same card, and from the same pay phone.

WHAT ABOUT PAGERS?

A pager is a simple radio receiver tuned to a single frequency. Each pager has its own unique phone number. When called, the pager network sends out your page through all of its transmitters simultaneously (since pagers are passive and don't broadcast a *"Here I am!"* NAM signal, as do cell phones). While your messages *can* be intercepted, your *location* can never be known through a pager.

In my 1997 *Bulletproof Privacy* I went into great detail on pagers. In the past twelve years, however, much has changed. (Motorola left the business in 2000, and stopped making pagers years ago.) There aren't many service providers out there any more, but www.allpage.com is one to consider.

In my view, pagers are no longer routinely necessary for privacy. To achieve maximum value, all your callers would have to use payphones (with powered down cellphones), and who wants to go through *that?* If you're the exception, just find a used copy of *Bulletproof Privacy* and photocopy Chapter 12.

IN SUMMARY

Your goals are really quite simple: ❶ not to draw attention to yourself, and ❷ to give snoopers no place to go even if you *do* draw attention to yourself. This is accomplished with a voice communications system which employs your three major tools of VoIP, Internet voice mail, and prepaid cellphones. With public/private accounts in all three, you divide your comm and thus conquer the snoops. If using aliases, be certain that each personality has its *own* comm channel. Watch out for any crossovers. Strict compartmentalization is the key.

By having a some kind of answerable phone number and a street address (postal drop with no useful address on the application), by not acting like a drug courier or a Romanian spy, you've melted into the crowd. You're enjoying the modern miracle of fiber-optic, satellite telecommunications and VoIP without having it work against you. As I explained at the beginning of this chapter, using voice comm with discretion is the hardest part of one's overall privacy stance. Beat that, and you'll win.

It's a good idea to change cellphones, VoIP accounts, code names/numbers, and calling habits often and unexpectedly. The Germans lost WWII because of lazy, overconfident communication habits. **Mix it up, stay alert, and *trust your feelings.*** If you get an eerie read about something, *disengage immediately* — however inconvenient or costly. Then change your codes, tighten up your procedures, and lay low for a while. Correlate any new or unusual experience/person with your suspicions. If something/somebody is too good to be true, then it probably *is*. Remember to keep a relaxed perspective!

PASSPHRASES

User ID for systems are authenticated by one of the below, or some combination of them:

> What you *know*
> What you *have*
> Who you *are*

Passphrases are the prime example of something you *know*. (If a keyfile, say with TrueCrypt, is used then that adds something you *have* — perhaps on a USB drive. A biometric fingerprint pad would be using something that you *are*.)

Computer security is hard. Software, computer and network security are all ongoing battles between attacker and defender. And in many cases the attacker has an inherent advantage: He only has to find one network flaw, while the defender has to find and fix every flaw.

Cryptography is an exception. As long as you don't write your own algorithm, secure encryption is easy. And the defender has an inherent mathematical advantage: Longer keys increase the amount of work the defender has to do linearly, while geometrically increasing the amount of work the attacker has to do.

Unfortunately, cryptography can't solve most computer-security problems. **The one problem cryptography can solve is the security of data when it's not in use.** *Encrypting files, archives — even entire disks — is easy.*

— *How Does Bruce Schneier Protect His Laptop Data?*
Bruce Schneier, Wired News, November 29, 2007

passphrase terminology

Good basics I've quoted from www.grc.com/passwords.htm:

"random" vs. "pseudo-random"

There are ways to generate absolutely random numbers, but computer algorithms cannot be used for that, since, by definition, no deterministic mathematical algorithm can generate a random result. Electrical and mechanical noise found in chaotic physical systems can be tapped and used as a source of true randomness, but this is much more than is needed for our purposes here. High quality algorithms are sufficient.

The deterministic binary noise generated by my server, which is then converted into various displayable formats, is derived from the highest quality mathematical pseudo-random algorithms known. In other words, these password strings are as random as anything non-random can be.

A beneficial property of these maximum entropy pseudo-random passwords is their lack of "inter-symbol memory." This means that in a string of symbols, any of the possible password symbols is equally likely to occur next. This is important if your application requires you to use shorter password strings. Any "sub-string" of symbols will be just as random and high quality as any other.

dictionary attack

30MB dictionaries that are floating around the 'Net that contain just about every word you can imagine.

HOW PASSPHRASES ARE GUESSED

Algorithms are subject to being cracked (through brute forcing), but this almost never occurs. Rather, it's much, much easier to guess/hack a human-generated passphrase.

cracking encryption . . . *not!*

It is generally infeasible to crack modern open-source algorithms of large key size. But, the *human* element remains the natural weak link. Passphrases that are simple, or written down are merely grass doors on a steel hut.

You must protect your computer against both access and surveillance (virtual and physical). Virtual would be planted software to log in your keystrokes, or data sniffing. Physical surveillance would be a camera planted to record your typing in passphrases. A computer which is "stand alone" (*i.e.*, never online), and not accessible to tampering (*e.g.*, a laptop that is either always with you, or locked up) would be very secure.

Linux machines can have their boot sectors encrypted, which basically prevents installation of Trojan Horses, etc.

Know your enemy and his tactics, for he certainly knows yours. Passphrase hacking has become very sophisticated, and you will have to constantly keep ahead. Most passphrases consist of a root and an appendage. Dictionaries for them exist:

. . . Password Recovery Toolkit goes through a series of increasingly complex root dictionaries and appendage dictionaries. The root dictionaries include:

* *Common word dictionary: 5,000 entries*
* *Names dictionary: 10,000 entries*
* *Comprehensive dictionary: 100,000 entries*
* *Phonetic pattern dictionary: 110,000 entries*

The phonetic pattern dictionary is interesting. It's not really a dictionary; it's a Markov-chain routine that generates pronounceable English-language strings of a given length. For example, PRTK can generate and test a dictionary of very pronounceable six-character strings, or just-barely pronounceable seven-character strings. They're working on generation routines for other languages.

PRTK also runs a four-character-string exhaustive search. It runs the dictionaries with lowercase (the most common), initial uppercase (the second most common), all uppercase and final uppercase. It runs the dictionaries with common substitutions: "$" for "s," "@" for "a," "1" for "l" and so on. Anything that's "leet speak" is included here, like "3" for "e."

The appendage dictionaries include things like:

* *All two-digit combinations*
* *All dates from 1900 to 2006*
* *All three-digit combinations*
* *All single symbols*
* *All single digit, plus single symbol*
* *All two-symbol combinations*

*AccessData's secret sauce is the order in which it runs the various root and appendage dictionary combinations. The company's research indicates that **the password sweet spot is a seven- to nine-character root plus a common appendage**, and that it's much more likely for someone to choose a hard-to-guess root than an uncommon appendage.*

How good is all of this? Eric Thompson estimates that with a couple of weeks' to a month's worth of time, his software breaks 55 percent to 65 percent of all passwords. (This depends, of course, very heavily on the application.)

— Secure Passwords Keep You Safer,
Bruce Schneier, January 15, 2007

your password is probably not good enough

There are dozens of very robust cryptological algorithms out there. They are not the weak link, and rarely ever were:

*For years, I have said that the easiest way to break a cryptographic product is almost never by breaking the algorithm, that almost invariably there is a programming error that allows you to bypass the mathematics and break the product. A similar thing is going on here. **The easiest way to guess a password isn't to guess it at all, but to exploit the inherent insecurity in the underlying operating system.***

— Secure Passwords Keep You Safer, Bruce Schneier

Nearly one in 50 will foolishly choose a passphrase from the Top Ten list, and one in 16 from the Top 100 list. (The top two are "123" and "password".)

In one survey of MySpace passwords which had been phished, 3.8 percent of passwords were a single word found in a dictionary, and another 12 percent were a word plus a final digit; two-thirds of the time that digit was 1.

In 2005 the Software Usability Research Laboratory (SURL) at Wichita State University conducted a study on password create, usage, and storage. Anything familiar here?

   54.6% use the exact same password for multiple accounts
   33.0% use a variation of the same password for multiple accounts
   74.9% have a set of predetermined passwords (3, on average)

35% use a predetermined character length, and between 5-9
85.7% use only lower case letters
56.5% use only numerals
54.9% use words from personal data
49.8% use numerals from personal data
59.7% do not vary complexity depending on the site
average usage time length: 31 months (2.5 years!)
52.7% "never" change their passwords
15% write down their passwords
28.6% use the "remember my password" software function

http://psychology.wichita.edu/surl/usabilitynews/81/default.asp

CREATING MEMORIZED STRONG PASSPHRASES

human generated passwords are weak in entropy

The entropy math assumes perfect randomness, so you should at least *double* your key length if it was not randomly generated.

NIST uses the following scheme to estimate password entropy (i.e., randomness):

   * the entropy of the first character is four bits;
   * the entropy of the next seven characters are two bits per character
   * the ninth through the twentieth character has 1.5 bits of entropy per character;
   * characters 21 and above have one bit of entropy per character;

*This suggests that, **in the absence of a sensible password policy,** an eight-character password has 18-bit equivalent strength. Yet, even with a password policy requiring at least one number, one symbol, and mixed case, an eight-character password only achieves an estimated 30-bit strength.*
   — http://en.wikipedia.org/wiki/Password_strength

A 50-character (easily memorizable) passphrase from a 95-character keyspace does not actually enjoy 328 bits (50 * 6.555 bits) of entropy. Using the NIST formula (which is the one to err on if you're truly concerned), it has barely over 60 bits of entropy — far short of the recommended minimum of 80.

what makes a good passphrase?

First of all, it must be 12+ characters long.   Robust security is not possible with shorter strings. Then:

> *Picking a good passphrase is one of the most important things you can do to preserve the privacy of your computer data and e-mail messages. A passphrase should be:*
> * * Known only to you*
> * * Long enough to be secure*
> * * Hard to guess — even by someone who knows you well*
> * * Easy for you to remember*
> * * Easy for you to type accurately*
> *   — www.diceware.com*

examples of bad vs. good passphrases

Examples of bad passwords include:
  * mydog2
  * bi11smith
  * yromem (memory backwards)
  * win4me

Examples of strong passwords include:
  * De2#vu
  * 5sd$oiP
  * er89TI
    — http://psynch.com/docs/choosing-good-passwords.html

random sequences vs. memorizable sequences

People are notoriously remiss at achieving sufficient entropy to produce satisfactory passwords. Some stage magicians exploit this inability for amusement, in a minor way, by divining supposed random choices (of numbers, say) made by audience members. In one analysis of over 3 million eight-character passwords, the letter "e" was used over 1.5 million times, while the letter "f" was only used 250,000 times. A uniform distribution would have had each character being used about 200,000 times. The most common number used is "1", whereas the most common letters are a, e, o, and r.
  — http://en.wikipedia.org/wiki/Password_strength

Random is the goal, but random is nearly impossible to remember after just a few characters. Conversely, what can be easily memorized is usually not very random:

> If the passphrase is a phrase in a natural language, the problem is much more difficult. There is a famous estimate due to Shannon that **the average entropy of written English is [only] about 1.3 bits per letter.** See Schneier's Applied Cryptography, 2nd Ed. p.234. However, applying this estimate to a passphrase is questionable. People are much more predictable than they think they are. In general, it is very hard to give a good estimate of entropy for a passphrase when any human judgment is involved.
>
> — www.diceware.com

> They guess intelligently. They don't run through every eight-letter combination from "aaaaaaaa" to "zzzzzzzz" in order. That's 200bn possible passwords, most of them very unlikely. They try the most common password first: "password1". (Don't laugh; the most common password used to be "password".)
>
> A typical password consists of a root plus an appendage. The root isn't necessarily a dictionary word, but it's something pronounceable. An appendage is either a suffix (90% of the time) or a prefix (10% of the time). One guesser I studied starts with a dictionary of about 1,000 common passwords, things like "letmein," "temp," "123456," and so on. Then it tests them each with about 100 common suffix appendages: "1", "4u", "69", "abc", "!" and so on. **It recovers about 24% of all passwords with just these 100,000 combinations.**
>
> Then the guesser tries different dictionaries: English words, names, foreign words, phonetic patterns and so on for roots; two digits, dates, single symbols and so on for appendages. It runs the dictionaries with various capitalisations and common substitutions: "$" for "s", "@" for "a", "1" for "l" and so on. With a couple of weeks to a month's worth of time, this guessing strategy breaks about two-thirds of all passwords.
>
> **But that assumes no biographical data.** Any smart guesser collects whatever personal information it can on the subject before beginning. Postal codes are common appendages.
>
> — *Passwords Are Not Broken, But How We Choose them Sure Is*, Bruce Schneier, November 13, 2008

what *never* to use for passphrases:

no blank passwords	(*i.e.,* leaving the field empty)
no repetitions	(222222, hhhhhhh)
no reversals	(drowssap)
no common sequences	(qwerty, mnbvcxz)
no common numerics	(*pi* 314159, 12345678, ZIP Codes, etc.)
no doubled words	(treetree, glassglass)
no dictionary words	(in any language)

no phonetically spelled words
no swear words or names of celebrities
no software or website names
no common quotations   (includes movies)
no default passwords from system vendor: (admin, guest, user, etc.)
no words with number substitutions: (password1, deer2000)
no words with simple obfuscation: (p@ssw0rd, g0ldf1sh)
no listed roots/appendages (www.accessdata.com)

and, no — *absolutely no* — personal or biographical data:
names (yours, nicknames, logins, relatives, friends, pets, etc.)
dates (birthdays, anniversaries, graduation, etc.)
ID numbers (SSN, license plate, etc.)
telephone numbers (past and current)
places (birthplace, honeymoon, schools, restaurant, etc.)
things (your car, favorite gun, etc.)

length, width, and depth of good passphrases

Given the average maximum passphrase length allowed by most software (*i.e.*, 8-20 characters), you simply cannot create a robust passphrase with just numerals or lower case characters. Assuming an 8-character passphrase, 8^10 (1,073,741,824) or 8^26 (3.022314549037 x 10^23) are not excessive possibilities for computers to crunch.

		# of characters
digits only	(0-9)	10
single case letters	(a-z) or (A-Z)	26
single case letters and digits	(a-z, 0-9)	36
mixed case letters	(a-z, A-Z)	52
mixed case letters and digits	(a-z, A-Z, 0-9)	62
mixed letters, spaces	(a-z, A-Z, _)	84
all of above, plus metacharacters	(~!@#$%)	94
all of above, and Alt+ characters		256

However, using upper/lower/digits/metacharacters means that *each* passphrase character could be one of 94 possibilities. An 8-character passphrase mean 8^94 possibilities, or 7.77 followed by *84* zeroes. Even with only 8 characters, using a wider variety of keys translates into *exponentially* more difficult hacking.

NOTE: Alt+ characters are not accessible from every device, and not all software will accept them in a passphrase. Although they greatly increase the overall character set from 94 to 256, try them out before you rely upon them.

if you choose a root/appendage passphrase

You must break up the root, according to Schneier:

mix upper and lowercase in the middle of your root
add numbers and symbols in the middle of your root
drop your appendage in the middle of your root
use two roots with an appendage in the middle

"bit strength threshold"

symbol set		N	entropy/char.
digits only	(0-9)	10	3.32 bits
single case	(a-z) or (A-Z)	26	4.70 bits
single letters and digits	(a-z, 0-9)	36	5.17 bits
mixed letters	(a-z, A-Z)	52	5.70 bits
mixed letters and digits	(a-z, A-Z, 0-9)	62	5.95 bits
mixed letters, spaces	(a-z, A-Z, _)	84	6.39 bits
all of above, plus metacharacters	(~!@#$%)	94	6.55 bits
all of above, and Alt+ characters		256	8.00 bits

. . . adding a bit of entropy (or its equivalent) to a password doubles the number of guesses required. On average, an attacker will have to try half the possible passwords before finding the correct one.

If a passphrase is selected from a universe of N possibilities, where each possibility is equally likely to be chosen, the entropy is log2(N). The symbol "log2" stands for the base-two logarithm. Most calculators don't have a button for base-2 logarithms, but you can use the formula:

$$log2(N)=log(N)/log(2)$$

If the passphrase is made out of M symbols, each chosen at random from a universe of N possibilities, each equally likely, the entropy is M*log2(N). For example, if you make a

*passphrase by choosing 10 letters **at random**, the entropy is 10*log2(26) = 47.0 bits.*
— http://en.wikipedia.org/wiki/Password_strength

So, by using upper/lower/numerals/meta, you are increasing entropy by 1.85 bits/character over mere lower case. That's a 39% gain. (Omitting the space bar, which cannot be used everywhere, there are 32 metacharacters such as #$%^&.)

Using one Alt+ 256 character increases entropy to the theoretical maximum of 8 bits of entropy per character. However, not all software will allow an ALT character, so this is more theoretical than useful.

You don't have to employ equal numbers of symbols from each character set to gain the increased entropy. Just one per set will increase the universe of possibilities.

minimum passphrase length

OK, so now how many bits should a very robust passphrase be? Let's survey some expert opinions.

(FYI, the NSA recommends 128 bit for Secret and 256 bit for Top Secret.)

Today's 80 bit random/96 bit nonrandom key is only just adequate. 96 bit random/115 bit nonrandom, IMO, begins decent long-term protection (up to year 2018).

128 bit random/154 bit nonrandom is currently the maximum for many software, such as Hushmail's 128 bit.
— www. diceware.com

Some basic benchmarks have been established for password bit-strength to protect against certain types of password cracking. In 1999, an Electronic Frontier Foundation project broke 56-bit DES encryption in less than a day using specially designed hardware.[7] In 2002, distributed.net cracked a 64-bit key in 4 years, 9 months, and 23 days.[8] Currently, distributed.net estimates that cracking a 72-bit key using current hardware will take about 403,784.9 days or 1,105.5 years.[9]

No currently expected increase in computer power will be sufficient to break 128-bit or 256-bit encryption using random keys via a brute-force attack. Due to currently understood limitations from fundamental physics, there is no expectation that any digital computer (or combination) will be capable of breaking 128-bit or 256-bit encryption via a brute-force attack.[10][citation needed] Whether or not quantum computers will be able to do so in practice is still unknown, though theoretical analysis suggests such possibilities.[citation needed]

As a result, there can be no exact answer to the password strength required to resist brute force attack in practice. **NIST recommends 80-bits for the most secure passwords,** which can nearly be achieved with a 95-character choice (e.g., the original ASCII character set) with a 12-character **random** password (12 x 6.5 bits = 78).

In their February 1996 report, "Minimal Key Lengths for Symmetric Ciphers to Provide Adequate Commercial Security" a group of cryptography and computer security experts — Matt Blaze, Whitfield Diffie, Ronald Rivest, Bruce Schneier, Tsutomo Shimomura, Eric Thompson, and Michael Weiner — stated:

"To provide adequate protection against the most serious threats... **keys used to protect data today should be at least 75 bits long.** To protect information adequately for the next 20 years ... keys in newly-deployed systems should be at least 90 bits long."
— http://en.wikipedia.org/wiki/Password_strength

Here is a very detailed synopsis by ECRYPT, a network of excellence in cryptology:

1   Attacks in "real-time" by individuals
Only acceptable for authentication tag size   32 bits

2   Very short-term protection against small organizations
Should not be used for confidentiality in new systems   64 bits

3   Short-term protection against medium organizations,
medium-term protection against small organizations   72 bits

4   Very short-term protection against agencies,
long-term protection against small organizations
Smallest general-purpose level,
protection from 2009 to 2011   **80 bits**

5   Legacy standard level protection
from 2009 to 2018   *96 bits*

6   Medium-term protection
protection from 2009 to 2028   *112 bits*

7   Long-term protection
Generic application-independent recommendation,
protection from 2009 to 2038   *128 bits*

8   "Foreseeable future"
Good protection against quantum computers   *256 bits*

The 32 and 64-bit levels should not be used for confidentiality protection; 32-bit keys offer no confidentiality at all relative to any attacker, and 64-bit offers only very poor protection. Nevertheless, there are applications where these levels may be necessary if security is to be provided at all, e.g. for integrity tags.

*While both 80 and 128-bit keys provide sufficient security against brute force key-search attacks (on symmetric primitives) by the most reasonable adversaries, it should be noted that 80 bits would be practically breakable and 128 bits might correspond to an effective 80-bit level, **if one considers attack models based on pre-computation and large amounts of available storage.** As a simple rule of thumb, one may choose to double the key size to mitigate threats from such attacks.*

—www.ecrypt.eu.org/ecrypt1/documents/D.SPA.28-1.1.pdf
Yearly Report on Algorithms and Keysizes (2007-2008),
D.SPA.28 Rev. 1.1, IST-2002-507932 ECRYPT, 07/2008.

comments from www.diceware.com

Diceware is the use of 7,776 random words and strings chosen from its dictionary by dice throwing. (Each word averages 13 bits of entropy, and are strung together.) While I find the resulting passphrases difficult to memorize, their security protocol/bit length commentary is very helpful to keep in mind. *I.e.*, what point is there in a robust 128 bit random passphrase if your computer is easily accessible in an unlocked office for a keylogger hack?

Another way to think about passphrase length is to consider what security precautions you take to physically protect your computer and data. Here is a list of possible passphrase lengths and commensurate security precautions. The list of precautions is not intended to be complete. I am not trying to discourage anyone from using longer passphrases if they feel up to it, **but the added strength without comparable physical security for your computer is of limited value.**

52 bits
Four diceware words are breakable with a hundred or so PCs.

* You would be content to keep paper copies of the encrypted documents in an ordinary desk or filing cabinet in an un-secured office.

65 bits
Five diceware words are only breakable by an organization with a large budget.

* You need or want strong security, but take no special precautions to protect your computer from unauthorized physical access, beyond locking the front door of your house or office.

78 bits
Six diceware words appear unbreakable for the near future, but may be within the range of large organizations by around 2014.

* Your computer is protected from unauthorized access at all times when not in your personal possession by being locked in a room or cabinet in a building where access is controlled 24 hours a day or that is protected by a high quality alarm service.

* Routine cleaning and building maintenance people do not have physical access to your computer when you are not present.

* You regularly use an up-to-date anti-virus program purchased off the floor at a computer store.

* You have verified the signatures on your copy of PGP or your installed Hushmail 2 client.

* You never run unverified downloaded software, e-mail attachments or unsolicited disks received through the mail on your computer.

Note: However I do encourage using six or more words on systems that use the passphrase directly to form a transmission key. Such systems include Hushmail, disk encryption (e.g. Apple's FileVault), Ciphersaber, and WiFi's WPA.

90 bits
Seven diceware words and longer are unbreakable with any known technology, but may be within the range of large organizations by around 2030.

* You take all the steps listed under 6 words above, and:
* Your computer is kept in a safe or vault at all times when it is not in sight of you or someone you trust.
* Your computer was purchased off the floor at a randomly selected computer store.
* All the software used on your computer was distributed with a strong, independently verified electronic signature that you checked, or was purchased off the floor in a randomly selected computer store
* Your computer has never been repaired or upgraded by anyone you do not trust completely.
* All disks and tapes used with your computer are either kept in a safe or physically destroyed.
* You take precautions against audio and video surveillance when entering passphrases.
* You change your PGP encryption key regularly (at least once a year).
* You have taken precautions against TEMPEST attacks. See the chapter "Commonsense and Cryptography," in Internet Secrets, from IDG Books Worldwide, for a discussion of what this involves.

Of course, if you are worried about an organization that can break a seven word passphrase in order to read your e-mail, there are a number of other issues you should be concerned with — such as how well you pay the team of armed guards that are protecting your computer 24 hours a day.

103 bits
Eight diceware words should be completely secure through 2050.

OK, so how many bits should my passphrase be?

The general consensus is that 80 bit random/96 bit nonrandom bits is today's absolute minimum. (Nonrandom strings require at least a 20% length increase, if not doubling.)

One could only begin to relax at 96 bit random/115 bit nonrandom, and then only until about the year 2018.

passphrase strength checkers
Various webtools can gauge strength, but I prefer to know the bits of entropy/character and multiply by character length.

> www.securitystats.com/tools/password.php
> www.passwordmeter.com/
> http://passwordstrength.net/
> http://rumkin.com/tools/password/passchk.php
> www.geekwisdom.com/dyn/passwdmeter

best tip: turn sentence into passphrase
The basis should be easily recalled, and then add a simple algorithm to scramble it a bit. Think of a punchline, such as:

> I was sitting in this refrigerator, minding my own business!

It's got upper and lower, ASCII characters (the , and ! and many spaces), but no numerals. Now, you could replace every "s" with a "5" and every "e" with a "3", which would make:

> I wa5 5itting in thi5 r3frig3rator, minding my own bu5in355!

Although it dosn't have much natural entropy (randomness), such is somewhat compensated by its *60* character length.

creating more entropy
"This little piggy went to market" could be "tlpWENT2m". It's easy to remember, yet contains good randomness. Here's another example, with layers of added complexity:

My son Aiden is three years old	msaityo
My SoN Ayd3N is 3 yeeRs old	MsAy3yo
MySoN 8N i$ 3 yeeR$ old	M$8ni3y0

The truncated versions are only 8 characters, but M$8ni3y0 does offer decent entropy. Either choose a longer sentence source, or use multiple sources and string them together.

(Some users develop mnemonic phrases and use them to generate high entropy (more or less, random) passwords which are nevertheless relatively easy for the user to remember. For instance, the first letter of each word in a memorable phrase.)

Tp4tci2s4U2g! — built from a phrase that a user can memorize: "The password for (4) this computer is too (2) strong for you to (4U2) guess!" — mixes types of character. If the phrase is not 'well-known' (e.g., published in a quotation compendium), this password should have high entropy for an attacker, and be easier to remember than many passwords.

But note carefully that, since these example passwords have been published in this Wikipedia article, they should never be used as real passwords.

— wikipedia

That Wikipedia example is 13 characters from a 94-character set. It has fair (and only that) entropy, mathematically, at 85 bits (13 * 6.555). Actual entropy of anything memorizable cannot reach the ideal of 6.555 bits/character, but this must come pretty close. (More on bit length and entropy later.)

recite poetry for good sentence sources

Poetry (and songs) has an easily memorized cadence. Never use poem or song that you are known to recite. Much of Shakespeare feels like poetry on the tongue:

To be, or not to be, that is the question. Whether tis nobler to suffer...

The first letters of each word do add up: TbontbtitqWtnts

Now, it needs some complexity with numerals and metacharacters: 2b0n2bt1tqWtnt$

These 15 characters from the 94-character universe work out to a total entropy of 98 bits — which is pretty strong even accounting for imperfect randomness.

German poetry is even better!

Proper nouns in German are capitalized, which naturally provides strong case-sensitive strings. A poem by Georg Heym:

Schon haengen die Lampions wie bunte Trauben
An langen Schnueren ueber kleinen Beeten
Den gruenen Zaeunen, und von den Staketen
Der hohen Bohnen leuchtend in die Lauben

Each line can be harvested for their first letters:

ShdLwbT
AlSukB
DgZuvdS
DhBlidL

All four together makes:

ShdLwbTAlSukBDgZuvdSDhBlidL

That's 153.9 bits of entropy (27 x 5.7 bits). Add a numeral:

ShdLwbTA1SukBDgZuvdSDhB1idL (notice the two "1")

And you've got 160.6 bits of entropy (27 x 5.95 bits).
Now, substitute a metacharacter:

$hdLwbTA1$ukBDgZuvd$DhB1idL (notice the three "$")

And you're now up to 176.9 bits (27 x 6.55 bits). Anything over 128 bits is probably overkill and thus unnecessary. Most SSL software that you'd be entering passphrases in (*e.g.*, Hushmail) max out at 128 bits, anyway. Meaning, for passphrases larger that than, it would be mathematically easier to attempt to crack the software's algorithm vs. your 128+ bit passphrase. That's a very uncommon scenario because most passphrases never approach a software's maximum encryption. Passphrases are usually very easily guessable, and have puny entropy.

256 bits is considered safe for the "foreseeable future" against even quantum computers.

So, if 128+ bits of entropy is currently a waste, then we can achieve lesser (though ample) entropy with less intricate hashing. We can eliminate numerals altogether.

If the software allows spaces, add them because it not only increases entropy, but it'd be easier to recall and type out the four stanzas that way:

ShdLwbT AlSukB DgZuvdS DhBlidL

These three spaces increase total character length to 30, and bump up keyspace per character from 52 to 84 because the space key is a metacharacter (i.e., from 5.7 bits to 6.39 bits of entropy). Total entropy is 191.7 bits, a whopper. Since it is much more than you need, just use the first three lines:

ShdLwbT AlSukB DgZuvdS

This 140.6 bit passphrase (22 x 6.39 bits) is an excellent balance between entropy and user convenience.

Latin phrases also work great

Siquis in hoc artem populo non novit amandi . . .
— Ovid

So, you can't remember German poems or Latin phrases?

OK, sign of the times, but there's one last hope for you: *popular songs*. Words put to music are easily recalled. *"Who ya gonna call? Ghost Busters!"* would produce:

Wygc?GB!

Here's the refrain from "Cold":

Cold, been excommunicated cos I'm cold
My temperature's been rated and I'm cold
Bring to me my big old sweater
Nothing more will make me better

Capitalize the first word of each line, and use spaces:

Cbeclc Mtbralc Btmmbos Nmwmmb

That's 29 characters times 6.39 bits of entropy each, for 185.3 bits of total entropy.

Even just the first two lines with 14 total characters provide 89 bits of entropy, which is still a very strong passphrase and good enough for most people. To be on the safe side, I'd use three lines and not just two — giving in this 22 character example 141.6 bits. It's not much trouble to type in the third line, and it provides entropy in excess of 128 bits. This will protect you until the year 2038 at current projections.

Make sure, however, that you don't pick a song which everyone knows you sing at Kareoke.

Also, if you are of extreme interest to somebody, and if they suspect that you're using song lyrics for passphrase character strings, it is not an infeasible operation to catalog every song in your computer and CD collection for probabilities. (Don't forget that Windows Media Player files will inform forensic investigators which songs you listen to most often. *Thanks, Bill!*) Assume you had 1000 albums of music, with an average of 15 songs each, and that each song has 40 character string blocks from lyric word first letters. That's a "dictionary" of 600,000 character blocks, which is child's play for any PC. Assuming a test speed of only 900 tries/second of the Password Recovery Toolkit program against your PGP file, and the sample passphrase of:

Cbeclc Mtbralc Btmmbos Nmwmmb

could be hacked between 5.5 and 11 . . . minutes. Not years or months, but *minutes*.

This is why it's vital that you never share any clues to anyone about how you construct your passphrases. (On this note, I would not highlight this part in your book. Maybe you should well hide this book after you've read it!)

Finally, to thwart such attacks, it's a simple matter to add a prefix or suffix to your song passphrase. Choose something that is memorable only to you, such as a funny one-liner that you often chuckle about to yourself. Joke punch lines work well for this, such as "*Yeah, but you should have seen the other guy!*" Add that to your song for:

Cbeclc Mtbralc Ybyshstog!

If you have enough of these one-liners going through your head, you can string two or three together for a sufficiently strong passphrase, and nothing in your computer will seed a dictionary attack against you.

entering your passphrase

Many passphrase entry windows will hide your characters with a ************ or XXXXXXXXXX or even nothing at all. That makes entering these characters strings more difficult (though it does become easier with practice). You could type them in the clear in a temporary Notepad window, then copy/paste into the passphrase window. Do remember, however, that your copied/pasted passphrase will stay in the RAM buffer (even during Standby mode) until you fill it with something else. (Not to make you paranoid, but it wouldn't surprise me if Windows keeps a record of everything once stored in its RAM buffer. That would seem a prime tactic from the Big Brother statists of Redmond.)

a tip for creating unique logons per website

One of the most interesting approaches for websites is to come up with sort of a personal hash of the domain name of the website.

What I'm thinking of is imagine a simple algorithm that you can memorize which is a way of, like, mutating the domain where you're visiting in a way that is unique to you. For example, take every other letter from the domain name, or every third letter. Come up with a rule for capitalizing them. Swap some letters around. You know, just sort of make up your own algorithm - and you don't share with anybody else, and don't use anything that I've talked about on the show, of course - and use that to create a password. The beauty is that it'll be unique, it'll not be in a dictionary - unless you don't have a very good algorithm. But once you know what it is, you don't have to remember the password any longer because you can always regenerate it. And wherever you are, you can regenerate it. I mean, it might take a little bit of pencil-and-paper work, depending upon - or maybe it's something that you can sort of type in as you look at the domain name. So, like, you know, reverse the order of certain groups of letters. Change the capitalization in a special way. Maybe take the name and, like, mix in the year of your birth, alternating that with the letters. I mean, you can get creative. But the beauty is, it's your own - basically it's your own password-hashing algorithm that takes the domain, mixes something that's unique to you in, and maybe tack on a couple gibberish characters that that part you don't ever change, but the gibberish is completely made up, you know...

So if I'm on nytimes.com, I could, say, intermix my year of birth at every other letter, and then uppercase every third letter, so I'd have n1Y9 and so forth, and that would not be a guessable password.

— www.grc.com/SecurityNow.htm#4

using the keyboard as a crypto device

Another way to create pseudo-random character strings is to purposely *mistype* the phrase. We've all done it by accident; beginning on the wrong row. This can create strong roots:

	we'reinthemoney
(up one, right one)	34]549j6u4k0j47
(up one, left one)	23[438h5y3j9h36
(down one, right one)	sdfdk gnd l dh

This will work only if you can full-finger type without looking at the keys or screen. Just reposition your fingertips and imagine that you're typing the phrase. (Phrases with spaces don't work well, as the thumbs don't nicely type letters.)

If someone were trying to crack it, you know, and they thought this might be what you were doing, they might look at the keyboard and try to figure out what way you went. But you could do other things like, you know, go left, up left for the first character, up right for the second one, down left, I mean you could get some - you know, again, that's sort of a variation on a personal algorithm that is very unlikely to be cracked.
    — www.grc.com/SecurityNow.htm#4

While I would *not* use keyboard crypto as my only method, it does have its usefulness as a prefix or suffix with other methods to easily increase passphrase length.

Diceware Passphrase   **www.diceware.com**
The complete list contains 7776 short English words, abbreviations and easy-to-remember character strings. The average length of each word is about 4.2 characters. The biggest words are six characters long.

I mention Diceware out of thoroughness, but I am still convinced that first-letter character strings from song lyrics, poems, jokes, etc. are much more easily remembered, and more robust. (Diceware's entropy is just 3.1 bits/character.)

PASSPHRASE GENERATORS

If you need a long string of nearly perfectly random characters, then there are many free sites for you. This is the best way to create ideal entropic passphrases, and to replace them easily. At www.grc.com is a free, brilliant passphrase generator (up to 64 characters) employing all ASCII characters. While as mathematically random as can artificially be:

IjMNI7c1iA0LW4vii654R3MwbECsdQQQEflTNr6sg7dl79Wjt2K495cX

. . . however, this gibberish cannot be remembered, obviously.

storing your list of perfect entropy passphrases

Your best bet is to store such within a symmetric encrypted PGP file and retrieve the inner passphrases only when you need them (such as to open a TrueCrypt volume, which deserves such a strong passphrase).

Or, they should be stored in an encrypted passphrase manager, and its master passphrase (which only has to be entered at the beginning of each session) should be a *very* strong one and never written down. String two of the previous types of examples together, for instance:

M$8ni3y0 + Tp4tci2s4U2g!

That 24-character random passphrase has *157* bits of entropy! It cannot be guessed, and no brute force attack could succeed. This is a viable example of what kind of strong passphrase should protect all the rest in an encrypted passphrase manager.

Steve Gibson's GRC www.grc.com/passwords.htm

While there are other random passphrase generators, they are *not* SSL secure, meaning they are transmitted to your computer in the clear. No need to chance this, or poor algorithms! Truly, Steve Gibson's free service is the best in every way.

Transmitted by SSL, Steve calls it a "Rijndael (AES) block encryption of never-repeating counter values in CBC mode."

The result of the combination of the 256-bit Rijndael/AES secret key, the unknowable (therefore secret) present value of the 128-bit monotonically incrementing counter, and the 128-bit secret Initialization Vector (IV) is 512-bits of secret data providing extremely high security for the generation of this page's "perfect passwords". No one is going to figure out what passwords you have just received.

How much security do 512 binary bits provide? Well, 2^{512} (2 raised to the power of 512) is the total number of possible combinations of those 512 binary bits — every single bit of which actively participates in determining this page's successive password sequence. 2^{512} is approximately equal to: $1.34078079 \times 10^{154}$, which is this rather amazing number:

13, 407, 807, 929, 942, 597, 099, 574, 024, 998, 205, 846, 127, 479, 365, 820, 592, 393, 377, 723, 561, 443, 721, 764, 030, 073, 546, 976, 801, 874, 298, 166, 903, 427, 690, 031, 858, 186, 486, 050, 853, 753, 882, 811, 946, 569, 946, 433, 649, 060, 084, 096

As far as the crypto experts know, the only workable "attack" on the Rijndael (AES) cipher lying at the heart of this system is "brute force" — which means trying each one of those many combinations of 512 bits. In other words, the passwords being generated by GRC's server and presented for your exclusive use [here], are safe.

for WEP routers
64 random hexadecimal characters (0-9 and A-F):
Each of the 64 hexadecimal characters encodes 4 bits of binary data, so the entire 64 characters is equivalent to 256 binary bits — which is the actual binary key length used by the WiFi WPA pre-shared key (PSK).

WEP key strength (key length) is sometimes confusing because, although there are only two widely accepted standard lengths, 40-bit and 104-bit, those lengths are sometimes confused by adding the 24-bit IV (initialization vector) counter to the length, resulting in 64-bit and 128-bit total key lengths.

However, the user only ever specifies a key of either 40 or 104 binary bits. **Since WEP keys should always be specified in their hexadecimal form to guarantee device interaction,** *and since each hex digit represents 4 binary bits of the key, 40 and 104 bit keys are represented by 10 and 26 hex digits respectively.* **So you may simply snip off whatever length of random hex characters you require for your system's WEP key.**

Note that if all of your equipment supports the use of the new longer 256/232 bit WEP keys, you would use 232/4 or 58 hexadecimal characters for your pre-shared key.

for WPA routers
63 random printable ASCII characters:
The more "standard" means for specifying the 256-bits of WPA keying material is for the user to specify a string of up to 63 printable ASCII characters. This string is then "hashed" along with the network's SSID designation to form a cryptographically strong 256-bit result which is then used by all devices within the WPA-secured WiFi network. (The ASCII character set was updated to remove SPACE characters since a number of WPA devices were not handling spaces as they should.)

for WPA routers with noncompliant devices
63 random alpha-numeric characters (a-z, A-Z, 0-9):
If some device was not following the WiFi Alliance WPA specification by not hashing the entire printable ASCII character set correctly, it would end up with a different 256-bit hash result than devices that correctly obeyed the specification. It would then be unable to connect to any network that uses the full range of printable ASCII characters.

Since we have heard unconfirmed anecdotal reports of such non-compliant WPA devices (and since you might have one), this page also offers "junior" WPA password strings using only the "easy" ASCII characters which even any non-fully-specification-compliant device would have to be able to properly handle. If you find that using the full random ASCII character set within your WPA-PSK protected WiFi network causes one of your devices to be unable to connect to your WPA protected access point, you can downgrade your WPA network to "easy ASCII" by using one of these easy keys.

And don't worry for a moment about using an easy ASCII key. If you still use a full-length 63 character key, your entire network will still be EXTREMELY secure.

one-time passphrases

One-time passwords (S/key is the most commonly used) are just that. They can be used only once. This requires carrying a list of passwords or having a special password calculator or SecureCard, but can be a very reliable method of password security.

As long as the passphrase is random and longer than the message, it is unbreakable through cryptographic means. You could find a trusted generator of one-time pads, or string together many of GRC's outputs. I heard of a guy (later with the NSA) who generated 700meg one-time pad CDs. Very cool.

USING & PROTECTING PASSPHRASES

test your passphrase for strength and usage
run it past a password checker, or calculate it yourself
This will calculate relative entropy for you, and judge it for strength. You can figure this out yourself pretty easily, though. Microsoft has one; it's cheesy and untrustworthy.

will the system accept your passphrase?
Learn its protocols first, such as length, and are spaces and metacharacters allowed? Some systems are shockingly limited to <10 characters, and all lower case.

tips on protecting your strong passphrases
don't reveal them to others, unless *absolutely* necessary
Even with trusted friends and family, ask them to please turn away while you enter a passphrase.
Extreme tip: have them leave the room first.

never divulge *how* you create your own passphrases
Your personal algorithm will greatly help attackers:

> Whenever it can, AccessData collects whatever personal information it can on the subject before beginning. **If it can see other passwords, it can make guesses about what types of passwords the subject uses.** How big a root is used? What kind of root? Does he put appendages at the end or the beginning? Does he use substitutions? ZIP codes are common appendages, so those go into the file. So do addresses, names from the address book, other passwords and any other personal information. This data ups PRTK's success rate a bit, but more importantly **it reduces the time from weeks to days or even hours.**
> — *Secure Passwords Keep You Safer,*
>   Bruce Schneier, January 15, 2007

protect your recorded passphrases
I disagree with security expert Bruce Schneier only on one major point: writing down your passphrases. Yes, people do default to overly simplistic passphrases from memory (which

Schneier claims is less secure than a piece of paper in their wallet). But, people do also lose their wallets often.

Strong passphrases are more difficult to remember, especially if you have (as you should) many of them. Probably the best solution is an encrypted password manager, which I will discuss shortly.

never provide a passphrase over email

Unless 128-bit or better encrypted, you should consider email about as secure as a postcard. This plaintext is easily intercepted in transit. (Every U.S. email goes through at least one government node. The Internet, if you'll recall, *began* as an ARPA network between defense contractors.)

Any company which alleges by email to require your passphrase to "update your account" is "phishing" for private info. Many people have lost their entire savings that way. Warn any elderly friends and family about this scam, as they are the most trusting yet least sophisticated on the Net.

I would not even trust public-key encryption to send an important passphrase, because that security is only as strong as the *recipient*'s passphrase.

change your passphrases regularly and often

This is vital for <8-character passwords, which are not safe for longer than a week. Some difficult-to-guess 14+ character with good entropy would be safe for at least a year.

When to Change Your Password

*Perhaps just as important as how to choose a new password is when to do it. New passwords are most easily remembered if you start using them immediately, and use them often. Don't change your password at the end of the day, the end of the week, or before a holiday. **Instead, change your password in the morning, at the start of the week. Your mind will be clearer, and frequent use of the new password will reinforce your memory.***

— http://psynch.com/docs/choosing-good-passwords.html

A good rule of thumb is to change passwords as close to the actual account as possible. For example, if it's an ISP account, don't telnet through three other machines to change that password. If it's an office computer, users should be on that computer and not on a co-worker's when changing it.

Don't let anybody watch while typing the old and new passwords. If at all possible, the password should be changed over a secure connection like a secure shell (SSH).
— http://psynch.com/docs/choosing-good-passwords.html

never enter passphrases on others' computers

When a user enters his/her password, it might be intercepted at his/her workstation (by a keyboard monitor program), on the network (by a packet sniffer program), or on the server he is accessing (by a Trojan Horse program).

If an operating system without security features is used (such as DOS, Windows or MacOS), then an intruder only needs temporary physical access to the console to insert a keyboard monitor program. If the workstation is not physically secured, then an intruder can reboot even a secure operating system, restart the workstation from his own media, and insert the offending program.
— http://psynch.com/docs/choosing-good-passwords.html

Public computers are everywhere: Internet cafés, computer labs, shared systems, kiosk systems, conferences, and airport lounges. (They include computers of friends and family.)

If you were known to use a particular computer not your own, it would easy for the owner (or a third party) to install a keylogger without your knowledge. (A hardware keylogger will defeat SSH proxies.)

If you've recently switched from public computers to solely your own, then change all your online passphrases.

use unique passphrases for *each* account

This is especially vital if you have multiple email accounts through any one provider. An encrypted password manager will really help here.

never use the "remember my password" function

That is for dummies. All one would have to do is boot up your computer, and then all your software and accounts would think you're the owner because of the cookies and IP address.

Also, avoid all online storage of passphrases.

be careful where you allow passphrase show keystrokes

If an extremely security-minded target using very long/wide/deep passphrase were know to regularly get online at a local cybercafe, and prefer a particular table, his uncrackable passphrase could be circumvented. Merely install a prefocused mini-cam to record his keystrokes over his paranoid shoulder.

laptop theft at cybercafes is becoming more common

Imagine some Condition White (look it up) Yuppie sipping a latté while working on his MacBook Pro. He is prime meat for a grab-and-dash attack. By the time he fumbled for his Blackberry to call 9-1-1, the thief would be around the corner.

be very wary of passphrase reminder questions

The answer to the secret question is much easier to guess than a good password, and the information is much more public. I'll bet my childhood address is in some database somewhere. And worse, everybody seems to use the same series of secret questions.

The result is that the normal security protocol (passwords) falls back to a much less secure protocol (secret questions). The security of the entire system suffers.

— *Secret Questions Blow a Hole in Security,*
Bruce Schneier

Using your dog's name (which was Paris Hilton's mistake) can be easily foiled by another through either knowing your dog's name or running a name dictionary attack.

For the answer to a secret question (if such must be provided for registration) is to simply use the same robust passphrase. Granted, this won't give you any backup if you forget, but that's the price of security.

who can see/deliver your passphrase?

The other thing that we got many questions about is, what about the password managers that are built into some web browsers? Because clearly, you know, I guess the Mozilla Firefox browser has a built-in password management facility. And I'm a little nervous about that only because it happens to be built into a communicating application. The idea of a third-party password manager makes me feel safer than a password manager built into a browser.

— Bruce Schneier

An important factor to hacking is the encryption program's key-escrow system.

bits of your passphrase may be on your HD

Even so, none of this might actually matter. AccessData sells another program, Forensic Toolkit,
http://www.accessdata.com/products/ftk/

that, among other things, scans a hard drive for every printable character string. It looks in documents, in the Registry, in e-mail, in swap files, in deleted space on the hard drive ... everywhere. And it creates a dictionary from that, and feeds it into PRTK.

And PRTK breaks more than 50 percent of passwords from this dictionary alone.

What's happening is that the Windows operating system's memory management leaves data all over the place in the normal course of operations. You'll type your password into a program, and it gets stored in memory somewhere. Windows swaps the page out to disk, and it becomes the tail end of some file. It gets moved to some far out portion of your hard drive, and there it'll sit forever. Linux and Mac OS aren't any better in this regard [if swap/paging file is not turned off].

I should point out that none of this has anything to do with the encryption algorithm or the key length. A weak 40-bit algorithm doesn't make this attack easier, and a strong 256-bit algorithm doesn't make it harder. These attacks simulate the process of the user entering the password into the computer, so the size of the resultant key is never an issue.

— *Secure Passwords Keep You Safer,*
    Bruce Schneier, January 15, 2007

Yet another compelling reason to install extra RAM, and then disable and shred swap/paging files. Then, shred all unused disk space and file cluster tips, defrag, and shred again.

Quite frankly, I'd go to Puppy Linux for all your online needs, and once comfortable with Puppy (run from a live CD) then DBAN your entire HD and reinstall Windows. (Be sure to re-disable the swap/paging file "feature" after reinstallation.)

If Windows is *not* a home computer surveillance tool, then any difference is indistinguishable.

OS and application dependencies
Unix and Linux users beware!
Many Unix-based systems allow access to the file containing the encrypted passwords (/etc/password) and limit you to 8 character passwords.

This is a serious security flaw, since it allows an attacker to test millions of trial passwords in a matter of minutes. Unfortunately, many Unix programs assume this approach and it is therefore widespread. (See The Ambitious Amateur vs. crypt(3) by Kurt Hockenbury. Since this paper was written, in 1997, computers have become much more powerful, increasing the threat.)

If you have to use such systems, your sole defense is to pick a good password. Only a completely random string of 8 characters, preferably chosen from all possible printable characters, provides strong protection against attacks, and even that may be vulnerable to an attacker with a very large budget. In particular, Unix "root" passwords should always be constructed in this way! You can use dice to select a string of 8 random characters using the tables below. If you install Unix systems frequently, we suggest you learn our method for creating a strong password using only coins and a computer keyboard. You might also consider our password generating applet, PassGen2. Select the "MMMMMMMM" template from the pull down list.

If security is important, ask your systems administrator to switch to more modem login password system that allows longer passwords and shadows the password file. Even better is a safer authentication method like Stanford University's Secure Remote Password Protocol SRP. If you are accessing a Unix or Linux system remotely, always use SSH.

— www.searchlores.org/password.htm

some software is easier to crack
Software varies widely in how easy it is to run passphrase attacks on.

So the security of your password depends on two things: any details of the software that slow down password guessing, and in what order programs like PRTK guess different passwords.

Some software includes routines deliberately designed to slow down password guessing. Good encryption software doesn't use your password as the encryption key; there's a process that converts your password into the encryption key. And the software can make this process as slow as it wants.

The results are all over the map. Microsoft Office, for example, has a simple password-to-key conversion, so PRTK can test 350,000 Microsoft Word passwords per second on a 3-GHz Pentium 4, which is a reasonably current benchmark computer. WinZip used to be even worse — well over a million guesses per second for version 7.0 — but with version 9.0, the cryptosystem's ramp-up function has been substantially increased: PRTK can only test 900 passwords per second. PGP also makes things deliberately hard for programs like PRTK, also only allowing about 900 guesses per second.

When attacking programs with deliberately slow ramp-ups, it's important to make every guess count. A simple six-character lowercase exhaustive character attack, "aaaaaa" through "zzzzzz," has more than 308 million combinations. And it's generally unproductive, because the program spends most of its time testing improbable passwords like "pqzrwj."

— *Secure Passwords Keep You Safer*,
    Bruce Schneier, January 15, 2007

passphrase wallets and vaults

And then the other Palm sits right by my side. And again, I don't dock it, and it does not touch my computers because I don't want anything to crawl into it. But that's sort of my offline reminder of which one of my collection of passwords I used on a particular day, you know, whatever mood I was in.

— Steve Gibson, www.grc.com

A simple solution is to create a simple .txt Notepad file with all your passphrases, and then PGP it with a fat single key. Open it up, and copy/paste where needed.

Password Safe

Password Safe allows you to manage your old passwords and to easily and quickly generate, store, organize, retrieve, and use complex new passwords, using password policies that you control. Once stored, your user names and passwords are just a few clicks away.

Using Password Safe you can organize your passwords using your own customizable references — for example, by user ID, category, web site, or location. You can choose to

store all your passwords in a single encrypted master password list (an encrypted password database), or use multiple databases to further organize your passwords (work and home, for example). And with its intuitive interface you will be up and running in minutes.
    — http://passwordsafe.sourceforge.net/index.shtml

This is a free and open-source software. (PRTK can test only 900 Password Safe 3.0 passwords per second, which is very good slowness.) Bruce Schneier recommends it.

PINS   www.mirekw.com

PINs is a free feature-rich Windows program for safe and comfortable storing of any secure information like passwords, accounts, PINs etc. PINs uses a secure 448 bit Blowfish algorithm to ensure the data are not crackable. The password used for securing access to stored data is not saved anywhere.

PINs does not require installation and does not need any special dlls, drivers or system files which can mess up your system. This means that PINs can run directly from floppy - including data files - without installing anything. This is extremely useful if you wish to easily access your data on other computers as well.

PINs is OSI Certified Open Source Software.

Selected features

*   * Secure 448 bit Blowfish encoding.*
*   * Unlimited number of entries and data files.*
*   * A clear tree-like data organization which allows logical grouping of systems and accounts.*
*   * Automated login into Internet services (SuperPaste).*
*   * A powerful random passwords generator.*
*   * Safe files wiping using Gutmann, DoD and custom methods.*
*   * Embedded hyperlinks launching.*
*   * Unlimited in size, multi-line descriptions.*
*   * A flexible data import/export in text format.*
*   * Multiple user accounts on a single PC.*
*   * Accounts sorting using any column as a sort criteria.*
*   * Comfortable accounts adding, editing, and deleting.*
*   * Compatibility with popular clipboard extenders.*
*   * Passwords masking.*

* *Copy logins and passwords to the Windows clipboard.*
* *Find/find next functions.*
* *Expired passwords tracking.*
* *Running from a floppy without saving settings to registry.*
* *Multilingual versions.*
* *Full source code available.*

KEYLOGGER THREATS

Covertly installed keyloggers are increasingly used by governments and other nefarious types, so you Windows sufferers might install some sort of countermeasure, such as:

KeyScrambler
www.qfxsoftware.com

KeyScrambler Personal is a free plug-in for your Web browser that protects your username and password from keyloggers. It defeats keyloggers by encrypting your keystrokes at the keyboard driver level, deep within the operating system. When the encrypted keystrokes reach your browser, KeyScrambler then decrypts them so you see exactly the keys you've typed. Keyloggers can only record the encrypted keys, which are completely indecipherable. Unlike anti-virus and anti-spyware programs that depend on recognition to remove keyloggers that they know about, KeyScrambler will protect you from both known and unknown keyloggers. What's more, KeyScrambler provides protection without getting in your way. You don't have anything to learn about the program and you don't have to do anything differently, but with KeyScrambler your important personal information will be a whole lot safer.

KeyScrambler Professional gives you complete input protection. *Anything* you enter in the Web browser is protected against keyloggers: your login data, your important personal information such as social security number, credit card numbers, search terms and email messages you type.

Whereas KeyScrambler Personal encrypts keystrokes of your username(s) and password(s), KeyScrambler Professional encrypts keystrokes of all your input, be it a credit card number or a whole page of email message you type out on the Internet.

COMPELLED DISCLOSURE

If you look at all the ways security can be compromised, you become discouraged and say "why bother?" I don't think that is good. To me it's just like other skills. You start out basic, and then add more security as you go along. Plug the most obvious holes first. Nothing is ever going to be perfect, but often it does not have to be. It just has to be "good enough". If the NSA is on your case, probably no security will work because "rubber hose cryptography" is just around the corner anyway. By that point you put the computer away and pick up the rifle.
— Paul B., from the FSW Forum

The law is still trying to come to grips with the new and urgent issues related to the Internet and robust encryption. The current battle is the crucial one: the battle for the *metaphor*. Upon the metaphor, all else hangs as if on scaffolding. Presently, these rubrics are floating about in contemplation:

car	(weak Fourth Amendment protection)
language	(strong First and Fifth Amendment protection)
house	(strong Fourth Amendment protection)
safe	(fair Fourth Amendment protection)

My own view is that passphrases not stored in physical form, but contained only within the mind of the user are protected under the Fifth Amendment. Would the last two users of a dying language have to decrypt their conversation if on trial for conspiracy? No. Furthermore, the First Amendment protects works of art so obscure that only the artist understands them, and that seems to protect encrypted speech.

There *is* an individual right to encryption. You have every right (at least for private, noncommercial use) to make your data and traffic nontransparent, just as you are not obliged to live in a glass house to increase the scope of plain view for probable cause. You also not required to provide house keys to the police for them to use in future warrants. Finally, you are not required to structure your private communications to make police eavesdropping easier.

It is difficult to predict how the public and the courts will come to finally view widespread strong encyption. It will boil down to which they fear more — the Terrorist . . . or Big Brother.

COMMON PASSWORDS

Here is a typical list, from www.searchlores.org. Do you recognize any of them in *your* passphrases?

!@#$% !@#$%^ !@#$%^& !@#$%^&* 000000 00000000 0007 007 007007 0246 0249 1022 10sne1 111111 121212 1225 123 123123 1234 12345 123456 1234567 12345678 1234qwer 123abc 123go 1313 131313 13579 14430 1701d 1928 1951 1a2b3c 1p2o3i 1q2w3e 1qw23e 1sanjose 2112 21122112 2222 2welcome 3 369 4 4444 4runner 5 5252 54321 5555 5683 654321 666666 6969 696969 777 7777 80486 8675309 888888 90210 911 92072 99999999 @#$%^& a a12345 a1b2c3 a1b2c3d4 aaa aaaaaa aaron abby abc abc123 abcd abcd1234 abcde abcdef abcdefg abigail about absolut academia access action active acura adam adams adg adidas admin adrian advil aeh aerobics after again aggies aikman airhead airplane alan alaska albany albatross albert alex alex1 alexande alexander alexandr alexis alfred algebra aliases alice alicia aliens alison all allen allison allo alpha alpha1 alphabet alpine always alyssa ama amanda amanda1 amber amelie america america7 amiga amorphous amour amy an analog anchor and anderson andre andrea andrew andromache andy angel angela angela1 angels angie angus animal animals ann anna anne annie answer anthony anthropogenic antonio anvils any anything apache apollo apollo13 apple apple1 apples april archie arctic are aria ariadne ariane ariel arizona around arrow arthur artist as asdf asdfg asdfgh asdfghjk asdfjkl asdfjkl; ashley ask aspen ass asshole asterix at ate ath athena atmosphere attila august austin author avalon avatar away awesome aylmer azerty aztecs azure babies baby babylon5 bacchus bach badboy badger bailey baker balls bamboo banana bananas banane bandit banks barbara barber barbie baritone barnes barney barry basebal baseball basf basil basket basketb basketba bass bassoon bastard batman be beagle beaner beanie bear bears beater beatles beautifu beauty beaver beavis because been beer beethoven before bell belle beloved benjamin bennett benny benoit benson benz beowulf berkeley berliner bernard bernie bertha beryl best better betty beverly bfi bicameral big bigbird bigdog bigfoot bigmac bigman bigred bilbo bill billy bingo binky biology bird bird33 birdie bitch biteme black blackie blaster

blazer blizzard blonde blondie blowfish blowme blue bluebird
bluesky bmw bob bobby bobcat bond007 boner bonjour
bonnie booboo booger boogie bookit boomer booster boots
bootsie boris boss boston both bowling bozo bradley brandi
brandon brandy brasil braves brazil brenda brewster brian
bridge bridges bridget bright bring broadway broncos brooke
brooks brown browns bruce brutus bryant bubba bubba1
bubbles buck buddha buddy buffalo buffy bull bulldog bullet
bullshit bumbling bunny burgess business buster but butch
butler butthead button buttons buy buzz by byteme cactus
caesar caitlin californ call calvin camaro camera campanile
campbell camping can canada canced cancer candy canela
cannon cannonda canon cantor captain cardinal carl carlos
carmen carol carole carolina caroline carolyn carrie carry
carter cascade cascades casey casio casper cassie castle
cat catalog catfish catherine cats cayuga cccccc cedic celica
celine celtics center cerulean cesar cfi cfj cgj challeng
champion champs chance chanel change changeme chaos
chapman charity charles charlie charlie1 charlott charming
charon cheese chelsea cherry cheryl chester chester1 chevy
chevy1 chicago chicken chico chiefs china chip chipper
chiquita chloe chocolat chris chris1 chrissy christ christia
christin christina christine christop christopher christy chuck
chucky church cigar cinder cindi cindy claire clancy clarence
clark class classic classroo claude claudia cleaner cleat
clipper cloclo clover clusters cobra cocacola coco coffee coke
cold coleman colleen college collins colorado coltrane
columbia come commrades compaq compton compute
computer concept condo connect connie conrad control cook
cookie cookies cool coolman cooper copper cornelius corona
corrado corwin cosmos cougar cougars could country
courtney couscous cowboy cowboys cox coyote cracker craig
crapp crawford creation creative creosote cretin cricket crow
cruise crystal cuddles curtis cut cutie cyclone cynthia cyrano
daddy daemon daisy dakota dallas dan dance dancer daniel
danielle danny darren darwin dasha database dave david
david1 davis dawn day daytek dead deadhead dean death
debbie deborah debra december deedee defense defoe
deliver delta deluge demo denali denise dennis denver
depeche derek design desperate detroit deutsch develop
dexter dgj diablo diamond diana diane diaz dickhead did
dieter digger digital digital1 dilbert direct1 director dirk
discovery disney dixie do doc doctor dodger dodgers does

dog dogbert doggie doggy dollars dolphin dolphins dominic domino don don't donald done donkey donna doobie doogie dookie doom doom2 doris dorothy doug dougie douglas down dragon dragon1 dragonfl draw dream dreamer dreams drink drizzt drought drums duck duckie dude duke duncan dundee dustin dusty dwight dylan e-mail each eager eagle eagle1 eagles earl easier easter eat eatme eclipse eddie edges edinburgh edward edwards edwin edwina eeyore egghead eiderdown ; eight eileen einstein elaine electric elephant elizabet elizabeth ellen elliot elsie elvis elwood emerald emily emmitt energy engine engineer enigma enter enterprise entropy enzyme eric ernest ersatz espanol establish estate etoile euclid eugene europe evans evelyn every excalibu except explorer export express extension fail fairway faith falcon family far farmer farming fast felicia felix fender fermat ferrari ferret fgh fiction fidelity find finite fiona fire fireball firebird fireman first fish fish1 fisher fishers　fishing five flakes flamingo flash fletch fletcher flight flip flipper float flores florida flower flowers floyd fluffy fly flyers foobar fool foolproof footbal football for ford foresight forest format forsythe foster found fountain four fourier fox foxtrot fozzie france frances francis francois frank frankie franklin fravia freak1 fred freddy frederic freedom french1 friday friend friends frighten frodo frog frog1 froggy frogs from front242 frosty fubar fucker fuckme fuckoff fuckyou fugazi full fun fungible funny future gabriel gabriell gaby galaxy galileo gambit gandalf garcia garden gardner garfield garlic garnet garrett gary gasman gateway gator gauss gave gemini general genesis genius george georgia gerald german gertrude get ghost giants gibson gilles ginger give gizmo glacier glenn global gloria gnu go goalie goat goblue gocougs godzilla goes gofish goforit going gold golden goldie golf golfer golfing gone gonzales gonzalez goober good goofy gopher gordon gorgeous gorges gosling got gouge grace graham grandma　grant graphic grateful gray graymail green greenday greg gregory gretchen gretzky griffey griffin groovy grover grow grumpy gryphon guess guest guido guinness guitar gumption gunner guntis guru gymnast h2opolo hacker had hal9000 hall hamlet hammer hamster handily hanna hannah hansolo hanson happening happy happy1 happyday harley harmony harold harris harrison harry harvey has hatton have hawaii hawk hawkeye hayes hazel he health heart hearts heather hebrides hector heidi heinlein helen hell hello hello1 help helpme henderson hendrix henry her herbert here herman hermes hernandez hershey hiawatha hibernia hill him his history hobbit hockey hockey1 hola hold holly home homebrew homer honda honda1 honey hoops hootie horizon hornet hornets horse horses horus hot hotdog hotrod house houston how howard hughes hunter hunting hurt huskers hutchins i ib6ub9 icecream iceman idiot if iguana iloveyou image imagine imbroglio impala imperial in include indian indiana indigo info informix ingres inna innocuous insane inside intel intern internet into ireland irene irish irishman ironman is isaac isabelle isis island it italia italy its jack jackie jackson jacob jacqueline jaeger jaguar jake jamaica james james1 jamesbond jan jane janet janice january japan jared jasmin jasmine jason jason1 jasper jazz jean jeanette jeanne jeff jeffrey jenifer jenkins jenni jennifer jenny jenny1 jensen jeremy jerry jesse jessica jessie jester jesus jesus1 jewels jim jimbo jimbob jimmy jixian jkm joan joanna joe joel joey john john316 johnny johnson jojo joker jonathan jones jordan jordan23 jose joseph josh joshua josie joyce jsbach juan judith judy juggle julia julian julie julie1 jump junebug junior jupiter justice justin justin1 karen katherin katherine kathleen kathryn kathy katie kayla keep keith kelly kelly1 kelsey kennedy kenneth kermit kernel kevin kevin1 khan kids killer killme kim kimberly kind kinder king kingdom kingfish kirkland kitten kitten12 kittens kitty kleenex knicks knight knights know koala koko kombat kramer kristen kristi kristin kristy krystal lacrosse laddie ladle lady ladybug lakers lakota lambda lamer lamination larkin larry larry1 larson laser last laugh laura lauren laurie law lawrence lazarus lebesgue ledzep lee legend leland lennon leon leonard leroy leslie lestat let letmein letter lewis library light like lillian lincoln linda lindsay lindsey lionking lisa list little live liverpoo lizard ljf lloyd logan logical lois london long look looney lopez lori lorraine loser louis louise love lovely loveme lover loveyou lucas lucky lucky1 lucy lulu lynn lynne mac macha macintos macintosh mack maddock maddog made madison maggie maggot magic magnum mailer mailman major majordom make malcolm malibu mantra many marc marcel marcus margaret maria mariah marie marilyn marina marine marino mario mariposa mark market markus marlboro marley mars marshal martha martin martin1 martinez marty marvin mary maryjane master master1 masters math matrix matt matthew maurice maveric maverick max maxime maxwell may mayday mazda1 me medical megan melanie melissa mellon memory

COMPUTER DATA

This will be one of the most involved chapters of the book, and certainly the most technical. Do not, however, skip this or stray. Any ignorance here can easily be your Achilles Heel of privacy, but you won't know this until it's too late. Three Commandments cover most of it:

Thou Shalt *Encrypt* Thy Data

Thou Shalt *Shred* Thy Files And Not Merely "Delete" Them

Thou Shalt Back-up Thy Data

DEFINITIONS

Every subset of knowledge requires its own definitions, so here's a basic introduction to what's involved in Windows.

Definitions (from Privacy Software Report)

http://www.privacy-software-review.toptenreviews.com/privacy-software-definitions.html

Application Logs

Under Windows 98, logs are kept on how often you run your programs. This option enables secure destruction of those logs.

Clipboard Data

After you finish using programs or performing copy/paste operations in Windows, all kinds of data can be left behind in the system's memory. Other programs and other users can obtain this data.

Common Dialog History
Common Dialogs are the standard Windows file open/save boxes that most programs use to open and save files. Some versions of Windows maintain hidden history for these boxes.

File Slack Space
A file with "slack space" refers to the unused portion of a cluster on a hard drive that a file is stored on.

Find/Search History
This is a history of files you have searched for using the Windows Find/Search program.

Index.dat Files
There are multiple Index.dat files in different directories that keep a copy of whatever there is in that folder and they continue keeping those records even after you have deleted the contents of those folders. These files can be very hard to find and erase. If you are in Windows, even with "Show hidden files and folders" enabled, these files are not visible and cannot be found if you do a search for these files. The reason that these files are so invisible is that they are not just hidden, they have been designated as "system" files. System files and folders are treated differently in DOS and Windows and are effectively cloaked from casual searches.

Windows Media Player History
If you have Windows Media Player installed on your system, "Most Recently Used" (MRU) lists are stored on your computer. The MRU lists contain links to the last 5 or 10 items that have been used and are found in Windows Media Player application under the OPEN, SAVE AS, and other options.

Windows Media Player Playlists
If you have Windows Media Player installed on your system, playlists that have been created for easier access to your media are stored on your computer.

MS Office
If you have MS-Office the "Most Recently Used" (MRU) lists are stored on your computer. The MRU lists contain links to the last 5 or 10 items that have been used and are found in MS-Office applications under the OPEN, SAVE AS, Insert Picture, and

other options. These lists show the MRU for Word, Excel, Access, Photo Editor and PowerPoint.

Recently Opened Documents List
On your Start Menu, the last 10 or 15 documents you read are stored in the Documents folder.

Recycle Bin
This is a special area on your computer that holds all deleted files until they are permanently deleted from your computer.

Registry Backups
These special directories contain backups of registry entries.

Run History
This is a history of all files you have run using the Run command.

Scan Disk Temporary Files (*.chk)
After one of your programs crashes, or Windows experiences a glitch, errors can accumulate on your drives. One of the common minor errors to appear on most drives over a period of time, is that Windows gets confused about the amount of free space on the drive. To help fix these files, the Windows utility Scan Disk can create a lot of .CHK files at the root directory of drives. These files usually contain junk data and can be erased to help keep drives clean.

Start-Menu Click History
There is a hidden encrypted database in the system registry which remembers a wide range of information about what you have clicked on your start menu. The dates and times of mouse clicks are stored with the names of programs started.

Start-Menu Order History
When items are moved around on your Start Menu, it makes a separate memory of their names and their positions.

Swap Files
A swap (or paging) file is an area on your hard disk used as virtual memory and contains data and information that has been accessed on your hard drive. (Best to have much extra RAM and thus disable the swap file option.)

Temporary Files/Directories
Windows creates temporary files in a folder named "Temp" that stores files used during installation of a program or files used while an application is running.

Deletion Overwrite - Number of Times
This is the number of times the privacy software application will overwrite a particular file on the hard drive. There are many Department of Defense Standards and non-governmental standards in what should be the optimum number of times for overwriting. In most cases, a 1 pass overwrite clears the file, and a 3 pass overwrite sanitizes the file. There is much debate on this issue, with some recommending 7 to 9 passes (or more!) for the complete removal of any file's data.

PROTECTING YOUR DATA

Keeping your stored data secure is *much* easier compared to Internet privacy (especially on PCs vs. Macs and Linux machines). You need two utilities:

robust encryption (with lengthy and complicated passphrase)

comprehensive file shredder (shredding slack/unused space)

Both exist in several excellent forms, and many are even free. I'll cover in their own sections: encryption, and file shredders.

passphrases

This subject deserves and gets its own chapter, but meanwhile here are some basics to keep in mind. The strength of a lock is related to the complexity of its key, and data encryption software is no different. While PGP is a very strong program, what's the point if your passphrase is only your son's birthday? You *must* use passphrases of sufficient:

length (8+, if not 20+ characters)

character dimensionality (not just lower case, but upper case, and numerals, and ASCII characters such as @ #$%^&* and the spacebar)

randomness (such can be computer generated, but is nearly impossible to humanly recall, and requires some sort of encrypted list to copy/paste from)

DATA ENCRYPTION

Encrypted data is data that only you (or your designated) can read. Everything else is in plaintext, which is readable by anyone. Since you can never know what data may be/become incriminating, or who will eventually read it, simply encrypt *all* of it.

file encryption

While it is much easier to protect data with an on-the-fly encrypted volume (acts like a disk drive), file-based encryption programs such as PGP certainly have their uses.

Pretty Good Privacy   http://web.mit.edu/network/pgp.html

PGP is one of the old standards here, and still a great software with Windows and browser plug-ins. For your own files that are not shared, you don't have to use public key encryption. Use versions which generate no Alternate Decryption Key (ADK), such as 6.5.8.

steganography
(research on www.searchlores.org)

This encryption software allows you to hide your private data such as email messages inside files, such as executable, music, and graphics (.jpg, .gif, .tiff, .bmp, etc). The image is still viewable as an image, but it also contains the encrypted version of your secret message. Some products are:

S-Tools
http://members.tripod.com/steganography/stego/s-tools4.html

4t HIT Mail Privacy Lite
http://www.4t-niagara.com/hitmail.html

Camouflage
http://www.camouflage.freeserve.co.uk/

disk encryption

Often, it is infeasible to encrypt/decrypt dozens of common working files. It then makes more sense to encrypt a large portion of your HD or USB drive as a "virtual disk" (which is assigned a drive letter and treated just like a drive). When not open for use ("mounted"), the encrypted portion can be copied and moved about just like a file. Awesome.

There are several excellent disk encryption software for this (PGPDisk and BestCrypt come to mind), but I see no reason to look any further than TrueCrypt.

TrueCrypt   **www.truecrypt.org**
Free open-source (no backdoors!) disk encryption software for Windows Vista/XP/2000, Mac, and Linux (kernel 2.6.5 or later). For Puppy Linux install (with debian files open):

truecrypt-6.1a-ubuntu-x86.tar.gz

Encryption is automatic, on-the-fly and transparent. Creates a virtual encrypted disk within a file and mounts it as a real disk, or it can encrypt an entire hard disk partition or a storage device such as USB flash drive. One of the best computer security products today. *Extremely* well thought out, powerful (AES-256, Serpent, and Twofish), yet easy to use. Steve Gibson raved about it in http://media.GRC.com/sn/SN-041.mp3.

provides two levels of plausible deniability . . .
. . . in case an adversary forces you to reveal the password:

❶ No TrueCrypt volume can be identified as such (volumes cannot be distinguished from random data).

❷ Hidden volume inside a known volume (like as "false bottom" in suitcase).

This second feature is just brilliant. Even if you were somehow forced to open up your known/outer TrueCrypt volume (which British courts can demand), it could *not* be discerned if you had a hidden *inner* volume as well (which contains all the good stuff). There is no way to prove that the unused space contains an inner volume because TrueCrypt always fills the entire outer volume with random data when it formats it. Thus, you could confidently deny any existence of that inner hidden volume. (Naturally, this inner volume should have a radically different passphrase and keyfiles.) Don't shred outer volume slack space, or it could point to the hidden volume.

other great security features of TC

Settings are kept in an .xml file and not the HD's registry, a Traveller Mode exists to use TrueCrypt off CD or USB drive from other machines, up to 64 character passphrases and concurrent use of keyfiles (which hampers keystroke loggers), ability to run apps from a volume, auto dismount during hibernation or screensaving, and transportable volumes across different OS versions. Not even which algorithm (or algorithm chain) used to encrypt the volume can be known because TrueCrypt doesn't store such info. (When you type in your passphrase, it simply runs it past *all* the algorithms.) Also, TrueCrypt does not keep track of when you accessed the volume, or revised internal files. You can back up and restore volume headers. You can even store the volume on an FTP or web server for ultimate back up. TC can be operated in Traveller mode, usable on other computers.

Since 64-bit block algorithms (Blowfish, CAST-128, and Triple DES) are now obsolete, create volumes with a 128-bit-block encryption algorithm (AES, Serpent, Twofish). TrueCrypt 5.0+ won't mount older 64-bit block alogorithms.

A good intro is at: http://en.wikipedia.org/wiki/TrueCrypt
Total newbies should read: http://truecrypt.blogspot.com
A helpful forum is at: http://forums.truecrypt.org

use at least version 4.1 of TrueCrypt

This 25 Nov 2005 version (and all later) use the LRW mode of encryption, vs. the older and less secure CBC mode. (Older TC legacy volumes will still mount from 4.1 or later.)

disable your XP paging (*i.e.,* swap) file!

This will avoid Windows saving portions of your mounted volume in unencrypted form to your hard drive. Windows 2000 users cannot completely disable their paging file, and thus must reconfigure their security settings to clear the paging file automatically during shutdown.

disable Windows hibernation mode!

Hibernation mode writes RAM content onto the HD, whereas Standby does not.

multi-user environment warning

Switching users does not automatically dismount a TC volume, thus other users may access your data.

unencrypted data in RAM buffers (*i.e.*, text copy)

Even when dismounted (forced auto, or not), these buffers will retain what you copied from your previously mounted volume until the computer is turned off. Until then, you can easily open a new Notepad box, type in some jibberish and Control-C that to overwrite the previous buffer.

do not store your TC volume in the TC folder

Since the unmounted (*i.e.*, not yet decrypted) volume is utter random data without any "TrueCrypt" signature, you have plausible deniability that it is even such a volume at all. Therefore, why show your hand by storing it in the TC folder?

naming your TC volumes

An unmounted TC volume appears to consist of nothing more than random data, without any kind of "signature." Free space and data cannot be distinguished; it's all random data from the outside.

Since it is impossible to identify it as a TC volume, you can give it whatever misleading name you wish. Then, give it a false file extension (which TC ignores), such as .raw, .dll, .iso, .img, .rnd, etc. Then, stuff it deep within the bowels of C:\Windows or a software folder to look like a program file.

Do understand that very large volumes (*i.e.*, over 1gig) are much more difficult to mask as .dll, etc. since such files are very rarely that large.

create an outer volume with the hidden volume option

. . . even if you've no current plans to use the hidden portion, because you may need it later and it can only be created at the beginning. Its passphrase should be much different from its parent volume, and with different keyfiles.

which hash algorithm to choose?

From this is derived your new volume's header key. I'd pick either Whirlpool or RIPEMD-160 over SHA-1 (an NSA product which is more vulnerable to future mathematical "collisions").

use the keyfile option in passphrase setup

A keyfile mixes its content with the passphrase. The purpose of using keyfiles is defeat keyloggers and sniffers. While mouse activity can be covertly logged, this is more difficult to accomplish than keystroke logging. Keyfiles also bolster the strength of passphrases.

You could have your keyfile only on removable media, thus making your computer's TC volumes unmountable without the simultaneous possession of the CD or USB drive.

This keyfile can be any number of files (the order submitted during mounting doesn't matter), or even a complete subfolder of files (though files later added to such a folder would prevent volume mounting because the subfolder has changed). (To keep my further discussion simple, I'll refer to keyfiles in the singular, even though you should use more than one.)

Use at least three files (preferably from different directories) of at least 512k in size. (Only the first 1024k of a keyfile is used, for performance issues, so larger files offer no additional security.) Choose files which are "static" in their composition (*i.e.*, they are not routinely modified). Examples include system files of software never to be updated or deleted, or compressed files such as .mp3 song files, .jpg photos, etc. Avoid easily modified files such as .txt, .doc.

TC does not modify keyfile contents, nor can such files betray their use as keyfiles.

If TrueCrypt volumes are to be opened in Traveller mode on other computers from CD or USB drive, make sure that the keyfile is present on such removable media, vs. existing only on the computer which generated the volume. (The original path of the keyfile during setup does *not* have to be used when mounting a volume, as long as the keyfile is identical.)

Tips on keyfiles: have at least dozens of potential keyfiles available on the removable medium, which increases hacking difficulty.

which algorithms to select?

Though I'm hardly any expert, my choices would be (in descending order) of **Serpent** (highest safety factor for all AES finalists, but slower), **Twofish** (uses key-independent S-boxes), and **AES** (Rijndael-256, chosen by the USG for Top Secret encryption); any one of which on its own is sufficient (although TC allows certain combinations of algorithms to be used in cascade).   Bruce Schneier of TwoFish recommends only algorithms using at least 18 passes (called "rounds").

I would avoid Triple-DES (an older and weaker algorithm, and the suspicious product of IBM and NSA), and CAST5 (*i.e.*, CAST-128) which uses small key and block sizes.

Whichever algorithm cascade you choose, TC doesn't store your choice, but runs your passphrase/keyfile(s) past *every* algorithm option in its menu. Very slick.

Never Save History

There is no need for TC to save its own history of when your volumes were mounted and revised. (Windows will kindly do that for you in its prefetch files, which you should shred.)

configure mounting as "removable media"

This prevents Windows from creating unwanted "Recycled" and/or "System Volume Information" folders.

do not use Auto-Mount

. . . else Windows will store on the HD the fact that you have a TC volume, where it is, and (if you allow) a cached passphrase.

avoid caching passphrases

Mount volumes the safe, *olde*-fashioned way! Type it in!

activate Auto-Dismount option

You can configure your laptop to go on Standby whenever the lid is closed, and thus TC to dismount whenever the computer is in Standby. This would be a sound tactic for those often in public environments who may wish to dismount quickly/automatically.

There are other Auto-Dismount options, such as user log-off and launching of screen saver. You can also configure hot keys (*e.g.*, Ctrl+F12) to force dismount all TC volumes.

back up your TC volumes on removable media

You can create volumes of nearly any size, and tailor them for CDs (<700meg), DVDs (<4.7gig), and USB drives (up to 16gig so far). You must use FAT (and not NTFS) during volume creation, and FAT is good only up to 4095meg. A rewritable CD-RW or DVD-RW is a very inexpensive way to continually back up data. (Disks can "tire out" after a dozen or so rewrites, so they aren't as reliable as USB drives. Use high-quality disks such as DVD RAMs and original Taiyo Yuden DVD-Rs.)

You can even keep all volumes on removable media (thus off your HD), making volume ownership very difficult to attribute. (If so, I'd rely only on USB drives and not disks.)

For even more plausible deniability, you could even avoid having TC software on your computer as you open USB TC volumes from Puppy Linux.

create unique passphrases for each volume

There is a natural temptation to create a single handy-sized volume (*i.e.*, for CD, DVD, or USB drive), and then clone it in order to hold different data. Yes, copying a blank volume will save in creation time, but filling them with different data will aid in cryptanalysis because the volumes all share a common key.

backup TC volumes

Beware of unwanted old info on them. Volumes containing different contents but sharing the same passphrase are a real boon to forensic cracking of that passphrase. Never encrypt different data with the same passphrase! Backup volumes should always contain the exact same content as the working volume. Write over with the current volume, and destroy any old CD-Rs.

destroying CDs

First, scratch them up thoroughly on concrete. Then, break them in pieces before discarding in discreet trashcan. This is the next best thing to melting them down.

If you believe that any backup copies have been or may be seized, you should immediately change the passphrase of the master volume. That way, the backup volumes' passphrase can't be used to mount the master volume on your HD.

software not used in startup should be in a TC volume

I would install everything having to do with Internet in a volume, primarily because that softwares' logs avoid being entered on C:\. Your PalmPilot backup software should be in a TC volume. All your web browsers. All your database and word processing. (This means uninstalling these software from

C:\Program Files and reintstalling in a dedicated TC volume solely for Program Files. Remember, volumes appear to your computer as a disk drive in nearly every respect. Hard drive C:\ or a TC volume's J:\ "drive"--the software "doesn't care" where it's installed. Some of these programs are expected by Windows to run at startup, so you will have to experiment here.

I'd have one TC volume for all the data sensitive program files, and other volumes for the data.

backup a copy of your TC volume header file elsewhere

With it, you'll be able to mount your TC volume if the hard drive's header file is ever corrupted or lost. (Restoring a volume header also restores the original passphrase.)

mount your TC volume(s) with the same drive letter(s)

This will help prevent you from confusing data of one volume from another. You could name different volumes with their intended drive letters in mind.

never step away from a *mounted* TC volume

Your mounted TC volume is the most valuable area of your computer. This is especially crucial while using a laptop in public places. Allow a TC volume to be mounted only in your personal presence. Otherwise, always dismount! (It takes a snoop only minutes to copy a volume.) Never run an errand, walk outside, or even make a trip to the bathroom. Do not leave mounted while you sleep. **Never rely on Windows Standby mode. Dismount first.** It takes only seconds to remount a volume, and this security is worth the moderate inconvenience.

don't forget to still encrypt *really* sensitive files with PGP

This will help protect such data in case your TC volume passphrase is ever compromised. Symmetric key is fine.

using the TC hidden volume feature

This can be exposed through Windows if you specify a unique drive letter for it. Let's say that your normal TC volume is mounted as K:\ drive. Then, you occasionally mount that volume's hidden inner volume as M:\. Any file operations to/from M:\ will show up somewhere in Windows, probably even after the most diligent of MRU shredding by multiple programs. (If, for example, you worked on a MSWord file in M:\

with repeated saves, that will be noted as Restore Point links in the hidden folder C:\System Volume Information\.)

While you could deny any existence of a hidden inner volume and "explain" (if forced) that you mistakenly opened your (only) volume as M:\ (instead of K:\), don't expect this to seem credible to an investigator experienced in computer forensics. A hidden inner volume is what he will suspect, and there may be enough evidence of it on your hard drive to create probable cause for a search warrant (thus, forcing you to open it if a court so orders).

"Why not open the hidden inner volume as the normal drive letter of K:\ ?" one might ask. Trouble is, the outer volume must first be mounted, and kept open. Thus, the drive letter K:\ is already taken and unavailable for any other volume. What you could do, then, is to mount the hidden volume in a drive letter normally reserved for USB drives, such as E:\ or F:\. This is the only way I've figured out how to not expose the existence of a hidden TC volume through its drive designation. (Not that I use the hidden volume feature. Just being hypothetical.) Even still, Windows is so utterly thorough in its user surveillance that a clever investigator might be able to ascertain from Event Viewer or Prefetch or whatever that the E:\ port was not used by a USB drive at the time you were trying to make it seem so. (Yet another reason to emigrate from M$ products into Puppy Linux.)

Traveller mode

Allows you to run TC off others' computers, but TC drivers must be installed on them (which isn't always possible). Better used in conjunction with BartPE (which boots XP from a CD, with registry files, etc.), or best yet, use Puppy Linux.

other recommended precautions

Make copies of all your PGP keys, a text file of all your secret account numbers and passwords and the other details for your [digital gold] accounts, full details of your Virtual Debit Card account, copies of INI files for critical programs, your anonymous Email account details plus anything else that is so critical your life would be inconvenienced if it were lost. All these details should now be stored in a folder called "Safe" on your encrypted drive. A copy of this folder should be stored on

an encrypted CD, preferably within the hidden part of a TrueCrypt container and stored off-site.
-- www.privacy.li/security_faq.htm

for optimal Windows security, encrypt drive C:\

Windows acts *so* devoutly as an activity surveillance tool that it is vanishingly improbable for such to be coincidental. Meaning, Microsoft has designed XP and Vista to keep track of your computer's usage through dozens of .txt logs and .dat files (generally arcane and unreadable, as "system" files).

For example, look in the directory C:\WINDOWS\Prefetch. Every software .exe you ran will be displayed there, including the time opened. Regarding your use of TrueCrypt, this folder will distinguish between having created a TC volume (truecryptformat.exe) vs. merely having mounted one already created. These persistent .pf files are very difficult to wipe from Windows, but can be done under Linux.

While some of these (*e.g.*, within Documents and Settings) can be wiped before shutdown, you'll never be able to locate/wipe them all as many are system files not able to be wiped while running from Windows. (You'd have to boot from a CD into DOS, and then wipe them.) Obviously, this is all an absurd inconvenience, especially if done daily.

The major defect of Windows is that the boot drive cannot be within an encrypted volume. Meaning, all your C:\Windows system and log files are available for analysis. Being able to encrypt the boot drive would go a *long* way in securing an otherwise-unsecurable Windows computer. This is sort of possible under XP with a dual-boot partition with DCPP, but what a hassle.) Or, you can use BartPE and run XP in RAM.

BartPE (booting XP off CD and running Windows in RAM)

This freeware transforms a Windows XP installation CD into BartPE (thus avoiding the HD entirely for your XP operating system). Thus, Trojan horses and other viruses cannot be loaded into your Windows Registry, temp files, etc. are all stored in RAM (another reason to have lots of it in your computer). Use only a CD-R (and not a CD-RW) to prevent its contents from being unknowingly altered, and burn "closed."
www.nu2/nu/pebuilder/

what about going to a Mac?

From a privacy standpoint, a Mac is world's better than a PC, but it's not as secure as Linux. (The new Macs can now run Windows software through the "Parallels" software.)

best yet, avoid Windows entirely and use Puppy Linux

I've tried BartPE, and it's a clunky temporary measure. You'll eventually want to go to Puppy Linux, anyway.

> *I have migrated my email and browsing over to Puppy, and spreadsheet work, which is where I spend most of my time on the computer. Thus my emails and browsing history are all encrypted with no fuss . . . . It's on a laptop (no separate keyboard) and I boot from a CD so there are few worries about keyloggers. Actually soon I plan to move over to booting from USB flash drives, and storing my data there as well, so I can take it with me everywhere and have even less to worry about with such threats.*
>
> *There is no spyware to deal with, no viruses (few linux folks bother running virus checkers), and only a simple firewall. And no mandatory software updates every couple of days. Sure beats the Windows world!*
>
> — from an Internet forum

I recently switched to Puppy Linux myself, and should have done it long ago. Details in their own chapter!

FILE SHREDDERS

Merely "deleting" a file does not delete it all; it only allows the file to be later overwritten if no unwritten disk space remains. This is why one may easily restore files long after they've been "deleted." (Col. Ollie North did not know this.) Few computer users understand how important it is to *securely* shred data from the magnetic memory of floppy disks and hard drives. This will prevent not only software, but hardware, recovery or reconstruction of your data.

Computers are simply a megalopolis of magnetic switches which read either ON (a "1") or OFF (a "0"). Each switch is called a "bit" and there are 8-bits to a byte (which is 2^8 or 256 possible permutations making up just one character). A 100-gigabyte drive stores 800 billion bits of binary information.

On a drive or diskette, disk platters serve as the magnetic medium, the surface of which consists of what are called magnetic domains, sort of like strands of carpet. These act individually like microscopic magnets with positive and negative poles. To save what the read/write head recognizes as just 1-bit of information requires *millions* of magnetic domains. Let's say 10,000,000, for example. Imagine a dense carpet with 10 strands per inch. To contain 10 million strands (*i.e.,* magnetic domains) for just 1-bit of binary information means a room-sized carpet about 26 feet per side.

Remember, this is only for *one* bit. To store just one character would require 8-bits, or a carpet 74 feet square. A square *mile* of this carpet would store about 375k of data (which is about 75,000 words of an average 5-character length). A 100gig hard drive would be the equivalent of 16.3 *miles* on each side. Now, just imagine that city-sized carpet shrunk down to the size of a cigarette pack, which is how small a 100gig laptop hard drive is these days.

When writing to the disk platter, the read/write head passes over the surface and flips the magnetic domains towards one direction, just like a vacuum cleaner does to carpet. By creating, altering, and deleting files, magnetic domains are overwritten (*i.e.,* revacuumed) many times.

What is now important to understand is that *each* time the read/write head passes over the magnetic domains, it does so with *imperfect* overlap. Let's say you smoothed a carpet in one direction (writing data on it, so to speak), and then sloppily vacuumed it in the *opposite* direction. Anybody could see that old information (*i.e.,* from the original smoothening) remained in the medium even after deletion (*i.e.,* from the vacuuming).

Even if you had *carefully* vacuumed, some strands would either have been missed, or stubbornly kept their orientation (*i.e.,* polarity) from the original smoothening (data). Just *one* magnetic domain (*i.e.,* one strand of carpet) retaining previous polarity is old information which had not been securely deleted. If enough magnetic domains exist with recoverable old information, then chunks of possibly sensitive data could be pieced together. "Deep Chip", a reader/friend of mine and security tech for a major computer firm, and had this to say:

Hard drives write in concentric circles. These circles get out of round over time. That means by using a very skinny head, you can pull data from the area next to an over-written track.

This assumes the data was [originally] *written a while before it was over written.*

This is precisely what government agencies rely upon to retrieve data deleted beyond software recovery methods. By employing hardware techniques such as magnetic force scanning tunneling microscopy (STM), they may analyze a particular disk sector's magnetic domains for old "layers" which have not successfully been "revacuumed" through overwriting. The Federal Government even has a specific laboratory in Linthicum, Maryland called the Defense Computer Forensics Lab (www.dcfl.gov) dedicated to retrieving data regardless of hard drive or diskette condition.

They are good at their work.

Thus, the trick to deletion overwriting is to make sure that *every* strand of carpet is vacuumed, and in a random series of particular passes to totally clear the magnetic orientation of the old layers. There are several methods of overwriting. (The DoD 5220-22.M standard is quite fast and moderately effective, but should not be relied upon for shredding sensitive data. The Government doesn't trust it for Top Secret data.)

Gutmann standard

This was devised by Dr. Peter Gutmann of the University of Auckland back in the mid-1990s, and this is the default method in Sami Tolvanen's widely acclaimed Eraser program (www.tolvanen.com). Eraser uses Gutmann's 27 deterministic passes (the order of which is shuffled by the Tiger hash function) preceded and followed by 4 passes of random data (created by the ISAAC pseudorandom number generator), totalling 35 passes. This should overwrite all data despite drive encoding (the middle 27 passes wipe the older formats of MFM and RLL, and the two bookend pairs of 4 passes wipe the modern PRML drives). Eraser installs (as **Erase**) in the Windows Explorer File command structure and is supremely simple to use. Click and shred.

avoiding cluster tip data trails

I use Notepad frequently for lists, saving them after each revision. For example, the Notepad file I'm using now to jot down these notes has a size of 10.4k. However, its allocated "size on disk" is larger: 12.0k. That 1.6k extra is called "slack space" or "cluster tips". (It's sort of like how a plate is always larger than the meal on it. As the meal is eaten, you can still discern how large it was.) Every file has some, and it will contain previously "deleted" material as a smaller file is saved. (Just because you can't see it in the file doesn't mean it's been eliminated from the HD.)

Cluster tips are overwritten *only* if and when there is no other free disk space. Depending on one's computer use, it could take months or even years for such plaintext data to be overwritten—or never at all. Therefore, it is vital that the shredding process (both for individual files and for unused disk space) overwrite all file cluster tips.

Most free space overwriting programs do *not* overwrite cluster tips! This is because although cluster tips may indeed be empty of data, they are necessarily allocated to their particular files and thus *not* listed by the computer's file system as actually being part of the disk's free space. Only a high-quality shredder program such as Eraser or BCWipe (which I now prefer, www.jetico.com) accounts for this and shreds all empty cluster tips still attached to their files.

Overwriting cluster tips across an entire drive takes a bit of time, and most files either don't have anything sensitive there (ever, or after the previous cluster tip wipe). One way to keep on top of the cluster tip issue is to copy/paste the working text into a new empty file, save it, and then shred the old one (which will include not only just the 10.4k you see, but the entire 12.0k of the file's space on disk.) Obviously, this is a hassle for too many files, and is not meant to replace regular cluster tip shredding. However, if you're working regularly on just a few sensitive files, this technique is a real timesaver.

a faster way to overwrite cluster tips

Since most files are software and not data, it makes sense to manipulate your data from a large folder (in a TC volume), and limit your regular cluster tip overwrites to that folder.

cluster tips vs. unused disk space

Now, let's say that I took out about half this 10.4k file's text, and re-saved it. That 5.0k of deleted text would then be separated from its parent file (which now uses less "space on disk"), becoming merely unused disk space. At some point, that deleted 5k of text could get randomly overwritten by new or enlarged file, but it's more likely to be left in the clear in a nearby cluster (thus easily reconstituted through a recovery program). It's always best to regularly shred a drive's unused space and its cluster tips. (Defrag after that for greater security and improved file access speeds. Then, shred again if can.)

how many times to overwrite data?

"Deep Chip" remarked:

> What you really want [for modern PRML hard drives] *is a pseudo random overwrite done several times (several ranges from 3 to 10 depending on your level of paranoia. My level is about 30) and then finishes with "0's" so that it looks the same as any place else on the drive. Second, NSA level data recovery is very advanced and can recover data that has been overwritten, but this is only used on national security type cases (or big time industrial espionage) because of the expense.*
>
> *I use several programs to overwrite data. For data scattered around the drive like browser cache, temp files etc... I use window washer from webroot.com. For specific files that I want to delete, I use PGP diskwipe. That pretty much obliterates the data and makes recovery almost impossible.*
>
> *There are two very important points to consider regarding data destruction. If you want data absolutely positively destroyed, you have to disassemble the hard drive, and grind off the surface down to the platter. That will make the data unrecoverable by anyone. The second thing is that securely deleting your file doesn't help if your system is already compromised. It is important to secure your system and keep intruders off. I use Linux because I don't trust Windows, although that is difficult for some people.*

Are 35 Gutmann passes required for modern drives?

Use Gutmann for any older non-PRML encoded drives. For PRML and EPRML, Gutmann's 35 passes are overkill as 8-10 overwrites with pseudorandom data are likely sufficient. As Peter Gutmann himself explained:

> *In the time since this [1996] paper was published, some people have treated the 35-pass overwrite technique described in it more as a kind of voodoo incantation to banish evil spirits than the result of a technical analysis of drive encoding techniques. As a result, they advocate applying the*

*voodoo to PRML and EPRML drives **even though it will have no more effect than a simple scrubbing with random data.** In fact performing the full 35-pass overwrite is pointless for any drive since it targets a blend of scenarios involving all types of (normally-used) encoding technology, which covers everything back to 30+-year-old MFM methods (if you don't understand that statement, re-read the paper). If you're using a drive which uses encoding technology X, you only need to perform the passes specific to X, and you never need to perform all 35 passes. **For any modern PRML/EPRML drive, a few passes of random scrubbing is the best you can do.***

— www.cs.auckland.ac.nz/~pgut001/pubs/secure_del.html

Hence, I wouldn't use 35 Gutmann passes on modern HDs, and never on USB drives (which wear out much more quickly from excessive overwriting). 3-10 passes are likely enough.

can intelligence agencies really read overwritten data?
One expert, Daniel Feenberg, calls it an *"urban legend."*

Gutmann claims that "Intelligence organisations have a lot of expertise in recovering these palimpsestuous images." but there is no reference for that statement. There are 18 references in the paper, but none of the ones I was able to locate even referred to that possibility. Subsequent articles by diverse authors do make that claim, but only cite Gutmann, so they do not constitute additional evidence for his claim.

Gutmann mentions that after a simple setup of the MFM device, that bits start flowing within minutes. This may be true, but the bits he refers to are not from from disk files, but pixels in the pictures of the disk surface. Charles Sobey has posted an informative paper "Recovering Unrecoverable Data" with some quantitative information on this point. He suggests that it would take more than a year to scan a single platter with recent MFM technology, and tens of terabytes of image data would have to be processed.

In one section of the paper Gutmann suggests overwriting with 4 passes of random data. That is apparently because he anticipates using pseudo-random data that would be known to the investigator. A single write is sufficient if the overwrite is truly random, even given an STM microscope with far greater powers than those in the references. In fact, data written to the disk prior to the data whose recovery is sought will interfere with recovery just as must as data written after - the STM microscope can't tell the order in which which magnetic moments are created. It isn't like ink, where later applications are physically on top of earlier markings.

The requirements of military forces and intelligence agencies that disk drives with confidential information be destroyed rather than erased is sometimes offered as evidence that these agencies can read overwritten data. I expect the real explanation is far more prosaic. The technician tasked with discarding a hard drive may or may not have enough computer knowledge to know if running the command "urandom >/dev/sda2c1" has covered an entire disk with random data, or only one partition, nor is it easy to confirm that it was done. How would you confirm that the overwrite was not pseudo-random? Smashing the drive with a sledgehammer is easy to do, easy to confirm, and very hard to get wrong. The GPL'ed package DBAN is an apparent attempt to address this uncertainty without destroying hardware.

Surveying all the references, I conclude that Gutmann's claim belongs in the category of urban legend.

Or it may be in the category of marketing hype.

— www.nber.org/sys-admin/overwritten-data-guttman.html
NBER Website, 5 January 2006

He purports that magnetic domains are *not* layered like ink, and the only previous data which is theoretically readable are those existing *between* disk head passes, not under them. My source "Deep Chip" disagrees:

> Data also seeps into the drive platters. **You can actually plane off the face of the drive platter to read older data underneath.** Both of these are beyond commercial recovery services, [but] are well within the capability of the gov't.

Modern hard drives are very precise and efficient, and thus far less exploitable in this regard than the older MFMs.

Nevertheless, it can't hurt to choose 3-7 passes when shredding files or slack space. (Don't stress out thumb drives with 35-pass Gutmann, as they are not designed for such.) You're far more likely to get tripped up by old .log or paging swap files or restore points or something else similarly arcane in Windows than not having overwritten old data enough times.

BCWipe   www.jetico.com/bcwipe3.htm

My current favorite, especially for wiping cluster tips and free space (which Eraser never seemed to do very well, according to Disk Investigator). You can even devise your own unique wipe protocol. Works also on virtual drives (USB, TC).

Eraser   www.tolvanen.com

It's open source, and has been tested/used by thousands of computer professionals. It works on Windows 95, 98, ME, NT 4.0, 2000 and XP (all versions, with or without service packs). This was once about the best shredder, but BCWipe is superior according to my testing.

Q: "Overwriting is the key to ultimate security, isn't it?

A: Wrong. When overwriting data, you are simply trying to fix a security leak that already has happened, the best way to deal with this is to prevent the data from getting written to the disk in the first place - use strong encryption. E4M and PGP can get you started, **but cannot help you with Windows-related security holes.** *If you must use Windows, use NT/2000. If you are serious about your security, try Linux, or even OpenBSD.*

Q: "I have been using Eraser to overwrite all sensitive data from my drive. Is it really gone now?"

A: It depends on how much money and effort people trying to restore your data are willing to use. Erased data cannot be recovered with any software utility, and even if the hard drive electronics are bypassed and disk platters are examined, recovering data will be extremely difficult, if not impossible.

— http://tolvanen.com/eraser/faq.shtml

A useful Eraser forum discussing many issues:
www.cipherserver.com/

Webroot Window Washer

A very solid program with a very simple interface (with oodles of plug-ins and good scheduling). Not as tunable as BCWipe, but nonetheless a good choice for most non-techs.

One glitch is that my free version does not recognize any drive but C:\, so I cannot slace space shred TC volumes and USB drives. No worries since this is what I use BCWipe for.

CCleaner   http://majorgeeks.com/download4191.html
This is very lean freeware system optimization and privacy tool, and it works fast. You should have several shredders, and this is one of them.

ZAPEMPTY
To wipe unused space on your drive I recommend ZAPEMPTY. Although a Dos based program, it runs easily even within Win XP. This is a part of a zipped file of wipe utilities called Wipeutil.zip. Extract ZAPEMPTY onto the drive you wish to clean up and double click it. **But do not use it or any other disk wipe tool on your encrypted drive or it may be a pointer to where the hidden container lies.**
    -- www.privacy.li/security_faq.htm

ZAPEMPTY is extremely simple (only 324 bytes!) and fast. Keep a copy on every USB and SD card. Run it routinely when you're machine is otherwise idle.

East-Tec Eraser
www.east-tec.com/eraser/index.htm
This is fine software offering a myriad shredding options. 7 passes a good minimum, yet not too hoggy on time.

other misc. scrubbers and info
I would install and use several different ones, for thoroughness:

www.cs.auckland.ac.nz/~pgut001/pubs/secure_del.html
www.marcompress.com/AboutWipePro4.htm
www.thefreecountry.com/security/securedelete.shtml
www.hsinlin.com/software/privacy.html

Hard Disk Scrubber	www.summitcn.com/products.html
Evidence Eliminator	www.privacy-software-review.com
Clean Disk Security	www.theabsolute.net/sware/clndisk.html
AVG Anti-Rootkit Free	http://free.grisoft.com/
Sophos Anti-Rootkit	www.sophos.com

files to frequently shred
Regular use of your computer will have Windows regularly create (unbeknownst to you) *many* files which clearly

show what you've accessed, copied, moved, executed, etc. Most good shredder software (BCWipe, Window Washer, etc.) will have an extensive list of these already built in.

PGP keyring files

You should *never* leave these files in the clear on the HD:

> c:\program files\pgp\pgpmail\pubring.pubkr
> c:\program files\pgp\pgpmail\prvring.prvkr

At minimum they are evidence of all your PGP friends and proof of your own file encryption. At worst, they will assist the unwanted decryption of your data (especially if a keysniffer logged in your passphrase). Encrypt your keyring files! Where these files reside as far as PGP knows should be either in a TrueCrypt volume or on a USB drive. This is why installing PGP inside a TC volume is a good idea — the key files are never automatically in the clear on C:\.

various .log files

If you use Windows, beware of these. As one computer expert constantly quips, Windows is like using a virus for an OS. It will log everything you do, and these logs are *very* difficult to find. You'll never be able to get them all, much less shred them because too many are system files.

First, decide if you really need to have certain logs generated in the first place. If so, then at least change the default storage directory to one within a TrueCrypt volume or thumb drive. (Programs within the startup menu will *precede* TrueCrypt volume mounting, so you'll have to move them later. It's a hassle, but it could be worth your effort. Programs which are used after bootup, such as PGP and your internet firewall ZoneAlarm, can wholly reside within a TrueCrypt volume.)

For a list of .log files, go to c:\Program Files\ and conduct a search for *.log — you will be astonished at the number of them. Sort the listing by View/Arrange Icons/Modified to display in date order, which will show you the ones updated every time you log on. Good shredder programs (*e.g.*, BCWipe) will wipe many log files, which are stored at:

c:\Documents and Settings\user\Local Settings\Temporary Internet Files
c:\WINDOWS\Internet Logs

Beware of your firewall's *extensive* logging. It will log *all* the IPs you connected to. Even if you use a tunnel, the proxy's IP will be logged though the subsequent surfing will not. The date/time stamp of your proxy logon is exact enough to use in a search warrant for the proxy's logs (which, if kept, will contain your session history).

.jpg thumbnails are usually cached by Windows

You'll have to turn off this "feature" and then shred every file called thumb.db. The freeware anti-XPspy.exe fixes this.

your wifi's IP address is logged by Windows

Go to: Network   Connections\Wireless   Network Connection\Change advanced settings\Wireless Networks, look in the box Preferred Networks. There you will find a list of every wifi connection ever made. Windows stores them for future use. Yes, you can highlight them one by one and click <Remove>, but the removal is merely an illusion (just as <Delete> is for files). Your usage of the wifi name "Beckman home computer" (thus its IP and physical location) was logged deep within the bowels of Windows. A mere Windows Explorer search for "Beckman home computer" will find nothing; you'll have to use a powerful tool such as Disk Investigator to dredge your HD.

Primary locations are within C:\WINDOWS\asym.ini, and .bin files within C:\WINDOWS\SoftwareDistribution\EventCache\. which are a hassle to shred (especially the most current one). You'll have empty space shred, defrag, then shred again. Yet another reason to "*move away from the Windows*" for Puppy Linux (or at least run Windows from a BartPE disk).

software remembers last files saved to which folders

I noticed this with my scanner. Look for any log.txt files in the software's folder, and see if you can disable logkeeping. Meanwhile/otherwise, spoof entry the final file to the final folder, just to give the software some dead-end to save.

Scour C:\Documents and Settings\user\Application Data.

wipe slack space, defrag, then wipe slack space again

This is an excellent protocol which strengthens the wiping process by writing (either random noise or actual files) over previously used clusters. This should remove past wifi history of removed hotspots you previously used.

before a trip: wipe/shutdown, reboot/wipe, wipe/shutdown

Some files can only be overwritten after system startup vs. before shutdown. So, for best security before traveling (*e.g.*, embarking on a road trip, going through airport security, etc.), go through this extra measure. Also, a wipe/defrag/wipe of your drive's unused space and cluster tips is a good policy here, too.

Some Windows files can't be shred during a Windows session, so use Puppy Linux for that. Be careful not to shred important files, such as ZA firewall settings found at:

C:\WINDOWS\Internet Logs\IAMDB.RDB

MRU-Blaster

MRU-Blaster is a program made to do one large task - detect and clean MRU (most recently used) lists on your computer.

These MRU lists contain information such as the names and/or locations of the last files you have accessed. They are located ALL OVER your registry, and for almost ANY file type. By looking at these MRU lists, someone could determine what files you opened/saved/looked at, what their file names were, and much more! (And, in many cases, the lists are displayed in drop-down menus automatically.)

With additional plug-ins that allow you to clean out your Temporary Internet Files and Cookies, MRU-Blaster enhances the protection of your privacy!

   — www.javacoolsoftware.com/mrublaster.html

A good freeware to keep running in the background, which will clean many MRUs just after they were created.

Disk Investigator www.diskcleaners.com/files/diskinv.exe

With this handy free hex-editor, you can discover *all* that is hidden on your drives (for Win9x and beyond).

What is Disk Investigator? - Disk Investigator helps you to discover all that is hidden on your computer hard disk. It can also help you to recover lost data. Display the true drive contents by bypassing the operating system and directly reading the raw drive sectors. View and search raw directories, files, clusters, and system sectors. **Verify the effectiveness of file and disk wiping programs.** *Undelete previously deleted files.*

   — www.theabsolute.net/sware/dskinv.html

Don't trust your shredding programs; ascertain *exactly* what files might still be left afterwards. You'll be quite surprised! This utility is what woke me up to Eraser's occasional mediocrity and BCWipe's superiority.

Jpeg Scrubber

Reduce file size & remove private information from Jpeg images - with no change to the image! Did you know that most Jpeg files contain lots of secret hidden data? This increases the size of your files, and exposes privacy issues when published on your website.Jpeg Scrubber can batch process folders of Jpegs, removing the hidden data, reducing the file sizes, reducing download times and removing private information. For example, Jpeg Scrubber can take a 56 KB image and reduce it to 13 KB, without changing a single bit of the image.

—http://www.fileplaza.com/web_authoring/web_design_ut ilities/details/jpeg_scrubber.html

ID-Blaster Plus 2.0   **www.javacoolsoftware.com**

Destroy tracking tactics by randomizing GUID/Unique ID numbers found on your computer.

In Windows, many applications have something called a "product ID number", a "GUID" or a "Unique ID number". This number may be the same throughout Internet Explorer, Windows Media Player - even the operating system itself. Since this number nevers changes, it would be the perfect way a malicious person or even an advertising company could track your habits -- perhaps through a malicious website ActiveX control, or Java applet.

Why not just delete it? In this case, you would have a constant ID of nothing - and given the small number of people that might also have that "null" value, it could still be used to track you. ID-Blaster Plus works by changing these ID numbers frequently, destroying tracking tactics using these numbers. ID-Blaster can run from the system tray, using very little resources, and constantly protect you in the background.

ID-Blaster Plus is compatible with Windows 95, 98, ME, NT, 2000, XP. Freeware/donationware.

Another GUI scrubber is from www.vecdev.com.

misc. useful freeware

www.javacoolsoftware.com/products.html
www.karenware.com/powertools/powertools.asp
www.thefreecountry.com/
www.ajorgeeks.com

*Since I remove spyware so often as part of my day job, I have
a toolkit of sorts. Removing spyware almost always requires a
"cocktail" of spyware removal applications. The four that I use
most often are:*

HijackThis
CWShredder
Spybot Search & Destroy
AdAware
— http://icrontic.com/articles/defeat_spyware

DBAN, for when you dispose of/sell your computer

http://dban.sourceforge.net/faq/index.html

It's just common sense to overwrite old computer hard
drives before selling them, Darik's Boot and Nuke is the way to
go. You'll need either a floppy disk or a CDRom with a CDRom
burner, and then set your target computer to boot from either
floppy or CDRom (whichever option you choose). Be *absolutely*
sure you've gotten everything off the drive you want. Once you
run DBAN your hard drive will be utterly scrubbed.

Webroot's Window Washer can also create a bootable CD
with full disk shred potential.

monitor security

be able to instantly clear your screen in public

I really like the QuickLaunch tray. While the list of my
most used softwares needs two rows, and half the width of my
screen, it beats having all the icons visible on the desktop. In
the upper left corner of the tray is the icon for "Show Desktop".
Clicking it will instantly clear my screen of whatever I'm
working on, which is handy for those snoopy types who like to
wander by. (In Linux, just roll the mouse wheel one click.)

video of your keyboard

If you are reliably known to use your computer at the
same place, and if that building/room is accessible, a small video

camera theoretically could be installed to record your keystrokes. The mildly paranoid should use different public wifi, and sit in different parts of the room when they do.

monitors can retain data even after being turned off!

"Deep Chip" had also this to say:

Now, while I don't want to make you paranoid, your CRT will also keep about six to seven layers of data on it as well. There are several reasons [police] take the monitor [during a search].

1) There could be something physically hidden in it.
2) They can duplicate your drive and then boot the system with all original hardware.
3) They usually get to keep it after the case is over.
4) They can plant bugs in the hardware if they give it back to you.
5) They can examine the screen and see what was on it recently.

There aren't any countermeasures, but the screen info fades fairly quickly. Laptop and flat screens are less susceptible to this but it is still possible to get info from them. And of course reasons one through four above still apply. As a side note, flat screens have a much lower tempest signature.

printers can be *individually* identified

Thanks to the U.S. Secret Service, many laser printers encode every document with microscopic dots (called "banding") which makes output trackable back to the specific printer. Buy your printer with cash, and don't use it for anything publicly sensitive. For related info, read the fascinating page at:

www.wikileaks.org/wiki/Successes_and_three_near_misses_for_Wikileaks

media devices
digital cameras and their SD cards

They usually come with a very small media card, such as 16 or 32meg. While too small for general use, these small cards do have their place for privacy. A few sensitive photos could be taken on them, which are much faster to entirely overwrite than some huge 2gig card.

Although a quality multi-pass overwriting program (Eraser, BCWipe, Window Washer) will make impossible software recovery of former data, there will remain evidence that files were shredded. All file content and properties (date, size, etc.) are gone. However, any third party with Disk Investigator can tell that x number of files have been securely deleted because the deleted directory entry will still list the sector numbers where the files began. This, indirectly, is indeed information about the owner.

Such a technically sophisticated act is unusual (because most people would merely "delete" them through the camera itself), and would probably increase a snoop's interest in you. (Shredding files on a computer HD may not be too uncommon, but shredding SD files probably is.) One idea to counter this is to keep a sacrificial SD card in your camera with innocuous images (present and "deleted"), while you hide your other SD cards. (They are so tiny and flat that they could be hidden nearly anywhere, even in places too small for a USB drive. Use your imagination!)

All digital photos have a *lot* of embedded info in them, such as camera model, date and time. This "metadata" may be too sensitive (especially for online or emailed photos), and should be removed with a program such as Jpeg Scrubber from www.jpeg-scrubber.com. A clean copy will be generated (reducing file size for faster downloading), and you can then shred the original.

Having a cheap spare digital camera (I bought a used one for just $15) is a great idea for certain classed of photos you don't want possibly linked to you through your main camera.

BACKING UP DATA

Storage media are now so cheap and versatile, you've no excuse not daily backing up your data. A 20¢ DVD-R can hold 4.7gigs, which is probably more data than most users have.

do not utterly trust disks over time and frequent use

Writable optical media (CDs and DVDs) are notoriously fluky over long periods of time and often lose data. USB drives don't seem vulnerable to time, but excessive free space shredding (*i.e.*, overwriting) will stress them out prematurely. Certainly, you should use such media often, but have many secondary copies stored in a variety of places.

use an external hard disk drive (HDD) for backup
For the <$200, these 250gig (or more) drives provide an amazing amount of fast and reliable data storage. Your computer's HD should not be excessively large (*i.e.*, not over 100gig) for reliability's sake. Use an external HDD to warehouse most of your data, and to backup your system files. It should have its own TrueCrypt volume, naturally, and should be hidden somewhere off-campus as a backup of last resort.

store files on the Net
This is a good plan if you travel frequently, especially internationally, and wish to avoid carrying your only data set with you. That way, if your laptop is stolen, you can get back to work with a replacement machine and downloaded backups.
Returning travelers to the USSA are subject to having their laptops searched without probable cause. If you refuse to divulge passphrases, "Homeland Security" can seize your laptop, and good luck ever getting it back. The smart owner, before boarding a flight back home, will email or FTP his work files to an online data storage site, and then shred such on his laptop. (While you could chance keeping data on your person on disk or USB drive, a thorough search may find it.) Have an inexpensive spare laptop for travel that you can forfeit at the border if necessary, saving your main laptop for domestic use. See Chapter 20 for more details.

PHYSICAL SECURITY

keyloggers and *Magic Lantern* software
Since encryption and shredding is so effective, the smart adversary will try to ascertain your passphrase. Guard the physical security of your computers, to reduce the chance of surveillance software being installed without your knowledge. This is why physical privacy is important, and if your home address is difficult to learn, your computers are much safer.

What is a Tempest attack?

Tempest is an acronym for Transient ElectroMagnetic Pulse Emanation Surveillance. This is the science of monitoring at a distance electronic signals carried on wires or displayed on a monitor. Although of only slight significance to the average user, it is of enormous importance to serious cryptography snoopers. To minimize a tempest attack you should screen all the cables between your computer and your accessories, particularly your monitor. A flat screen (non CRT) monitor offers a considerable reduction in radiated emissions and is recommended.

-- http://www.privacy.li/security_faq.htm

IF YOUR COMPUTER IS SEIZED

Your primary goal is to "stay under the radar" of the modern Police State. If, however, your computer is ever seized (or even surreptitiously analyzed without your knowledge through a *USA PATRIOT* Act "sneak and peek" warrant), the fact that you have an unusual amount of spyware and file shredders will increase the feds' interest in you. Treble that if they have a difficult time piecing together your internet activity because of your thorough computer hygiene.

If your computer is seized and returned, I would DBAN the entire drive down to 00000000s, and then reinstall everything from a secure backup source (that remains uncompromised). This would be a good idea if you strongly suspect a "sneak and peek" attack. Better safe than sorry! For the truly concerned after a seizure, DBAN the drive, reinstall only the OS and then sell the thing. (Never using it again because a hardware keylogger could have been installed.)

Once you have nicely setup a new computer that you know has not been compromised, mirror the HD (with all its dandy security software that you installed), and hide that backup well.

Then, practice vigilant physical security over that computer. This is easy with a laptop, which can also double as your desktop machine. Keep it with you as often as possible, and otherwise locked up (preferably in a hard case).

Choose a laptop with readily replaceable HDs (such as the very rugged Panasonic "Tough Book" used by cops and soldiers), and mirror your work on multiple drives which are stored offsite. That way, you can be quickly up and running if your regular laptop HD ever crashes or is seized.

encryption and crossing the border

Can travelers crossing the U.S. border be forced to open encrypted files? It seems to be heading that way:

Feds: We will search through your laptop files at the border
http://tech.yahoo.com/blogs/null/90325

Airport Electronics Searches Truly Troubling
http://tech.yahoo.com/blog/null/71776

Clarity Sought on Electronics Searches
http://www.washingtonpost.com/wp-dyn/content/article/2008/02/0
6/AR2008020604763.html
http://blog.wired.com/27bstroke6/2008/04/border-agents-c.html

Judge: Man can't be forced to divulge encryption passphrase
www.news.com/8301-13578_3-9834495-38.html

DOJ: No comment on forcing encryption passphrases
www.news.com/8301-13578_3-9835392-38.html?tag=nefd.blgs

If you refuse to open up encrypted files or volumes, border agents are currently permitted to seize your laptop for further scrutiny. Thus, the wise international traveler will have a sacrificial, inexpensive, secondhand computer running Puppy Linux from live CD, with an unused Windows HD (or none at all). TC volumes should at least be on a hidden USB drive. Better yet, mailed ahead, or FTPed in advance to an online storage site (leaving you without any data, even encrypted, on your person). Shred all Application Data from any music and movie ripping. (More on border laptop security in Chapter 20.)

The Supreme Court has yet to rule if passphrase (*i.e.*, contents of your mind) are secure under the 5th Amendment. This will be *the* case of the early 21st Century! Even if SCOTUS rules that passphrase disclosures may be required, the police will have to prove that you haven't a faulty memory or that you haven't lost a crucial keyfile. Measure . . . countermeasure.

OVERVIEW

In the end, nothing is really anonymized — only obscured.

Again, I point out that I am no computer expert, but a very knowledgeable layman. No doubt I've missed some excellent products, but here is what I've come up with. Please take this overview as a starting guide for your own continuing research.

	Poor	Fair	Good	Superb
computer	home/off.	public (few)	public (many)	wifi laptop
OS	XP	Mac	Linux	OpenBSD
data storage	HD-clear	HD-PGP	HD-True Crypt	USB-True Crypt
shredder	"delete"	Eraser	Window Washer	BCWipe
browser	IE	Netscape	Opera	Firefox
log-on from	home	office	random DSL	random WiFi
email	Outlook	Eudora	Quicksilver	Thunderbird
firewall	Windows	Norton	ZoneAlarm	Comodo
spyware	Norton	Spybot	Spy Sweeper	Vipre, CCleaner
popups	Windows	Norton	Window Washer	Razor
IP proxy	Anonymizer	Neomail	Trilightzone	TOR or JAP
servers	local	U.S. proxy	offshore (one)	offshore (many)
encryption	none	SSL	VPN	SSH or OpenVPN
VoIP	Vonage	Skype	SIP over VPN	SIP/VPN/Zfone
how paid	credit card	e-gold	cash/M.O.	prepaid debit card
when used?	never	sometimes	often	always

INTERNET PRIVACY

This is *the* most technical chapter of the book. Do not, however, skip this or stray. Any ignorance here can easily be your Achilles Heel of privacy, but you won't realize that until it's too late. These Commandments cover most of it:

Internet Explorer, Norton, Skype, and Google Are Sinful

Thou Shalt Use ZoneAlarm

Thou Shalt Use Firefox or Opera

Thou Shalt Use Offshore SSH and OpenVPN Tunnels

Windows Is A Virus, Not An OS

Puppy Linux Will Set You Free!

Any communication on the Internet leaves all kinds of digital traces which can be automatically acquired, saved and analyzed. Some companies have thus specialized in creating individual user profiles from surfing related data. These databases are of high economic value since they allow an enterprise to comprehensively profile their costumers, that means you. This process is called data accumulation in data mining lingo.

There are many reasons why one should avoid leaving digital traces when surfing: part of the data collected advects into scoring systems which are used to evaluate loan requests, to create individually priced offers or to decide on eligibility for C.O.D. service. Employers may be generated a character profile of their job applicants from traces on the Net prior to hiring them. Freedom of opinion is limited by governments or institutions where they trace individual surfers

that use or edit certain web services or deny them any usage at all. Companies may recognize employees of other businesses or even those of their competition and subsequently annoy them with promotional calls or email spam. Browser related data exposes vulnerabilities in the surfing machine. An hacker may subsequently contact the computer directly and attack it.
    — http://anon.inf.tu-dresden.de/index_en.html

Three may keep a secret if two are dead.
    — Ben Franklin

Whenever you log on to the Internet, you are, in effect, speaking to people—even if you merely visit a website. Your visit there tells strangers many things about you and your computer. While it is possible to enjoy robust Internet privacy, it does require much research, diligence, and at least $200/year.

I will give you a solid education of what's involved, but you really should keep at least one computer as a "stand alone" machine which is never, *ever* connected. On this resides all your sensitive data, which is never shared with your Internet "promiscuous" computers.

There are three components of Internet privacy and anonymity, and they are dealt with separately:

location (virtual and physical)	use an SSH proxy
message content (what you say)	encrypt text with PGP
traffic (whom you email & when)	good browser & shredder

Definitions (from Privacy Software Report)
http://www.privacy-software-review.toptenreviews.com/privacy-software-definitions.html

Auto-Complete
Internet Explorer can store a record of almost everything that you type into any web site form. Form data can be things such as all the keywords you have ever typed into a search engine and personal information such as your name and address and passwords.

Cache (Temporary Internet Files)
When a web page is requested and delivered to your browser, the images and documents associated with the web page are

saved in a temporary Internet file or cache so that the next time they are requested; they are accessed from your computer and not over the web (unless a change has occurred).

Cookies
A cookie is a small message of text stored on your computer. The main purpose of cookies is to identify users and possibly prepare customized Web pages for them. When you enter a Web site using cookies, you may be asked to fill out a form providing such information as your name and interests. This information is packaged into a cookie and sent to your Web browser, which stores it for later use. The next time you go to the same Web site, your browser will send the cookie to the Web server. The server can use this information to present you with custom Web pages. So, for example, instead of seeing just a generic welcome page you might see a welcome page with your name on it.

Downloaded Files
Files and file components that you have downloaded from the web are stored in directories on your computer. Examples are Active X and Java Applets. Sometimes these files are harmless, sometimes they can contain virus, spy ware, or ad ware applications.

Favorites List
This is a list of all of the URLs or website addresses that have been saved on your computer for easy referencing later on.

History of Visited URLs
Is a complete history of every website that has been visited.

Plugins
Third party software applications (browsers, email, graphical editors, instant messaging, chat, P2P, image viewers, etc.) record activity like pictures viewed, websites visited, media played, and last used files. A plugin is a small piece of interface software, specifically designed for each application, that allows your computer to erase this information.

URL Error Logs
Logging files keep records of URLs you have tried to access that resulted in an error.

Registry Fragmented Files
Most programs leave garbage in the windows registry that can
be recovered. Evidence of Internet sites is one example that
remains until your Windows registry is rebuilt.

OPERATING SYSTEM (OS)

Your Internet privacy depends mostly on which OS you
use, followed by which firewall and browser. In descending
order of security they are: OpenBSD (mostly used by banks and
large servers), Linux, Mac, and Windows. 89% of the world's
home computers use Windows, so I'll discuss it first.

Windows
As I described elsewhere, the way of the world is usually
wide, downhill, well-lit, populated, and *wrong*. This is
Windows. (Skype and Google, too.) Beyond its ubiquity (which
is decreasing as Linux is becoming widely known), there is
nothing right about Windows. This could be only on purpose.

> *Windows is a closed source operating system which is a law
> to itself. Each new update that is released by Microsoft seems
> to need further updates to fix the security holes discovered in
> the previous releases. It has been an ongoing process over
> many years with no end in sight. These weaknesses can
> manifest themselves as security holes when on the Net. A
> further problem with this operating system is its seeming
> determination to write to your hard disk all sorts of information
> that may be hidden from your view in all sorts of places that
> could be found by a forensic examination of your computer.*
>
> *Thus we have a two fold problem. Firstly, the problem of
> Windows having the potential of security holes that might be
> exploited by snoops and hackers using the Net and a different
> security problem of writing all sorts of information to
> sometimes hidden folders that might not be obvious from a
> cursory check by you, but easily found by a forensic
> examination.*
>
> -- www.privacy.li/security_faq.htm

*The frightening truth is, there is no way for any of the
Windows 9x family of products (Win31, Win95, Win98,*

WinMe) to be truly secure, and although the Windows NT family (WinNT, Win2000, Whistler) can theoretically be secure, Microsoft has never enforced this built-in capability (and, in fact, Microsoft has been eroding it over time.) In practice this means that while using Windows there is no operating system enforced software "containment". Any program running in the system can do virtually anything it desires.

This was not a practical problem back in the "old days" where we were all amazed just to be able to compose and print a letter on a computer that we owned. But in today's world, security has become a huge problem (which Microsoft had better start getting serious about very soon.)
— www.grc.com

A perfect example of all this are those ample activity files at:

C:\WINDOWS\Prefetch\

Every software you executed will be listed, and by time/date. (Claim not to have mounted your TC volume in months because you "forgot the passphrase"? Prefetch will prove otherwise!) These are very difficult to shred, and you'll have to add the above subfolder to the shredder's task list. Same issue with all those index.dat files (many of which you can read with the free program IndexDatSpy210.exe).

The frightening truth is, there is no way for any of the Windows 9x family of products (Win31, Win95, Win98, WinMe) to be truly secure, and although the Windows NT family (WinNT, Win2000, Whistler) can theoretically be secure, Microsoft has never enforced this built-in capability (and, in fact, Microsoft has been eroding it over time.) In practice this means that while using Windows there is no operating system enforced software "containment". Any program running in the system can do virtually anything it desires.

This was not a practical problem back in the "old days" where we were all amazed just to be able to compose and print a letter on a computer that we owned. But in today's world, security has become a huge problem (which Microsoft had better start getting serious about very soon.)
BTP Note: Too late! Puppy Linux is here! ☺
— www.grc.com

I'll have much more to say about and against Windows shortly. In the long run, you should migrate to Mac if not Linux. Even better, *begin* your PC experience with Puppy Linux and avoid Microsoft altogether. (Leaving Windows is certainly possible, but the disorientation feels like having left a cult. One's sense of computer reality is affected.) Oh, and read:

> **advapi.dll an NSA backdoor in Windows**
> www.voxfux.com/archives/00000059.htm
>
> **Windows XP, Professional Bugging Device?**
> www.privacy.li/forum/viewtopic.php?t=383

Mac

Used by about 10% of the world's computers, it is *much* more inherently secure and resistant to viruses and spyware. Most Mac users don't even bother with virus checkers, etc. I have very little experience with Macs, thus cannot discuss in greater detail their security features. Never forget that it is the product of a mega-corporation, so how much can you trust it?

Linux

Open-source code developed often by passionate volunteers. Used by about 1% of the world's home computers, and there are dozens of "distros" such as Red Hat, Fedora, Ubuntu, etc. Dell will even sell you a new box with Linux installed, if you ask them to. Russian schools are trying to go to GNU/Linux, even though Microsoft has promised to invest $300 million over three years if they didn't. (Scroogle the story about "Dream Spark" and visit www.boycottnovell.com.)

There is no greater boon to your Internet privacy than using Linux for all your online activity. I'm a delighted "Microsoft refugee", having gone to the amazing Puppy Linux (which works from a live CD and not the hard drive!). There are plenty of apps to satisfy most users, and many helpful forums. (Puppy Linux has its own chapter.) The learning curve is a bit steep at first, and there are snags, but I'm 98% there.

✓ HARDWARE

This concerns your computer's "host name" (sort of like its SSN, which should be spoofed), MAC addresses, and routers.

your MAC addresses

Besides the IP address, the MAC address is probably the next most important datum to mask for Internet privacy, and it's the one which people know little about.

Unless you get online through a dialup modem, some form of Network Interface Card (NIC) adapter (LAN, WLAN, GPRS, UMTS, VPS, etc.) is used and all these have a unique Media Access Control (MAC) address burned into the hardware. So, instead of a dialup's username and password, your ISP registers (and tracks) the MAC address of the cable modem, broadband router, or PC that hosts the Internet connection. Look at the next connection info box when getting online, and you'll see that the IP is leased to a particular MAC address.

Often, your local ISP expects the customer's MAC address (whether that of the computer itself, or the router) to match its registered value. Changing your network hardware will change the MAC address (unless you spoof the new hardware to use the old value), and usually result in denial of service. Also, some software is registered to a specific MAC address.

Generally, the MAC address is known only over one hop and is *not* transmitted from your machine all the way to a visited site. The MAC (being in an outer packet, called Layer 2) is stripped out at each hop:

your wifi MAC
➡ router
➡ local ISP
➡ foreign proxy
➡ URL visited

The MAC is not included within the IP packet. *E.g.*, if you use a router, your ISP will register the *router's* MAC address and not the one from your wifi NIC. (This may *not* be the case regarding a VPN client, which has access to where the MAC is stored, in Layer 2 — one good reason to prefer SSH tunnels over VPNs. And, a MAC can be gathered by client side code such as Java or

ActiveX and placed inside the data layer — which is probably how the FBI's CIPAV works.) All that aside, *generally* a MAC address goes just one hop, because it's only needed for one hop and TCP/IP must be ready to receive the next MAC.

Those of you who use proxies don't have to worry about MAC addresses, as they are long since stripped off through the connection termination/reestablishment process.

Where MAC addresses are really vulnerable is the "air gap" of a wireless signal. (I see neighborhood routers' MACs all the time with my Linux wifi scanner.) It is a geek's no-brainer to grab with Wireshark any wifi MAC out of the air (computer or router), and spoof it if desired. This would not only circumvent any MAC filtering security you've got at home, but also allow a hacker to spoof your router/ISP relationship and act *as* you as far as the ISP knows. (This is much less of a concern if you directly connect your computer to DSL cable, thus eliminating the "air gap".) If a dedicated hacker knew of your OS, browser header, host name, and MAC addresses, he could easily spoof your computer and the ISP wouldn't know the difference. He could grab data packets meant for you (called a "man in the middle" attack), bypassing your router's encryption (even if WPA). While a router does generally mask your computer's MAC addresses, it's at the high price of security elsewhere. Use routers carefully and sparingly.

Spoofing your MAC (at least for wifi, since it's most often used) is a good idea, so that ISPs cannot track your history of connections. If your actual hardware MAC addresses were never seen by any router or ISP, then it would be very difficult to *ex post facto* link any online activity to your computer. Also, no ISP could discern if your computer were online, because no accurate (hardware) baseline of MACs had ever been made.

Can IP be determined from MAC?   Sometimes.

There is no universal mechanism for an end user to determine an IP address given a known MAC address, although it can be done in certain specific situations. The Address Resolution Protocol (Formerly known as ARP) allows a host to find the MAC address of a node with an IP address on the same physical network, when given the node's IP address. To make Address Resolution Protocol efficient, each

computer caches IP-to-MAC address mappings to eliminate repetitive Address Resolution Protocol broadcast requests.
—www.how-to-hide-ip.info/2008/03/11/determining-i
p-address-from-mac-address/

how to find your MAC (or "physical") addresses

It's a 12 digit hexadecimal string, *e.g.*, 00:73:JV:96:C8:J4.
Sometimes they are separated by hyphens, or not at all. Your
OS will display MAC addresses if you know how:

Windows 95 and newer	Run>CMD>winipcfg
Windows NT and newer	Run>CMD>ipconfig/all
Macintosh Open Transport:	TCP/IP Control Panel
	Info, or User Mode/Advanced
Macintosh with MacTCP	TCP/IP Control Panel - Ethernet icon
Linux and some Unix	ifconfig -a

changing your MAC addresses (Windows)

This can be done through software (most of it free), or by
hand. Here are some sites for more info:

www.nthelp.com/NT6/change_mac_w2k.htm
www.irongeek.com/i.php?page=security/changemac
http://en.wikibooks.org/wiki/Changing_Your_MAC_Address
www.klcconsulting.net/change_mac_w2k.htm
www.tech-faq.com/change-mac-address.shtml
www.nthelp.com/proggy/macshift.zip

Changing Windows MACs by hand is tolerably easy, though the
easier one requires a reboot. The other one involves Admin
User Rights (which you might not have) to change Registry
Keys, which isn't for the newbie or faint at heart.

Why bother? A nifty free software that automatically
randomizes/resets all MACs during boot is:

*MadMACs was designed with the privacy paranoid in mind.
The two main things a DHCP server records when you get an
IP from it is your host name and the MAC address of the
network card you are connecting from. This is identifying
information that not all users want to leave behind. MadMACs
allows you to randomize this information after it runs and
reboots.* (BTP: Experiment to make sure the program takes.)
— http://www.irongeek.com/i.php?page=security/changemac

changing your MAC addresses (Linux)

> www.hak5.org/wiki/MAC_Randomizer
> www.alobbs.com/macchanger

It's easy with just two script commands. For example, changing the Ethernet (eth0) adapter's MAC to 00:00:00:00:00:01:

> ifconfig eth0 down
> ifconfig eth0 hw ether 00:00:00:00:00:01
> ifconfig eth0 up

change MAC *before* connecting to the Internet

Startup programs such as MadMACs will change MACs before connection, but if changing them by hand be *sure* to have first turned off your wifi and/or unplugged the Ethernet cable.

changing your router's MAC address

While beyond the scope of this book, it's something to look into. Find out if your router supports it, and if your ISP will allow it without a lot of re-registration hassle (likely not).

Where changing a router's MAC makes sense is when you change service accounts or ISPs. You might as well begin with a new MAC to help cover your tracks.

your wifi router

do not rent a router — rather, buy it with cash

It wouldn't surprise me if router MAC addresses were somehow tied to the purchaser.

WEP encryption is easily breakable — use WPA instead!

WEP encryption is a joke, and anyone using Kismet for GNU-Linux or Retina Wi-Fi scanner for Windoze can bypass it pretty quickly. Traffic Injection, as my friend Cedric Blanchard pointed out a couple of months ago in Montreal, has dramatically decreased WEP cracking achievement time. And of course any 'Security professional' (and any 'Insecurity professional') should in my opinion have a look at Biondi's Scapy.

> — www.searchlores.org/Helsinki_.htm#bigbro

Note that while this "the longer the better" rule of thumb is always true, long passwords won't protect legacy WEP-protected networks due to well known and readily exploited weaknesses in the WEP keying system and its misuse of WEP's RC4 encryption. **With WEP protection, even a highly random maximum-entropy key can be cracked in a few hours.**

But the successor [to WEP], *called WPA, was specifically designed so that it could be retrofitted in older gear that only used the WEP encryption. So WPA is extremely strong. I mean, it's industrial strength. You can use it anywhere.*
— Steve Gibson, www.grc.com/SecurityNow.htm#11

Many public wifi hotspots are broadcast either in the clear or under WEP. A good packet sniffer can reconstruct WEP data from the raw, including POP logons (and their passphrases) usually in the clear. WPA encryption is *much* stronger. WPA routers are 802.11g standard (versus the 802.11b of WEP). Make sure that your wifi card supports 802.11g.

If, however, you use an SSH or VPN, your entire session is safe within a very robust encrypted tunnel. (Unless running stunnel.exe, SSL only encrypts page content — not headers, routing, etc., which the ISP and data hackers can read)

if you have a wifi router, enable the security option

Uninvited users slow down your own traffic, at the very minimum. At worst, strangers could access unsavory websites and download things that you'd never want linked to your IP and MAC (domestic ISP logs are forever). Use a very strong passphrase, and change the one your service tech provided.

try to randomize its MAC address

Many routers will allow a software override of its burned-in MAC address.

turn off your router whenever not in use

No data or MAC address can be sniffed if the router is off. Try to use the Ethernet cable whenever feasible.

FIREWALLS

A firewall ABSOLUTELY ISOLATES your computer from the Internet using a "wall of code" that inspects each individual "packet" of data as it arrives at either side of the firewall —

inbound to or outbound from your computer — to determine whether it should be allowed to pass or be blocked.
3rd party firewall is vital because the Windoze firewall allows outgoing connections and cannot be blocked.
-- www.grc.com

This is the most important piece of your armor. Think of a firewall as the security system around your house, and spyware as the roving dogs within the fence to capture successful intruders.   Some spyware includes a firewall, and some firewalls (*e.g.*, ZoneAlarm 6) have a bit of spyware, but such hybrid software is usually just a compromise somewhere. You'll need robust versions of both. www.smoothwall.org for Linux.

The standard Windows firewall is simply too porous (even after customizing its settings), and purposely allows *outbound* traffic (so that your computer can report to Microsoft HQ).

Many aftermarket firewalls (*e.g.*, Counterspy, www.kerio.com) are much better than Windows, but are either still too porous or run poorly with proxies.   Norton, quite frankly, sucks. If you use Norton, beware of its *extensive* logging (unless you disable it). ZoneAlarm 6 is a *much* better firewall, and keeps fewer logs (or none, if you say so). If you don't trust ZA, then try freeware Comodo (www.comodo.com). Install within a TrueCrypt volume for best security.

Unlike spyware (different software which can be run concurrently), firewalls are jealous creatures and it's not recommended that you run multiples together.   Go with ZoneAlarm, and disable Windows and Norton firewalls. Test for porosity with www.grc.com/lt/leaktest.htm.

Zone Alarm   **www.zonelabs.com**

I have learned that ZoneAlarm (and optionally the Tiny Personal Firewall) goes the extra mile of generating a "Cryptographic Signature" for every permitted program. This signature is then regenerated and compared before any program of that name is again allowed access. This completely prevents this simple form of trusted program impersonation, but NO OTHER FIREWALLS OFFER THIS CAPABILITY.
— www.grc.com

ZA was recommended to me by "Deep Chip" and I've found it excellent. Easy to use, yet very powerful. Its control of software (4 levels of Internet permission) is the most flexible I've seen, allowing you to specifically tailor your system. I had trouble using proxies before ZA, but not afterwards.

There is a free version that is adequate for most users, and pay-for versions with a few more features.

I would download/install ZA as the very first thing you do with your new computer. The free version setup file is about 30megs. Download a copy from a library computer to your thumb drive, and install on your computer before you get online for the very first time. I would set the security level on High for all zones, at first.

ZA popups will ask permission for each software's attempt to access the Net (often OK) or act as a server (rarely truly required; not even a proxy's putty.exe needs that). Experiment with denying permission and gradually acede as you must for system performance.

zones: "trusted" and "internet" (start with "trusted")

By granting access or server permission for the Trusted Zone, you enable a program to communicate only with the computers and networks you have put in that Zone.

By granting access or server permission for the Internet Zone, however, you enable a program to communicate with any computer or network, anywhere.
— ZoneAlarm

install ZoneAlarm in a TrueCrypt volume

That way, your activity logs and program control preferences are kept secure when you're offline. Since ZA then couldn't be loaded as a Startup program, you must remember to do so yourself after mounting that TC volume. You must also relocate the log archive *away from* C:\Windows\Internet Logs :
Alerts & Logs>Main>Advanced>Log Archive Location>Browse

be sure to turn off auto update!

Preferences>Check for updates>Manually
Also, deactivate auto updates for all software, else your ZA log will show your local IP (even for a blocked attempt).

BROWSERS

This interfaces your computer with the Net. What you choose is crucial to your privacy. Anything is better than MSIE.

Microsoft Internet Explorer (*Boo, hiss!*)

MSIE is a dangerous program designed by MS to allow remote servers to access your computer's registry. Although designed for use by MS to allow easy updating of the Windows Operating System, this feature could be used by any site to access your IP address, even your machine ID and your personal Credit Card details or worse, far worse, your saved passphrases. This can be done even if you have logged onto a site through a chain of proxies. In other words Microsoft Internet Explorer is an absolute no-no as far as anonymity is concerned.

-- www.privacy.li/security_faq.htm

Unnecesarily embedded within the OS (which compromises your whole box every time you're online), MSIE is an unholy mess. It is *riddled* with security holes and it creates/keeps far too many logs. It will log all IPs you connected to (have a look at your c:\WINDOWS\Internet Logs). Even if you use a proxy, the proxy's IP will be logged though the subsequent surfing will not. The date/time stamp of your proxy logon is exact enough to use in a search warrant for the proxy's logs (which, if kept, will contain your session history). MSIE is slow, too.

MSIE will allow your HD to be written with files from sites that you had never visited! (It is probably the open door through which the FBI's trojan horse CIPAV enters.) Finally, any regular user of it will need to download at least weekly the security patches. This is unheard of with Opera or Firefox.

I actually deleted the MSIE icon on my XP box. If you buy a new computer, I would not use MSIE even once. From a library computer download a copy of Opera or Firefox onto a USB drive and then install it on your own machine.

For more info about MSIE's surveillance "features" such as XML "userdata persistence" and "page hit counting" read:

The case for NOT using MSIE
www.searchlores.org/athei_06.htm

Netscape
The other horrible American browser, and really no better than MSIE. Avoid.

Opera   www.opera.com/download
Very good, but the 2006 version I used was limited about SOCKS proxies (maybe that's changed). It's lean (one-tenth the size of MSIE) but mean. Lots of great features, like blocking ad images on the fly (SHIFT+I), loading pages without their busy backgrounds, and deleting cookies immediately after use. Pestering ads and flash crap are a thing of the past. Opera has very strong control over what information is given out, such as referrer logging and automatic redirection. It's faster than even Firefox. A good overview at:

> Tutti all'opera!
> www.searchlores.org/tuttiope.htm

Mozilla Firefox   www.mozilla.org
A top choice to use with Windows, and it works nicely with all proxies. Good security features. And, it's *free*. (SeaMonkey is the Puppy Linux version.) Once you configure it nicely, it can match many of Opera's features (though not quite its speed).

misc. browser security tips
install your browser software in a TrueCrypt volume
That way, your bookmarks, settings, and activity logs (if retained) are kept secure when you're offline. Whatever program that does not *have* to be in the Startup menu should reside in TC Volume\Program Files. While your Windows .ini files will prove installation, that's all it will prove.

I'd have one TC volume for all such program files, and other TC volumes for the data. This kind of separation makes your computer much easier to scrub and modify.

do not use your browser's bookmark feature
I never save bookmarks in the browser, but in a .txt file within a TC volume. I can encrypt that file individually if I want to, and it keeps the browser files empty of helpful data. And, I can retrieve that .txt file to use with different browsers. It takes only a slight bit of extra work to copy/paste URLs, but it's

really no big deal and I find organizing them is easier in Notepad. (Plus, it's so simple to compile lists to include in emails or forum posts.)

deactivate auto updates!
These will leave local IP data in your firewall logs as they bypass your SSH and VPN tunnels.

delete: cache, cookies, history, and download
Set Opera and Firefox to delete these after every session. Assure yourself of their removal with frequent shredding of empty and slack space, followed by defragmentation.

install security plug-ins
Such as Firefox's No-Script and WOT.

EMAIL CLIENT

This is the interface between your computer and the email server, allowing you to quickly up/download your emails. Even though I don't use them, I do know that the worst email client is (of course) Microsoft's Outlook Express. Please use only open-source Quicksilver or Thunderbird. (Eudora is just OK.)

IP (Internet Protocol) ADDRESS

Everytime you connect from home or office, your session is given a particular IP address by your local ISP (Internet Service Provider), which is knowable by every site you visit. It is encoded in every email you send (click on "full headers" to read the originating IPs of your Inbox emails). This allows web forensic tools to collect much info about your operating system, Internet browser type and version, your physical location, and what you are viewing.

Your internet provider retains a log file that shows the times your IP address was used and where it connected to. Some internet providers save these log files indefinitely and they may give these files to whoever asks with or without a court order and this would mean every website you visited and

everything you did is no longer private. Your internet provider has your home address, name, phone, credit card etc. When this information is turned over to third parties your privacy has been violated big time and you don't even know it. The results of this can be stalking electronically or physically, identity theft, and other forms of harassment.
      — www.findnot.com/privacy.html

Even if you go online from a public computer, the terminal you use is tied with its temporarily assigned "dynamic" IP. This is easily correlated with that paper sign-up list most libraries keep. (Or, you may be recorded on camera using that terminal.)

If you use your laptop wifi at a coffee shop or hotel, their IP will be known in your emails and by the sites you visit. And, the local ISP has access to all nonencrypted content.

The log-on origin of your computer is specified by four numerals (*e.g.*, 207.195.240.197). Every ISP (Internet Service Provider) rents a block of IPs (*e.g.*, 207.195.240.0 through 207.195.255.255). Thus, even the most casually interested can visit ws.arin.net/cgi-bin/whois.pl and learn that 207.195.240.197 is owned by GBU Internet, LLC. Who is that? A Delaware LLC (*heh, heh*) which provides IP blocks to a well-known internet firm called anonymizer.com. And this nicely segues into the solution to exposed IP addresses:

anonymous surfing

An encrypted tunnel is what this is called, an encrypted tunneling service, where you would run some client software on your side. Basically you're using the wireless connection to get your machine on the Internet. Then you're creating an encrypted tunnel connection between your machine, client software running on your side, and this service, for example, the Anonymizer secure tunneling service, so that your traffic is encrypted through the air, across the Internet, to Anonymizer.com, where it is then decrypted in order to then transit from their location out over the Internet, just as you normally would if you were at home or in a corporate environment or wherever else. The point being that the vulnerable segment, where you're going over the air from your computer to the coffee shop or airport access point, that's encrypted. It's also encrypted all the way to where it gets to

Anonymizer, so you're safe against, for example, employees at the access point who might be able to sniff your traffic . . ..
    — www.grc.com

You can surf the internet and send emails without revealing your IP by the use of a proxy (which is similar to using a postal remailer to hide your origin). Only the proxy's IP can be seen (although the proxy will know your local IP). This is available even for iPhones and the like.

offshore servers

It is *highly* advisable to choose services who base their computers outside US jurisdiction. In the (Forever) War on Terrorism, U.S. companies are at the mercy of any fed with a badge and an attitude. Your U.S. records are simply not private in this increasingly Orwellian age.

For example, here is Anonymizer's privacy policy:

*...we disclose personal information only in the good faith belief that we are **required to do so by** [U.S.] **law**, or that doing so is reasonably necessary to: **comply with legal process**;...*
    — http://anonymizer.com/company/legal/privacy_policy.html

Several companies use offshore servers (*e.g.,* Netherlands, Germany, Malaysia, etc.) which are beyond leisurely reach of U.S. law. (Findnot was the leader in this regard, with 30+ servers located on 17 IP blocks spread amongst 6 countries, but their service mysteriously dropped in May 2009.) **Neomail** offers servers in Holland, and **Steganos** in Germany. **Privacy.li** is based in Lichtenstein. **Cotse** is in Europe.

A great comparison site is www.myvpnreviews.com.

always use a proxy, even if only a domestic one

While I strongly recommend using only foreign proxy tunnels, you may not need such extra protection.

For Wi-Fi users, a VPN protects your data by closing the "air-gap". The "air-gap" is simply the distance between your laptop and the internet access point. All the data that flows across that gap is unencrypted - meaning anyone within range of your internet access point can read all your emails, see the websites you visit, and steal all the website passwords . . . .
    — http://publicvpn.com/

It's based on redundant server clusters in Virginia and Los Angeles. You just configure your Mac or PC to use its native (not IPsec) VPN capabilities and point it at the HotSpotVPN servers. Your traffic will be encrypted through the tunnel between your computer and HotSpotVPN. From there it travels normally (in the clear or protected by SSL) to the Internet.
    — www.hotspotvpn.com

We have to admit, the iPhantom [www.iphantom.com] is one of the more clever ideas we've seen in a long time when it comes to road-warrior security. Without getting too deep into the nitty gritty on it, the iPhantom essentially appears to be a location-independent transparent VPN-tunneling proxy — in other words, this device encrypts all your outgoing traffic, sends it to a secure proxy node on Phantom's network, and forwards it for you.
    —www.engadget.com/2005/08/08/the-iphantom-transpare
      nt-vpn-tunneling-proxy/

the (mere) redirecting proxy

These are the most simple, but offer no content privacy. All they do is fool the website you're visiting as to your IP. (Often, that's enough.) There are many free proxies out there:

    www.thefreecountry.com/security/anonymous.shtml
    www.anonymouse.org

You cannot use these free services for any SSL (Secure Socket Layer) content, nor for http POST requests (*e.g.*, checking your Yahoo email account). These are fine for bland surfing, but these "rewriting" proxies do not mask content from anybody, nor even routing headers from your ISP. For that kind of privacy, you'll need an encrypted tunnel of either SSH or VPN.

you need an encrypted *session*

Otherwise your local ISP (or anybody else who might be intercepting your data packets) can read your traffic.

web-based rewriting proxy (creates https SSL connection)

These proxies do not require any downloaded software or plugins, so you can use them away from home and office (*i.e.*, on public terminals) as long as your browser is SSL-capable. It's not an encrypted tunnel (only an encrypted connection).

This is decent option for those who don't go online from home or office computers, and who use web-based email (Yahoo, Gmail, Hotmail, Mailvault, Hushmail, MyMail, etc.).

www.neomailbox.net offers this, and it's easy to use. Instead of visiting www.javelinpress.com directly, you'd enter:

https://neomailbox.net/p/www.javelinpress.com

A dialog box then appears asking you for your Neomailbox username and passphrase. (Only $29.95/year!) Then all data to/from www.javelinpress.com will be encrypted in SSL (as is typical with most credit card order pages).

It's not reliably effective against Java, JavaScript, Flash, Active X, and other active content — so disable these. (They recommend the free proxy connection software **stunnel.exe**.) Neverless, the rewriting proxy can come in handy on public computers as a fallback option in case you don't have your laptop, VPN, or SSH.. (Do *not* frequent the same public computers, as they're not under your control).

Understand that your local ISP knows the sites you visit through the SSL, but not the content. I wouldn't rely on an SSL connection to mask IP from Gmail (which is quite invasive).

What is neat about the Neomailbox SSL connection is that you can easily use it *within* an encrypted tunnel (SSH or VPN) from a provider (such as Relakks in Sweden). Relakks can't know exact content (privacy), and Neomailbox can't discern your identity or location (anonymity). This greatly reduces vulnerability from using a *single* encrypted proxy provider. For web pages without active content, this is a good strategy.

SSL connections require stunnel.exe, which works in nearly any computer (and there's a Firefox plug-in). Stunnel will secure non-SSL aware daemons and protocols (like POP, IMAP, LDAP, etc.). This connection is not very secure against Java, though it's stronger than a web-based SSL rewrite.

tunneling proxy (usually requires software), SSH and VPN

Even for those who are not privacy-passionate, using tunnels is still a must when wifi logging on from hotels, cafes, etc. because tunnels prevent your passphrases (and everything else) from being broadcast in the clear (which are frequently intercepted by credit card thieves). From public access points (especially wifi), I wouldn't visit *any* site which required a passphrase unless the session were within an encrypted tunnel.

SSH tunnels require putty.exe, meaning that you can use SSH only on downloadable computers. (*I.e.,* no SSH from the library computer, unless you reboot with a Puppy Linux live CD, and then activate the onboard SSH client through the Console command: ssh -D 1088 -p 80 username etc.) You will have to configure browsers (and other apps) to connect through your SSH tunnel. This is much more secure than PPTP VPN because no data will leak when the connection fails. Their only real downside is lack of auto-reconnect, but that's no big deal.

VPN tunnels require a VPN client on your computer (standard in Windows, but the Puppy Linux client is fussy). Besides being easy to set up, fast and very stable, an advantage of VPN over SSH is that your *all* traffic can be configured to go through VPN. Also, VoIP works sometimes *only* on VPN.

Dozens of providers exist (many are outside the U.S., such as Relakks, Blacklogic, Banana VPN, Metropipe, Trilight Zone, and Steganos). The most secure VPN is **OpenVPN** (not supported by many providers, but this is improving). Next in security is **L2TP**, but it's tricky to install and has issues. **PPTP** is quite insecure (I call it "the WEP of VPN"), and there's usually no reason to prefer it (though some Pocket PC devices use only PPTP). Google's Gmail can apparently pierce both PPTP and L2TP connections to ascertain a local IP. *Eeeeww!*

If sites are inaccessible after connection, then you must flush your DNS cache (Start Menu>Run>ipconfig/flushdns), check your adapter binding order ("send all traffic over VPN connection"), or manually assign DNS server to the VPN. Port 1723 must not be blocked by your firewall, software, or router.

For fantastic security, run OpenVPN, and then an SSH tunnel (from another provider) within that. Tunnels within tunnels are *extremely* secure.

Be sure to firewall force VPN as the *only* connection, else when the VPN drops, traffic will revert through your local IP!

cost for tunneling proxy service

For a quality SSH or VPN, $10-15/month, but it's worth it. The most expensive firm I've seen is Perfect Privacy (about $200/year). Their technology (from SSH-2 to OpenVPN) and service (over two dozen servers!) are *very* impressive, and they accept just about every kind of payment (including cash). And, they claim to have *disabled* logging, which is very rare. Most people spend much more than $200/year for DSL or satellite.

what will your local ISP know?

From an encrypted SSH or VPN proxy session? Only that an encrypted tunnel was connected to another server. The ISP can't tell with whom on the other side, much less what content was exchanged. Your proxy tunnel server is, in effect, your local ISP — and your ISP is little more than a (clueless) router. If you log on to a local ISP through public wifi, and have spoofed your MAC address, that local ISP is like a pass-through server.

In fact, your DSL cable could be spliced from just outside your computer and it wouldn't disclose anything but how many data packets were sent and received.

Your local ISP will, however, know your computer's "host name" (its serial number) and MAC address of the connecting device. Both of these can be randomized with MadMac.exe.

Millions of people every day use SSH and VPN tunnels in business and government, so these tunnels are quite common.

IM and VoIP supported?

Most quality tunnels will support IM and VoIP. For highest privacy, you *must* connect through an SSH tunnel (as VPN does *not* always hide your IP from IMs, "phone home" software, and other third-party logs, unless you've *really* buttoned down your firewall to guarantee traffic flow via VPN).

Be *very* careful when setting up this software, and before using it for the first time make *sure* that you've enabled the proxy setting as the *sole* connection for *all* apps. Otherwise, it will not "know" about your proxy and will instead connect directly through your local ISP, and this will be logged. (A superb firewall such as ZoneAlarm or Comodo will alert you to such an attempt before allowing the connection.) A computer geek friend is probably essential, to set this up reliably. Info at:

http://strongvpn.com/forum/viewtopic.php?id=294

no long-term storage of logs

While proxies will keep logs for 2-7 days (for their own system purposes), they claim to delete them afterwards. If so, then they'll have no records of your IP or your surf history.

We don't keep logs period so there is no record of your activity no matter who wants to know. Since we do not log anything related to our customer's internet activity, we have nothing to produce even we are requested to do so.

. . . The time required for an attorney to file a lawsuit, and then generate subpoenas usually runs into the months. Subpoenas typically require someone to comply within 10-30 days, depending on the subpoena. If one has no information to provide then the subpoena would be returned with notation that requested information is not in the possession of the entity served with the subpoena.
— www.findnot.com/privacy.html (now defunct?)

They claimed never to have received an enforceable subpoena. Since they claimed to delete their logs after 5 days, very little (if any) information would still be active even if they *were* ever properly served. (Presumably, they could warn their client, or simply terminate service for his protection, but don't count on this.) They also claimed not to keep any customer emails.

anonymous payment without *any* personal information

This means not having to use your credit card. Some proxies take cash or M.O.s, but you must be careful that your mailing location gives nothing away. Several (such as Neomailbox) take different forms of digitial gold, but your privacy is only as strong as you made it when establishing and loading such accounts. (More on digital gold payments elsewhere.)The best way to fund your proxy is with a nonreloadable debit VISA which can be used internationally (this rules out WalMart's cards!). Some companies accept Liberty Reserve, a good alternative.

Register the card, email contact, and tunnel from the same IP during one session — this provides great insularity.

I'd avoid anybody who processes credit card orders through the privacy-intrusive PayPal. That rules out at least two good foreign services (Perfect Privacy and Trilightzone).

Some firms (Cienen, VPN Privacy) insist on phoning you to provide your new PIN, and this may be too creepy for you (even with a prepaid cell phone). And, no, they won't phone you at your VoIP number — sorry.

confirm that you are actually running through a proxy

The easiest way is to set up one particular browser (not MSIE, of course) to use the proxy, and another for direct connection (if this is frequent).

There a many websites which will display your IP, such as www.whatismyip.com.   Search for more, and use several (perhaps one for each different proxy). Your browser's default home page should be one of these sites, so that you're assured from the beginning of your session that the proxy is active. Change these sites at least every month.

GeoIP is excellent. http://geoip.dmwtechnologies.com/

It is the all in one API, which can extract Country, Capital, State/Region, City, Area code, Metro code, PIN code, Currency, Calling Code, Current Conversion rate (with USD), Local Time, Current Weather, Latitude, Longitude and more information just from the IP address.

confirm *which* proxy with www.whois.net

Proxies change over time, and your batch file link to a Dutch proxy may later go to one in Chicago without notice. (Findnot was notorious about this.) This is a critical issue if you're trying to avoid domestic IPs. Know your foreign proxy's IP by heart so that any change is obvious during a www.whatismyip.com homepage download. Be wary of any key certificate change, and don't divulge your passphrase then.

frequently confirm that your local IP is masked

Some proxies are immune to Java tattling your real IP, while others are not. Test them (Java on and off) with:

> www.stayinvisible.com/cgi-bin/iptest.cgi
> www.lagado.com/proxy-test
> www.grc.com (their ShieldsUp! is probably the best)

is the connection stable?

Findnot's SSH tunnels dropped at least once/hour (and not all of their offshore choices are up and running), while Neomailbox's stunnel is *very* stable (though often Java transparent). You will have to experiment with several.

privacy policies

Read these *very* carefully before you sign up. Under which circumstances would they ever divulge personal info? Merely *"to comply with legal demands"* or only forced by court order? A *"good-faith belief"* of necessary disclosure to law enforcement

(Banana VPN) is hardly reassuring. Read privacy policies carefully, and research each company's reputation.

can you trust your proxy service?

Not infinitely. Even if the technology were perfect, the people running it are not. One proxy I do *not* trust is Anonymizer because they serve governments:

> *The Anonymizer® Enterprise Chameleon protects the government identity and provides information assurance when users are online.*
>
> Government Insight *provides government agencies white papers, articles and robust solutions to keep their online activities confidential.*

Yes, there are *"nefarious Web sites"* which likely deserve monitoring, but the fact that Anonymizer so actively courts government accounts encourages me to look elsewhere. They are too big for my comfort, and brazenly deal with governments. Also, they are US-based with US servers, under U.S. leverage.

Even if you've thoroughly tested your proxy's spoof IP with good diagnostics, I wouldn't utterly trust any tunnel to hide your local IP. Even if the proxy service indeed deletes their logs every 5-7 days as claimed, you have no firsthand knowledge who owns the company and where their loyalites really lie.

If you are really concerned about it, then *never* get online from home, not even via tunnels. Go to a public wifi, do your business, logoff, shred your MRU, etc. files, and then shutdown.

A final thought about trusting proxies: being online without an encrypted tunnel is *certainly* risky, while being online though a proxy provider *may* be risky. The NSA is downloading all cleartext Internet traffic, anyway, so logic says to go with a tunneling proxy service. You've really nothing extra to lose, and you're more secure from local hackers.

logging on from hotels and airports (don't trust them)

Most of the time, you will first have to directly connect to the Internet through their portal, and then change your browser back to proxy connection. (They do this to temporarily allow your computer access through MAC address filtering. Thus, your hostname and wifi MAC address is forever associated with the name and credit card of your check-in.)

After reverting back to your tunnel proxy, run some *thorough* diagnostics for IP traceback.

can a proxy be backtraced to your name or real IP?

Though usually very difficult, yes, it's theoretically possible, but "they" have to begin *somewhere*. Either from a site you're known to frequent, or from a proxy service you're known to use (*e.g.,* if you paid by credit card, or blabbed which proxy you preferred), or from some IP address that you've used before.

Assuming that you didn't order with your credit card (or used an anonymous nonreloadable prepaid credit card), then it's likely your email account or website will be flagged. That ISP (if US-based) *will* comply with requests for IP surf history, which then resolve to your proxy.

From your proxy to you, it's steeply uphill through traffic analysis. TA is the attempt to, for example, tie your Yahoo email account logs to your proxy's traffic (via timestamp data and packet size), and thus to your IP. (This is different from examining ISP logs days or months later; here I'm talking about monitoring realtime traffic.) Although you've a secure tunnel with your proxy, your proxy does *not* have a secure tunnel with the IPs you are indirectly accessing. *I.e.,* proxy traffic (address and content) on your behalf is in the clear. TA exploits this.

Proxy traffic in general is no doubt scrutinized by the NSA, etc. By packet matching incoming with outgoing, the proxy intermediary can be made transparent—though probably not in any real-time basis. (Only the NSA could answer this.) Hence, the wifi laptop road warrior could easily jump on and off the Net for brief sessions with confident security (although prior locations and thus a vector of travel could be assembled, which provides a great opportunity for a disinfo trail).

A customer-created proxy chain will complicate the backtrace, of course, but additional TA might prevail. I can't imagine any peaceable person worth such trouble. Only TOR or JAP has any real chance of completely muddying those waters.

Again, be sure that no software is allowed to auto update. Even if blocked by your firewall, a log records the attempt. Test your IP masking frequently with sites such as:

http://privacy.net/analyze-your-internet-connection/

TOR (The Onion Router)

Speaking of proxy chains, TOR is *truly* the ultimate. First of all, it's free, so there's no revealing payment history. Based on volunteer bandwidth contributions by thousands of TORries, a unique proxy chain is created at the beginning of *each* session.

Backtracing seems nearly impossible through TA because of the chain's randomness and complexity. (There are nested encrypted packets which are individually opened only at each respective proxy link. No link knows the whole chain.) While noticeably slower to use, it's the price one pays for such security.

There is the Videlia bundle for Firefox, which transforms that browser into a dedicated TOR surf vehicle. TOR requires a fairly high degree of technical sophistication to use, however, once installed a more basic user can be instructed on how to operate it. (Most people don't need the power of TOR, and couldn't run it, anyway.) Episode #70 of www.grc.com has some great commentary about TOR.

Consider helping TOR out with your own unused bandwidth when you're offline. It's safe for your computer, and this will help speed up service for everyone.

JAP Anonymity and Privacy Freeware

JAP uses a single static address which is shared by many JAP users. That way neither the visited website, nor an eavesdropper can determine which user visited which website. This allows anonymous surfing. How it works: Instead of connecting directly to a webserver, users take a detour, connecting with encryption through several intermediaries, so-called mixes. JAP uses a predetermined sequence for the mixes. Such a sequence of linked mixes is called a mix cascade. Users can choose between different mix cascades. Since many users use these intermediaries at the same time, the internet connection of any one single user is hidden among the connections of all the other users. No one, not anyone from outside, not any of the other users, not even the provider of the intermediary service can determine which connection belongs to which user.

The data sent by you is separately encrypted for every mix server and slightly altered in size and sequence so that nobody can eavesdrop on or guess your data stream.
— http://anon.inf.tu-dresden.de/index_en.html

This is all very ingenious, and should thwart TA. With the data packets changed in size and mixed up, there is no need for an elaborate proxy chain such as TOR. (In order to assemble the mix cascade, all intermediaries would have to cooperate with authorities — which is very unlikely.) The one downside I see to

JAP is that it requires *Java!* Such a dangerous browser plugin is warned against even by JAP's own website:

> *Webcontent accessible by browser plugins such as Flash, Java, ActiveX and Silverlight renders the Web more dynamic and colorful but also more dangerous, for they allow websites to execute code on your PC. If executed, these plugin contents are able to read some details about your computer and network configuration and send it to the web server. By certain manipulations they moreover can read and edit files on your machine and in an extreme case even gain complete control over it. Especially beware signed Java applets: by accepting its signature, the applet, and thereby the visited webserver, automatically receives all user rights on your machine. In particular, it may then read your IP address, your MAC address and even hard disk contents.*
>
> **Websites which demand usage of active plugins should be avoided if possible.**

It remains to be seen if JAP recognizes their paradox, and redesigns what seems to be an excellent idea to run Java-free. Also, JAP was allegedly forced by government to compromise itself, which was exposed through open source compiling.

redundacy in proxies

You should also have an unused backup array of tunnels and email accounts to employ post-seizure (and especially if you believe that prosecution is imminent). All of that must have been established on a separate computer, with dedicated prepaid dedit cards -- the works. Make certain you've absolutely no crossover links to your "normal" computer life. (If matters are dire, you will have to cease visiting your favorite websites and forums until everything blows over.)

don't bet the ranch on proxies!

If disclosure of your location, identity, or what you communicate would be devastating, then you'd be wise not to email it (not even through a foreign tunnel with robust open-source encryption). If a non-geek like me can come up with an apparently strong system as described in this chapter, then the FBI or NSA can probably pierce that veil if they really wanted to. *I.e.*, if you're worth the trouble, somebody will eventually *take* the trouble (such as the FBI and its CIPAV).

EMAIL PROVIDERS

There is no reason (much less *compunction*) to rely on plaintext message content and US-based Yahoo, Hotmail, Gmail, aol, etc. These companies store everything, fully cooperate with the feds, and will turn over your email history and content without a court order (thanks to the "*USA PATRIOT*" Act). Also, your plaintext email is like writing personal info and sending it by *postcard*.

Instead, go *offshore* based (to hinder US snooping), and preferably offer web-based encryption. There are many good options: Hushmail, Mailvault, Zipmail, etc., all providing encrypted email from within each other. (Do understand that message headers always remain in plaintext and thus readable. Keep your subject lines innocuous.)

Hushmail.com

My own opinion is weakened, due to news like this:

> *There has been at least one instance in which Hushmail has turned over e-mail messages to US law enforcement agencies [1]. In addition, Hushmail logs IP addresses "to analyze market trends, gather broad demographic information, and prevent abuse of our services." Hushmail states that a court order from a court of British Columbia, Canada is required for the release of user information. . . In the past, it was believed that possible threats, such as demands from the legal system to reveal the content of traffic through the system, were not as imminent in Canada as they are in the United States. However, Hushmail has turned over copies of supposedly private e-mail messages to law enforcement agencies under a Mutual Legal Assistance Treaty with the United States. One example of this behavior is in the case of U.S. v. Tyler Stumbo.*
> — http://en.wikipedia.org/wiki/Hushmail

There are two modes of encrypting your Hushmail: through client side Java applets (somewhat secure), and through server side SSL (less secure).

> *. . . in Java mode the level of trust the user must place in us somewhat reduced, although not eliminated.*

> *The extra security given by the Java applet is not particularly relevant, in the practical sense, if an individual account is targeted.*
> *Hushmail is useful for avoiding general Carnivore-type government surveillance, and protecting your data from hackers, but definitely not suitable for protecting your data if you are engaging in illegal activity that could result in a Canadian court order.*
> — Hushmail CTO Brian Smith, from *Wired* magazine

So, you've been warned: Hushmail can circumvent client side Java applet encryption. Nonetheless, it is far superior to plaintext Hotmail and Yahoo, and will thwart content vacuuming schemes through the ISP and nodes.

Mailvault.com

I think it's superior encryption to Hushmail, but their site is too often down for my taste. Give both a test drive.

However, never bet the bank on server side encryption!

how to send encrypted email to those who haven't PGP

As long as you can pose a difficult test question to the recipient that he is sure to answer, then go through the kind services of:

www.hushmail.com/services-send

The email content (though never sender, recipient, or subject) will be nicely encrypted in an SSL packet (hence the **https**).

Strengthen the passphrase with upper and lower case, numerals, and at least one metacharacter. Instead of asking just one question, ask two or three, with their answers strung together with, for example, a + sign. Sample questions could be:

your mom's favorite TV character+month and year birthday for "Mr. Hilarious"+city in which we ran out of gas

A sample multi-answer passphrase (so that the recipient clearly understands the format) would be:

Bob Newhart+March 1985+Des Moines

That's a fairly robust passphrase, and very difficult for any third party to crack. Your first encrypted email message could then contain a virtually unbreakable passphrase (generated by www.grc.com/passwords.htm) to be used thereafter.

Or, if you've a face-to-face meeting with the recipient in advance, why not establish a mutual passphrase? Yes, everybody using PGP would be ideal, but most people never will, so it's up to you to bridge the privacy gap with them.

~~PGP email~~ (good tutorial below)
PGP/GPG to Encrypt Your Email (Windows)
http://vertoro.com/enigmail.htm

SEARCH ENGINES

Avoid Google, as it is the most expansive and effective monitor of your interests and shopping habits ever devised:

www.criminaljusticeusa.com/blog/2009/25-surprising-things-that-google-knows-about-you/

Instead, **Scroogle** (an intermediary) is your friend. Add www.scroogle.org/cgi-bin/scraper.htm as "default search engine" to Firefox (search for the plug-in to add it to the search engine taskbar). **Clusty** is another cookie-free search engine.

SPYWARE

Spyware detects and/or defeats malicious programs that somehow got past your firewall. You can and should use several spyware programs together, as each have their own respective strengths and tend to cover each others' weaknesses. WebRoot's SpySweeper is one of the best.

malware threats

Keyfiles can be copied by appropriate malware, plus your OS could invisibly cache its contents, then leave them lying around after you've removed the media containing the keyfile.

ActiveX objects

These are executable code (*i.e.*, programs) that can be downloaded and executed inside Internet Explorer. Before these objects are downloaded there is usually a warning dialog in Internet Explorer, asking you if you really want to download and use this object, but depending on security settings and security flaws in Internet Explorer you might not even see this warning dialog. Once the ActiveX object has been downloaded to your computer, it can do practically anything, for example infecting the computer with viruses, or install keyloggers or other nasty spyware. These possibilities are indeed also used in large scale by the bad guys on the internet. Because of these risks, it is quite good to keep track of which ActiveX objects are actually downloaded to your computer, and be able to remove the unwanted ones.

   All-Seeing   Eye   from   www.fortego.com/en/ase.html notifies you of any added, modified or removed ActiveX objects in your computer, and also gives you the option to remove any of them immediately when they are detected.

Java and JavaScript

   Capable of bypassing your internet proxy service and displaying your true IP address.   (Neomailbox stunnel is vulnerable to Java. Test your tunnel for IP transparency.)

> *Both Hotmail and Hushmail (and the latest version of Yahoo) insist on you having both Java and Javascript enabled before they allow you to open an account. This is unacceptable to me. I would never recommend using any Email service with such a requirement.*
> *-- www.privacy.li/security_faq.htm*

webbugs

> *"Webbugs" are usually pictures of 1x1 pixels and therefore invisible to the viewer. However, they can also be coded into banner ads embedded in a website. The website contains a picture that is loaded from another server running a statistics service (such as Doubleclick, Google Analytics). Thereby the statistics service may set or edit a cookie in your browser unnoticeably. The browser will then send this cookie back to the statistics service with every new request for a site where any webbug of this service is embedded. If the service is used on many different websites, it can now track large parts of your browsing session. If the owner of the statistics service moreover collaborates with . . . your preferred search engine, he gets an almost complete picture of your internet activities.*
> *— http://anon.inf.tu-dresden.de/index_en.html*

the FBI's "CIPAV"

In 2007 *Wired* magazine broke the story that the FBI used its own spyware to identify the high-schooler who used the Internet to make bomb threats.

> *The FBI euphemistically calls its software a "computer and internet protocol address verifier," or CIPAV.*
>
> *In general, a CIPAV utilizes standard Internet computer commands commonly used over local area networks (LANs) and the Internet to request that an activating computer respond to the CIPAV by sending network level messages, and/or other variables, and/or information, over the Internet to a computer controlled by the FBI.*
>
>   — http://blog.wired.com/27bstroke6/files/timberline_affidavit.pdf
>   http://blog.wired.com/27bstroke6/surveillance/index.html
>   www.wired.com/politics/law/news/2007/07/fbi_spyware
>   http://blog.wired.com/27bstroke6/2009/04/get-your-fbi-sp.html

This CIPAV spyware was probably first extensively used just after 9/11, given this formerly classified March 2002 memo:

> *As many of you know, some investigators have begun to use an investigative technique referred to as an 'Internet Protocol Address Verifier" . . . While the technique is of indisputable value in certain kinds of cases, we are seeing indications that it is being used needlessly by some agencies, unnecessarily raising difficult legal questions (and risk of suppression) without any countervailing benefit.*
>
>   — March 7, 2002 internal memo from the DoJ's Computer Crime and Intellectual Property Section

. . . and within *months* it was being improperly used!

> *I think it's safe to say the use of such a technique raises novel and unresolved legal issues.*
>
>   — attorney David Sobel, of Electronic Frontier Foundation

While CIPAV has proven an effective tool in capturing actual criminals of property and violence, the fact that the DoJ admits to misuse sounds like it's been employed as an illegal surveillance tool (hence the *"risk of suppression"*) by multiple agencies on nonviolent people (hence the *"without any countervailing benefit"* language). Persons of interest are likely being located through the tool, even if CIPAV's information is inadmissible in court. For that reason, I have no moral qualms discussing CIPAV here.

what data CIPAV gathers and transmits

> IP address
> MAC address for the network card
> list of open TCP and UDP ports
> list of running programs
> OS type, version, and serial number
> default language of the operating system
> default browser and its version
> registered owner and registered company name
> currently logged-in username
> last visited URL (probably a referral URL)

CIPAV acts like a pen register of IP and URLs

It apparently does not record traffic content. (The Timberline warrant specifically mentioned this *three* times.)

why CIPAV seems dedicated to Windows

Three things in particular point to Windows:

> OS serial number
> registered owner and registered company name
> currently logged-in username

Only Windows is so anal about serial numbers, registered owners, and usernames. (Linux is an open-source OS which does not even *have* serial numbers! In Windows, however, the serial number is the 25-digit alphanumeric product activation key.) Granted, these criteria could also point to a Mac, but I don't think that Mac asks to register a "company name".

Finally, if any OS manufacturer were covertly helpful in developing CIPAV, it's Microsoft. (Remember their NSA backdoor file, the advapi.dll?)

infecting a (likely Windows) computer

The CIPAV will be deployed via a Uniform Resource Locator (URL) address posted to the subject's private chat room on MySpace.com.

First, the FBI had to know *where* to offer a URL to the Unsub. In this case it was his alias MySpace account, but had they known his email address they could have sent him the URL in some enticing email. My point is that for CIPAV to work the Unsub must have some known contact point, and then he must then participate by visiting the FBI's covert site.

So, the Unsub clicks the link, his browser (likely MSIE) loads the page, and in doing so a trojan horse (likely a plug-in such as Java or ActiveX) is delivered to his hard-drive.

speculating on the FBI's highly attractive URL

In a separate February 2007, Cincinnati-based investigation of hackers who'd successfully targeted an unnamed bank, the documents indicate the FBI's efforts may have been detected. An FBI agent became alarmed when the hacker he was chasing didn't get infected with the spyware after visiting the CIPAV-loaded website. **Instead, the hacker "proceeded to visit the site 29 more times,"** *according to a summary of the incident.* **"In these instances, the CIPAV did not deliver its payload because of system incompatibility."**

There are very few websites I've visited *29 times*, so it's interesting to contemplate what site could be so fascinating. My hunch is that the FBI was maintaining a dynamic high-quality porn site for CIPAV. (Stranger things have happened.)

If they were *really* clever they'd host an apparently effective anti-CIPAV site with lots of great technical info, covering all but a few vital areas. Anybody interested in foiling CIPAV unknowingly gets a download of it. If this notion strikes a chord in you, then visit all CIPAV oriented sites from a public computer, and save only the text into a simple Notepad file.

Oh, and that *"system incompatibility"*? CIPAV seems more and more to have been designed for Windows, and maybe only for MSIE. Sounds like "Mr. 29" used either Mac or Linux.

CIPAV transmission of info

That CIPAV can transmit a list of your visited URLs likely means that such log files were *already* created by your OS and/or your browser. This screams Windows and Internet Explorer. Linux does not create and keep "userdata" files with such information, but your Windows box does. CIPAV was apparently designed to read and transmit personal info from .dat and .xml files buried deep within Windows.

beware unknown links and attachments

This is just good security, regardless of CIPAV. You should have a unique IP address/tunnel/email account path which is never used to click on emailed links and attachments.

protecting your computer

. . . announcing use of the CIPAV would assist a person controlling the activating computer(s) to evade revealing its true IP address, other variables, and certain registry-type information — thereby defeating the CIPAV's purpose.

— page 16 of the Timberline warrant

There you have it: CIPAV is not invincible. It's probably easier to defeat than most would assume.

In order for this particular backdoor (CIPAV) and many others to be effective, the user needs to either visit a page in which they'll be infected, likely via a browser delivered trojan. This particular attack vector can be accomplished one of many ways and is likely ONLY to infect Windows based operating systems. I state this with certainty without having to get into a discourse on operating systems and their security.

Anyhow, the first thing I would do in a situation regarding Windows is download the following, and this is two fold, one it protects my machine from intruders, secondly it alerts me to any funny activity coming to or leaving my machine. Remember the key with this document is to prevent anything from leveraging my machine. An attack is an attack is an attack. If something is coming to or leaving my machine, I'd want to know about it, especially if its leaving my machine without me sending it.

— www.infiltrated.net/cipav.pimp

The author then recommends the below software and describes how to employ them effectively. This is fairly technical stuff, and requires an above-average computer ability.

Windows Protection Tools 101:

Mozilla Firefox NoScript plug-in
http://noscript.net/

Comodo Personal Firewall
www.comodo.com/products/free_products.html

Spybot Search and Destroy
www.safer-networking.org/

Lavasoft's AdAware
www.lavasoft.de/

Crap Cleaner
www.ccleaner.com/

AVG Antirootkit
www.grisoft.com/doc/download-free-anti-rootkit/us/crp/0

Avast Antivirus or Kapersky Labs AV
www.avast.com/

Autoruns (pre-Microsoft if you could find it)
http://download.sysinternals.com/Files/Autoruns.zip

Process Explorer (same as above)
http://download.sysinternals.com/Files/ProcessExplorer.zip

SpywareBlaster
www.javacoolsoftware.com/

The below 39 page report by Howard Fosdick is a superb overview of protecting your Windows machine. Since the .pdf version hasn't executable links, I've added an html version.

How to Secure Windows and Your Privacy, by Howard Fosdick
www.rexxinfo.org/How_to_Secure_Windows_and_Your_Privacy.pdf
www.osnews.com/story/19701/How_to_Secure_Your_Windows_Computer_and_Protect_Your_Privacy

Nevertheless, with all *that* trouble, it really is easier to just migrate to Puppy Linux for your online needs. I went quite far down the Windows security path, and the time and system load really became excessive. (The boot up/down sequence including all the searching and shredding was over 10 minutes!) It's a never-ending job trying to secure such a viral OS, because you won't *really* know if you've gotten everything. Even trying will soon foment increasing paranoia in the user, as there is always pressure to add yet another anti-spyware package.

At some point, just throw in the towel and get yourself a new Puppy running OpenOffice! I have an entire chapter on doing just that.

some misc. tips for all users
beware auto updates!

These are legion: spyware, firewall, MediaPlayer, Google, Explorer remotedesktop support, error reports, and in particular those ubiquitous and infernal Microsoft updates.

Switch to manual! Otherwise, they may bypass any tunnel you use, thus logging in your actual IP to the software company. Even if blocked your firewall will log the attempt and originating IP (which won't be that of your tunnel provider).

True story: When I first began using my laptop, I noticed a persistent and unwelcome parallel dialup connection made without my consent. And I didn't even have dialup, only DSL! Trying to disconnect it, the error window would read:

Protecting your connection to a newly detected network on adapter "WAN (PPP/SLIP) Interface"

What the hell? My WAN adapter was *disabled* but it would not allow being shut down! I'd pull the Ethernet cable, severing all internet connection, then reattach. Within minutes that dialup network icon would again start flickering. I was beginning to suspect a Trojan dialer. Then, it finally dawned on me to Scroogle the message text. Yep, I wasn't the only frustrated one. My ghost connection was Norton Symantec, running live updates. Gee, great. I installed ZoneAlarm and uninstalled Norton -- *all* of Norton. Solved. I'll say it again: *Norton sucks*.

how to securely update or register software

Assume that your proxy *will* be bypassed. So, when you choose to periodically and specifically allow updates, do so from a location and IP that are not sensitive. (A random hotel parking lot during a long road trip would be ideal.) Spoof your MAC addresses (if possible without conflicting with any registered MAC), don't have any TC volume open, and temporarily change your browser setting to "manually connect to the Internet" and then update. (This can take longer than you expect, so have a fully charged battery.) When finished, logoff, and reset your browser for the proxy connection.

Do not use that IP address any further, even through a proxy. If you must that day get back online as usual, logon from another IP some distance away, after respoofing your MACs.

This process may also be required when registering new software, which sometimes does not work well (or at all) through a proxy.

carefully read (and save) all User Agreements!

Under the section "Connectivity & Privacy" one software's agreement contained the following:

> *You agree and understand the Software will not function without Internet connectivity. Software makes several calls to our server(s), transmitting your hard disk volume serial numbers and product key. Hard disk volume serial numbers and other information acquired may be stored on our servers indefinitely.*

Facebook's is worse — *much* worse:

> *By posting Member Content to any part of the website, you automatically grant, and you represent and warrant that you have the right to grant, to Facebook an irrevocable, perpetual, non-exclusive, transferable, fully paid, worldwide license to use, copy, perform, display, reformat, translate, excerpt and distribute such information and content and to prepare derivative works of, or incorporate into other works, such information and content, and to grant and authorise sublicenses of the foregoing . . .*
>
> — www.spiked-online.com/index.php?/site/article/4482/

network and remote access

I presume that your computer is not used in a local area network (LAN), which is inherently insecure. Thus, you should disable all network functions. To streamline this, download the superb software from www.xp-AntiSpy.org, and check off nearly every possible box. (You can always reset any/all of them later.)

disable all scripting support

This is particularly vital in MSIE, which relies on scripting to amass its *goram* "userdata persistence".

switch off TCP timestamp

This will help to thwart reconstruction of packet flow to/from your proxy. (It may not work in Windows.)

use wifi only if you must

For regular home or office internet sessions, if you can plug in your ethernet cable instead of using wifi, do so as it's more private (encryption WEP keys can be cracked, though this is probably unlikely in your case). Cable is faster, too.

no referrer URL (copy/paste URL into new window)

If you click on a blue URL, that downloaded page will "know" from whence you clicked. I've noticed this in my website's security logs, and can see if somebody had Googled me (and by exactly which search terms). To avoid leaving about this kind of revealing info, copy/paste the next URL into its own new browser window.

buying software online

Always use a prepaid disposable (*i.e.*, nonreloadable and <$500) dedit card! Never use your real name and credit card for any internet purchase, particularly software. Pick a username to associate with each dedit card and register under that alias. (If an email address is required, you should have something *only* for that name, used *solely* for registration purposes.)

downloading security software

Do so only from trusted sites, and then check the PGP signatures of your files. Some software (*e.g.*, Skype) will ask to act as a *server,* thus bypassing your proxy unless you know exactly how to configure it otherwise. Don't take a chance. Instead, treat it as an update downloaded at a nonsensitive IP.

too much security software can overwhelm your RAM

. . . and thus defeat the utility of your computer. I noticed this while testing many different software products for *ONUS* research, and used up so much RAM that I couldn't even get online. Through Windows Task Manager I had to End Task a few processes. (I'd obviously reached the point of diminishing marginal returns, sort of like installing twenty deadbolts on my front door.) While you need only one firewall, you should have a few security programs running concurrently. Just don't go bananas about it. Also, 512meg of RAM for XP won't be enough (assuming you've properly disabled the swap/paging file), so 1-2gig of RAM is the answer. (You won't need that much RAM if you switch to Puppy!)

The new Norton suite is apparently very bloated:

The more I use Symantec Norton Internet Security 2009 the less I like it, I have to walk away before I get mad at how long it takes to use certain systems on my computer. As long as my computer is open, and I only do one thing at a time, it runs slower, but not a complete stop. However, very rarely do I simply have one window or system running at a time. I consistently get a delay that is so long that I get a "not responding message" while I wait for everything to get in "sync," or end up having to stop to attempt to reload pages all over again as the internet checking system took so long that the window timed out.

Since I can't have more than one application and browser window open, and my last attempt was for two hours, I uninstalled the system.

— www.identitytheftsecrets.com/symantec-norton-internet-security-2009.html

use some proper Netiquette when emailing

For one thing, stop sending your friends' email addresses in the clear with "To" as you forward. Cut/paste them from "To" into "Bcc" and put your own address in the "To" field.

Before forwarding every e-rumor that lands in your Inbox, run the story past one of these sites:

> www.truthorfiction.com/
> www.snopes.com/
> www.urbanlegends.about.com/
> www.hoaxbusters.ciac.org/
> www.symantec.com/avcenter/hoax.html
> www.vil.mcafee.com/hoax.asp

Once debunked, email the rumormonger with the truth. Together we can help vastly improve Internet hygiene.

USING PUBLIC COMPUTERS

For those without a wifi laptop, all is not lost.

CDs and USB drives can act as a portable computer

Usable third-party hardware is ubiquitous, such as at libraries, internet cafes, etc. What's lacking there is the software and data you regularly use, such as PGP and

TrueCrypt. The serious road warrior could run TorPark (www.torrify.com) and portable Firefox from his USB drive. Both are free programs.

With a CD and large USB drive, however, you've got portable "RNA" to "takeover" any host computer by booting up on your own OS. (You'll have to use a CD or DVD to boot from D:\, as most PCs will not boot from a USB drive.) Puppy Linux is perfect for using on a public host computer. Just reboot, and hit the <Esc> key to change the boot order to CD. (More later.)

SO, YOU'RE *STILL* USING WINDOWS?

XP is quite full of security holes as it is (although Service Pack 2 did remove those blasted raw sockets), and Vista is just more of the same. Stop at XP — I did! Since Windows is designed to collect, store, and send private information about you and how you use your computer, there is only so much you can do to limit that. (Limit, not *eliminate.*) Although modern shredding and anti-spy software do a very good job at reducing the sheer amount of tracks left all over Windows, there are always more buried deep within. For example, your system restore points can be found at:

c:\System Volume Information_restore{_____}

To view this, and other hidden items, click on:

Tools > Folder Options > Show hidden files and folders

So, what follows is basically what you need for your XP-afflicted machine. (The aforementioned software from the CIPAV subchapter is also recommended.) This will all help tremendously, but don't *fool* yourself that you've a manifestly secure system, because you don't — and you never will.

Before you ever even turn on your new XP box, use a Linux box and download a fat parcel of Windows security sofware. Before ever getting online, install the below on your XP box. The software needs to run in "learn" mode to establish a reliable baseline of what is (and should remain) "normal" for that machine.

Resolve *never* to use MSIE. In fact, delete the icon. (Don't try to uninstall MSIE, as it's bound within Windows and won't extract without bonking your system.) Use Firefox or Opera.

turn off all software automatic updates
This is the third time I've mentioned this, for good reason.

dump Internet Explorer for Firefox or Opera
www.mozilla.org/products/firefox/

dump Outlook Express for Quicksilver
www.quicksilvermail.net/

disable active content (ActiveX, Java, Javascript)
. . . which prevents website object code.

disable hibernation mode
. . . which would dump RAM content onto the HD)

disable and shred the paging/swap file
You'll likely need extra RAM to make up for this.

disable Windows firewall for ZoneAlarm
www.zonelabs.com

install Vipre Antivirus + Antispyware
www.sunbeltsoftware.com
This is a superb package, and all you'll likely need.

install www.xp-AntiSpy.org software
. . . and disable nearly every option.

install Advanced SystemCare   www.iobit.com
Excellent, simple, and thorough XP diagnostic software.

disable Write Behind Disk Cache
(Start > Control Panel > System > Hardware > Device Manager > Disk Drives - show devices > open the appropriate disk > Policies > uncheck Enable write caching on the disk)

disable Media Player's supercookie GUID
(Windows Media Player > Tools > Options > Player > uncheck box "Connect to the Internet")

use encrypted TrueCrypt volumes   www.truecrypt.org
Full details in the *Computer Data* chapter.

install and regularly use Windows Washer
www.webroot.com
One of the most highly regarded package shredders. This (and also BCWipe or Eraser) will remove data found in such files as:

MRU (Most Recently Used)

C:\Documents and Settings\your username\Recent\
HKEY_CURRENT_USER\Software\Microsoft\Windows\CurrentVersio
n\Explorer\RecentDocs\MRUListEx

install and regularly use a reputable SSH host proxy
Use putty.exe as the client:

Privacy.Li	www.privacy.li
Cotse	www.cotse.com/refs.htm
Trilight Zone	www.trilightzone.com
Perfect Privacy	www.perfect-privacy.com

install PGP 6.5.8
Avoid any version which generated ADKs! Some links:

www.panta-rhei.dyndns.org/downloads/PGP/pgp658ckt08.zip
web.mit.edu/network/pgp.html
www.axion.physics.ubc.ca/pgp-begin.html#index
www.skuz.net/pgp4dummies/
www.cryptography.org/getpgp.txt

install and use www.openoffice.com
Avoid all those MS embedded GUIDs!

install All-Seeing Eye   www.fortego.com/en/ase.html
When compared to e.g. antivirus software, All-Seeing Eye has two big differences:
*   * The first difference is that All-Seeing Eye is not actively preventing actions from taking place in your computer, but it is rather monitoring everything that takes*

place, and then alerts the user as soon as anything suspicious or out-of-the-ordinary is happening, providing the user with alternatives for possible actions.

    * The second difference is that it is not basing its monitoring and alerts on a list of known threats, but it rather learns what is normal for the specific computer in question, and then detects anything that is new or out of the ordinary. This way, it will detect also unknown threats, like for example a completely new spyware program, or a hacker breaking into your computer with a custom made tool.

    * Process Tracker
    * DLL Tracker
    * Driver Tracker
    * Event Log Tracker
    * Autostart Guard
    * Service/Driver Guard
    * ActiveX Object Guard
    * Browser Helper Object (BHO) Guard
    * Winsock Layered Security Provider (LSP) Guard
    * Hosts File Guard
    * File System Guard
    * Registry Guard

If you're committed to Windows, and have the time necessary to tightening up a hopeless OS, then this program is a must. It's tedious to set up while it learns what's normal.

install Sandboxie   www.sandboxie.com

    This runs new and/or suspicious Windows programs in an isolated and secured part of your HD.

now, for the final thing . . .

    OK, all that done and tested, here's the last bit: Create an image of this clean, well-understood, and (fairly) secure system and store it in several places (DVD, external HD, etc.). At least once a month DBAN (3-7 passes) your entire HD and then copy back your original system. Takes about the same length of time as formatting, and it's much more secure. This would be about as bulletproof as an XP box could be, yet I *still* would never take it across international borders subject to inspection/copying.

    If all this seems too extreme, then good luck and sweet dreams. Say hello to Santa Claus and the Tooth Fairy for me.

why you should *still* migrate from Windows

Our products just aren't engineered for security.
— Brian Valentine, Microsoft executive
www.infoworld.com/articles/hn/xml/02/09/05/020905hnmssecure.html

We all want progress . . . [but] if you're on the wrong road, progress means doing an about-turn and walking back to the right road: and in that case, the man who turns back soonest is the most progressive man . . . We are on the wrong road. And if that is so, we must go back. **Going back is the quickest way on.**
— C.S. Lewis

Windows is a typical American example of devoutly heading down the wrong road, and adding "fixes" along the way to try to make up for it. Eventually, the whole paradigm just sags with weight. It's like trying to carry enough gasoline with your car for a cross-country trip, rather than filling up as you need to.

Yes, I know that you're already up and running on Windows, but that just means you're skipping along on the wrong road. All the security products and tips I just described can never transform this wrong road into the right one (Linux). If you still believe I'm exaggerating, a serious hypothesis is that Microsoft has altered the Windows OS to reflect US military requirements and that its primary role is a 'bugging device'.

How long as Microsoft been programming Windows for? Ten, maybe fifteen years, and we are seriously asked to believe that a company with the financial resources of Microsoft cannot a create a bug-free Operating System?
— Windows XP, Professional Bugging Device?
www.privacy.li/forum/viewtopic.php?t=383

The article exhaustively catalogs dozens of Windows "features":

Search, Backup, Task Manager, Dr. Watson, Registry, Recycle Bin, Page File, Automatic Updates, Temporary Internet Files, index.dat files, thumbs.db, etc.

They are so blatantly surveilling and reporting in nature that the totality must have been done by design. (Otherwise, why three OS softwares from 1999-2001?) I describe all this for you not so much that you will feel secure, but to illustrate the futility of relying on an OS which purposely acts like a virus.

one option: encrypting Windows boot drive

This is a difficult and desperate measure:

> *Since you cannot prevent Windoze from behaving against your privacy interests, one option is surround it with a whole boot drive encryption program (such as DCPP -- DriveCrypt Plus Pack from www.securstar.com). The passphrase input is at the BIOS level, before Windows is even loaded, circumventing software keyloggers (but not hardware keyloggers). The below FAQ includes an installation tutorial on DCPP, as well as PGP, TrueCrypt, Stunnel, FreeCap, Privoxy, Tor, Quicksilver, Agent, and FireFox.*
>
> *. . . you are well advised to encrypt your whole drive to protect yourself from what Windows will write to your hard drive. There are so-called wipe and cleaner programs to remove cookies and many other files that Windows will save to your hard drive for future reference. But at the end of the day, the only truly effective counter measure against these potential weaknesses is to encrypt your whole boot drive.*
>
> *In some countries, even this might not be enough. Such countries can force you to hand over your passphrases to these encrypted drives by threatening imprisonment. As more and more judicial systems seem to be leaning ever closer to this sort of injustice (injustice because the culprit is being forced to self-incriminate himself which is in direct violation of Article 5 of the Bill of Rights; the right to refuse to be a witness against oneself), so it is more and more important for the individual to protect himself.*
>
> *Because of these encroachments on our liberty I propose in this Faq a method of plausible deniability. This means you can justify every one of the files and folders that are on your comp uter.*
>
> — www.privacy.li/security_faq.htm
> Security and Encryption FAQ - Revision 22.6.5

the much better option . . .

Encrypting Windows boot drive is unnecessary when you can just go to Puppy Linux! PL's boot drive is (if you specify) encrypted in the pup_save file, and the passphrase is given at the BIOS level. Then, Puppy runs all in RAM! (Do turn off the paging swap file feature.) In less than 8 hours, I was using SSH tunnel and TC volumes — basically 95% there in a new OS.

Have a great new life with your new Puppy!

OVERVIEW

In the end, nothing is really anonymized — only obscured.

Again, I point out that I am no computer expert, but a very knowledgeable layman. No doubt I've missed some excellent products, but here is what I've come up with. Please take this overview as a starting guide for your own continuing research.

	Poor	Fair	Good	Superb
computer	home/off.	public (few)	public (many)	wifi laptop
OS	XP	Mac	Linux	OpenBSD
data storage	HD-clear	HD-PGP	HD-True Crypt	USB-True Crypt
shredder	"delete"	Eraser	Window Washer	BCWipe
browser	IE	Netscape	Opera	Firefox
log-on from	home	office	random DSL	random WiFi
email	Outlook	Eudora	Quicksilver	Thunderbird
firewall	Windows	Norton	ZoneAlarm	Comodo
spyware	Norton	Spybot	Spy Sweeper	Vipre, CCleaner
popups	Windows	Norton	Window Washer	Razor
IP proxy	Anonymizer	Neomail	Trilightzone	TOR or JAP
servers	local	U.S. proxy	offshore (one)	offshore (many)
encryption	none	SSL	VPN	SSH or OpenVPN
VoIP	Vonage	Skype	SIP over VPN	SIP/VPN/Zfone
how paid	credit card	e-gold	cash/M.O.	prepaid debit card
when used?	never	sometimes	often	always

	local ISP	foreign proxy	website
no SSL			
(routing)	OOOOOOO		OOOOOO
(content)	OOOOOOO		OOOOOO
SSL, but no tunnel			
(routing)	OOOOOOO		OOOOOO
(content)	XXXXXXX		OOOOOO
SSH or VPN tunnel			
(routing)	XXXXXXX	OOOOOOOOOO	XXXXXX
(content)	XXXXXXX	OOOOOOOOOO	OOOOOO
SSH or VPN tunnel, with inner SSL connection (or P2P encryption)			
(routing)	XXXXXXX	XOXOXOXOXOX	XXXXXX
(content)	XXXXXXX	XXXX X OOOOO	OOOOOO

GET A NEW PUPPY! (LINUX)

OK, if by now you've had enough of Windows, it's time that I tell put you out of your misery. How would you like an OS that is:

- Free!
- Open-source (no hidden back-doors!)
- Includes all the applications required for daily use
- Works right out of the box
- Is easy to use, even for Linux newbies and Windows refugees
- Runs fast and performs well -- especially on limited hardware
- Runs on old computers, thin clients, and diskless workstations
- Installs and boots from any bootable device, including USB memory sticks, hard disks, Zip drives, LS 120/240 SuperDisks, CDs and DVDs, rewritable CDs and DVDs, and network interfaces

Puppy includes the full range of applications users want. This includes word processors, spreadsheet, browsers, image viewers and editors, instant messenger and chat, games, graphics applications, text editors, file managers, audio and video players, CD and DVD writers, backup utilities, web connections, dialers, and everything else. Nothing is missing.
— *An in-depth look at Puppy Linux,* Howard Fosdick
www.desktoplinux.com/articles/AT7455536044.html

Puppy runs in RAM!

Thus, the data, OS, apps, and all their settings are saved within an encrypted module on the USB drive. (Choose the "heavy encryption" option during setup.) Effectively, your boot drive is encrypted, something impossible to do under Windows! Very secure, and there's no OS snooping or virus nonsense to worry about. Running completely in RAM, there's no hard-drive to hijack. (Puppy has its own firewall, too.)

isn't Linux difficult to use?   *No!*

Puppy is the one to try, probably the easiest path for Windows refugees to take. Why?

1) It boots off CD. Push the CD drawer in, Puppy boots. Open the CD drawer, Windows boots. What could be easier? Actually there are numerous ways to boot Puppy, including off flash drive, but the way to start with it is on CD.

2) Since it boots off CD, you don't have to partition your hard drive, fool with dual boot programs, or any of that nonsense, like you would with mainstream linuxes. You don't (normally) install it to your hard drive either. A couple of files from Puppy will reside on the hard drive Windows partition - the c: drive - (unless you put them on flash drive or some other place) but that is all. You can download the iso, burn the CD, boot it, try it out, and throw it away if you want. No harm done to your Windows installation. It's just as crappy as ever!

3) Puppy is designed to look rather Window-ish, so linux newbies should feel pretty comfortable.

4) Puppy now offers encryption (add-on for version 2.14, but being mainstreamed next revision). This makes your data theft-proof, and may even give some protection against govt snoops although there is a bit of controversy how good the encryption Puppy uses actually is. Bottom line, everything in your "save" file is invisible - all your emails, all your browser bookmarks, etc. Pretty easy!

5) Word files? Use Abiword, or OpenOffice. Spreadsheet xls files? Use gnumeric or OpenOffice. Many other applications have linux analogs. Not as fancy as Windows apps, but not as bloated either. Win some, lose some.

Anyone who is frustrated with Windows really ought to give Puppy a try. It's just not that hard to get going. Oh, the support forum is a very helpful one also.

— from the FSW forum

how much RAM does Puppy need?   *less than Windows!*

Puppy is specifically designed to run on limited hardware. This includes older computers, thin workstations, and diskless PCs.

Puppy accomplishes this goal through several techniques:

* Puppy's bundled software covers all typical application needs, but the tools included require minimal system resources

* The operating system is minimalist

* The entire system loads into memory and runs from there by default

* Software is compressed and is transparently decompressed to run

* Puppy boots and runs from any available device -- your computer is not required to have specific devices like a hard disk or a bootable CD drive

Yet the Puppy download ranges from only 28MB to about 130M, depending on the version. While most Linuxes require a 700MB download, and some fill up multiple CDs, Puppy typically clocks in at less than 100MB. Puppy achieves this by carefully selecting the lightest program to satisfy each need. It also comes as compressed software, which it dynamically decompresses as needed.

The result is that Puppy requires less storage space on USB or disk or other device. It fits limited hardware. The exact amount of storage space required varies according to the kind of install you choose, the size of your working storage, the additional software you install, and your Puppy release. Most installs come in at under a gigabyte and are measured in hundreds of megabytes.

*To ensure quick interactive responses, Puppy loads completely into memory by default and runs from there. **Puppy requires at least 128MB to run from memory, up to about 320MB for a version that includes the full OpenOffice suite.***

— *An in-depth look at Puppy Linux,* Howard Fosdick
www.desktoplinux.com/articles/AT7455536044.html

what about device drivers?

Puppy Linux is pretty much there. It has a network setup wizard that recognizes a large number of cards; it handled one of mine just fine (but not the other). Each revision new drivers are added so new cards and USB wireless dongles are supported.

You have to realize, all these drivers are created and maintained by volunteer efforts. In most cases the card vendors don't even bother to put out information about the cards because they support Windows and no one else. This means the driver writers have to reverse-engineer the cards to come up with a driver, quite the arduous effort. There is simply no way Linux is going to have the coverage for drivers that a massively-funded corporation like Microsoft has. However there is a facility called "ndiswrapper" which is an interface that allows Linux to use the Windows driver to get the card working; that often is a good fallback when the Linux native driver does not work or is not available.

The way I look at it, is "hardware is cheap". If one $40 card does not work, try another one. I have no problem experimenting a little to get away from the problems I had to put up with using Windows. It is well worth it. What is your time worth? What do you pay for good virus checkers and spyware checkers? How much more do you have to pay for high performance hardware just to deal with Windows bloat? How much does that Windows license cost when you buy a computer? Either way, with Windows or with Linux, you are going to pay. Overall, in both time and money, I think Linux is cheaper. You do not have to be a geek to run Puppy Linux, but it is not like falling off a log either. But then, neither is working with Windows.

The Puppy support forum has over 5000 members. The vast majority of them are Windows refugees, not linux geeks, in my opinion.

*I have heard all the Linux criticisms before. In fact I used to make these criticisms myself. If you have used Windows for years, you are familiar with it, even if it has become a giant pain to deal with all the problems. I understand this. That is why I am so excited about Puppy Linux. **It is the easiest migration path away from Windows that exists today** (yes, lots easier than DSL). Some people are going to give it a try and like it. Some are going to try, run into a snag somewhere, and give up. Some are just going to stick with what they know, and put up with whatever problems come up.*

— from the FSW forum

aren't the Puppy applications limited?   *Not really.*

I forgot to mention, if you need heavyweight office applications you can have the openoffice .sfs file load at boot time (maybe it's just mounted rather than loaded into memory). Look at the Menu>System>Bootmanager application for this. I find the lightweight standard Puppy apps are fine for just about everything I need to do.

Puppy is kinda fun to fiddle with, and it's nice to have a friendly Puppy forum to ask questions in. One recommendation I would strongly promote: BACK UP YOUR PUPSAVE FILE BEFORE TRYING ANYTHING NEW OR INSTALLING ANY SOFTWARE. If you break anything, no big deal; just go back to the old pupsave. Of course you need to boot "pfix=ram" to back up the pupsave, which is an annoyance, but fortunately it is a pretty fast boot.

— from the FSW forum

Adding applications

Beyond booting and installation choices, options in saving session information, and Windows co-existence, a key aspect of flexibility concerns how easy is it to access and install additional software.

Puppy's answer is a package manager called PETget. Package managers make it easy to select and install additional applications. **PETget can install any of the 500+ packages on the official Puppy Live CD distribution,** *as well as a few hundred "unofficial" add-on products It can install these applications either from the Puppy CD or by connecting to the vast online Puppy applications repository.*

PETget's seamless download and install process manages applications from a single consistent interface. The result is that you can easily extend Puppy with mainstream Linux applications.

— *An in-depth look at Puppy Linux,* Howard Fosdick
www.desktoplinux.com/articles/AT7455536044.html

Will TrueCrypt work in Puppy?   *Yes!*

I got TrueCrypt to work in Puppy 4.1.1 by installing another version:

truecrypt-6.1a-ubuntu-x86.tar.gz *from www.truecrypt.com*

It's a Linux "zip" file. Select all to extract. Click the setup file.

You must then extract the .deb when it asks you to, then install.
(Save it in something other than .tmp folder, for perpetuity.)
It will open a hard drive TC volume just fine, and is not merely read-only!   File changes/additions work, just as through Windoze.
Get TC today, especially since Puppy's crytpoloop is weak.
— Boston T. Party, from the FSW forum

Puppy runs from live CD!

*You can boot and test Puppy Linux using its live CD, **without making any changes to your hard disk and without risk.** So you can ensure Puppy is fully compatible with your hardware and make sure it handles the video, system devices, and interface cards the way you want. Then, play with Puppy and learn about Linux while you determine if Puppy meets your needs.*

*If you run Puppy from a Live CD, you'll quickly discover another advantage to running the system from memory. **You can remove the CD and Puppy continues to run.** So after booting, you can listen to that hot new audio CD you bought, or write data to a CD or DVD disc. **Few other Linuxes free up the CD or DVD drive after you boot off that device.***

You can also use Puppy's unique multi-session CD / DVD capability. With any kind of writeable CD or DVD (+ or -), Puppy writes your session information to the disc so you pick it up the next time you boot. Puppy's included disc-burning tools write to the multi-session disk.
— *An in-depth look at Puppy Linux,* Howard Fosdick
www.desktoplinux.com/articles/AT7455536044.html

I generally encourage people not to install Puppy to the hard drive. Why? Because it is easier not to, and Puppy is designed to run as a live CD (or "frugal install" which is almost like a liveCD without the CD). Also, it removes the danger of trying to shorten a windows partition to make room for puppy, gets rid of multiboot PITA (open CD drawer, windows boots - close it, Puppy boots) and lots of other reasons. Lots of people start with liveCD and never go beyond it - I'm still using a live CD. The only case where you pretty much have to install is with very old machines with little memory (so that puppy could not be completely loaded into ram - which would make it a dog). But in such old machines, you are not usually trying to protect a windows install and trashing the whole partition is no problem.

BTW, trying to shorten a Vista NTFS partition will give you grey hairs (doable with XP). I finally had to reinstall Vista on one of my machines because Gparted, the partition editor, broke Vista.

— from the FSW forum

can Puppy boot from USB?   *Yes!*

The USB option didn't show up in BIOS on the first try on a fairly new (two-year-old) Toshiba Satellite running XP. I was stymied and thought "this is NEVER going to work on the five-year-old ThinkPad I ordered.

But the "trick" I figured out was that the USB has to actually be *connected* to the computer for it to show up as a BIOS option on my box. This may seem obvious, but it didn't to me, because my newer desktop shows options for all the ports, regardless of whether or not they're in use.

So I ran Pup from the CD, use the installer to format the USB drive, then installed Pup to the USB, then rebooted, and it showed up as an extra option, as "USB DISK 2.0."

Interestingly, the only format option that worked was the one that said "DO NOT USE, THIS IS STILL EXPERIMENTAL AND HAS A BUG."

— from the FSW forum

can Puppy and Windows be used alternatively?   *Yes!*

There is another way as well, the way I use in fact. I have a few windows applications that I need occasionally. I just open my CD drawer and instead of booting Puppy on the CD, Windows boots instead. I don't get on the internet any more in Windows (I'm done with being a masochist). Fortunately, the applications I use the vast majority of the time are the ones that Puppy handles very well: browser (Seamonkey, derived from Firefox), email client (Seamonkey, derived from Thunderbird), spreadsheet (gnumeric, with access to OpenOffice Calc if I need something heavier), word processor (Abiword, with access to the OpenOffice word processor if I need it), editor (vi, geany, etc.) and various other smaller apps like ftp clients and encryption tools and the like. Only lately have I had any need at all for Wine, because of this server work I am doing.

— from the FSW forum

I cling to Windows, but rather to not allow a need to use Windows for some things to get in the way of migrating to OSX or Linux for everything else. Once someone gets on an alternate OS, even if they still have to use Windows for some subset of their work, then Windows becomes the secondary issue, and weaning off of it becomes easier.
— from the FSW forum

can Puppy be installed on the hard drive?   *Yes!*

Puppy also offers two install-to-disk options, both of which co-exist with Windows. Puppy's frugal disk install allows you to install Puppy to your hard disk simply by copying four files from the Puppy Live CD into any existing Windows partition (including NTFS partitions). You can perform the copy manually or by selecting a Puppy menu option. The frugal disk install does not require any changes to your disk partitioning but still yields the benefits of loading from disk.

Or you can perform a regular full install of Puppy to the hard drive. Simply start up the Puppy Live CD, and use its GParted tool to add a disk partition for Puppy. Then select the menu option for the Puppy Universal Installer and away you go. Puppy detects Windows' presence during the install process, so you can tell it to install its boot selection menu program (called GRUB). Next time you start up your computer, you'll see a boot menu that allows you to select either Windows or Puppy for your session. (Puppy provides for free the kind of boot selection facility you might otherwise buy in a tool like System Commander.)

If you tried Linux a few years ago, you may have (justly) felt some anxiety about how well Linux would co-exist with Windows. Would trying Linux put your Windows system at risk? These concerns have been put to rest. Puppy offers a range of methods to use and/or install Linux on Windows computers. The risks of exploring Linux and dual-booting systems have been eliminated.
— *An in-depth look at Puppy Linux,* Howard Fosdick
www.desktoplinux.com/articles/AT7455536044.html

does SSH and VPN work in Puppy?

Puppy has both clients built-in. While the SSH works perfectly, the PPTP VPN client seems to have DNS routing issues. A small patch should fix it, according to the PL forum. I'd also install an OpenVPN GUI.

Puppy testimonials from Windows refugees

Wow, wow....I just really never though Linux would work for me, but Puppy is wonderful. **I also sent a 20-dollar donation to Barry Kauler,** *the guy who made Puppy. He seems like a fun guy, semi-retired engineer living in rural Australia, with his puppy. Pix of his digs are here: http://www.puppylinux.com/bkauler/*
— from the FSW forum

Overall, for just my first day of use, I'm very impressed with Puppy.

Free, safe, and easy to use (once you've got the hang of it). Don't install it on your HD. No real need to! Get a 16gig USB drive if you must have such storage. All you current XP sufferers should really try this out.

It's so simple, fast, and clean that you initially can't believe it. It feels great emerging from the XP haze. And you can run it completely away from a hard drive. HD crashed under Windows? So what? You've an instantly workable backup system, using the same machine! Buy a used laptop with wifi and USB ports for <$300, and you're in business. Truly, it's a wonderful product.
— Boston T. Party, January 2009

Rotten wood cannot be carved, and you can't polish a turd. *XP is the last Microsoft OS I will ever use. If Microsoft imagines that I am going to "upgrade" from XP to Vista, they are all on the crackpipe. I can't speak for others, but this felt good to me:*

> *Select the essential XP software I still may use (though nothing web-related)*
> *Save those setup.exe files to external HD*
> *Make XP boot disk with WindowWasher (a BartPE disk is a good idea, too)*
> *DBAN the entire HD! (This will take a long time, like overnight.)*
> *Reinstall XP and chosen software*

Now, I run Puppy for the Net and most offline use, and (very) occasionally XP for only a few offline things. No more goram XP updates, virus scans, adware, malware, etc. Data is secure in a TrueCrypt volume, which Puppy loads just fine.

I am done with Windows; ain't never lookin' back!
— Boston T. Party, a few days later, January 2009

what about other versions of Linux, such as Ubuntu?

The reason I don't care for Ubuntu, Fedora, etc for this initial step is that they generally require installation on the hard drive, which means partitioning the hard drive, dual booting (and shortening up a Windows partition is risky and even will break a Vista installation). The live CD versions (of Ubuntu, etc) are not designed to be run as live CDs indefinitely; they are intended only as samplers to let people see what the OS is like. Their performance is very poor compared to Puppy Linux which is designed to run as a live CD all the time (and that's the way I run it).

— from the FSW forum

HOW TO INSTALL PUPPY LINUX

What follows is from a very helpful post on:
www.fundamentalsoffreedom.com/fswforum/index.php?topic=7120.0

There are lots of howtos out there, but I thought I'd throw something together here to get people off the dime about trying something other than Windows.

❶   Go to

http://distro.ibiblio.org/pub/linux/distributions/puppylinux/

and download

http://distro.ibiblio.org/pub/linux/distributions/puppylinux/puppy-4.1.2-k2.6.25.16-seamonkey.iso

to some place on your hard drive. If you are on dialup and 94MB takes too long to download, one of the CD vendors like http://distrowatch.com/kokoku/linuxcdorg.php can supply one for you for under $2, or you can find a friend with broadband to download it.

❷   You need to burn this .iso file to a CD. You may already be set to do that; if so go ahead. Otherwise get

http://ftp//terabyteunlimited.com/burncdcc.zip

and install it in Windows; it is a nice simple and reliable burner application. Burn the CD "closed", not "open".

❸　　Stick the CD in your CDROM drive and reboot. One of two things will happen. If you get Puppy booting, all is well. If you get Windows, your BIOS is not set up to boot first from CD. You can either reboot and use the boot device menu (which you would have to do for every boot), telling it to boot from CD; or you can get into your BIOS and set it up for the same thing (which would make it try to boot from CD first permanently, provided anything is in there). Many PC's are set to boot from CD by default. It might take an F1, F2 or F10 during early boot to kick it out of its normal process and get it into the BIOS.

❹　　Assuming you got it to boot Puppy, you might want to check the integrity of the download. Normally this is more important if you are going to depend on Puppy. For just trying it out, you might skip this step. It boils down to mounting the disk that the .iso file got downloaded to (in Puppy you manually mount and dismount volumes while in Windows the mount part is automatic). If you see some disk icons, clicking on them will mount the volume and leave a green dot on the icon to show it's mounted. Then you download

http://distro.ibiblio.org/pub/linux/distributions/puppylinux/puppy-4.1.2-k2.6.25.16-seamonkey.iso.md5.txt

small file to the same place you put the .iso file, and from the same place you got the iso. Then open a console window, go to that place (usually the command will be cd /mnt/home) and check the checksum by entering md5sum puppy-4.1.2-k2.6.25.16-seamonkey.iso.md5.txt (or whatever the name of the small file you just downloaded). It will say if it is OK which means the download worked OK.

❺　　On your mounted volume, try opening a .doc or .xls file, or something of that nature. By default .doc's will open with Abiword which is a lightweight "Microsoft Word", and .xls's open with gnumeric which is a lightweight "Microsoft Excel".

❻　　Getting your internet going is the next step. Run Menu>Setup>Network Wizard to get your wireless or ethernet connection going. (There are other applications for dialup but I haven't used them for a while; look in Menu>Network and start pupdial or roaring penguin.) With luck the wizard will work right off. Otherwise you will need to get on the forum and start asking questions, or ask me in this thread (although it may take a day or two for me to respond). Network setup tends to be a bit difficult in linux, although it is way better than it was a couple years ago. Once it is set up, click the "browse" application to get on the internet (starts Seamonkey which is basically Firefox and Thunderbird in one application).

❼   When you are done, reboot. On shutdown it will ask you if you want to save your setup stuff in a pupsave file. Say yes. You can encrypt this if you want. Your emails go there by default, and you can put other sensitive files there, although it is not the top grade of encryption. Most folks go for a 512MB pupsave file at first. You can start smaller and it is easy to expand later if need be. When your system comes up again it will use the pupsave file and you won't have to answer questions about your machine again because it will be using the setup info in the file.

That's it in a nutshell. It does not affect your Windows install, because you are not actually doing a Puppy install. The only thing that happens is that two files get written to your hard drive in the top directory. The first is your pupsave file, which holds config data and installed programs and emails and so forth. The second file is pup_412.sfs which is puppy itself, copied from the CD down to your hard drive so your boot goes much faster next time around (the hard drive is much faster to read from than the CDROM is).

If you don't want to use Puppy, these two files can simply be deleted from within Windows.

use Puppy for online stuff, and Windows offline

There is a solution that is not all-or-nothing.

Boot Windows but do not connect to the Internet. Most of your security problems are now solved, yet you can run all the regular non-Internet applications.

To connect to the Internet, boot Puppy Linux (or any other linux really). All the regular mainstream Internet applications like Firefox, Thunderbird, etc. are available. Linux is relatively secure on the Internet (certainly compared to Windows). Most linux users don't even run virus checkers, never mind spyware checkers. A firewall is about it.

This won't work too well if you are constantly going back and forth, because of boot times; but otherwise I can tell you it works fine because that's what I do! I boot Puppy from a CD, and have Win 98SE on the hard drive for the occasional rare use. Puppy boots fast and runs fast - a friend was over here trying it out and he was amazed how fast applications opened. Works well on old hardware too.

You can run Wine under linux which allows you to run Windows applications (it's a Windows emulator), but I haven't bothered. It is not 100%, but a lot of people like it.

— from the FSW Forum

install Puppy on cheap used laptops

The result is that you can take an old Pentium III or II computer, install Puppy, and enjoy excellent performance. Memory access is way faster than disk access. Just make sure that the computer has sufficient memory to run Puppy from RAM.

To show how this works, read this earlier article about my experience installing Puppy on a 550MHz Pentium III desktop with 448MB memory and an 8 gig hard drive. Running Puppy, this turn-of-the-century hardware runs typical applications as fast as my 2.6 ghz Celeron with a gigabyte of ram runs equivalent Windows XP programs!

Another example: I installed Puppy on an old IBM Thinkpad 770Z laptop, a 366MHz Pentium II. I had hauled this machine directly out of the trash bin. I upgraded system memory from 128MB to 256MB by buying a used memory stick for $20. Even this old laptop is responsive with Puppy in memory when word processing, creating web pages, and delivering presentations.

For systems lacking sufficient memory -- for example, old Pentiums with less than 128MB -- Puppy runs fine but with reduced performance. For these systems, you need to create a swap file on the storage media so that Puppy can use virtual memory. Puppy's minimum hardware requirements are a 166MHz processor and 128MB of memory (64MB for older releases). Enthusiasts report decent results with systems down to 75MHz CPUs and 40MB of RAM and a 233MHz machine with 32MB RAM.

Puppy breathes new life into old hardware and runs well on diskless PCs and thin workstations. Needless to say, it's a total speed demon on state-of-the-art hardware. While I've emphasized Puppy's special role on constrained hardware, the product is fully competitive on current systems. My friends and I run it on our newest computers, too.
— *An in-depth look at Puppy Linux,* Howard Fosdick
www.desktoplinux.com/articles/AT7455536044.html

I was inspired to buy an extra laptop on eBay, I'm gonna wipe windowz from it and make it Puppy only. Bought it from a seller with nothing but positive feedback. It's a used, good-condition, working IBM Thinkpad A31 Laptop,1.6Ghz, WiFi, 15" LCD, CD-RW, 512MB RAM, 30GB hard drive, and a USB port. 200-dollars. Should run screamingly fast with Puppy.

I have a friend who's working her way through college, she's smart and geeky, but under employed. I suggested to her that she buy lots of older working laptops with no OS (you can find them on eBay for like 50 bucks sometimes if you buy five or ten of them), install and configure Puppy, and sell them for a small profit to help with college expenses. She might do it. And that's permitted in the Puppy license.
— from the FSW forum

misc. Puppy tips

Disable the paging swap file. Setup with heavy encryption (vs. "none" or "light"). Keep all data in a TC volume.

misc. Puppy Linux websites

www.freesoftwaremagazine.com/articles/free_computing
www.puppylinux.com/cd-puppy.htm
www.freeveda.org/linux/puppy/index.htm
www.freeveda.org/linux/puppy/PupWinQE.htm
www.freeveda.org/linux/puppy/PupWinQE.zip
http://www.murga-linux.com/puppy/   (Puppy forum)

donation to Barry Kauler

www.puppylinux.com/bkauler/

YOUR PRIVATE HOME

Your home should be a sanctuary; a dike holding back the vast ocean of humanity. With proper planning and discipline, its location will be an utter mystery to interested parties.

GOING PRIVATE FROM PUBLIC

Most of you are currently living in an informational fish bowl, totally visible to outsiders. Once your address is public knowledge, there's no making it private. You'll have to *move*. Correctly handled, a move cancels all ties to your old address.

get your new place long *before* you need it

Remember Pascucci's hunt for the Nazi Koziy? Had he set up his second "flee-to" house *before* he needed it, his number wouldn't have been on the list of newly connected phones (or utilities). Arrange for your new home at least several weeks before moving so it's not flagged by some post-move activation date of phone, gas or electricity.

buying a new place with privacy

This *can't* be accomplished in your own name. This also *can't* be accomplished through a mortgage. It will work *only* if you've the funds to buy a house outright, *and* if the house is purchased by an entity (which you control).

the entity

This is a trust or a corporation (Nevada, Wyoming or Delaware, which allow for *undisclosed* directors and stockholders). It has its own postal drop and voice mail. Your name should *not* appear as trustee, agent, etc. You discreetly move assets to the entity's bank account and have *it* buy the house, establish phone/utility connections, pay property taxes, etc. Under an alias, you can "rent" the place from your entity and pay with M.O.'s.

Not only is this utterly private, but you've separated ownership and control. Since there is peril to ownership, you want to merely *control* the asset. In a lawsuit, your house couldn't be taken away from you any more than your rental car. You just "live" there and pay rent, remember?

what about "allodial" titles?

An "allodium" was land given to Roman centurions, with title utterly free and clear of state encumbrance. All land in the U.S.A. *used* to be allodial. Part of the reason behind the Homestead acts was that the 160 acre parcels were allodial, and thus incapable of being stolen from the homesteader by scheming banks and speculators. Allodial land cannot be mortgaged or bonded against by government — therefore no property taxes, zoning restrictions or building codes apply. Allodial land is *your* land, utterly. We got tricked *out* of our allodial titles by the "fee simple" deed through the State.

While you can "re-allodialize" your land, it must be fully paid for and the process involves a public notice in your newspaper and notifying the tax assessor, etc. Obviously, not a very private process. I've *heard* that it works, that property taxes cease and the bureaucrats go away (after a long fight) — but I don't *personally* know of these success stories. Therefore, I cannot recommend the allodial position at this time, especially since it totally violates your locational privacy. However, I am willing to be convinced of any success story, so please write me if you've firsthand proof.

renting a new place with privacy

It would be pointless to merely exchange one credit-checked apartment for another. You want to avoid giving out your SSN. Though difficult, it is not impossible to find places which will rent to you without a credit check or ID — I've done it all my life. In fact, I've *never* rented under my own name, nor have I been subjected to a credit check. (The secret is an honest face, lots of smiles and a hefty cash deposit.)

This is easiest in small college towns. Roommates are constantly needed, and if you don't look like a scumbag you're in with little ceremony. Cash deposits quench uncertainty.

> ...[A] *university is perhaps the best place in the world to lay low while establishing your new identity. The social climate is generally free and easy, jobs without strings attached are readily available, and the world in general doesn't make the kind of demanding requirements on college students that it expects of the average working stiff.*
> — Doug Richmond; *How To Disappear Completely*

If you've a family, then you probably don't want to share a place and you'll need a house or apartment to yourselves. This is most difficult still, and you'll probably need false ID as it's very unlikely (though not impossible) to be rented on your good looks alone — unless they know you or somebody who knows you. Farming communities are best. Trust is high there.

If you're heavily sought after, have a trusted friend rent a place *for* you. Pay your rent by mail and the landlord will never see you. If he drops by and asks where Fred the tenant is and asks who *you* are, reply that Fred is travelling and you're just watching the place for him. Smile and invite him in for coffee so that he can see you haven't trashed the place.

the utilities

Try to have the landlord handle this and reimburse him monthly. Explain that you can't afford the $50 new account fee, and offer to give him a cash deposit. I've done this all my life, too. (Once, I rented from Patriots who were glad to do this to help lower my exposure—but don't rely on such luck. I don't.)

If your landlord isn't keen on this (after all, there's nothing in it for him but extra hassle and risk), then all's not lost. You can, in smaller communities, obtain service without credit and ID. (By law, utilities must be provided, if for no other reason so that tenants don't freeze in the winter.) You'll just have to leave them a fat deposit. Pay your bills and go easy on the kwatts, or else the electric company will report you as a possible pot-grower using indoor lamps, and you *will* get a visit.

your landlord

Pay your rent on time, *without fail*. **No excuses.** Sell your valuables if you have to, but *pay your rent*. Keep the noise down, and don't get the cops called on you. Avoid any domestic disturbances. Keep the place clean and tidy. Take care of the lawn. Show some pride in your own appearance. Offer to make small repairs yourself, and give him the receipt. Tether your dog and keep him quiet. No wild parties.

Don't talk about radical politics, philosophies or religions. **Never talk about guns.** (If the subject comes up, say you had a .22 as a boy, but don't have guns now. This will appease everybody. Gun-owners will think you're still salvageable, and the gun-haters will praise you for "growing out of it.")

Before you sign your lease, firmly limit the "inspection rights" of the landlord. Insist on a change of locks (with full possession of *all* keys) and a 24 hour advance notice of any inspection (unless the place is flooding, on fire, etc.). Any presence of his outside the stipulated terms should constitute breaking and entering. You want your landlord to respect your privacy, and if he seems reluctant to do so during lease negotiations, find some other place.

I once rented a room in a friend's beach house. Since the place was constantly teeming with overnight guests and I was often travelling, I insisted on putting a lock on my bedroom door. I should have clarified this *before* moving in, but I didn't anticipate his unreasonable reaction. Even though he could have the spare key, he threw a *fit*. He insisted that *his* overnight guests shouldn't be *"forced to sleep on the floor when there's an unused bed in the house."* He called me *"unsociable and paranoid"* and just couldn't understand why I didn't want strangers in my room and in my bed. (A semblance of rationality eventually prevailed, though not without strain on the friendship. I soon moved out.) Moral: work all this out *first*.

the timing of your move

Unless you want to simply be followed from your old job to your new place, you should (suddenly, without notice, if you think you're under surveillance) quit your job the day *after* your "public" move. In my chapter *Earning A Quiet Living*, I'll get into more detail. A job, unless paid in cash, is never private because of SSN tracking. You should have your own cash economy business.

You shouldn't move *during* scrutiny, but months *prior*. While it can be difficult to know just *when* you will come to the attention of somebody, guess earlier than later.

the moving sequence
Here's how it's done, in these easy steps.

❶   establish a landlord-dedicated prepaid cell phone
This is the number you'll give to real estate agents and prospective landlords. You don't want *any* of their calls going to your old home number or its replacement voice mail number. Remember, *no links* between the old and the new. Use this cell only for tenant-related calls only. Keep it for the entirety of your lease, and let it die when you move again.

❷   get a P.O. box for your *private* correspondence
Never use this for anything but receiving letters from friends, or else it'll quickly get on a mailing list owned by TRW, etc.

Receive at your *new* home any mail which is unavoidably *directly* related there (utilities, phone, property taxes, etc.). See, if the electric company *already* knows your *home's* location, then why inform them of your P.O. box, too? (*Never* provide additional information if you don't *have* to.) Also, if your P.O. box is ever monitored, your home's location won't be indirectly discovered through the electric company.

❸   establish a second prepaid cell phone
Get it from a different provider. This will become your new number for *trusted* friends. They will be instructed *never* to give out this number. *Extreme tip:* have them call you from pay phones and avoid creating MUDs on their home or cell.

❹   change your "official" address to a *street* mail drop
This is done weeks or months before moving. Have *all* your official and business mail rerouted there. Change your license and registration, credit cards, library card, voter's registration, checks, etc. Filing a postal change of address form goes a *long* way in creating the desired false trail, as it's provided to over 70 direct mail marketers.

Extreme tip: get the mail drop in another city nearby enough to service once a month or so.

However, the most cursory of investigations will reveal your "home" address to be merely a mail drop. So, either use my RR box ploy, or:

> Set up a "legal" address somewhere else, such as a closet at a friend's house, containing some misleading personal effects

(books on [benign] *subjects you have no interest in, and clothes a few sizes away from your own). He can thus point to something if ever questioned; but, of course, he hasn't the slightest notion when you'll be returning from India...*
  — *100 Way To Disappear and Live Free;* Eden Press

❺   establish Internet voice mail; drop your old home number
This is also done at *least* several weeks before moving, and from a totally different provider. Get all your acquaintances, "mere" friends and public used to it. This number will serve as a calling buffer to hide the timing of your move. Otherwise, your home line being suddenly disconnected would send an *"I've just moved"* message to anybody who called. Check messages from pay phones only, *not* from your new home.

You will *not* be able to change your home number to the voice mail number through the phone company. The voice mail provider leases a block of numbers from the phone company, so the phone company cannot therefore deal directly with you.

❻   do *not* hire a mover — *gradually* do it yourself
   do *not* have a "moving" sale or make announcements
The logic of this should be obvious. You *don't* want your neighbors to know that you're moving. If possible, move from an enclosed garage over a period of several weeks — the last trip being a couple of months before your disappearance date. Well done, you simply evaporated and your old neighbors never knew you *had* moved out — much less *when.*

Your neighbors probably cannot help but notice a trip or two, however, so you'll have to yarn them with *"some stuff is going in storage"* or whatever.

If you must sell some stuff before your move, do so *weeks* before disguised as a *yard* sale. Do not have a yard sale at your new place, as some unwanted person is bound to show up.

Since you will be living in your old place for weeks *after* your unknown move (to maintain the *appearance* of normal residency), leave a car load of necessities there. Once you're leaving for the *last* time, scour the place (especially the trash) for *anything* which might enlighten an investigator. Unwanted stuff you should drop off at the Salvation Army or Goodwill.

Don't alienate your old neighbors. Return any borrowed items and make good on any promised favors. Once they discover that you've actually *moved*, they'll be at least a little hurt if not downright pissed-off, so you want to have in advance ameliorated as much bad feeling as possible.

If you need help to move, pick some trusted *best* friends. Throw a nice party or dinner for them afterwards. Instruct them that your new place is to be private.

❼   leave some false leads

If you think it's clever to leave utterly *no* leads, then think again. By leaving *no* leads, you'll frustrate and fascinate the investigator and make him *really* sink his teeth into your case. You don't want your case to become his Cause.

Your false leads should be *shrewd*. The more *subtle* the better. Weeks *before* moving, create a MUD to a local travel agent. Go visit her and explain that you are moving to San Diego and ask for info. From your old home, make a few phone calls to the San Diego Chamber of Commerce and receive some brochures. Mention to your mailman, gossipy friends and neighbors that you've always loved San Diego — but say nothing about *moving*. Establish a mailbox there and have your nontrusted people write you after you've split and done ❽.

Don't make your misinfo ridiculous. Don't spread the word that you're moving to Alaska when it's common knowledge that you hate cold weather. Keep the B.S. plausible.

The more time an investigator spends on false leads which have been "confirmed" from several angles, the less time he can spend on *real* leads. Digging through your trash, he already found a bookstore receipt for *Guide to San Diego*, so he's hooked. If you keep your misinfo subtle and let *him* make the links between your bogus triggers, he'll *stay* on the false trail. (Remember, he's not accustomed to anybody as *smart* as you who's using a book as *good* as this.) As more and more time passes, the case becomes more and more stale. Assuming that you're no great crime figure, and that you haven't personally pissed him off, your case will be quickly back-burnered.

❽   After some months, cancel the Internet voice mail number

Keep it only if need it for "public" or "legal" reasons (job, classified ads, etc.). Remember, you should be dropping many people from your life. Since privacy measures complicate things, you must simultaneously whittle down your social sphere. *"Three can keep a secret if two are dead."*

Your method of "social triage" is up to you. You'll be somewhat amazed (and hurt) at the small number of your "friends" who actually miss you and make any *real* effort to keep in touch. If you're not appreciated once gone, then you probably weren't very appreciated when around. Ghost out, and the social fluff won't really notice. *Nothing personal* — it's just the way most people are these days. If they ask, reply that you've *"been travelling"* and *"we'll get together soon."* That'll hold most of them. Tell the pushy ones that you're in-between places and just staying with friends for now.

in review

Your business/official mail gets shunted to a street addressed postal drop, which has only an RR box#. The buffer VM has only that postal drop address. Your old phone number has no linking MUDs or long-distance records to your new place. Your trusted friends have a separate channel to call and write you, and even if they *are* pen registered, all that can be learned is a prepaid cell phone. Big deal.

The only way you could be found is if you or a trusted friend were actually *followed* to your new place. But to be followed *to*, one must first be followed *from*. Anybody under such intense, expensive surveillance should move out of town (if not the state), drop *all* previous contacts and not return to regular haunts (bars, restaurants, dry cleaners, grocery stores etc.) Examine your cancelled checks and credit card records to learn what these old haunts are — *he* will. Don't have magazines, newspapers and mail orders sent to your new place.

Think things through, use wisdom in which friends you trust and lay low for a while. The feeling of new freedom and personal control will prove incredibly refreshing.

ONCE AT YOUR NEW PLACE

drop all old spending habits

Don't use the same: pest control, delivery or security service, housekeeper, yardboy, etc. Don't update newspaper or magazine subscriptions; buy them at the newsstand. (The traitorous Christopher Boyce — "The Falconer" — was caught by resubscribing to a falconing magazine from his Oregon hideout.) I'd even change hairstylists. Go through your cancelled checks and credit card records and list all the past businesses you must now avoid. (I repeat this for emphasis.) It should *appear* as though you've moved overseas, even though you maybe only moved just across town.

modify or drop all past associations

Be *very* careful about which friends and relatives know your new address and number. Trust me on this: if your privacy measures are tight, then an investigator will focus on finding you from your friends and family — either by interview or surveillance. Pen registering their phone lines is an easy way to find you. Have them call your national 800 pager from a pay phone, and return their call there by prepaid calling card. If the feds are *really* serious about you, even *this* wouldn't be safe enough, in my opinion. Cease communications entirely.

don't blow it by getting all paranoid

O.K., so you've made a slick move and regained the privacy of your domicile. Don't stupidly draw attention to yourself by being overtly covert. The best example of this is a Duluth guy known to every UPS deliveryman as "The Hand." Whenever "The Hand" receives a parcel to be signed for, a mere hand darts from a cracked doorway for the clipboard, signs it within the bowels of his house and returns it, by hand only. Although his face has never been seen, he's *blown* his privacy. I don't personally know "The Hand." I heard about him only *third*-hand (ha, ha — pun unavoidable). **Moral: suspicious activity *will* get you talked about far and wide.** Don't be *too* cagey with your new neighbors.

appear middle-class and keep a low profile

Barry Reid wisely recommends not living in a place more expensive than the average cop can afford. Anything more expensive paints a big *Sue Me! —Raid Me!* target on your head.

Pay your rent, don't alienate your neighbors and keep your mouth shut. Keep your shades drawn. Don't be effusive, either. Don't show them your guns or books. Don't discuss politics or religion, however tempting. *Never* carry your actual address on you or in your car.

don't take in boarders, renters, or casual guests

While you may like the rental income, the sacrifice of your privacy probably isn't worth $350 a month. Such people will pick up all sorts of useful information on your habits and plans. Remember, at least 95% of those you know will roll over on you with enough carrot or stick. (For a real landlord scare, watch *Pacific Heights* with Michael Keaton.)

Handy Boston tip: If you *truly* need to give somebody a house or padlock key, make successive copies of it, which by the 3rd or 4th generation will not work. Give out the *penultimate* copy, which is an inadequate master from which to make copies.

hidden caches

There are many books on this subject. There are two kinds of home caches: the instantly accessible and those which require time and tools. (Buried caches should be off-property.)

Have a "fall guy" safe with a bit of cash, benign diskettes, and valuables to satisfy any raid or burglary, while your extremely well-hidden floor safe goes untouched. Great caching locations include ceiling beams, electrical outlets, solid-core doors, bookcases, stairways and ceilings. Use imagination and quality carpentry. (Small fire-resistant lockboxes start at $30. Use them for cash and valuable papers.) Bury some of your stuff on and off your property.

burn, don't throw away sensitive trash

Be *scrupulous* about this. I throw away nothing which has names, data, handwriting, or addresses on it. In fact, I burn nearly all printed and packaging material, receipts, etc. All anybody would learn by going through *my* trash is what kind of breakfast cereal I eat. If you can't burn in town, lock away the papers in a briefcase and drive to the country.

dealing with unwanted persons at your door

Never allow salesmen, religious doorknockers, etc. inside. Even a casual glance inside your home can be educational, and investigators are very good at posing as innocuous passersby. Speak to these people only through the door or intercom. If an emergency is claimed, offer to make a phone call *for* them, but do not allow them inside. (If you need convincing on this point, watch *A Clockwork Orange* — otherwise *avoid* that movie.)

store your extra stuff

Do not keep all your worldly goods at your new place, even if it's roomy enough. Spread your eggs out into at least a couple of baskets. That way, if your house is cleaned out (by fire, flood, theft, or seizure), you can still start over. **Never have *all* of your cash, books, guns, computers, data, vehicles and trade tools at home.**

a motor-home or travel trailer parked in the country

This the best choice, in my opinion. Stock it for self-sufficiency with tools, books, food, guns, clothes, cash, gold/silver coins etc. Set it up in the country on some old couple's farm for $50-100 a month, or in exchange for helping them out. Not only have you solved your storage needs, but you've created an inexpensive retreat to go to for vacations or in times of trouble. For shoestring budgets, read *Travel-Trailer Homesteading Under $5,000*. (Although I wouldn't want to *live* like author Kelling, such makes for a great cheap retreat.)

Travel trailers shorter than 24' are too cramped, and those longer than 30' are a real pain to drive or tow (requiring a heavy-duty tow rig). Buy something at least five years old (for good value) and post-1995 for good style and function. Although you can get lucky and find a $4,000 cream puff, expect to pay up to $12,000 for a decent one. Pressurize the water system for 24 hours and carefully check for leaks. Buy it under an alias different from your rental alias. If you won't drive or tow it very often, don't bother registering it — it's more private and saves $.

I have lived and vacationed in a trailer for years. I've even written several books in it. Mine has hundreds of books, a good stereo, CDs, breadmaker, TV and DVD with lots of movies, electric piano, computer and laser printer, reloading equipment, toaster, blender, juicer, dehydrator, and lots of stored food/water. They can be comfortable to near luxury. Within their limitations, they're pretty neat. Being cute and cozy, your date will even think it's romantic.

They make great guest homes for your out-of-town friends. You could even have several RVs salted about the country in your favorite places. You'll have no hotel bills, less packing and the safer geographical diversity of your stuff.

Or, it could serve totally as your ultimate privacy pad. Your home is squeaky clean, while the RV contains your sensitive material, books, guns, reloading equipment, etc.

storage units

I don't care for them. They're expensive and get broken into fairly often. However, if the RV route isn't for you, or if you've got too much furniture, you'll have to rent a unit.

Since any tenant-landlord face-to-face is probably only during the rental, have a friend rent it for you. Your name won't be on the lease and the manager will never have seen you.

Pick a place with a security gate, as this dramatically cuts down on the petty burglaries. Usually, there will be a 6 or 12 month deal, and you should go for it. It's cheaper, and there's less of a paper trail than by paying monthly. Pay by mail with M.O.s from another town.

For your "home" address, do not give your public mail drop, and do not give your P.O. box. Use a one-time apartment or hotel address (without mentioning any room number). They'd only use the address to notice you of the auction of your stuff for unpaid rent, anyway.

You might find somebody willing to rent out their *garage* for storage space. This alternative is cheaper and more private, though not as safe as a security-gated storage facility.

Keep utterly *no* records or receipts of the unit at home. Hide them in the unit itself, or someplace nearby. If transported in your car, keep them in a locked briefcase.

FINAL THOUGHTS

Quit worrying about your precious stuff. You weren't born with it and it's not going with you after death. Rather, take some quality precautions and give 'em hell! We may indeed suffer a 21st century Dark Age in America, but by God, let's at least make them *earn* it. Let's face it: if you're not at least a *plausible* annoyance to the draconian forces, if you don't bang your head against the rules, if you don't have some assets and personal freedom on the line — *then what good are you*? The human capacity for obedience probably borders on the infinite, but how often is such obedience deserved by *government*?

Be a barnacle for Liberty, and slow down the ship of Tyranny. If there are enough of us barnacles, then perhaps we'll eat through the hull.

THE CENSUS & ACS

Never doubt that a small group of thoughtful, committed citizens can change the world. Indeed, it is the only thing that ever has.
— Margaret Mead

In order to apportion Representatives and direct taxes to the States, the decennial census was authorized by the Constitution in Article 1, Section 3:

The actual enumeration shall be made . . . every . . . ten years, in a manner as they (Congress) *shall by law direct.*

Nothing in the Constitution requires Americans to answer any Census question beyond the number of people in one's household. This is *all* the Federal Government needs to fulfill its constitutional duty of apportionment.

Sadly, the Government has transformed the Census into an unconstitutional invasion of your privacy. The 1870 Census asked only five questions. By 2000 it was 53. The 2010 Census will pose *over 70* questions ranging from your ethnic background, education, work, income, health, your relatives and housemates, and how many flush toilets you have.

Oh, and for 2010 and beyond, the census "enumerators" will be using GPSs:

I'm down in Colorado house-sitting for a friend, and just caught an "official census taker" wandering around this private property with a GPS unit, marking the positions of all the buildings and taking notes, right down to the old camper.

> *When I confronted her, she handed me a "Form D-31",*
> *told me they were trying to find all the places people lived for*
> *the 2010 census, and took off.*

GPS? That seemed pretty outrageous, but was easily verified:

> *Robert LaMacchia, head of the Census Bureau's geography*
> *division, says they'll capture the latitude and longitude of the*
> *front door of every house, apartment and improvised shelter*
> *they find.*
> *"We will actually knock on doors and look for hidden*
> *housing units," he says. "We will find converted garages; from*
> *the outside, it may not look like anybody lives there."*
> —www.lfb.com/index.php?action=help&helpfile=aug06arc
> hive.html#080206

The Government cannot tolerate not knowing about every possible "housing unit". That's just plain creepy, if not paranoia.

is answering census questions required by law?

Apparently, but it's unconstitutional on several grounds.

> *(a) Whoever, being over eighteen years of age, refuses or*
> *willfully neglects, . . . to answer, to the best of his knowledge,*
> *any of the questions . . . shall be fined not more than $100.*
> *(b) Whoever, when answering questions described in*
> *subsection (a) of this section, and under the conditions or*
> *circumstances described in such subsection, willfully gives*
> *any answer that is false, shall be fined not more than $500.*
> *(c) Notwithstanding any other provision of this title, no*
> *person shall be compelled to disclose information relative to*
> *his religious beliefs or to membership in a religious body.*
> — 13 USC § 221.
> Refusal or neglect to answer questions; false answers
> www.law.cornell.edu/uscode/13/221.shtml

The $100 fine for refusal seems to apply per person, and not per question, although the *Morales* case posits otherwise. It's a moot point since nobody has been prosecuted for it since *1960*. Just two people had to cough up the $100 . . . fifty years ago! You've more risk getting nabbed by the mattress police for tearing off those tags than being prosecuted by the DoJ for standing on your 1st, 4th, and 5th Amendment grounds.

Again, I say that the Census Bureau itself is, of course, not an enforcement agency. It wouldn't prosecute. **The Department of Justice would have to do the prosecution, and we don't recommend that.** *As most of you know, not since 1960 has there been any attempt to prosecute someone who did not complete the census form.*
        — Census Director Kenneth Prewittt, 2000

Mail and phone compliance with the long form census has been dropping, from 83% in 1980 to just 60% in 2000. *Boo, hoo.* In fact, the Census Bureau doesn't really like to talk about refusal and noncompliance because they don't want to inform people about even the possibility that they may decide not to answer. Government officials will mention "undercounts" and "missing some people" but not refusals to answer.
        To refuse on Fourth Amendment grounds, consider the privacy theories of **Griswold v. Connecticut,** 381 US 479 (1965) and **Roe v. Wade,** 410 US 113 (1973).

HISTORICAL CENSUS MISUSE

Satan rose up against Israel and incited [King] *David to take a census of Israel . . .* **This command was also evil in the sight of God . . .**
        Then David said to God, "I have sinned greatly by doing this. Now I beg you to take away the guilt of your servant. I have done a very foolish thing."
        — I Chronicles 21:1,8

1086 England: Wililam the Conqueror

Domesday Book (also known as Domesday, or Book of Winchester), was the record of the great survey of England completed in 1086, executed for William the Conqueror, that was similar to a census by a government of today. William needed information about the country he had just conquered so he could administer it. Whilst spending the Christmas of 1085 in Gloucester, William "had deep speech with his counsellors and sent men all over England to each shire ... to find out ... what or how much each landholder had in land and livestock, and what it was worth." One of the main purposes of the survey was to find out who owned what so they could be

*taxed on it, and the judgment of the assessors was final —
whatever the book said about who owned the property, or
what it was worth, was the law, and there was no appeal.*
  — WikiPedia

1864:   Sherman's march through Georgia

*Census officials began treating the collected information as
confidential, although no law required them to do so. The
custom didn't keep the Union Army from turning census data
into a weapon, however,* **thereby providing one of the
earliest proofs of the second and third laws of data
dynamics: that information produced for one purpose
will be used for other purposes and eventually will
cause harm to those who supplied the Information.**

*In 1864 Union General William Tecumseh Sherman
concocted an audacious plan — a full-force march from
Atlanta to the sea, which Civil War historian Bruce Catton
called "the strangest, most fateful campaign of the entire war."
Sherman set out not to engage another army; but to destroy
the Confederate economy and to convey the message that
the United States, in Sherman's words, "has the right, and
also the physical power, to penetrate to every part of the
national domain, and that we will do it . . . that we will remove
and destroy every obstacle — if need be, take every life,
every acre of land, every particle of property, everything that
to us seems proper." With the help of the census office — it
was not yet called a bureau — he made a pretty fair try at
fulfilling that promise.*

*He planned a fast, lean march. Doing so meant he would
not be able to maintain conventional lines of supply; in those
days before helicopter gunships and Harrier jets, an army was
only as good as its ability to protect the roads, rivers, and
railroads down which it had already traveled. Sherman would
have to live off the countryside to a degree no Union or
Confederate army had done before.*

*From the start of the war, Census Superintendent Joseph
C. G. Kennedy had been earnestly providing the war effort
with maps and census information on southern population
and industry but had sparked only limited interest. Sherman,
however, saw in Kennedy's annotated maps the key to his
campaign.*

**In practical effect Kennedy had provided Sherman
with a kind of Mobil guide for the plunder of the**

Confederate countryside, using data produced in more settled times by the very people Sherman encountered along his route. He gave his troops explicit orders to forage, a practice that until then was technically against the law. The army's mission included destroying mills, cotton supplies, railroads, anything of economic or military value. An Illinois sergeant wrote that his colleagues seemed "to take savage delight in destroying everything that could by any possibility be made use of by their enemies."

After the campaign, Sherman dropped Kennedy a thank-you note:

"The closing scene of our recent war demonstrated the, value of these statistical tables and facts, for there is a reasonable probability that, without them, I would not have undertaken what was done and what seemed a puzzle to the wisest and most experienced soldiers of the world."

— Erik Larson, *The Naked Consumer*
(Penguin 1992) ISBN 0-8050-1755-0, pp. 33-34

For a powerful visual rendition of Sherman's march to the sea, Scroogle to find "The Four Minute Civil War".

1942-1946:　U.S.A. internment of Japanese

Recall the law-abiding 110,000 Japanese-Americans who were rounded up during World War II and herded into concentration camps? Tar-paper shanty prisons erected where nobody had lived before, and nobody has lived since. With just 6 days of notice to report to the *"Reception Center"*, nearly all lost their possessions, homes, farms, and businesses. Most of their pets were destroyed.

This *"evacuation"* was ordered by FDR's Executive Order 9066, defended by both houses of Congress unanimously, and upheld by the Supreme Court in 1944 *Korematsu*. The rationale was based on the media/government paranoia that Japanese-Americans (Nisei) and their immigrant parents (Issei) were naturally loyal with Japan and could not be trusted:

JAPANESE HERE SENT VITAL DATA TO TOKYO

JAP AND CAMERA HELD IN BAY CITY

TWO JAPS WITH MAPS AND ALIEN LITERATURE SEIZED

CAPS ON JAPANESE TOMATO PLANTS POINT TO AIR BASE

When the baseless and hysterical warnings of imminent sabotage did not occur, government officials twisted that calm to mean that the conspirators were simply biding their time:

> *Unfortunately [many] are of the opinion that because we have had no sabotage and no fifth column activities . . . that means that none have been planned for us. But . . . this is the most ominous sign in our whole situation . . . The [sabotage] that we are about to get, are timed, just like the invasion of France, and of Norway . . . I believe that we are just being lulled into a false sense of security . . . Our day of reckoning will come.*
> — California Attorney General Earl Warren, February 1942

This sounds like the Bush administration claiming that the failure to find WMDs in Iraq was proof of their existence because they must have been spirited off to Syria. And, Bush's *"the Constitution's just a goddamned piece of paper!"* is echoic of 1942 Assistant Sec. of War John J. McCloy's *"the Constitution is just a scrap of paper to me"*. Other parallels include false information dissemination by the military, suppression of evidence in court proceedings, and denial of the writ of *habeus corpus.* (*Plus ça change . . .*)

The mass roundups of WWII were all for nothing:

> *. . . . after careful investigations on both the West Coast and Hawaii, there was never a shred of evidence found of sabotage, subversive acts, spying, or fifth column activity on the part of the Nisei or long-time local residents.*
> — U.S. Navy Lt. Commander Kenneth D. Ringle

Not only that, but the Japanese segregated 442nd Regimental Combat Team was the most decorated unit in the U.S. Army, winning 18,143 individual medals. Yet most of these same soldiers had family languishing in American camps!

The camps were finally emptied by March 1946, but it took decades for the inmates to achieve any redress.

> *The promulgation of Executive Order 9066 was not justified by military necessity, and the [mass detentions] were not driven by analysis of military conditions. The broad historical causes which shaped these decisions were race prejudice, war hysteria and a failure of political leadership.*
> — *Personal Justice Denied,* the 1983 Redress Commission

Korematsu *remains on the pages of our legal and political history . . . As historical precedent it stands as a constant caution that in times of war or declared military necessity our institutions must be vigilant in protecting constitutional guarantees.*
> — U.S. District Court Judge Marilyn Hall Patel, 1983, in voiding the indictment/conviction of Fred Korematsu

Only a half century later was the Government forced to apologize and offer some minuscule $20,000 reparations for the Japanese-Americans' loss of freedom and property. Most of those harmed had died long before.

Well, how did the Government ever know their ancestry?

From the 1930 and 1940 Census!

Knowledge is *power!*

The Census Bureau tried to defend themselves by alleging that they gave out only generic "block data" which the Army re-identified to actual persons:

> *Census Bureau spokesman Ray Bancroft insists that this was not a breach of confidentiality because the bureau did not give out the names or exact addresses of Japanese-Americans.*

This was proven in 2007 to be a lie by researchers William Seltzer and Margo Anderson:

> *Their paper "Census Confidentiality under the Second War Powers Act (1942-1947)", prepared for the Annual Meeting of the Population Association of America, March 30, 2007, New York, New York, documents actual examples of the Census Bureau revealing both personal and business records during the war hysteria of World War II. In 1943, the Census Bureau looked up and revealed every Japanese citizen or alien in Washington, DC to the Secret Service. It's no longer conjecture; here's the listing in black and white from the National Archives. (BTP Note: see the following page.)*
>
> *(The researchers blacked out the name and house number of each person when republishing this document in 2007. The original 1943 document revealed all the names and addresses.)*
> — www.toad.com/gnu/census.html

DEPARTMENT OF COMMERCE
Bureau of the Census
Washington

JAPANESE RESIDING IN THE METROPOLITAN AREA OF WASHINGTON, D.C., APRIL 1, 1940

Address	Sex	Age	Marital status	Citizenship	Work status	Occupation
Franklin Park Hotel	Male	24	Married	Alien	Employed	Performer -
Franklin Park Hotel	Male	25	Single	Native	Seeking work	Performer -
1st St., N.W.	Male	68	Married	Alien	Employed	Own account
1st St., N.W.	Female	64	Married	Alien	Not in labor force	Housework -
1st St., N.W.	Male	29	Single	Native	Employed	Clerk - Reta
10th St., N.W.	Male	59	Married	Alien	Employed	Clerk - Deli
Massachusetts Ave., N.W.	Male	55	Married	Alien	Employed	Artist and r
Massachusetts Ave., N.W.	Female	42	Married	Alien	Not in labor force	Housework -
Massachusetts Ave., N.W.	Male	18	Single	Native	Not in labor force	Student
Massachusetts Ave., N.W.	Female	17	Single	Native	Not in labor force	Student
Massachusetts Ave., N.W.	Female	33	Single	Native	Not in labor force	Student
R St., N.W.	Male	47	Married	Alien	Employed	Writer - New
20th St., N.W.	Female	28	Married	Native	Not in labor force	Psychologist
20th St., N.W.	Male	54	Married	Alien	Employed	Housework -
Massachusetts Ave., N.W.	Female	56	Married	Alien	Own account	Maid - Apart
Massachusetts Ave., N.W.	Female	22	Single	Native	Employed	Secretary -
P St., N.W.	Male	28	Married	Native	Employed	Architect -
P St., N.W.	Female	24	Married	Native	Not in labor force	Housework -
Y.M.C.A. (17th and I Sts., N.W.)	Female	32	Single	Alien	Not in labor force	Student
P St., N.W.	Female	60		Native	Seeking work	Trained nurs
P St., N.W.		90	Married	Native	Employed	Chemist - L.

1933-1945:   Nazi Germany and Holocaust

In 2001 a groundbreaking book was published which proved the partnership between IBM Germany and the Nazi government. *IBM and the Holocaust* by Edwin Black fully describes how IBM punch card technology was designed and employed to identify German Jews and other "undesirables."

> *After decades of documentation by the best minds, the most studied among them would confess that they never really understood the Holocaust process . . . How could it happen? How were they selected?* **How did the Nazis get the names? They always had the names.**
>
> *What seemingly magical scheduling process could have allowed millions of Nazi victims to step onto train platforms in Germany or nineteen other Nazi-occupied countries, travel for two and three days by rail, and then step onto a ramp at Auschwitz or Treblinka—and within an hour be marched into gas chambers. Hour after hour. Day after day. Timetable after timetable. Like clockwork, and always with* blitzkrieg *efficiency.*
>
> *The survivors would never know. The liberators would never know. The politicians who made speeches would never know. The prosecutors who prosecuted would never know. The debaters would never know.* **The question was barely even raised.**
>
> — Edwin Black, *IBM and the Holocaust* (2001), p. 425-426

The process of genocide goes like this: First, the government desires the technology. Once it has that, then come the laws. After the laws comes action. IBM took governments (US and Nazi Germany) into the information age back in the 1930s. Today, Microsoft, Oracle, and other amoral computer companies are taking the Government into the next generation of omniscience.

> *In using statistics, the government now has the road map to switch from knowledge to deeds.*
>
> — Friedrich Zahn, German Statistical Archive (1936)

> *Theoretically, the collection of data for each person can be so abundant and complete,* **that we can finally speak of a paper human representing the natural human.** (Black *op. cit.*, p.304)
>
> — 1936 journal of the German Statistical Society

*We are no longer dealing with general censuses, **but we are really following individuals**.* (Black *op. cit.*, p.323)
    — René Carmille of the National Statistical Service of 1941
      Occupied France

It possessed the technology to scrutinize an entire nation.
    *...No one would escape. This was something new for mankind. Never before had so many people been identified so precisely, so silently, so quickly, and with such far-reaching consequences. **The dawn of the Information Age began at the sunset of human decency.*** (Black *op. cit.*, p.104)
    — regarding IBM in Nazi Germany (Dehomag)

A special envelope containing a so-called Supplemental Card was created. This all-important card recorded the individual's bloodline data and functioned as the racial linchpin of the operation. Each head of household was to fill out his name and address and then document his family's ancestral lines. Jews understandably feared the newest identification. Census takers were cautioned to overcome any distrust by assuring families that the information would not be released to the financial authorities. (Black *op. cit.*, p.170)
    — regarding Nazi Germany's 1939 census

*Another sign that bodes ill: Today, notices informed the Jewish population of Warsaw that next Saturday there will be a census of the Jewish inhabitants . . . **Our hearts tell us of evil; some catastrophe for the Jews of Warsaw lies in this census. Otherwise there would be no need for it.***
    *The order for the census stated that it is being held to gather data for administrative purposes. That's a neat phrase, but it contains catastrophe . . . We are certain that this census is being taken for the purpose of expelling "nonproductive elements" . . . **We are all caught in a net, doomed to destruction.***
    — October 1939 diary of Warsaw Jew Chaim Kaplan

*The evacuation (i.e., deportation to concentration camps for disposal) of Poles and Jews in the new Eastern Provinces will be conducted by Security Police . . . **The census documents provide the basis for evacuation.***
    — Reinhard Heydrich's 1939 memo
      Evacuation of the New Eastern Provinces

Without the intimate collaboration between IBM and the Nazi government, the Holocaust could never have happened. If the Jews had not obeyed the command to register themselves during the census process, the Nazis simply would not have known whom to roundup, or where.

The German people of the 1980s protested so much over their intrusive census questions, that the Constitutional Court stopped the census in 1980 and 1983. The last census was in 1987. (A similar situation happened in the Netherlands, cancelling any census since 1991.)

FUTURE CENSUS MISUSE

The bureaucrats who run the Census Bureau are building a fortress from which they cannot be dislodged.

The ACS is designed to shield the Census Bureau from criticism and to allow them to hire permanent workers to replace the army of temporary workers that were chasing down the non-responders in the real 10-year Census.

By inventing a new term "data customers", they are justifying their own positions and building a secure empire. That's what bueaucracies do.

More permanent workers means promotions for those on board now. More funding means more resources. What's not to like? It's a unholy alliance, alright. The Census Bureau bureaucrats, bureaucrats from various agencies, Congress and K Street special interests ganging up on taxpayers to squeeze data out of them so they can all expand their power.

Now if those pesky citizens would just shut up and cooperate, everything would be hunky-dory. And please don't mention those poor misguided citizens of Germany and the Netherlands who got rid of their Censuses.

— suinmd, December 29, 2006

The census performs many useful functions for society. However, there is widespread evidence of the misuse of census data. Hitler notably used the European Census in his conquests across Europe. The misuse of census data can be found in much of the world, including in our own nation. Even recently, privacy risks lead to public statements by politicians regarding the intrusiveness of census questions. The Washington Post quoted Former Senate Majority Leader

Trent Lott of encouraging citizens not to answer invasive questions.
    — www.epic.org/privacy/census/

marketing firms

Up-to-date small area address counts from ACS operations will be beneficial to private companies conducting surveys, small area data on characteristics, such as race and ethnicity, will help them stratify their area samples, and general-purpose data products from the ACS will allow the private sector to develop new specialized data products that contain current, rather than outdated, information.
    — www.ogc.doc.gov/ogc/legreg/testimon/106s/prewitt0720.htm

Consumer marketing companies use the census to evaluate much more then income, race, gender, and the location of potential customers. Companies can evaluate the workplace, leisure activity, and consumption patterns of individuals. This can be attempted through "geodemographic segmentation," which combines the population and housing census information from several categories. Using geographic, demographic and psychographic (focusing on lifestyle rather than demographic information as a basis for describing segments of data) approaches, marketing companies can use the census information to construct lifestyle profiles. The marketing companies Claritas, CACI Marketing, Mediamark Research, Inc., former R.J. Reynolds Tobacco Company, and others have used various types of census based marketing systems.
    — www.epic.org/privacy/census/

This is allowed by 13 USC 401, just in case you aren't already getting enough junk mail, email spam, and telemarketing calls. By the way, those free 38 minutes of your time the Bureau insists from you are sold in a compiled CD package for $1,200.

more government/corporate incest

In addition, the Census Bureau relies heavily on strong support from corporate interests to collect, scan, archive, and conduct follow-up work related to surveys unwittingly filled out by individuals under the false pretense that their responses will be kept 'strictly confidential'.

Indeed, the Census Bureau and its contracted help will all tell you that your responses are protected by statute and any unauthorized disclosure is punishable by severe fines and prison time. What they don't tell you is that the number of 'authorized' disclosures is expansive and corporations and individuals working with the Census Bureau have unfettered access to your personal information while under contract with the Bureau.

A close look at several corporations such a Lockheed Martin and Evolver, Inc., shows a strong connection to other government agencies such as Homeland Security, the Department of Defense, and various Intelligence agencies. Additionally, Lockheed Martin has not only been a major player in previous decennial census efforts in the United States but has also been a major contractor for National Census efforts in other countries such as Canada and England. In the case of Canada, Lockheed's participation resulted in an uproar from the public that is still being heard today.

— www.checkpointusa.org/Census/Census.htm

more welfare programs

The Census Bureau just released statistics showing that 51% of women now live alone, which is straight from the ACS. Now we have people in government agencies and lobbying groups trying to figure out if that's a problem and what can they do about that. I have no doubt they'll be able to gin up some silly program to address whatever they think is the problem. Giving the Feds more data is like matches to a 5 year old.

But, the Census data helps get government money to grandparents raising their own grandchildren!

If those grandparents had done a better job raising their own kids, they wouldn't be stuck raising their grandchildren. What we DON'T need is some goof-ball, well-intentioned, but flawed Federal Government program to rectify that situation. But that's what the ACS is all about ... inventing crisises from statistics and then proposing or justifying Federal spending on programs that feel good, but don't work. That's why all those bureaucrats and lobbying firms love it. All they need to do is get the right questions asked in the right way and it's a bonanza for them.

individual re-identification from aggregates

Public use datasets contain 'anonymous' microdata, information on individual people and organizations where the explicit identifiers have been stripped away. Microdata can then be transferred even in blocks of just a few individuals. Under 13 USC § 9, the Census Bureau is required to make sure that the identities cannot be "reasonably deduced." Concepts of "reasonable deduction," however, are changing quickly.

Re-identification is the process of linking anonymous data to the actual identity of an individual. Carnegie Mellon Professor Latanya Sweeney has demonstrated that anonymous data sets can often be readily re-identified. In one experiment, Sweeney, using 1990 Census data, demonstrated that individuals often have demographic values that occur infrequently. Since these values occur infrequently, they allow the re-identification of individuals in putatively anonymous datasets.

> *— www.epic.org/privacy/census/*

social security numbers are next

About 21,000 American households received a census form asking respondents for that all-important nine-digit number, in addition to the typical inquiries on race, gender and age. It was a little-noticed experiment conducted by the Census Bureau to see how Americans would respond to being asked for the figure...

> *— www.stevefriess.com/archive/sun-sentinel/census.htm*

The use of the Social Security Number on public documents remains one of the most controversial topics in privacy regulation. Recently, the Census Bureau has engaged in a study to see whether the public will object to the collection of Social Security numbers on census forms. The Census Bureau has created a program called SPAN, Social Security Number, Privacy Attitudes and Notification Experiment. The experiment would consist of asking 20,000 people to fill out their special census form, which would include their SSN. Meanwhile, the Census Bureau has begun to expand interagency sharing of Social Security numbers. In 1998, Commissioner of the Social Security Administration approved the Census Bureau's request for the file of SSN applicants (also called the Numident File).

*The Administrative Records Steering Committee continues **to assess whether or not a public outcry would follow the use of SSNs in the Census.** Their studies have recognized that there are numerous considerations, particularly due to issues of controlling data.*

— www.epic.org/privacy/census/

If the ACS data are supposedly not individualized and only kept in aggregate form, then why would forms need SSNs?

why not also ask about gun ownership?

That way, the feds could concentrate on areas with an "inordinate" number of "assault weapons" and would the hiders will be in the coming gun confiscation raids.

increasingly empowered government

This new program will cost taxpayers well over $150,000,000 a year and is envisioned by Census Bureau personnel as a permanent fixture to the new American police state. It was developed and implemented by unelected career bureaucrats at the Department of Commerce in close consultation with other government interests including but not limited to the Department of Justice, Health and Human Services and Homeland Security.

— www.checkpointusa.org/Census/Census.htm

By providing reams of information, the census allows politicians to further manipulate people's lives. The more information government collects, the more control government can exert.

The Constitution mandates that an enumeration of the citizenry be conducted every ten years in order to apportion seats in the House of Representatives. Citizens should never be required to answer any question except for the number of residents at an address. A partial boycott of the census questionnaire was necessary to safeguard our liberties and, therefore, it was good that a large number of Americans have refused to answer all the questions. Rather than a promise of confidentiality, the government's census forms should come

> *with a Miranda warning: Any answers you give can be used against you.*
> — James Bovard, in 2000

The audacity of the ACS questions stupefies.   Truly, the mandarins of government believe that nothing is outside their domain. They see themselves above all restraint:

> *According to a view that is widely held (although it has been challenged by the Nuremberg principles), the state itself is an entity that is not subject to the moral law; it is free to do anything it deems necessary to protect or promote the national interests. The central authorities, in acting for the state, are similarly not subject to moral restraints that might operative in their personal lives . . . According to this view, the freedom from all restraint devolves on the central decision maker [e.g. Hitler] from a higher authority, the state, of which he is merely the servant. . . . He too claims that he had no choice in that he was responding to authoritative demands . . .* **The whole doctrine is, of course, extremely dangerous because of its total circularity.**
> — Herbert C. Kelman, psychologist, *"Violence Without Moral Restraint: Reflections on the Dehumanization of Victims and Victimizers"*
> Journal of Social Issues 29(4): pp.45-46 (1973)

loss or theft of census data

Klaus Fuchs was delivering our A-bomb secrets to the Soviets before we had even tested Trinity in July 1945. I'm not impressed with Government's security of information.

> *The census forms the most inclusive federal database of American citizens. The information it contains is protected under law from disclosure, yet with the advent of technology many of the traditional legislative protection are inadequate. The recent use of computers has dramatically altered the structure of the US census. It has allowed the Census Bureau to retain information in an efficient format, while also challenging the traditional methods of information collection. Along with this growing technology, the potential harm has grown exponentially. Technology has allowed the collection of information to move at remarkable speeds and the protection of such information remains a struggle.*
> — www.epic.org/privacy/census

AMERICAN COMMUNITY SURVEY

This is an *annual* version of the Census 2000 "long form" which was widely detested and ignored. The negative response from some 20 million households was too much to manage, so the Census Bureau leveled out their work-load to 250,000 monthly forms given out by fewer, but better trained, staff.

The ACS is *not* the census, as it is administered in off-years. It is sort of a "rolling census" and the Bureau hopes that the lessened impact per year will reduce mass noncompliance. By affecting just 10% of households each year, mass anger does not reach a flashpoint. It's a clever plan, but it's failing.

The questions are very intrusive, inquiring into the daily and personal habits of each member of your household. For example, under "Housing" you are asked how many vehicles you have; monthly fuel, water, and electricity costs; monthly rent or mortgage; estimated value of your property and annual property insurance. Forty-two questions are listed to be answered by each person in your household.

Disturbing questions in this section include a question asking if you have any physical, mental, or emotional conditions that would make it difficult for you to go shopping or go outside the home, involvement of the grandparents in raising the children, and the exact time you leave for work and name of your employer. It's difficult to imagine a legitimate reason for a government entity to demand this kind of information from its citizens. If you have concerns about Big Brother becoming too interested in your private affairs you will not like this survey.

Oh, and who is behind the ACS? A bunch of special interest groups, marketing firms, megacorps, bureaucrats, and sociology professors.

intrusive ACS questions

Oh, you're gonna love these. It is difficult to imagine what the ACS does *not* ask.

What type of house do you live in?
When was it built?
When did you move into it?
How many acres is it on?
How many rooms are in the house?
How may bedrooms are in the house?
Does the house have plumbing?
Does it have a complete kitchen?
Is there telephone service available?
How many cars are kept at the home?
What fuel is used to heat the home?
How much did you spend on electricity last month?
How much did you spend on water and sewer?
Did anyone receive Food Stamps?
How much are Homeowners Association fees?
How much would you try to sell the home for?
How much are the real estate taxes on the property?
How much was insurance on this property?
Do you have a mortgage?
How much is the mortgage?
Does the mortgage include real estate taxes?
Do you have a second mortgage?
How much is the second mortgage?
Are you a citizen of the United States?
Have you attended school in the past three months?
What is the highest grade attended?
Do you speak a language other than English?
How well do you speak English?
Where did you live one year ago?
What medical conditions do you have, and do they affect your ability to
dress or bathe youself, or go outside the home?
Do you have any grandchildren?
Have you ever been on active duty in the military, and for how long?
Did you work last week?
Where did you work?
How did you get to work?
How long did it take you to get to work?
What time did you leave for work?
What is your chief job opportunity?
What were your wages?
What was your interest from investments?
What was your income form Social Security, public assistance,
retirement, and/or the VA, child support, or alimony?

the hollow farce of "it's only statistical data"

By just clicking a few census tracts, I found one with a population of 26. The tract number is 118200. How can they keep data private for such a small sample?

Here what I know about that tract.

11 homes, 2 of which are vacant seasonal homes.
All 9 occupied homes are owned by white owners.
4 family households.
5 single person households - 2 male and 3 female.
1 of the residents of the tract is American Indian.

It can't be difficult to do just a little more research and find out who the 1 American Indian is, where he/she lives, how much he/she makes, if he/she lives alone, when he/she goes to work, etc.

So much for being private.

As most Americans are tied to their home residences by a myriad of records, their re-identification is a simple matter. There is great risk of privacy intrusion and even identity theft:

The risks that accompany the electronic compilation personal information include re-identification, which is the practice of linking individuals identities to anonymous census records; marketing solicitations; and even more serious consequences of political abuse. The use of information to identify individuals rather than for the statistical collection of information offers room for abuses of privacy and confidentiality.

— www.epic.org/privacy/census/

the ACS is not the census

Frequently posters on this board take the position that all they all constitutionally required to disclose is the number of people residing at a residence.

If ACS was the constitutionally-mandated 10 Year Census, I'd agree.

But the ACS taken in a non-Census year, isn't a Census.

It's something else trying to make itself look like a census.
It's a survey the government is trying to peddle as a Census.

It's being administered by the Census Department. And they are trying to stretch the law covering the Census to make it fit.

> *I don't see where we are obligated to make any response. Not the number of people in the home. Not the electric bill. Not the race of the residents.*
>
> *This isn't a Census.*
>
> *And they sure don't want the Courts involved in this obvious subterfuge.*

the ACS and Big Brother government

> *This information could be shared with county officials in case of an emergency need to lock down schools, close post offices, isolate a neighborhood, or evacuate part of a hospital.*
>   — ACS brochure

That reads like something much more helpful to *Heimat Sicherheitsdienst* (Homeland Security) than to building new roads and senior citizen centers. Besides, county officials *already know* about their own schools, post offices, neighborhoods, and hospitals. The goal of the ACS is not to share redundant information with local officials, but to empower the federal government to rule locally if it so chooses.

According to the Libertarian Party Press Release of 2000:

> *Remember, Americans were promised by our government that our Social Security numbers would be used only for Social Security. We were told that confidential FBI files could never end up in the White House. And we were assured that IRS employees would never browse through individuals' tax returns just for fun. So why should we trust politicians about the Census?*
>
> *The government should put the Census form on a postcard containing only one question: How many people live at your address," he suggested. "That would raise response rates dramatically, protect Americans' privacy, and comply with the Constitution. It's an inexpensive, obvious, and practical solution — no wonder the politicians refuse to do it.*
>   — "Strike a blow for privacy: Refuse to answer nosy Census questions"

Go to the Census Bureau website to discover that the ACS is only the tip of the iceberg. Read about their "Final Plan" at:

www.census.gov/acs/www/Downloads/OpsPlanfinal.pdf

RESISTING THE CENSUS & ACS

How dare they demand that I give them an additional 40 minutes of my life in addition to the 2 days a week I already work to keep them in pork? If I had 40 additional minutes, there are many other things I could do with the time — all of which would be none of their business!

Contrary to popular belief and Government propaganda, you are *not* constitutionally required to answer anything on the Census beyond how many people are living in your household. (On the ACS, don't even answer *that.*)   Do not let the Government try to intimidate you; the fine for not answering questions is only $100.   Congress may have unlawfully expanded the Census, but they have not required you to waive your rights to privacy.

The founders never authorized the federal government to continuously survey the American people. More importantly, they never envisioned a nation where the people would roll over and submit to every government demand. The American Community Survey is patently offensive to all Americans who still embody that fundamental American virtue, namely a healthy mistrust of government. The information demanded in the new survey is none of the government's business, and the American people should insist that Congress reject it now before it becomes entrenched.
— Congressman Ron Paul
www.house.gov/paul/tst/tst2004/tst071204.htm

Over 90% of what the Government knows about you and your family is information that came directly, or indirectly, from *you*.   From warranty card info to credit applications, Americans snitch on *themselves* daily and this information (*i.e.,* power) is used against us! 2010 is for many where that ends.

You can choose *not* to answer intrusive Census questions.

You can choose *not* to speak with Census-takers.

You are *not* required by law to allow Census-takers in your home.

More and more, Americans are protecting their privacy. So much so that the Census Bureau must lie about compliance, claiming a preposterous 96%. Only 61% of the sample answers by mail or phone, leaving only a third of the remaining 39% to be visited in person:

> *What they are really saying that by making the assumption that the 1/3rd of the 39% that don't respond to the mail or phone attempts are representative of the 26% they make no attempt to visit in person.*
>
> *They try to make the ACS look like a Census so they can stretch the laws covering that to include the ACS. They mislead people on the response rate. They suggest that people will be fined, even though they know it won't happen.*

The Census is of an unconstitutional scope, and with an evil purpose — to register the characteristics, assets, and habits of Americans for the purpose of selection, ostracization, and confiscation. We are told that the information collected will not be shared or misused, that our privacy will be protected.

That is a *lie!*

That has always *been* a lie!

Ask the Japanese-Americans of 1942. Ask the Jews under Hitler. We are poised for a 21st Century cataloging of *"extremists"* and *"religious fanatics"* and *"survivalists"* and *"gun nuts"* and other groups of concerned peaceable folk.

The Jews of 20th century Europe may not have had any warning of what was in store for them. It had never before happened, and to contemplate systematic genocide was unimaginable. But, 21st century Americans will have no excuse to be surprised.

Registering yourself during the 2010 Census is like sending a list of your household valuables to a burglars' guild. Do not invite — no, *guarantee* trouble for yourself. Do not participate with oppression! The sooner enough of us refuse to complete the ACS the sooner it will be abandoned as unreliable.

Tyranny cannot succeed without its victims' cooperation.

Tyranny cannot succeed without *your* cooperation.

the Census Bureau process

First, we must understand their methods and timeframe:

In the training given to ACS callers, they are only supposed to make a total of seven calls. The section under data collection indicates that their protocol is to harass you by phone until you refuse twice. Then you have the chance of being contacted in person. However, the total harassment period should last no more than three months . . . which is their data collection timeframe.

First they send a pre-notice letter.

Second, they send an initial questionnaire package four days later.

Third, they send a post card three days later.

Three weeks later they send another questionnaire package.

This mail phase takes a month. You can throw it all out as you get it.

If you don't respond, they will attempt to call and interview you over the phone. This phase lasts a month and someone suggested that they will try and call seven times. Just screen your calls.

If they can't get ahold of you on the phone, then they will go to the Personal Interview phase. That lasts a month. But there's only one chance in three (33%) that they will try and come to your house.

If you refuse to be interviewed, then their supervisor may mail you or call you. But essentially that's the end of it.

The whole cycle is 90 Days. 30 Days for mail to work. 30 Days for telephone. 30 days for visits.

Then they'll be gone to pester someone else.

don't waste your time and energy with . . .
writing your Congressman

He's heard it all before, and doesn't care:

I regret that you and I have a difference of opinion on the issue of the American Community Survey. While we might disagree on the right course of action on this situation, I am sure there are many other issues that we have a similar opinion on, and I sincerely appreciate your willingness to

*share your thoughts with me on this issue and I will continue
to value your input in the future.*

Or, how about this one:

*I understand that you find the questions on the American
Community Survey to be intrusive, and you feel they violate
your right to privacy. However, federal law requires that
household selected for participation act in compliance with the
survey, specifically in Title 13, Sections 141 and 193.*

(Translation: *Tough shit!*)
Here's another example, but with some lubricant:

*By posing a host of demographic and lifestyle questions, the
US Census Bureau uses such data to provide critical
information that helps the government determine how to best
distribute scarce resources that can affect your daily life from
school districting to police force levels to even the number of
US Congressional delegates allocated to each state.*
  — Senator Barack Obama, in 2006

*". . . to even the number of US Congressional delegates allocated
to each state"*? Talk about rubbing our noses in it — that is the
sole constitutional mandate for the census in the first place!

dialoguing with a Census Bureau senior official
They've also heard it all before, and won't renounce his
holy mission. (What, do you expect to convince the guy to quit
his job?) If anything, you only help train him to argue better for
the next citizen (who isn't likely as informed or resolute as you).

arguing the privacy to the Census "enumerator"
If these drones cared about your personal privacy, then
they wouldn't be crawling around your premises with a GPS,
sitting in your driveway for 15 minutes making notes, or trying
to cajole your cellphone number from your neighbors.

suing for your constitutional rights
It's likely fruitless at this stage, as a U.S. District case has
upheld the intrusive questions: ***Morales v. Daley*** (2000)
www.census.gov/dmd/www/pdf/morales.pdf

you can't answer what's not been asked

The paper-tiger legal requirement aside, let's think tactically here. You can't answer questions which you've not allowed them to ask. They can be foiled at every stage:

the form mailed or FedExed to you

The mailed survey does not ask you (not you specifically) any questions that you are required to answer. Since the survey is addressed to "The Resident of," you can confidently ignore it.

There is no proof that you even *received* the form, especially if you don't sign for the FedEx. (Don't even mark it "Return To Sender" as that betokens delivery with subsequent refusal.)

However, do not throw out the form! Snip out your address and the form's serial number, and then show it widely. Most will not have yet seen the thing, and its questions will shock them. Explain how to handle it when it's their turn.

the phone calls

If an agent calls you on the phone, you are not obligated to answer any questions. Either hang up when the agent identifies him/herself, or state that you have no way of verifying the identity of the person asking the questions and therefore will not respond.

Seems to me the easiest way to handle this is to answer the phone and tell them in no uncertain terms that you are refusing to participate and then just hang up. If you stay on the line they will argue with you until they run through their whole book of prepared scripts.

If they do decide to send someone to interview you, just tell them you are not going to participate. Don't get into any discussions as they are pointless.

The key to this is to refuse and then do not let them get you into an argument about why you are refusing. Don't get into arguments with these people. They don't care what you think and they are never going to agree with you. They are trained to keep you engaged in any conversation and they are armed with memorized answers to address your objections.

Dodging their phone calls shouldn't be any different from dodging the telemarketers that already pester you.

Just a hint, but when my caller ID shows a number I do not recognize I answer with "may I help you" because the dialing computers are set to connect you to a live person when the word "hello" is spoken. This gives you about a 3 second lag and you can hear that it is being transferred, that's when I hang up. Works great with telemarketing calls as well.

the house visit

If they send someone to your house — which probably won't occur — tell them you aren't going to respond. Be polite, but curt.

As I read more about how the Census Bureau implements the ACS, certain mysteries start to clear up.

Why are they satisfied when they talk to you over the phone or at your doorstep with far less information than they asked for in the survey?

There's a simple answer. They are going to fill in the form themselves by guessing at what your responses would have been by comparing the answers you gave to others who did fill in the whole thing completely.

Now, they don't like to do that, but they will. That's another way they get to that phony "96% response rate" they advertise.

If you tell them "nothing", they can't do that.

And they know that "response rate" is the key to the whole thing. Their "customers" will lose faith in the data and the whole ill-advised thing will collapse.

He said: I represent the Department of Commerce US Census Bureau. I am doing a follow-up interview to the census survey that was mailed to this address. Do you live at this address?

I said: We do not participate in surveys or accept any solicitation.

He said: I am not soliciting, I am gathering necessary census data.

I said: That sounds like soliciting.

He said: I'm going to ask you a number of questions related to you, your residence, and others residing at this address.

I said: I will not answer any questions.

He said: You are required by law to respond to the survey questions.

I said: Are you an enforcement officer of some department with jurisdiction here?
He said: I am not a law enforcement officer.
I said: Are you trying to detain me?
He said: NO! I'm not trying to detain you.
I said: I'm leaving now. Please excuse me. [I stepped back and started to close the door.]
He said: Is there a better time to complete the interview?
I said: It will never happen. [I finished closing the door.]

If an agent comes to your door:
    1) Do not invite them in.
    2) As soon as he/she begins to identify him/herself, step back inside and close the door -even if he/she is in the process of showing you identification.
    It is a simple matter of not being asked. If you are not asked, you cannot be fined for not answering.
    Title 13 may require you to answer questions that are asked, but it does not allow for you to be detained for that questioning. Don't worry about being rude. Just think about how rude the Department of Commerce has been to you by asking the questions in the first place and then hounding you over it when you had the nerve to try to reserve a little bit of privacy.
    Deal with these people just like you would with any annoying telemarketer.

an intriguing legal angle

The ACS back page reads:

Respondents are not required to respond to any information collection unless it displays a valid approval number from the Office of Management and Budget. This 8-digit number appears in the bottom left on the front cover of this form.

There is no number in the bottom left on the front cover. Since it's in the bottom right, it does not comply to OMB regs. Perhaps it is a "bootleg" form? That could be legal grounds not to trust it, nor the person handing it out. *Heh.* These legal snags can be surprisingly effective. (Remember Sam Lowry in *Brazil* demanding the Form 27Z-6?)

idea for rural properties

Those on farms and ranches vulnerable to vacant fields trespassing could post frequent signs reading:

WARNING! The entire private property behind this fence is daily used as a shooting range with unscheduled and unannounced live-fire activity. There are dozens of prepositioned targets throughout and all visitors must have an escort. For your own safety, do not enter this property without the express permission and/or prior knowledge of the owner.

Requests for appointment to visit must be made at least 30 days in advance by writing the owner at P.O. Box ___. (Include your full name, home address and phone, DOB, DL#, and SSN for a preauthorized background check.) A mailed request to visit the property does not indicate receipt of such, nor does it guarantee owner's permission.

If you are not expected, leave now to avoid unintentional injury from practice gunfire on this property. Trespassers have been duly warned, and the owner and his assigns are not responsible for any consequences arising from property intrusions.

That should keep out nosy strangers. (You may even want to also post a Spanish version.) If you post something like this, be sure to first inform the neighbors, friends, the propane guy, etc. I admit that this approach will garner you some attention, so you must weigh the cost:benefit ratio for yourself.

create your *own* form for the "enumerator"

Along the "permission to enter" and "know your visitor" scheme of the above:

I have seen a questionnaire intended as a defense against telephone solicitors. I have tried it and it worked well. The person called simply turns the interview back on the unwanted caller by requiring a bunch of specific identification before answering anything. Perhaps this method would deter the ACS operators. We can take our lead from the ACS form and ask for much of the same questions.

What is your full name?
SSN?
Marital status?
What is your mailing address?
What is your home address?
What is your home phone?

What is your annual income?
How many children live at your residence?
Do they go to public school?
What time of the day are you and the other adults of the residence away from home?

These are just some "harmless" questions. I won't tell anyone else your answers.

Explain that without the full information you cannot know the caller is not just another unsolicited call selling something or attempting identity theft.

A sample form can be downloaded from:
http://faemalia.net/PublicServantQuestionnaire.pdf

some websites to peruse

www.census.gov/acs/www/
www.toad.com/gnu/census.html (defiant)
www.epic.org/privacy/census/ (solid analysis)
www.checkpointusa.org/Census/Census.htm (excellent sources)
www.checkpointusa.org/Census/ACS/docs/2005questionnaire.pdf
www.survivalarts.com/archives/001095.html (very lengthy, but good)

some sample questions and answers

From my research, the quickest and easiest way to finally be left alone from these pests is to simply refuse to answer all objectionable questions. However, you may not be able to resist, so here are some ideas.

"Your information is important for social services."

So you claim. Even if that were true, I don't want your "services".

"96% of Americans reply."

No, they don't. Only 50% of Americans send the questionnaire back in. Only 10% respond to your harrassing phone calls. Less than a third of the rest reply. The compliance rate is 74% at best.

"Completion of the form takes only 38 minutes."

I do not work for free, and cannot be compelled to do so. My rate for consultations is $500 per hour, with a two-hour minimum, paid in advance with cash. Do you accept?

"The information will not be shared with others."

That's what they said about the Social Security Number. "*Not to be used for identification.*"   Remember?   You claim that census data is protected. Are you willing to place your own property as security bond?

"Census data is protected against unlawful disclosure."

Yeah?   Well, have you found those 1,100 Census Bureau laptops that went missing?   Anybody been prosecuted, convicted, and sentenced to that $250,000 fine and 5 years in prison? (Didn't think so.)

What about those 26.5 million veterans who had their personal data stolen?   Look, I don't believe the Bureau's promise to protect private information, and neither do half of all Americans.

"You're not required to give your name."

Really?   Then why does the form specifically *ask* for it?

"The Cenus Bureau needs your input."

Here's your "input".   I refuse to provide the requested information. I know that I will not be prosecuted. I resent the government making empty threats. I do not trust the government to do anything worthwhile with that information, much less keep it secure.

"You can be fined if you do not answer."

Perhaps, but nobody has regarding the Census since 1960 when just two people had to pay $100. Regarding the ACS, nobody has ever been fined. My privacy is worth a $100, and I'll take my chances. Just review your booklet about "*Techniques for Non-Responders and the Hard to Interview*" and consider me as such. Good day.

"Then I must report your refusal to the Justice Dept."

See you in court! (laughing)

❖ 17

PRIVACY & YOUR GUNS

Note: *Boston's Gun Bible* is essential reading for more details!

THE PURCHASE

buying privately

In some 25 states Americans can still privately buy and sell firearms without any forms, paperwork or registration. In many cities there is a classified ad section for guns (if not under "Guns" or "Firearms" then often under "Sporting Goods"). Call from a pay phone and pay cash.

Or, go to a gun show and seek out the private sale tables (they'll usually advertise this with a little sign). At gun shows, beware of anybody suggesting that you participate in any unlawful activity, such as "straw sales" (buying a gun on behalf of somebody forbidden to do so themselves). If this happens, it's probably a BATF agent trying to set you up. Threaten to alert the police if he persists. BATman or not, he'll leave at once.

These lawful, peaceful, and historic shows are now (May 2009) under attack by the "Gun Show Background Check Act":

www.freedomsphoenix.com/Find-Freedom.htm?At=0054892&From=News

Attend your local gun shows while you can!

the FFL

If you buy or sell through a federal firearm licensee (FFL), then you must fill out a Form 4473. These forms are, illegally, being photocopied or scanned by BATF agents for the growing national database. Avoid FFLs where legally possible.

OWNERSHIP

First rule: *Keep your mouth shut.* Do *not* tell your neighbors, landlord, acquaintances or casual friends that you own any guns (much less what kind and how many). When Confiscation Day comes (and it *will* come), there will be toll-free fink lines. Will Americans snitch on fellow Americans? Count on it. They'll see it as their civic duty as law-abiding citizens. The $1,000 reward won't hurt, either. (For a memorable scene about this, read *Neither Predator Nor Prey* by Mark Spungin.)

Fugitive-from-injustice Gordon Kahl was ratted out by a daughter of his hosts. For $25,000. The feds crept up on Kahl from behind and shot him in the head. (Kahl was sitting in a chair, watching TV with the volume way up, as he was hard of hearing.) When the sheriff blanched at that, the feds shot *him* and blamed it on Kahl. They then chopped off Kahl's hands and feet with an ax, then doused the place with fuel to hide the evidence. (The concrete structure didn't burn down, and a reporter later found a foot under the fridge.) In a privately funded exhumation and autopsy, famed L.A. coroner Thomas Noguchi confirmed that the foot had indeed been intentionally severed and the body purposely set ablaze between two mattresses. Any skeptics of this should order the documentary video *Death and Taxes* from retired Phoenix officer Jack McLamb's *Police Against the New World Order* (602-237-2533).

Moral: Reward money *works*. Keep your mouth shut.

record and encrypt your guns' serial numbers

Have a data sheet for *each* gun to prove ownership if necessary. *Never* make a *list* of your guns — one sheet per gun only.

the concealed carry permit

Some 40 states have now passed CCW's or liberalized their laws to Florida-style *"shall issue."* Now, the government knows the identity of several million Americans who have the *temerity* to actually *bear* arms.

I firmly believe that gun ownership and gun bearing will eventually be outlawed through a U.N. convention on "Gun Trafficking" or "Disarmament." **Such a U.N. convention could *constitutionally* overturn these state CCW permits.** (Yes, the 2008 *Heller* case protects handgun ownership, but did not touch on carry in public.) Naturally, it will be challenged in court (as was the Brady bill) and will probably be upheld (as was the Brady bill). It is good to recall that registrations invariably lead to outright confiscation. Ask the British, the Canadians, and now, the Australians.

So, before you run out and get your permit, think long and hard about the possible consequences down the road. Do you *really* want to be fingerprinted and pay $50 per year for something that is your *right* — only to suffer confiscation five years hence?

I won't do it. Self-defense is my right, and I won't beg for permission to exercise that right. I'll keep my name off the master list and carry privately, thank you. I'd rather be tried by twelve than be carried by six, as it's much easier for my family to get me out of jail than the cemetery.

carrying discreetly without a permit

In open carry states, no permit is required. However, open carry not only compromises your privacy, but you risk unknowingly passing within 1,000' of some school two blocks away and committing a federal felony! H.R. 3610 has all but *killed* open carry rights — rights normally untouchable by the feds — and is the beginning of the final onslaught of gunowners.

So, how to carry *de facto* concealed without a permit? Usually, a gun in its *"holster"* is not considered to be *"concealed."* A holster doesn't necessarily have to be the classic leather hip holster. The SafePacker from Dillon Press (800-762-3845) is a square Cordura *"holster"* (by judicial agreement, I understand) which resembles a cell phone case. Gun fanny packs and gun purses can stretch the legal definition of *"holsters"* so check it out in your state.

If you don't live in an open-carry state, and want to conceal carry without a permit, you'll have to technically break the law. *Boo, hoo.* The only ways you'd be found out are if you were frisked, or if you had to defend yourself. The odds on either are pretty remote. A behind-the-back holster underneath a vest or jacket works well. Shoulder holsters print obviously, and gun fanny packs are too well-known. Ankle holsters are cumbersome, create a limp, and hold only small pistols. Gun attache bags are fairly indiscreet. For *deep* concealment, use something like ThunderWear which holds your pistol inside the front of your pants.

buying accessories

Do so at gun shows with cash. Or, alias order with prepaid debit card from a pay phone and pick up your package at a mail receiving service. Don't *subscribe* to gun magazines. Never buy gun related stuff by check or credit card. Ideally, there should be absolutely no records to indicate that you're a gun owner.

storing your guns privately

At home, keep only what you *need* for self-defense. You won't need your full arsenal to stop a burglar, and your full arsenal won't stop the federal ninja. (Besides, they're going to confiscate what they find in your house anyway, so keep the rest elsewhere.) No more than one pistol and/or one rifle or shotgun per person at home is necessary.

If you have more than that (and you *should*), store them elsewhere *not* under your real name. I wouldn't *bury* them unless you *really* know what you're doing. Underground caching has its place, but don't go crazy. You want most of your guns *accessible*. Digging up cached guns and cleaning them up takes a lot of time. Would you bury your only fire extinguisher?

shooting your guns privately
the gun club and range

I would *support,* but not join, your local gun club. Have a friend tell you the combination to the gate, or go with him as his guest — but do *not* join the roster. Send them an anonymous M.O. for the dues, *but stay off of their list*. Gun club members will one day be rounded up for questioning and home searches.

on public land

Done sparingly and in varied locations, this isn't a problem. Keep the sessions short and lock up your guns, ammo, brass, gear, etc. in the *trunk* before you go. Have nothing in your interior's plain view to even suggest that you're a shooter.

on private land

There are two trains of thought on this. The first is: Don't draw attention to yourself and alert your neighbors to your gun ownership. The other is: Damn it, it's *my* land, I can shoot on it legally, and I *want* the neighbors to know that we're armed. I can sympathize with both.

Some of my neighbors have been shooters, while others were not. I guess it all depends on where you live and who's around. One thing I would *never* do is fire fully-automatic Class III weapons on private land — not even the perfectly legal "Hellfire" devices (which sound just like fully-automatic fire). This will likely alarm even your gun owning neighbors, and the Sarah Brady's will certainly call the feds.

SELLING YOUR GUNS

In a word, *don't*. I'd sell a kidney before I sold off my guns. Guns should not be merely a hobby or some form of recreation. Guns are *"liberty's teeth"* (George Washington) and to sell off the teeth is to guarantee your future slavery. It is the 2nd-Amendment which protects the other nine. Keep your guns.

If you *have* to sell a gun or two to streamline your battery, then get an *ad hoc* voice mail number just for the classified ad. Pick up your messages and return calls from a pay phone only! Meet the buyer in a discreet place (*e.g.*, a gun store parking lot where gun handling is normal) and accept only cash. It is illegal to knowingly sell to out-of-state buyers, minors, convicted felons, fugitives, those under the influence of drugs, and other *"prohibited possessors"*. Do not break any laws.

TRACKING OWNERSHIP

The trail ends with the first private sale wherein no state or federal paperwork is made. Such private sales exist primarily in the South and the West. If you sell or pawn a gun to an FFL, a receipt must be filled out. To get that gun back, you must fill out a Form 4473 — even if you'd bought it privately.

Avoid having to fill out the Form 4473. I know people who have dozens of guns, all purchased privately with cash. There's not a scrap of paper, not a cancelled check, not a charge card record, not a magazine subscription, not a CCW permit—*nothing* to indicate that they are vociferous gun owners. This situation terrifies the government. There are now more guns in America than Americans. The feds will *never* find them all.

THE COMING GUN GRAB

I'm not worried about a successful gun confiscation program in America. I just don't know if enough Americans will have the guts to shoot government thugs. *That* is the only relevant question regarding future gun control. On this point, I quote from a speech by the late novelist Taylor Caldwell:

> *I'm going to castigate all you men here for what you have done to America — every mother's son of you.*
>
> *How did we arrive at this disastrous hour in time? I will tell you.* **You men . . . abdicated your manhood!** *You deserted the Republic. Aristotle said two thousand and five hundred years ago: "Masculine republics decline into feminine democracies and democracies into despotism." That is what has happened to America now. We call ourselves a free country. We are not free! Tomorrow the tyranny will be overt instead of covert as it is now.*
>
> *Is there any hope? Well, only a little, and I'm afraid that few men will take advantage of it.* **One:** *Challenge your government and, if you suffer for it, to hell with sweet peace.* **Two: Fight gun control!** *It is your right to bear arms under the Constitution but the tyrants want to take away your arms so you won't be able to offer any resistance to bayonets!*
>
> *Gentlemen, you can restore your dead Republic. But be again the masters of your government and be again the masters of your women or will you meekly say: "Hail, Caeser, we who are about to die salute you."*

Don't worry that they'll get your guns. Worry that *you* might not have the *guts* to use them. Will you let federal barbarians storm your neighborhood, breaking down doors — or will everybody on your block rain a torrent of copper-jacketed lead on these thugs? It's about to hit fan — will you be courageous?

If *you* can't imagine — gasp! — defending *your* rights and *your* property and *your* family against the Government, then sell your guns to a *real* man. Who are you fooling — you don't deserve a Zeiss-scoped Sako any more than a .22 Jennings. Give up your guns now and spare yourself the embarrassment later. **The 2nd Amendment is for *men* — not hobbyists.**

❖ 18

A QUIET LIVING

*With five notable exceptions, nearly everyone in our society works at a job of some kind and is automatically suspect . . . if he doesn't work. The exempt classifications: The very rich, who obviously don't need to bother working, the very poor, who also don't need to work because the Welfare State takes care of them. Then housewives, students and retirees. Everyone else in the U.S. and Canada is expected to work **or at least have the appearance of working**.*
— Doug Richmond; *How To Disappear Completely* (1986)

Much has changed since 1986. A *sixth* exemption should now be added: the home-based entrepreneur, which I discuss later in this chapter. Although ideal privacy is attained through one's own small business, not everyone is, or can be, an entrepreneur.

PRIVACY ON THE JOB

Most people work for a company. I will show you how to increase your job privacy, although jobsites are not private:

SSN tracking
This will become total through the coming E-Verify (*"Get Permission to Work from the Feds"*) system and the EDL. No SSN, no job. The DHS is trying to move the SSA under it vulturous wing, if that's any clue to where all this is going.

employer spying
Once you are hired, there is virtually no limit to the information your employer can [legally] gather. He may listen to your telephone conversations, monitor your keystrokes on a com-

*puter terminal, and even ask your neighbors to describe your
habits at home. If you* [claim] *worker's comp . . . , he may
place your name in a computerized database that other employers may consult when they are making hiring decisions.
He may even hire informants to spy on you.*
— Mark Nestmann; *How To Achieve Personal & Financial
Privacy In A Public Age,* Fifth Ed. (1993), p. 91

filling out the job application

To avoid suspicion, you *must* have what *appears* to be a
street address and home phone. Unless you are to go through a
security background check for job clearance, your "official" address street mail drop and voice mail will serve just fine.

Your work time line must not contain any curious gaps
which imply periods of unemployment. While references are
rarely checked, make sure that yours do not contain any great
triggers to your current domicile, activities, etc. Any particularly nosey questions should be answered N/A (not applicable).

For SSN, I'd leave it blank *until* you are hired. Once you
are hired and on the job, *then* you should spring any untax
posture on your new employer. (Visit **www.losthorizons.com**)
Even if you *do* allow SS and "income" tax withholding from your
untaxable private-sector remuneration, there's no reason to
sprinkle about your SSN to every *prospective* employer.

Beware of any waivers of personal privacy which you
might be asked to sign. These would include submission to drug
tests (which are often inaccurate) and polygraphs (which
actually measure stress, and not prevarication). There are
often state and federal restrictions on use of the "whiz quiz" and
"the box." Also, companies *so* suspicious might not be worth it.
How much you are comfortable with signing away is up to you.

If, by the time you are reading this, some form of national
ID workers' card has been instituted, avoid getting one at all
costs. Instead, show the prospective employer your records of
birth, or passport. If unacceptable, start your own business —
but refuse to get a federal cattle brand!

the job interview

Don't act weird or covert. Seem personable and outgoing
— you *like* people. You are *sociable,* not a hermit. It does not

enhance your privacy for it to be *known* that you savor your privacy. Also, show moderate excitement to be working for them, and express a desire to make it your "home."

on the job behavior

Have no illusions: your email and phone calls are easily (and legally) monitored by your company. Be discreet. Also, many companies prohibit firearms, so conceal *well*.

your new coworkers

They will naturally want to get to know you. Do not shy at having dinner or drinks if invited. Do not discuss politics, religion or philosophy. Do not rail against the government any more than the general level of discontent. Do not admit that you own any guns, even if your coworkers do. Trust somebody only if you *can* and if you *need* to.

> ...[A]*void giving background information to fellow workers. If you're planning to stay . . . only a short while, however, make an effort to plant false and misleading information in the minds of the other workers, such as your favorite pastimes, places you'd like to travel or live someday, and your plans for the future. Insulate your private self by keeping your personal interests and ideas to yourself alone.* **Share the spurious with the curious.**
> — *100 Ways To Disappear and Live Free*; Eden Press, p. 14

leaving employment

The odds are that you won't be working for Wonka Widgets for the rest of your days, and that you'll eventually leave — or be fired. The general rule is to *leave on good terms*.

how to quit

They'll *know* why you're quitting — no Hamletonian soliloquy is necessary. Be gracious and act with style. Give them fair notice (usually 2-4 weeks). Train your replacement well. Make them sorry to see you go, even if you were kind of a pain. Don't leave bad feelings behind which can fester into lies.

what if you're fired?

Same rules apply — be gracious. *"But I was 'discriminated' against!"* Yeah, so *what*? Can you refuse to marry somebody based on their race, creed, color, religion, "sexual orientation," economic status, education, or personal hygiene? Certainly! People "discriminate" (show bias) every day against others. Only government hasn't any right to "discriminate" because it exists by us all, for us all.

So, why don't private *companies* deserve the same right? Because the Supreme Court says it *"affects interstate commerce."* So what, you got fired. Just because not everyone on the planet *likes* you, don't be a big baby and file an EEOC suit. Even if you sincerely believe you were fired for being a left-handed Lithuanian lesbian, *drop it.* Find a company *owned* by left-handed Lithuanian lesbians and go work for *them.*

START YOUR OWN BUSINESS

By the year 2020 "Self" will be the largest employer. Such is *the* key to not only financial privacy, but to financial success. Wealth comes from profit and capital gains, *not* salaries.

what *form* of business?

I tried a partnership years ago, and they're like a marriage. While they *can* work, be cautious of whom you get involved with and write down a comprehensive agreement on duties, responsibilities, etc. Beware of the "mutual agency" of partnerships; each of you is liable for the debt and obligations incurred by the other. Finally, partnerships rarely end on pleasant terms — so, your privacy can be deeply compromised.

Corporations and trusts have their place, but learning enough about them may be too demanding at first. Begin with a sole-proprietorship *in your own name* and avoid having to file a DBA (doing business as) form.

An LLC (Limited Liability Company) is probably the way to go for any business with significant assets or lawsuit risk.

what *kind* of business?

Whatever we do for money is usually oriented towards:

> **People** (sales, health care, hairstylist, therapy, etc.)
> **Information** (computer programming, research, etc.)
> **Things** (car mechanic, inventor, construction, etc.)

I recommend that you develop marketable skills in *each* of the three areas. For example, an individual competent in tutoring, bookkeeping, and locksmithing could grow a successful business *anywhere* in the country. There is safety in diversity.

Not everybody, however, can be such a generalist. If, for example, you are *not* a "people-person" or mechanically inclined, then only the Information field is open to you. So, if you are clearly attracted to a single area, try to develop several marketable skills *within* your area. Being a plumber is fine, but learn how to fix cars and computers, too.

Whatever it is, *do what you love doing*. That's the only *real* "secret" to success. If you're not doing — *right now* — what you'd *rather* be doing, then change it — *right now*. Probably 90% of people die with deep regret how their lives "went" — and they generally had no excuse for it but themselves. Live *your* life.

the main thing to remember

Your eternal enemies will be Envy and Greed. These are personified by bureaucrats, gossipers, thieves, and moochers. They share a dilemma which complicates the lives of cannibals: no reusable victims. They're always looking for a new meal.

be private. *Don't...*

get an Employer Identification Number (EIN) or DBA
hire employees
allow "public access" to your home
get a business phone unless the Yellow Page ad is vital
get a business bank account
get a business or professional license
charge or collect sales tax
advertise too publicly
attract attention of the bureaucrats
let disputes sour into lawsuits, formal complaints, etc
accept checks, if possible
offer receipts — make them ask for theirs
declare this *"remuneration"* as taxable *"income"*
keep your expense receipts at home — hide them if kept
don't brag about your success or speak of your affairs
ever admit that you're engaged in a *"trade or business"*

be private. *Do...*

insist on cash, or *postal* M.O.'s (cashable at any P.O.)
offer prompt, quality service and honor your word, *always*
quietly operate under your own name — avoid "retail" sales
pay your independent contractors in cash
get a separate voice mail number for business calls
get a separate P.O. box or mail drop for business letters
appear *moderately* successful, but not wealthy

consider a mail-order business

It has little or no local visibility, therefore the city, county, and state bureaucrats will probably never notice you. Also, it's very low-key financially (no 1099s filed on you), so the IRS will probably never notice you, either. Receiving cash and M.O.s (which you can either cash or endorse to make them bearer instruments) creates far less records than depositing checks at a bank. Also, cash and M.O.s do not bounce like checks do.

Almost *anything* can be (and is) sold by mail. There are forums available for any product, especially on the Internet. Payment comes in; product goes out — simple and quiet. You can (and probably should) operate out of your house. Work in a suit, or in your underwear — it's your choice. If you're painfully shy or just plain ugly, who'd know? Customers like your ad and buy your product. You never have to see or talk to them! For privacy and flexibility, nothing beats mail-order in my experience.

◆ **19**

THE PRIVATE CAR

It is amazing the number of people who take their cars with them when they disappear. When they do, it makes the Missing Persons Bureau's job so very, very easy. All they have to do is wait until the current license or registration expires, then get their information from the renewal or switch. Whether you sell it, swap it or ditch it, your car will be a very valuable and readily discovered clue to your new location and identity.
— Doug Richmond; *How to Disappear Completely*, p. 39

Vehicular privacy depends on: how you buy and sell it; how you register it; and how you drive/park it.

PURCHASING YOUR CAR

If at all possible, you should purchase your car with cash. Most private sellers will appreciate cash. Dealers, however, are not so keen on it. If the amount is over $3,000, a dealer (though not private seller) is supposed to report the transaction with a CTR to be cheerfully filled by yourself. Simply purchase several postal money orders (M.O.s). They're available up to $1,000. You do not have to produce ID during their purchase. Be careful that you do not engage in "*structuring*."

Another reason to not buy from a dealer is that they usually won't help you reduce sales tax by writing up a lower price. Private sellers, however, are delighted to help. (I've bought dozens of vehicles throughout my life and only *once* did a seller refuse this. He was a crusty Olde Pharte. I walked away from the deal. You should have heard him splutter.)

If your assets are considerable, then you should own your rolling stock through entities (corporations, trusts, LLCs, foundations, etc.) These entities may hold bank accounts and tender checks.

REGISTERING YOUR CAR

First of all, try to get the seller to simply sign off the title, omitting a date. Explain that you'll probably resell the car soon, or that you're not sure exactly how you'll register it since the car may go in your new company. Write up a single bill of sale for yourself, which you keep. Most sellers will have no problem with this — they just want your money and to be rid of the car.

The advantage of a signed title is that you can sell the car without first having to register it yourself. The car is still in the seller's name, and after many months he won't remember your name if asked. You can probably get away with renewing the plate tags as the registered owner, though you might have to show "proof" of insurance (which is easily created on any home computer). Just don't cause the seller any problems by racking up unpaid parking tickets or robbing banks. I've bought many cars this way, kept them for up to 3 years and sold them without a problem. My name was never affiliated with those cars. Pretty ghostly, eh?

Some states (*e.g.*, Washington) thwart this practice by requiring the seller to fill out a detachable sales invoice and sending it in the DMV. Know the peculiarities of your state. You won't be able to pull this off forever, so keep sharp.

if you have to register your car

There are many Sovereign Right-To-Travel plates running around, and while I admire the daily courage and tenacity of these folks, such isn't for me. *Technically,* they're right — a car is a private conveyance free of all licensing requirements, and a *"motor vehicle"* is operated in commercial capacity, thus subject to registration and regulation. Unrequired registration turns a car into a regulated *"motor vehicle."*

Practically speaking it's a weekly hassle. Impoundment is common, and I've yet to hear of *anyone* getting their car back through even the best legal arguments. The *"vehicle"* vs. car battle will *someday* be won, however, it's not *my* battle. I use motorized conveyances to *enhance* — not impede — my travel.

So, to travel around without hassle, you'll need some form of government-issued plate. Simple reality. **Never register a car in your *own* name** — use an *entity* (trust, corporation, etc.) as your "heat shield." Make sure the address is a dead end. I hear that Tennessee doesn't require insurance or smog tests.

insurance

This is tricky, because nearly every state requires either insurance or *"proof of financial responsibility"* (which is beyond the scope of this book, but well worth checking into).

If you must procure liability insurance, your name will be linked to that vehicle. This is very unprivate! One way around this is for the car's company owner to simply get a "fleet policy" which covers all drivers of your age bracket and history. Talk to a savvy insurance agent about this.

Whatever insurance company you go with, very carefully read their policy to make sure that none of your privacy components (*e.g.,* spoof address in another state) will forfeit your right to future claim.

USING YOUR CAR PRIVATELY

As I say repeatedly, *don't draw attention to yourself.* Don't drive like a maniac, don't have glaring equipment faults, and don't park it inconsiderately.   Having an understated econobox, Ford Taurus, or OldsmoBuick wagon helps to lower your profile.   Unless obviously a work van, vans attract the cops. You might want to even remove identifying stickers and nomenclature for that extra generic look.   Use an enclosed garage, if possible. Pay off parking tickets — or better yet, feed the meter and don't get parking tickets. Avoid valet parking.

mechanical repairs

If you're mechanically minded, do your *own* repair work to avoid exposure at the dealership. Buy the parts with cash, from different stores. Don't become a regular at the local NAPA. If it requires a professional mechanic, choose a small independent garage over a dealer if you can. Remove all interesting items and use an alias for the work order. Carefully think through any phone number you give them. Pay in cash, obviously.

19 states do not require an official front license plate
> . . . *these states being Alabama, Arizona, Arkansas, Delaware, Florida, Georgia, Indiana, Kansas, Kentucky, Louisiana, Michigan, Mississippi, New Mexico, North Carolina, Oklahoma, Pennsylvania, South Carolina, Tennessee, and West Virginia; U.S. territories Puerto Rico, U.S. Virgin Islands, and Guam also do not require an official front license plate.*
> — http://en.wikipedia.org/wiki/License_plate

Such a state-tagged car will enhance your privacy (as you can back into parking places and "anonymize" your car), and they reduce the photo-radar potential.

Do be aware that if you travel to any noncontiguous front-plate 31 states, and their cops are not used to it (such as in Oregon and Washington), you will possibly get pulled over (especially if your rear plate is anyhow obscured).

stuff in your car
paperwork
Have your driving paperwork *handy* (not in glovebox) to show a cop. For any paid tickets, have copies of the M.O. and certified mail. This will effectively rebut the *prima facie* evidence of an erroneous FTA warrant.

mail and packages to send
All this should be face down, or in a locked briefcase.

preparedness gear
Inside the passenger compartment, and within a *locked* bag, I would have: binoculars, scanner, and ham radio. Keep an overnight bag on the rear seat (with clothes and toiletries) to pose as a traveler, if need be.

Inside the trunk, I'd have 5 gallons of water, tools, car parts (belts, hoses, plugs and wires, cap and rotor, drain plug, oil, coolant, etc.), and backpack filled with end-of-the-world gear (pistol, jacket, hiking boots, hunting knife, tent, bag, etc.).

travel rifles

It's May 2009 and the old days of bargain guns and ammo are *over*. Primers are no longer $15/1,000, but $50+. Surplus FMJ at 15¢/round? You'll pay at least 75¢, if you can find a willing seller at all. Oh, you read my *Boston's Gun Bible* in 2007 and *now* are interested in a $200 SKS? $400, Bucko! Send Obama a letter in thanks for all this, since he's quite rightfully scared the shit out of the gunowning public.

Even Lee-Enfields (former <$100) have doubled in price. If you aren't competently armed by 2010, it will be very difficult and costly to become so after then.

There is one rifle/ammo bargain left: the 7.62x54R Mosin-Nagant carbine. The 7.62x54R cartridge is 90% as powerful as the venerable 30-06 and the Mosin is a war-proven rifle.. It's quite powerful, reliable, and accurate. I can hit a Bad Guy-sized target at 400 yards from standing with a tree rest. If stolen or confiscated, you're out a whopping $200. Store it unloaded together, with ammo, in a $25 hard case. Accompanying it should be the fine .22 Marlin Model 60, especially for only $80.

The point of such survival gear in your car is to have options if you are stranded or cut off from home. It is decidely unprivate to have no options.

privatizing your car travel

Pay for gas with cash — do *not* use credit cards (one of Ted Bundy's many tactical errors). Do not drive at indiscreet speeds. Wear a touristy T-shirt of the area so I'll look like Joe Roadtrip if stopped. Have all sensitive stuff in the trunk.

If you travel with a pistol, keep it in an unlatched combination-lock briefcase on the front seat. If stopped, quickly unload it, put the mag and ammo in the glove box, lock your pistol in the briefcase, and the pistol is no longer *"on or about your person."* (This tip from my *You & The Police!*) Refuse consent to *any* search.

Keep your EZ-Pass toll tag in a shielded pouch, and attach to the windshield by Velcro whenever you approach a toll booth.

CBP agents at borders and checkpoints

With greatly increased computer capacity and requirement of machine-readable documents (soon the RFID chipped EDL), all land border traffic (passport and license plate info) is now logged into IBIS.

Northern Border Inspection Systems (NORBIS)

The CBP has beefed up its presence on the nation's northern border since the terrorist attacks of Sept. 11, 2001, adding more than 1,100 agents -- or four times its presence before the attacks. To tighten up the loose rural border with Canada, many unstaffed locations have newly installed devices: PortPASS readers, interactive audio/video terminals, and license plate readers. Some individuals will be directed to a staffed POE for secondary inspection. See 21.9 of the CBP Inspector's Manual for more details.

inland CBP checkpoints

The CBP would like to fool you that you have no rights there (as at the border or its "functional equivalent"). An excellent overview of the relevant portions of the CBP Manual regarding suspicionless checkpoint seizures:

www.checkpointusa.org/blog/index.php/2008/03/13/p89

(a) Mere suspicion: At the border or its functional equivalent, an inspector needs only mere suspicion to justify a search and comply with the requirements of the Fourth Amendment. This is because the person is attempting to enter the United States from abroad and may reasonably be required to demonstrate that the person and his or her belongings are entitled to enter the United States.

(b) Reasonable Suspicion: Before an inspector may constitutionally detain a person (non-entry related case), the inspector must have reasonable suspicion that the person is an alien and is illegally in the United States. This higher degree of suspicion arises generally in questioning persons encountered in and around the port who are awaiting persons referred to secondary. This suspicion is based on questioning of alienage alone and also involves specific articulable facts, such as particular characteristics or circumstances which the inspector can describe in words.

(c) Probable Cause: Probable cause is the degree of suspicion which an inspector must have before constitutionally making an arrest under either civil or criminal

law. An inspector has probable cause to arrest or search if evidence and circumstances which would lead a reasonable person to believe that an offense has been or is being committed are known by the inspector.

*(e) Checkpoints: The Border Patrol conducts two types of inland traffic-checking operations; checkpoints and roving patrols. Border Patrol agents can make routine vehicle stops without any suspicion to inquire into citizenship and immigration status at a reasonably located permanent or temporary checkpoint **provided the checkpoint is used for the purpose of determining citizenship of those who pass through** it, and not for the general search for those persons or the vehicle. Inquiries must be brief and limited to the immigration status of the occupants of the vehicle. The only permissible search is a "plain view" inspection to ascertain whether there are any concealed illegal aliens.*

In contrast, INS officers on roving patrol may stop a vehicle only if aware of specific articulable facts, together with rational inferences from those facts, that reasonably warrant suspicion (reasonable suspicion) that the vehicle contains illegal aliens. Absent consent, a more in-depth search requires probable cause for both types of inland traffic-checking operations.

*Chapter 12 of the field manual makes clear that any inspection is to be terminated as soon as the inspecting agent has reason to believe the individual is a U.S. Citizen: "**When you are convinced that an applicant for admission is a citizen of the United States, the examination is terminated.**" To clarify, the manual goes on to say: "**Temporary detention of a U.S. citizen for extensive questioning generally requires reasonable suspicion that the person is involved in illegal activity.**"*

An interesting 28 minute checkpoint exchange at:
www.freedomsphoenix.com/Find-Freedom.htm?At=045286&From=News
Some choice bits from the agents:

"Anything outside normal occurrence is suspicious."

"The reason you're being referred to secondary [inspection] *is because you are acting in a suspicious manner."*

"You are not free to go until the inspection is complete."

> *"We're detaining you for mere suspicion of illegal activity."*
> *"You're interfering in a federal investigation."*
>
> *"Your lack of cooperation* [with the inspection] *in and of itself* [creates suspicion]. *"*
>
> *"I have no idea* [of what illegal activity to suspect you of]. *"*
>
> *"Right now you're in violation of the law because you refused to present a valid ID."*
>
> *"Did you get the idea to do this through CheckpointUSA.org?"*
>
> *"Our superiors feel that we've got better things to do than play this game with you, Sir, so we've been ordered to allow you to, uh, depart the checkpoint."*

The agents there were clearly wrong to confuse "mere suspicion" detention authority at actual border crossings with the more stringent requirement at inland checkpoints of "reasonable suspicion". Also, mere 5th Amendment refusal to answer questions cannot by itself create "reasonable suspicion" much less PC.

The driver's resolve to stand upon his rights was commendable, but he was uninformed about PC and the "automobile exception to the warrant requirement" as well as "reasonable suspicion." He mistakenly believed that the full force of the 4th Amendment was in effect, when it was not. All this needlessly stretched out the matter. Had the driver:

❶ been knowledgeable of the existing (though limited) authority of CBP officers at inland checkpoints, and

❷ allowed Agent Hutchins to complete his sentences before trying to refute him

. . . then he would have victoriously been on his way in just a few minutes instead of nearly a half-hour. You've nothing to lose by declaring your USA nationality. Carry your *expired* U.S. passport for these inland checkpoints. It is sufficient for citizenship proof, yet its loss or seizure would not be nearly as inconvenient as your current passport.

a cool Boston tip on counter-rousting gear

A foolproof way for the cops to create probable cause (PC) is to have a drug-sniffing dog "alert" to drug scent planted on your trunk lid. How does the dog handler plant the scent? By touching a twig of pot in his pocket and wiping the scent on your car. It's guaranteed PC on demand. I know; it happened to *me*.

My countermeasure: Make the dog *terrified* of your car. How? With the **Dazer** from U.S. Cavalry (888-888-7228; stock #N9539; $34.95 plus $7.95 s&h). I thought of this idea while writing *You & The Police!*, but couldn't find the equipment.

> [This ultrasonic dog deterrent is a] *high-tech alternative to chemical sprays or physical violence. A 2-3 second burst or quick on/off action deliver a discomforting yet humane, high-frequency sound inaudible to humans.* **Aggressive dogs become dazed or confused and retreat to a safe distance. Effective up to 15' away.** *Includes a long-life 9V battery. Measures 2"x4½". Weight: 3 ozs.*

During a detention you will not be permitted to hide your hands, much less hold the Dazer. So, you will have to mount it in your car. To hardwire it, buy a 12V to 9V power jack for cigarette lighters (KMart, Radio Shack, etc. sell them for $8. Keep the 9V battery as backup). I'd replace the Dazer's internal switch with a switch/oscillating relay hidden under your dash or in your glovebox. (The oscillation turns the Dazer rapidly on and off for best effect.) The Dazer itself (or at least its speaker) should be mounted under the car, probably pointing at the ground. (Left inside the car it might not be loud enough.)

I'd activate the Dazer whenever you are on the public roads or parking lots. That way, your car is protected while you're inside a store, etc. Also, you might not have the opportunity during a traffic stop if detained outside your car.

If you properly refuse consent to a search of your locked trunk or car, the cop will often call for a drug dog. Then the fun begins, but *do* try to keep a straight face. Immediately tell the K-9 to *"Back off!"* He won't get *near* your car. In fact, he'll want only to run to the squad car and cower on the back seat.

The cops will be extremely baffled and disturbed by this. "Explain" that you've always had a "way" with animals and that they obey you. No sniff, no alert, no PC, no search.

Do *try* to keep a straight face.

SELLING YOUR CAR

If you need to dump your car, sell it yourself to a private party for cash. Be careful not to reveal anything to this person about your real plans or reasons for selling. He would be an ideal source of information...for snoopers, thanks to the efficiency of auto registration systems throughout the country. **The buyer will, of course, be an excellent place to dump your fake information...**
— *100 Ways to Disappear and Live Free;* Eden Press

If the car is registered in your own name, set up an *ad hoc* voice mail number for the classified ad. Meet the buyer somewhere public. Be honest about the car's condition and mechanical history — don't lie to him. Price your car fairly, with slight room for negotiation (but not too much, say 10-15%).

Politely insist on cash. Explain that you don't have time to wait in line at the bank. Offer to leave the sale amount on the title blank and he can fill in a lower amount to reduce the thieving sales tax. Nearly all buyers will appreciate that. Once, I sold a car to a company and since they wanted to record the *full* purchase price (deductible as a business expense), my offer had no leverage. Also, they insisted on paying by check for the paper trail. Since I needed the money and there were no other prospective buyers on the horizon, I took the check.

avoid car dealership trade-ins

Your old car is forever linked to your new car, so any privacy measures of name/address change will be negated.

PRIVATE TRAVEL

It's becoming extremely difficult to travel *incognito*, but it still *can* be done.

THE BUS

Nobody travels by bus in America because they *want* to. I would almost ride a bicycle than ride the bus. DEA and INS agents patrol the bus stations like hungry sharks. Your travelling companions will seem from another planet. A long-distance bus is more often than not a rolling bad neighborhood, and the ride is a working definition of eternity. Sorry to be such a snob, but is saving a few bucks over a flight really *worth* it?

THE TRAIN

I've heard conflicting reports about Amtrak passenger security screening (especially regarding carry-on bag checks), so I can't offer any helpful info. I tend to think that their terminals will soon go the way of TSA measures.

RENTAL CARS

While a couple of companies (*e.g.*, Enterprise) will rent you a car with cash deposit, the rest require a credit card. (*Credit* card, not a debit card.) While you can pay with cash once the car is returned, the card voucher is made through the *electronic* card reader, thus the card company will know of your location and car rental.

For increased privacy, have a friend rent the car for you. (Drivers over 25 years old may use another's rental car.) This is very low key as long as you don't get pulled over for a traffic offense.

Most rental companies no longer sticker their after enough foreign tourists in Florida got carjacked and killed. The reason carjackers preyed on rental car drivers is because they were likely from at least out-of-state, if not overseas, and therefore would *not* be one of 340,000 Floridians with a lawfully concealed pistol.

MOTELS & HOTELS

While motels generally don't ask for ID, most *hotels* do. It's also difficult to avoid having to cough up a credit card for the room deposit, though it can be done with the right attitude and a reasonable desk clerk.

Don't make *any* calls directly from your room — *no exceptions!* If it's a *really* sensitive call, don't use the pay phones in or even near the hotel. Logging online through their wifi is risky unless you use an encrypted proxy and a spoofed MAC address. Leave a "Do Not Disturb" sign on the door to discourage routine housekeeping (but be pleasant to the maids in the hall).

A paid room is considered a *"house"* for warrant requirements. Don't open your door to the police; speak to them *through* the door. Don't allow officers inside without a warrant. Don't get the cops called on you in the first place.

COMMERCIAL AIR TRAVEL

From 1996 to 2001 was the "Computer Assisted Passenger Prescreening" program run by the FBI and FAA. CAPPS selected passengers for additional screening of any checked luggage for explosives. (Such selected passengers did not undergo any additional security screening at checkpoints.) Although CAPPS had selected 8 of the 19 hijackers on 9/11, it failed to prevent their actions.

Shortly after 9/11, CAPPS II was unveiled, a profiling system (fed by airline data) which ranked passengers by security risk score for additional screening. Congress killed it in the summer of 2004 due to public outrage.

The DHS didn't give up, and has since tried to roll over CAPPS II into another program called "Secure Flight". After DHS lied to Congress about the existence of pre-approval testing and that American Airlines had provided 1.2 million passenger records for prototype testing, Congress postponed its implementation until the DHS can pass 10 tests for accuracy and privacy protection. (Folks, this is just window-dressing.) "Secure Flight" should be fully implemented by 2010.

the DHS future of air travel

Even the new "Secure Flight" program will not assuage the paranoia of the DHS. What they are interested in is new shock bracelet technology to immobilize onboard passengers at the whim of the cabin crew. I wish I were making this up:

> An official with the Department of Homeland Security says the U.S. should consider having airline passengers wear electronic bracelets that could track their movements, hold personal information and be triggered like a Taser to stun them into immobility.
>
> **Paul S. Ruwaldt of the DHS Science and Technology Directorate wrote the inventor of "the immobilizing security bracelet,"** a Canadian company, saying he looked forward to receiving a written proposal, according to Washington Times columnist Jeffrey Denning.
>
> **"It is conceivable to envision a use to improve air security, on passenger planes,"** said Ruwaldt's letter, posted on website of the company, Lamperd Less Lethal.
>
> The video says passengers could be fitted with "electronic ID bracelets" they would wear until they disembark their flights. The device would replace a ticket, carry passenger information, track passengers through terminals and track carryon luggage.
>
> **But the key feature is that the bracelets could be discharged, as a gun, and leave the wearer "immobile for several minutes"** although without causing "permanent injury."

"For a businessman on his way home, to a young family going south for a winter holiday, wearing an EMD bracelet during flight is a small inconvenience to assure their safe arrival," says the company. "Many, if not most, passengers would happily opt for the extra security."

The U.S. government has expressed interested in such 'bracelets' for air travelers

The company acknowledged on its website the negative response to Denning's story about its product: "It is amazing how much controversy our new research project has created."

[DHS] Ruwaldt wrote in his letter to the company, 'To make it clear, we [the federal government] are interested in the immobilizing security bracelet, and look forward to receiving a written proposal."

The Canadian company responded to the publicity about its proposal with a website statement:

"We wish to clear up any misconceptions regarding the EMD Safety Bracelet for Airline Security," the company said. "The bracelets remain inactive until a hijacking situation has been identified. At such time a designated crew member will activate the bracelets making them capable of delivering the punitive measure — but only to those that need to be restrained. We believe that all passengers will welcome deliverance from a hijacking, as will the families, carriers, insurance providers etc. The F-16 on the wingtip is not to reassure the passengers during a hijacking but rather to shoot them down. Besides activation using the grid screen, the steward/stewardess will have a laser activator that can activate any bracelet as needed by simply pointing the laser at the bracelet -- that laser dot only needs to be within 10 inches of the bracelet to activate it."

Lamperd, of Sarnia, Ontario, Canada, also provides training and designs specialized civil defense-related equipment. It boasts of expertise in "less-lethal tactics and equipment" used by military and police departments around the world for crowd control and "peacekeeping."

— "Shock bracelets for all airline passengers"
July 08, 2008, WorldNetDaily
www.lamperdlesslethal.com/news/upload/pg2Homelan
dSecurity7_06.pdf

So, forget all about low-tech passenger intervention (as with the attempted shoe-bomber, and allegedly Flight #93). No, the

DHS wants us all strapped in our "ConAir" seats, and ready to be wrist-tasered by some stewardess guard. (This about the most *warped* thing I've heard in years.) Why not just put all passengers under general anesthesia during the flight, and revive them at their destination? Wouldn't that be safer still? I mean, a really clever terrorist just might remove his bracelet in-flight *before* he tried to take over the plane. *Duh.*

What really gets me is how stunned those cretins at Lamperd, Inc. really are at the public outrage. Their website response was absurd: *"Oh, don't worry, the stewardess won't shock you unless you really deserve it! And the F-16 won't shoot down your plane unless it has to!"*

If "Secure Flight" and all the passenger security screening were so effective, then why would DHS be so fascinated by "Electro-Muscular Disruption" bracelets? Conversely, if DHS is so insecure about the effectiveness of airport screening, then why are we submitting to such a worthless hassle?

Every stupid TSA procedure just broadcasts the fact that TSA doesn't believe in what they claim they are doing.

Remember the silly *"Take Shampoo Away"* excitement? The limitation of carry-on liquids and gel was a *sham.* Ostensibly, the TSA is worried that Liquid A and Gel B can be mixed to form a binary-component explosive. So, what's their brilliant safety plan at the airport? To seize your Liquid A and Gel B and toss them into the *same* trash barrel, along with everybody *else's* — many of them *leaking.* That the American public believes this sham is a disgrace. (The rules have relaxed since 2006, and 3oz clear containers in a 1-quart ZipLoc are permitted in carry-on bags. *Ooooh, thanks!*)

TSA "Selectee" and "No Fly" lists

Imagine a list of suspected terrorists so dangerous that we can't ever let them fly, yet so innocent that we can't arrest them - even under the draconian provisions of the Patriot Act.

This is the federal government's "no-fly" list.

There is no recourse for those on the list, and their stories quickly take on a Kafkaesque tone. People can be put on the list for any reason; no standards exist. There's no ability to review any evidence against you, or even confirm that you are actually on the list.

And, for most people, there's no way to get off the list or to "prove" once and for all that they're not whoever the list is really looking for. It took Kennedy three weeks to get his name off the list. People without his political pull have spent years futilely trying to clear their names.

There's something distinctly un-American about a secret government blacklist, with no right of appeal or judicial review. Even worse, there's evidence that it's being used as a political harassment tool: environmental activists, peace protesters, and anti-free-trade activists have all [been listed].
— www.papersplease.org

Being on the TSA Selectee list gets you a secondary screening. Being on the TSA No Fly list prohibits you from US commercial air travel. During airline check-in, if you get a boarding pass, you're clear. If your boarding pass and bag tags have an "SSSS" on it, then prepare yourself (and luggage) for "Secondary Security Screening Selection" (which means hand inspected carry-on, explosive detectors, and hand-held metal detectors).

The TSA will not divulge if you're on the list, and is trying to threaten the airlines with a $25,000 fine per disclosure to passengers. The numbers of names on the list is rumored to be in the hundreds of thousands, though this was denied:

> [DHS secretary Michael Chertoff claimed in October 2008] *the No Fly list contained only 2,500 names, with an additional 16,000 "selectees", who "represent a less specific security threat and receive extra scrutiny, but are allowed to fly."*
> — www.cnn.com/2008/TRAVEL/10/22/no.fly.lists/index.html

The Canadian government has its own version, which they charmingly call "Passenger Protect". It contains 500-2,000 names, incorporated from domestic and foreign intel data, including the TSA No Fly list.

these TSA lists legally apply only to international flights!

*The [TSA] No Fly [and Selectee lists are] disseminated to airlines on a daily basis to be used as a watchlist for comparison against **passenger manifests for all flights that enter or depart U.S. airspace.***
— *The Federal Bureau of Investigation's Terrorist Watchlist Nomination Practices*, Appendix II, p. 70
U.S. Department of Justice, Office of the Inspector General, Audit Division, Audit Report 09-25, May 2009
www.usdoj.gov/oig/reports/FBI/a0925/final.pdf

Although these lists are applied to domestic flights, I may be the first author to point out that they are apparently limited in law only to flights *"that enter or depart U.S. airspace"*.

what TSA lists really say to the public

If these TSA lists were limited only to those wanted for questioning or arrest, that could be understood. But it's much more than that because people are prohibited to fly — without reasonable suspicion or probable cause. You cannot know why you were placed on the list, and there is no quick or reliable protocol for being removed. (The courts have so far ruled that since you are not guaranteed any right to commercial air travel, no constitutional injury occurs.)

What really gets me about this stupid list is that it proves the TSA is *not confident* about their own airport security procedures. For example, even if an individual were on the list (yet without any warrant for his arrest), search him more thoroughly if need be, but after that why not let him fly? What's the risk, unless the security screening is lousy? In fact, if I were the Government, I'd *want* such "watched" people to fly, because it places them in a controlled environment (where their behavior and associates can be monitored), and more can be learned about their travel habits than if they drove (which can still be quite private, even today).

what will likely get you on the TSA Selectee list

Since neither the TSA nor the airlines run a background check at the time boarding passes are issued, immigration status and criminal records do not come into play here.

The list criteria for being on "double-secret probation" (unavoidable reference to the movie *Animal House*) by the TSA are deemed too sensitive to disclose:

> The criteria for No Fly list is defined by the Homeland Security Council Deputies Committee. The original criteria were established by the committee on October 21, 2004. On February 8, 2008, this committee established revised criteria for the No Fly list which are not listed here because the criteria has [sic] been deemed sensitive by TSA. (p. 70)
> — DoJ report (op cit.)

. . . but here are some pretty good guesses:

having a one-way reservation
paying cash for your ticket (that got me snagged once)
booking a flight on the day of departure
being a "no show" for any leg of your flight
flying to countries like Iran
random selection (admitted by TSA spokeswoman Amy Von Walter)

what could get you on the TSA No Fly list

Any significant kind of public dissent (done in your own name) will probably land you on the No Fly list.

> *Walter F. Murphy, McCormick Professor of Jurisprudence at Princeton, reported that the following exchange took place at Newark on 1 March 2007, where he was denied a boarding pass "because I [Professor Murphy] was on the Terrorist Watch list."* **The airline employee asked, "Have you been in any peace marches? We ban a lot of people from flying because of that."** *"I explained," said professor Murphy, "that I had not so marched but had, in September 2006, given a lecture at Princeton, televised and put on the web, highly critical of George Bush for his many violations of the constitution." To which the airline employee responded,* **"That'll do it."**

This is just more proof that the whole DHS/TSA thing is really about cementing our national compliance to government. *"Have you been to any _____? We ban a lot of people from flying because of that."* The No Fly list is supposedly for people are a credible threat to civil aviation, not political dissidents. If anybody gets turned away at the counter subsequent to having attended an April 2009 "Tea Party", please let me know. Those who suspect being on the No Fly list ought to digitally record the ticket counter check-in procedure.

Adopting the Muslim religion can also apparently get you on the TSA No Fly list:

> *Yusuf Islam, a singer and pop star formerly known as Cat Stevens. Author of song "Peace Train." His flight from London was diverted and forced to land in Maine once the government realized he was aboard, and he was barred from entering United States.*
>   — http://abcnews.go.com/2020/News/story?id=139607&page=1

Diverting an international flight because *Cat Stevens* was onboard? Just insane.

Having a very common name like "Gary Smith" or "John Williams" will greatly increase your odds of being listed.

All that aside, the TSA No Fly list includes (or has included) serving members of Congress, airline pilots, Saddam Hussein (while in U.S. custody!), and 14 of the 19 hijackers of 9/11 (*after* 9/11!). This kind of junk data only inconveniences innocent travelers, and wastes security assets and time. Not one terrorist has been caught because of the TSA No Fly list.

watch out for *SPOT!*

Not the dog Spot, but the TSA's "Screening Passengers by Observation Techniques":

Select TSA employees will be trained to identify suspicious individuals who raise red flags by exhibiting unusual or anxious behavior, which can be as simple as changes in mannerisms . . . . Those who are identified as suspicious will be examined more thoroughly; for some, the agency will bring in local police to conduct face-to-face interviews and perhaps run the person's name against national criminal databases.... If such inquiries turn up other issues [such as] countries with terrorist connections, police officers can pursue the questioning.

— www.time.com/time/nation/article/0,8599,1195330,00.html

Try not to look "*anxious*" making a tight connection, or you may be SPOTted by an overzealous "*select TSA employee*".

the future of air travel and privacy

Two major issues have emerged in the last year in relation to personal data about travel: (1) The overall goal of the government of the USA in its various policy initiatives on "travel security" has become increasingly clear. The USA is seeking to establish a global norm that:

1. Government-issued identity credentials should be required for all forms of travel, domestic and international.

2. All travel transactions should be recorded in a lifetime "travel history"

3. Pre-departure government permission should be required for all travel (based on the identity credential and the associated historical dossier), particularly for air travel or international travel.

These goals have been implicit in US practice, but became explicit policies in 2008 with the changes to the "Advance Passenger Information System" APIS) rules (which added an explicit permission requirement to what was previously only an information-submission rule for international flights to and from the USA, the similar "Secure Flight" rule (which established for the first time explicit ID and permission requirements for domestic flights within the USA), and the "Electronic System for Travel Authorization" (ESTA) rule (which established an additional permission requirement for visitors to the USA from many EU and other countries). . . . The conversion of "identity verification" systems into systems of surveillance ("reporting" or event logging) and control ("clearance" or "vetting") raises questions that are broader than any specific policy or the limited perspective of "data protection":

> *1. Should identity credentials be required for routine movement of innocent citizens?*
> *2. Should governments keep records of the travels of people who are not suspected of any crime?*
> *3. Should travel require government permission?*

The USA has been reluctant to label its individual policy initiatives as measures for surveillance or control, for fear of public reaction. But since these are the real underlying issues, these questions should be confronted directly, through widespread public and political debate.
> — Recent developments in the USA in travel data
> www.papersplease.org/wp/

buying your tickets

First rule: *never* buy your tickets at the counter with cash. This is typical behavior of drug couriers (who imagine they're being really sneaky). Many airline tickets agents will alert the airport DEA office, in hope of a reward. (America is the land of the snitch.) Instead, go to any travel agency, arrange your flight and pay for your tickets with cash. Or, buy online (preferably with a prepaid debit card)

at the travel agency

Do not balk about providing a phone number or address — you should have *already* established your postal drop and Internet-based voice mail (as I outlined earlier). Remember, you'll be expected to have ID matching the ticket name. (Those who are proficient at the ID game, reserve some ID just for air tickets and alternate their use. They fly under one name, rent a car under a second, and hotel check-in under a third.

With the travel agent, be polite and *moderately* friendly, but do not get too chummy. If asked a personal question, *lie with the truth*. Spin a yarn with something you know. If you say "Baltimore" without ever having been there, it'll be your bad luck if she grew up there and wants to reminisce.

I realize that good travel agents are hard to find, but use different agencies from various cities. You don't have to buy your tickets in the same city you're flying from.

buying airline tickets online

Online booking has nearly killed off the travel agencies. TA commissions were limited in 1995 and it now costs them $28 to issue a ticket — so, it's not worth it for the cheaper flights.

What this all means for privacy is clear. We might soon be required to key in our DNA ID number with every reservation, or some similar B.S. I'm glad that I got most of my travel done years ago, when it was much more free.

Airlines compare your name (called the Passenger Name Record, or PNR) to government watch lists before a flight. If on the No Fly list, you will be allowed to book a flight (which is illogical) but *not* get a boarding pass. You cannot print a boarding pass at home (which could be a handy thing, saving you a lot of hassle at the airport) or at airport kiosks and must go to an airline check-in counter with ID to show you are not a suspected terrorist.

This is difficult to do in the case of a "false positive" because your ID must substantially differentiate you from the banned name. (Having a copy of your passport would be helpful here.) If cleared, the rest of your flight (including the return) should be hassle-free, but you'll have to go through the whole thing for subsequent air travel. If you cannot differentiate your name from the banned name, the airline will refuse to issue a boarding pass and have you contact the TSA.

packing for privacy, comfort, and convenience

This should be done with great forethought, especially if you lawfully fly with a firearm. In Chapter 11 of my *You & The Police!* I explain how to do this. Make *absolutely sure* no stray ammo or spent brass are left in your luggage or pockets.

I strongly urge against the carrying of any sensitive paperwork, receipts, business cards, etc. While computer data can easily be encrypted and hidden, papers are vulnerable to inspection and being copied. Business travellers take a great risk by often carrying with them company documents that contain proprietary, legally privileged, or trade secret information. FedEx such materials ahead, if feasible.

what to wear

Your goal is to be comfortable, yet not draw attention to yourself. Americans are the poorest dressed passengers in the world, so if you dress down a bit you'll fit right in. A good wardrobe is chino-type slacks and a simple button-down shirt. It's informal, comfortable, yet has at least a *bit* of style. Avoid flashy shirts, hand-tooled leather boots and expensive jewelry. Ladies, if you'll dress up a bit you'll be less bothered by officials.

Make sure that you've removed all telling personal items from your wallet and pockets, such as business cards, lists, etc. Carry a digital voice recorder for any confrontation with airport cops. (Many cell phones will work nicely for this.) If you don't tape the Scene, they can claim that you consented to a search.

belt ("fanny") pack

These are just too "metrosexual" (*i.e.*, gay) for general use, but I do wear them on international flights. In it go *all* metallic pocket items (leaving me to walk through the metal detector without a beep, because a second beep garners a secondary screening), copies of your necessary travel info, any data storage medium such as CD or USB (containing color photos of your bags in case they are lost), and any personal comfort items. For example, here is what I stuff in mine for Africa:

> toothbrush, small tube of toothpaste
> earplugs in a 35mm film can (flying is ear-damaging noisy)
> inflatable neck pillow
> blindfold (for sleeping on the plane)
> safety razor

Bandaids
Ziploc bag of unscented baby wipes
eyedrops
coughdrops
Ziploc bag with latex gloves
small bottle of hand disinfectant
small clear spray bottle mister (very refreshing on long flights)
dysentery pills
energy bars
paperback novel
small notepad and pen
digital camera
one of your two GMRS radios (your partner has the other)
copies of misc. paperwork (insurance, passport, etc.)

Yes, you *could* keep these things in your day pack, but accessing it frequently from the overhead bin is a hassle. Also, a worn belt pack is less likely to become lost or stolen. If a belt pack isn't your style, then a good travel vest would work well.

neck wallet (an absolute *must*)

Protect your passport, international DL, travelers' checks, backup credit card, and some cash. Wear that neck wallet *everywhere* — without exception. If empty of anything metallic, you can even wear it through the magnetometer.

ankle wallet

This contains travelers' check receipts (always keep separate from the checks!), a spare credit card and drivers license, some cash, copies of passports (yours and your friend's) and any other vital paperwork. If this seems redundant to your neck wallet, trust me that it is not. Modularity and multiple "baskets" for your "eggs" is what protects you against Murphy.

slip-off shoes

Given the shoes-off silliness of airport "security" you will enjoy travelling in easily slipped off footwear, such as Roper walking boots. Such can also serve as your about-town shoes, casual or dress-up. Some quality replacement insoles can really make a comfort difference. Try out the gel-packs.

And have a pair of sacrificial slippers or spare socks for the shoeless shuffle. Public airport floors are filthy. TSA used to provide slippers, but no longer.

non-metallic belt buckle

Be able to wear your belt through the metal detector, versus holding your pants up like an idiot.

pack intelligently

You want to be able to comfortably survive with what you have *with* you, because checked bags are frequently delayed (though rarely lost permanently), or you could be stuck at an airport for many hours. Your carry-on bag should have enough to sustain you, such as a change of clothes, hat, spare batteries, some books, and personal hygiene items. (Readers of *Safari Dreams* have already thanked me for this tip!)

Get a *quality* nylon backpack with 2500-3500in² volume — about the maximum size allowable in overhead storage bins. If there's some local disturbance while you're traveling, you may be on your own for a while, and a good pack (no bright colors) then becomes tactical gear. It should have wide and thickly padded straps, at least one outside pocket, an organized interior, and a *very* rugged bottom. REI and other quality outdoors stores will have good choices. (Most will be made in Asia, but avoid packs made in Communist Vietnam. Chinese products may be nearly unavoidable these days, but you've no excuse supporting *Hanoi*.) I like the Kelty Redwing 3100. The Vaude Seattle 65 Travel Pack is versatile choice (www.eigerequipment.com), as it looks like a small suitcase, but has hidden shoulder straps. Whatever you choose, walk twice around the block with at least 30lbs of weight for comfort trial.

Leave your carry-on 20% empty in case your checked bag is overweight and you need to empty it of some things. Know your airline's weight limits, and actually weigh bags at home.

scour and secure your laptop, PDA, etc.

This is especially true for any international travel because CBP agents are now overtly permitted to read and copy your data. With 400 million travelers entering the country each year, secondary inspections generally occur only from lookout lists or agent suspicion. (More on that later in this chapter.)

luggage tags and locks

It is suspicious to *not* have tags on your baggage. Use the kind, however, which cannot be publicly read. Have secure luggage tags on the outside *and inside* of all bags (including carry-on). Reliable contact info (such as a prepaid cell phone) is a must, yet can still be private. Your address should match the one (if any) you gave the travel agent.

Use TSA locks for your checked luggage; at least you'll know if they pawed through them. Have a spare set inside just in case the original pair are mistakenly cut off, or damaged.

checking in

Your goal is to get your boarding pass and check your bags without being remembered. Get there early enough to avoid looking harried, and have your stuff ready (bags tagged, ticket ready, etc.) Do not act furtive. You're on vacation and you're happy, remember? You're merely a grain of passenger sand on an airport beach. Request a forward, window seat. You'll exit the plane more quickly and you can unobtrusively doze against the bulkhead. (I use foam earplugs and sleep perfectly.)

confirm your flight and reservation within 48-72 hours

Some airlines require this. Your travel agent will advise. Do not skip this vital step, as your flight could have been cancelled or merged into another, or your reservation lost.

at the airport, *verify* boarding/departure times

One international flight left 20 minutes earlier than ticketed, and I barely noticed it in time. (*That* was exciting.)

board *early*

The masses arrive late and wait. Breeze through earlier. This also gives you plenty of time to unravel any snags, especially if they're related to being on the TSA No Fly list.

showing ID at ticket counter

Ever since the Unabomber's threat to down a 727 out of LAX in spring 1995, passengers have been obliged to show ID during check-in. (This was *supposed* to be, of course, "temporary" just like the WWII 5% "Victory Tax" on wages. This kind of crap is never temporary; it's merely the latest click of the tightening ratchet.)

The real reason wasn't to prevent terrorism, but so the airlines could kill the unused ticket resale business (called "bucket shops"). I once flew from Europe to the USA on a bucket shop ticket in the 1980s, and was even upgraded to First Class by the counter agent (so that a family in Economy could all sit together).

> [W]*hile the photo ID requirement is presented as an antiterrorism security measure, it is really an airline-business security measure* [to kill sales of unused tickets].
> *So business is why we have the photo ID requirement in the first place, and business is why it's so easy to circumvent it. Instead of going after someone who demonstrates an obvious flaw that is already public, let's focus on the organizations that are actually responsible for this security failure and have failed to do anything about it for all these years. Where's the TSA's response to all this?*
> *The problem is real, and the Department of Homeland Security and TSA should either fix the security or scrap the system. What we've got now is the worst security system of all: one that annoys everyone who is innocent while failing to catch the guilty.*
> — "The Boarding Pass Brouhaha", Bruce Schneier
> www.wired.com/news/columns/0,72045-0.html

Until 2008, you could still check-in for a flight without ID if you accepted secondary screening (*Gonzales v. Gilmore*). That wasn't widely known, and few who knew about it tried it.

The public didn't complain loudly enough about the "*Your papers!*" environment, so today the TSA generally will not process you without government ID:

> *Effective June 21, 2008, adult passengers (18 and over) are required to show a U.S. federal or state-issued photo ID that contains the following: name, date of birth, gender, expiration date and a tamper-resistant feature in order to be allowed to go through the checkpoint and onto their flight.*
> *Passengers who do not or cannot present an acceptable ID will have to provide information to the Transportation Security Officer performing Travel Document Checking duties in order to verify their identity. Passengers who are cleared through this process may be subject to additional screening.*

Passengers whose identity cannot be verified by TSA may not be allowed to go through the checkpoint or onto an airplane. Acceptable IDs include:

* U.S. passport
* U.S. passport card
* DHS "Trusted Traveler" cards (NEXUS, SENTRI, FAST)
* U.S. Military ID (active duty or retired military and their dependents)
* Permanent Resident Card
* Border Crossing Card
* **DHS-designated enhanced driver's license**
* Drivers Licenses or other state photo identity cards issued by Department of Motor Vehicles that meets REAL ID benchmarks (All states are currently in compliance)
* A Native American Tribal Photo ID
* An airline or airport-issued ID (if issued under a TSA-approved security plan)
* A foreign government-issued passport
* Canadian provincial driver's license or Indian and Northern Affairs Canada (INAC) card
* Transportation Worker Identification Credential (TWIC)

Non-US/Canadian citizens are not required to carry their passports if they have documents issued by the U.S. government such as Permanent Resident Cards. Those who do not should be carrying their passports while visiting the U.S.

This standardization of the list of accepted documents better aligns TSA with other DHS components, including Customs and Border Protection, and REAL ID benchmarks.

— ID Requirements for Airport Checkpoints
www.tsa.gov/travelers/airtravel/acceptable_documents.shtm

beware excess baggage weight fees!

You're allowed two checked bags, weight 50lbs each. Between 50-70lbs they will charge you $50, but over 70lbs is a whopping fee. Weigh your bags *before* you leave home, and allow extra space in your carry-on in case you need it.

remove your baggage claim stubs from ticket jacket

Place these *immediately* in your neck pouch. Do not step away from the ticket counter until you've done this!

detach your return ticket and place in neck pouch
> If you don't, it can easily become separated and lost.

do not walk about with your passport or ticket in hand
> Keep these secured until you must provide them.

airport security tips
> Modern airport security installs a steel door on a grass hut, since the airport workers go through far less screening. Also, the *shoes-off, no-shampoo* drill is no doubt calculated to dehumanize and condition passengers. (What indignity will people *not* put up with these days?) While you can't avoid the process, reduce its unpleasantness by packing in this fashion:

front pants pocket
> Outbound ticket and ID in one pocket, and most of your cash in the other. Remove all metallic items.

neck pouch inside the shirt
> This contains all vital paperwork: passport, baggage claim checks, return ticket, some cash, travelers' checks, and a spare credit card. Have nothing metallic inside so you can wear it through the detector.

belt pack
> *All* pocket metallic items go in here: coins, watch, keys, cell, etc. Your goal is to pass the detector without beeping.

going through the metal detector
> I place my things in trays in this order: shoes, belt, belt pack, vest/jacket, laptop, rucksack. Thus, I am dressing on the other side while they are screening my rucksack (which has the most items and takes the longest to clear). The reverse order begs for trouble, and it's embarrassing to have to wait for your belt, etc. while the TSA agent is opening up your carry-on bag. You also project much more authority and dignity dealing with those people when you're fully dressed. It makes a difference.

your attitude with TSA staff
> The most important thing is to always remain calm, even when angry. Be either cheerful or icy (depending on your mood

and their disposition), *but never kiss their ass.* While you cannot avoid their shoes-off shampoo silliness, you can avoid stroking their egos with any hint of groveling. If you can pull it off without a whiff of sarcasm, ask questions such as, *"Where can I get such cool blue gloves like yours?"*

Always be prepared mentally to forego your flight and recollect your checked luggage, rather than accept rampant indignities. Remember that you may be just one question away from a cavity search if TSA gets nervous for being inquired about their patently inane procedures or demanding to know if the AirServ dweeb actually works for TSA.

> [T]*he TSA has crafted its procedures so that the demand for identification credentials is made neither by the TSA itself nor the airline, but by a third party whose identity and authority are entirely unverifiable to the traveller, and who is accountable to the traveller neither through government legislative and regulatory procedures nor through enforcement of contractual rights (since they have no contractual relationship to the traveller).*
>
> *To give an added* frisson *of resemblance to countries with corrupt or dysfunctional police and governments, the people in uniform demanding people's credentials are lying about being government employees. The real government employees watching them don't care. And if, like me, you so much as ask a few polite questions about what is going on, you are detained, threatened with arrest, searched, investigated, your papers copied by the government for your permanent (I can only presume) dossier, and the unaccountable third party (and, in the case of an RFID passport, anyone else within range with a reader in their luggage) left with the unregulated legal "right" to use and sell any data obtained from its government-coerced scrutiny of your credentials.*
>
> — Edward Hasbrouck, "Unanswered questions at Dulles Airport"   www.hasbrouck.org/blog/archives/001066.html

airport behavior

Enroute to your gate, just do what everybody else does. If in a hurry, jog. If you've plenty of time, casually make your way, stopping at the gift shop. Do not go to the bathroom directly before or after clearing security. Such is done by drug couriers who are constantly adjusting the parcels taped to their bodies. You shouldn't be smuggling anything, so don't worry about it.

I advise against making *any* **pay phone calls, however innocuous.** Airport pay phones are routinely pen registered and even monitored at the direction of a surveilling agent. If cell phones were monitored at airports, it wouldn't surprise me. You should have made your calls beforehand. Your pickup party should know to check your flight number in case it's running late, so you won't be expected to call him.

I prefer to get to my gate straightaway, sit down and read. When I say read, I don't mean just turn the pages — I mean *read*. If you've caught some agent's attention, he will look you over with binoculars across the terminal from behind a mirrored window. He will scrutinize your eye movements, and spot any nervous hand/foot movements. Therefore, pick a seat which is not easily observed, sit down and *read*.

If you need to use the bathroom, by all means do so — but only *once*. Repeated trips to the bathroom are typical of drug couriers. Do not make frequent trips to the water fountain — such implies nervousness.

If accosted by TSA or DEA, they will demand to see your tickets and ID. You are under no legal obligation to comply unless detained or arrested. Start your digital voice recorder. **You should** *never* **go where** *"we can talk more privately."* Stay put — make a quiet scene if you have to. Demand to see and scrutinize their credentials — write it down. (If they refuse, express disbelief that they are truly officers or agents, and thus powerless to detain you. *Then* they'll show you their badges.) Keep asking if you are free to go. If they claim *"reasonable suspicion"* to detain your luggage and it contains something politically incorrect, state your possessory right to it (so that they can't claim you abandoned it) and excuse yourself to get your lawyer. Leave the airport *immediately*. You should have already read my *You & The Police!*

onboard behavior

If there was ever an example of how *not* to behave during a flight, this is it:

> *In October* [1995], *Gerald Finneran, described as one of the leading authorities on Latin American debt, was arrested at*

JFK airport in New York as he disembarked from a United Airlines flight from Buenos Aires. According to passengers and crew, he had lost his temper when flight attendants refused to serve him more liquor, assaulted them, **defecated on a serving cart,** cleaned himself with the airline's first-class linens, and thus left an odor that remained in the cabin for the remaining four hours of the flight. (BTP Note: From Buenos Aires to Malos Aires. Here comes the best part.) *(The flight could not be routinely rerouted to land sooner because one of Finneran's seat neighbors was the President of Portugal, and flights containing heads of state are harder to divert.)*
— from *News of the Weird*

His client fined $5,000, the attorney for "Exlax" whined, *"Maybe the skies aren't so friendly anymore."* I know $5,000 is a stiff fine, but Finneran got his money's worth. I mean, what would *you* pay to assault flight attendants and crap on a serving cart beside the President of *Portugal?* $5,000 seems a *bargain.* I once called a flight attendant *"Darling"* and farted next to a Guatemalan Air Force general and was fined *$4,000!* Just think what a mere $1,000 *extra* would have bought me. (That's what I get for not reading the brochure.)

Anyway, once aboard you're home free, *if* you can possibly manage to restrain yourself from crapping on the serving cart. I realize this is impossible for leading authorities on Latin American debt, but do *try.*

picking up your bags

Go to baggage claim without delay. At some airports, baggage handling is so efficient that it sometimes beats the passengers. Get there before somebody walks off with it, as stub verification by airport personnel is almost nonexistent.

Pick up your bags, and *leave.* Airports are hazardous environments, full of federal agents. I prefer my party to pick me up *outside* baggage claim and therefore not have to park. You should have arranged this before your flight and not need to call them upon arrival.

Also, I prefer to dropped off at the curb and not have them come in with me. I like a simple, clean *Bon voyage!* on the outside, so I can concentrate on making my flight.

INTERNATIONAL FLIGHTS

Most of the same tips for domestic flights apply here.

what to wear

Dress in quality clothes. For myself, I prefer to wear a suit and tie and fly Business Class. I've never had problems. Officials generally don't mess with successful businessmen. (Once, I was even asked if I was a diplomat!)

check-in

Get there *way* early. Relax and act excited about your trip. If you schmooze the ticket agent about this being your — *gosh!* — very first flight on TransOceanic Airlines, she might even upgrade you to Business Class for free. If no upgrade is possible, then ask for an exit row bulkhead seat (they have the most legroom).

clearing foreign Customs and Immigration

They are primarily concerned if you have enough traveling funds to avoid becoming a welfare case in their marvelous Socialist country. For young people, having a gold VISA or American Express card goes a long way in smoothening your way. (And leave your ratty jeans at home, please.)

If asked where you'll be staying, mention an upscale hotel. (If you're *really* serious about your cover story, then you should have already made reservations there, in case they check.)

If you're visiting Israel or some other sensitive country, ask that your passport *not* be stamped, or at least a stamped paper be merely stapled inside. This is a fairly common request.

staying in foreign hotels

The desk clerk will invariably want to see your passport, if not photocopy it — if not keep it during your stay. Do not allow this. Explain that you took it to the Fulmarian Consulate for a visa. Show/give them a photocopy instead.

Do not let the hotel hold your room key while about town. You don't want the front desk knowing precisely when you come and go. If your key is generic (without the hotel's name), then keep it on your person. If not, then hide it somewhere in the hotel, or nearby. I devised a clever way to hide mine, but I can't tell anybody — not even *you*. Sorry.

be nice to the hotel maids

Leave a $2-5 tip every morning for your maid. My mother convinced me of this, calling it inexpensive theft insurance. Neither of us have ever suffered pilfery by the housekeeping staff. Even if you're only staying one night, leave a tip. It's thoughtful, *and* you might leave something in a room one day. Which maid is likely to turn it in — a tipped or untipped?

getting around overseas

Planes, trains and automobiles. Europe, for example, is so compact that air travel isn't really necessary. Take the train. Forget Eurail passes; they force you to stay on the move to get your money's worth. Simply buy your ticket and step aboard.

The *MitFahrGelegenheit (MFG)*

The *MFG* is a neat thing. In German it means "passenger opportunity." *MFG* agencies are in nearly every town across Europe and will (for a fee of $3-12, depending on trip distance) put you together with a driver going your way. With gasoline being $7.00 per gallon, most Europeans can't afford to drive alone for long distances. So, a driver calls up the agency and says that he's going to Munich on the 8th and has room for 2 passengers. He pays no fee to the agency. The passengers pay the agency's fee, and an agreed maximum of roughly 5¢ per mile to the driver. The agency won't ask for your ID. Reserve your *MFG* by phone, drop by, pay the fee, get the driver's name, call him and arrange the price and pickup. The driver doesn't have to know your real name or your address. I prefer to be picked up outside the train station. If you don't care for the driver, the agency will make another introduction for you without charge.

I've used *MFG*s many times, without a hitch. I made some good friends, and never did the drivers charge me the full rate. I've ridden with all kinds of folks, from student musicians to an army captain. The *MFG* experience is faster, cheaper and more personable than the train. You might have to wait a couple of days to find a tricky route, but you'll always be able to get close enough to take a short train ride. Take along some fruit to share or a guitar to play, relax and enjoy your trip.

ENTERING THE U.S

This is real fun. I once returned home through Atlanta, and DEA was there to greet our plane, all suited up in black ninja gear. Barking at us to stand in line and place our bags to the left, our bags were sniffed by two drug dogs. There was no *"Good afternoon, ladies and gentlemen. We are drug enforcement agents and this spot-check is purely routine. We apologize for this delay and welcome you to the United States."* It was like getting off the cattle car train in Auschwitz — an utterly disgusting display of naked power.

In 1997 I opined that customs officials were seemingly trained by the *Sicherheitsdienst*. Now, with the DHS hiring ex-Stasi chief Markus Wolfe as a consultant, I now I was right.

Treasury Enforcement Communications System (TECS II)
The first checkpoint will be the TECS II counter where your passport will be scanned. If you are wanted in the NCIC, suspected/convicted of smuggling, drug dealing, or tax evasion, or wanted for jumping bail you will be detained at the very least. If you are snagged here, remain silent, reserve your rights and state that you wish to speak to your attorney.

clearing U.S. Customs

The one thing to be profoundly aware of is that you have no Bill of Rights at the border (or its *"functional equivalents"* such as international airports).

CBP can review and copy all your laptop data

One of our most important enforcement tools in this regard is our ability to search information contained in electronic devices, including laptops and other digital devices, for violations of U.S. law, including potential threats," said Jayson Ahern, deputy commissioner, U.S. Customs and Border Protection, in an online post in June.

— www.wikileaks.org/wiki/DHS_Report_Says_Leave_Laptops_At_Home

Without probable cause, reasonable suspicion, or even "mere suspicion", CBP agents can review any electronic data. This is a new policy, cancelling a 1986-2007 higher standard requiring PC before material could be copied. (The 1986 directive stated that customs officers *"as a general rule . . . should not read personal correspondence."*)

All that is gone now. Today, if you refuse to boot up or open obviously encrypted files, they can seize your computer and analyze it at leisure over weeks.

The policies cover "any device capable of storing information in digital or analog form," including hard drives, flash drives, cellphones, iPods, pagers, beepers, and video and audio tapes. They also cover "all papers and other written documentation," including books, pamphlets and "written materials commonly referred to as 'pocket trash' or 'pocket litter.' "

When a review is completed and no probable cause exists to keep the information, any copies of the data must be destroyed. Copies sent to non-federal entities must be returned to DHS. But the documents specify that there is no limitation on authorities keeping written notes or reports about the materials.

Customs Deputy Commissioner Jayson P. Ahern said the efforts "do not infringe on Americans' privacy."

— "Travelers' Laptops May Be Detained At Border"
Ellen Nakashima, *Washington Post*
August 1, 2008; Page A01

CBP policy was upheld by the 9th Circuit Court in the April 2009 ***US v. Arnold*** (www.eff.org/cases/us-v-arnold).

As we all know, CBP's data collection capabilities have been widely discussed in the law enforcement community and we have been asked by many various agencies to copy and transmit documentation being carried by travelers for legitimate law enforcement reasons.

— unnamed CBP agent in a 11 July 2007 email to colleagues

All this has been internationalized thanks to the 2009 *ACTA* ("Anti-Counterfeiting Trade Agreement") treaty regarding pirated movies and music (which allegedly finance terrorism). How the treaty reads we do not know, because the documents are withheld for purportedly containing *"information that is properly classified in the interest of national security pursuant to Executive Order 12958."* (Classifying treaties affecting passenger luggage? More paranoia. So much for Obama's promise of government *"transparency".)*

Some delegate, however, used his cell phone to photograph the draft text, and sent it to www.wikileaks.org.

Article 2.6: Scope of the Border Measures

*3. Where a traveller's personal baggage contains goods of a non-commercial nature within the limits of the duty-free allowance and there are no material indications to suggest the goods are part of commercial traffic, **each Party may consider to leave such goods, or part of such goods outside the scope of this section.***

"May consider" to not inspect your laptop? Gee, thanks!

This probably seems curious if you are not aware there is a consensus among government officials, some industry leaders and liberal think tanks that counterfeiting music and movies is connected to organized crime, which is connected to TERRORISM. So, of course, what is needed is a Piracy Patriot Act.

The government officials of the treaty nations are devising ways to monitor the contents of your computer and iPod to prevent such things as downloading through peer to peer networks . Of course, any interesting stuff, incidentally discovered in rummaging through your hard drive, would be referred to the proper law enforcement agency, like the IRS, DEA, your ex-spouse — whatever.

However, these government hackers are savvy enough to realize that people will not readily buy the idea that a twelve year old girl, downloading a Hannah Montana Movie bittorrent, is connected to the International Jihadist movement. So they feel it best, for the time being, to hide behind the National Security shield, while they work out ways to efficiently rummage through our hard drives and mp3 players:

The privacy of your laptop is something that has to be forfeited in the New World Order.

I guess we will just have to give up some of our quaint American customs in favor of the hip ways of the New World Order. One of those is embracing the culture of surveillance.

In suspicion we trust.

— Becky C., "Obama's Culture of Surveillance"
www.girlinshortshorts.blogspot.com/2009/04/obamas-c
ulture-of-surveillance.html

Privacy expert Bruce Schneier has this advice:

Encrypting your entire hard drive, something you should certainly do for security in case your computer is lost or stolen, won't work here. The border agent is likely to start this whole process with a "please type in your password". Of course you can refuse, but the agent can search you further, detain you longer, refuse you entry into the country and otherwise ruin your day.

You're going to have to hide your data. Set a portion of your hard drive to be encrypted with a different key - even if you also encrypt your entire hard drive - and keep your sensitive data there. Lots of programs allow you to do this. I use PGP Disk (from pgp.com). TrueCrypt (truecrypt.org) is also good, and free.

While customs agents might poke around on your laptop, they're unlikely to find the encrypted partition. (You can make the icon invisible, for some added protection.) And if they download the contents of your hard drive to examine later, you won't care.

So your best defence is to clean up your laptop. A customs agent can't read what you don't have. You don't need five years' worth of email and client data. You don't need your old love letters and those photos (you know the ones I'm talking about). Delete everything you don't absolutely need. And use a secure file erasure program to do it. While you're at it, delete your browser's cookies, cache and browsing history. It's nobody's business what websites you've visited. And turn your computer off — don't just put it to sleep — before you go through customs; that deletes other things. Think of all this as the last thing to do before you stow your electronic devices for landing. Some companies now give their employees forensically clean laptops for travel, and have them download any sensitive data over a virtual private network once they've entered the country. They send any work back the same way, and delete everything again before crossing the border to go home. This is a good idea if you can do it.

If you can't, consider putting your sensitive data on a USB drive or even a camera memory card. Encrypt it, of course, because it's easy to lose something that small. Slip it in your pocket, and it's likely to remain unnoticed even if the customs agent pokes through your laptop. If someone does discover it, you can try saying: "I don't know what's on there. My boss told me to give it to the head of the New York office." If you've chosen a strong encryption password, you won't care if he confiscates it.

Lastly, don't forget your phone and PDA. Customs agents can search those too: emails, your phone book, your calendar. Unfortunately, there's nothing you can do here except delete things.

I know this all sounds like work, and that it's easier to just ignore everything here and hope you don't get searched. Today, the odds are in your favour. But new forensic tools are making automatic searches easier and easier, and the recent US court ruling is likely to embolden other countries. It's better to be safe than sorry.

— "Crossing Borders with Laptops and PDAs"
www.guardian.co.uk/technology/2008/may/15/computing.security

I suspect there will soon come a time when travelers' laptops are simply downloaded as a CBP routine. Schneier's advice is sound, which I supplement with some ideas of my own:

> have a spare, inexpensive, sacrificial laptop for border crossings
> > lean (no data other than necessary during travel)
> > an OS *not* Windows (Puppy Linux is optimal)
> > have a CBP and a private pup_save.sfs boot file
> > a scrubbed (or new/empty) hard-drive (or no HD at all!)
> > free of any music or video files, even legal archive copies
> > all data kept in a TrueCrypt volume, and already emailed home
> > the TC volume backed up on well-hidden USB drive

The real key to this is learning Puppy Linux, as described in Chapter 14. You'll *never* plug all Windows security holes — not if the feds have unlimited time to analyze your laptop. The Puppy Linux boot sector can be encrypted, and runs from USB drive. Thus, the box doesn't even *need* a hard-drive, and even if it has one no data or TrueCrypt installation must reside there. Whether or not you choose to hide a backup USB is your call, but not even that is necessary since you can store the TC volume somewhere on the Web.

You could email home your normal pup_save.sfs settings file, shred it from your USB, and open the second .sfs file which is a very basic replacement for the border inspection, containing not even a whiff of any online history. **This *tabula rasa* aspect is impossible with a Windows box** unless you DBANed the entire HD (that takes hours) and reinstalled

Microsoft's crappy OS — and even then I still wouldn't trust it. The Puppy Linux *tabula rasa* plan can be done in just minutes, on your arriving flight. You'll have full use of your computer right up until you land, and it is useless to CBP thereafter.

If the CBP agent is naturally astonished over the unusual Puppy Linux box operating by live CD without a hard-drive, explain how you only use the machine to check email and don't download anything. Tell him that a travel vacation to you means little or no computer work (and don't forget to chuckle). Rather than look like a fool for seizing a computer without storage device, you will likely be quickly on your way.

You've got a proper machine that is sacrificial, without costing you any data or much money, and without possibility of incriminating you. Used laptops are commonly under $200, so just figure this into your trip budget.

Or, you can sell it overseas just before you return, but after you've emailed or FTPed your data back home. (Good used laptops are popular in other countries.) Suffice to say that there are many ways to "skin this cat". Anybody caught flat-footed on arrival with their brand new $2,000 data-rich Mac PowerBook seized by CBP is simply ignorant.

Oh, and don't forget to either file shred your camera's SD card, and/or swap it out for the "public" version.

if your laptop is seized/returned, *never* use it again

You would never be sure if a keylogger had been installed. Another possible surreptitious device is a real-time VoIP watermarking engine (Scroogle CCS05-VoIPTracking.pdf) which increases by 3ms your VoIP inter-packet arrival times. This effectively "fingerprints" your VoIP calls, and is proof of whom you spoke with. (The test computer was modified in a lab, so sneaking it on *your* box would take leisurely access.) Read of other active timing-based attacks at www.crypto.com. These are no Internet trojan horses, but require full access to a target's computer, which reinforces why to keep yours secure.

If it's ever seized/returned, DBAN the HD and sell it.

final BTP thoughts on entering Customs

I prefer to bring less than the full allowance, declare nothing and go through the green lane. Focus on the person ahead of you, and walk straight through without glancing at the agents to your side. Flit your eyes about and they'll call you over for a baggage search.

Avoid bringing back certain furs and leathers, ivory, etc. and you'll have no surprises. Also, you're supposed to report over $10,000 in *"cash"* (cash, bearer notes and bonds, blank or *endorsed* checks and M.O.s, etc.), so know that in advance. If they find unreported cash beyond $10,000, it *will* be confiscated and you'll be arrested. It's nice to live in such a "free country".

If detained, don't raise a fuss. Coolly cooperate, but don't forget to record the incident. (Practice covertly activating your digital voice recorder or cell phone. Twelve states require consent of *all* parties to record — know which ones.)

leaving the airport

If you were hassled by the feds or the airport police, do *not* use the pay phones. You should have already arranged for your ride home. If things were really dicey clearing customs, or even if you just have an eerie feeling, beware. The authorities may already have probable cause on you and are waiting for you to charitably lead them to the friend picking you up, or to your car in airport parking. Wave off your ride with a covert signal (*e.g.*, scratching your nose) and take a cab to some prearranged meeting point (*e.g.*, a mall, etc.). Similarly, do not walk to your parked car. Take a cab and come back later for your car.

HOW TO AVOID LOST & FOUND

Everybody loses and misplaces things, and would like them returned. But how to do so effectively and privately? Fortunately, there is a viable and trustworthy intermediary in the company www.stuffbak.com. Basically, you register/pay (privately, of course) your purchased tags with them, and if the tagged item is ever found Stuffbak pays a cash reward to the finder and arranges the item's return (at a mutual meeting point, or sent on its way through a neighborhood UPS Store).

Without StuffBak, recovery rates are less than 5%. With StuffBak, the odds are raised to over 75%. Why? StuffBak is easy for finders and works across the broadest spectrum of real world circumstances (the service is not reliant on battery power and works whether or not device passwords restrict access to contact info).

PRIVATE ENTITIES

You must begin to cultivate a change of thinking regarding business structures. Sole proprietorships and partnerships leave the owners vulnerable to business risk. What you must do is to *separate ownership from control* to create a legal posture of limited liability. While corporations can accomplish this, they offer little privacy in exchange for increased regulatory hassles (unless chartered in Nevada, Wyoming, or Delaware).

TRUSTS

Trusts are the common-law antecedents to modern corporations. Not only is ownership separated from control and your privacy protected, but trusts can lower your taxes.

Tax avoidance is *legal*. Tax evasion is *illegal*.

Tax evasion is like walking out on your dinner bill. Tax *avoidance* is using a free-dinner coupon to legally avoid paying. Or, say there were two bridges next to each other — free and toll. To sneak across the toll bridge without paying is evasion, but it's legal avoidance to use the free bridge.

The only thing is...the road to the *free* bridge is uphill, inconvenient and obscure, and the bridge itself is long, dark, narrow, and seemingly rickety. Conversely, the road to the *toll* bridge is a downhill highway and the bridge is short, wide, well-lit and secure — *everybody* seems to be using it! And they are. What they don't realize is that it eventually leads to a *cliff*.

There is nothing illegal or immoral about using your constitutional rights and statutory loopholes to minimize (or even eliminate) your tax burden. There is no obligation to pay one penny more in taxes than the legal requirement.

what is a trust?

A trust is a contract whereby A (the **Trustor** — the one who *trusts*) entrusts the ownership of his property to B (the **Trustee** — the one who is trust*ed*) to manage on A's behalf. Parents, for example, act as trustees for their children's funds. Since your right to contract for lawful purposes is unlimited, a trust is perfectly legal if there is no fraud or mental incompetence involved. Trusts may be revocable or irrevocable.

For tax purposes, the less power the Trustor has over the Trustee's management and disposition of the trust assets, the better. In short, the less control the Trustor has, the more unassailable the trust. When the Trustor has too much direct control of the trust, the courts may disallow the trust as a separate entity because **a Trustor *cannot* be his *own* Trustee.**

what's in it for the Trustor?

The Trustor has merely nonvoting Certificates of Beneficial Interest (CBIs — similar to corporate nonvoting common stock) which he can sell or redeem when the trust is liquidated.

So, the Trustor exchanges his assets for these CBIs and holds on to them tax-free while the trust's net worth grows. Once he sells the CBIs for cash, then the capital gain is *de jure* taxable — but we live also in a *de facto* world. In order for capital gains to be taxed, the IRS must first *know* about them. If the CBIs are sold out of the country and the proceeds transferred to the Trustor's *foreign* bank account, who is the wiser? This, however, would be construed as tax *evasion*.

Since we want tax avoidance and not tax evasion, the Trustor should *borrow* against his CBIs. **A collateralized loan is *not* a sale and the funds received are *not* income.** The Trustee has a foreign investment entity for just this purpose — to be the Trustor's bank. Though the Trustor must pay regular interest to maintain formalities, whether or not he actually pays off the *principal* is legally immaterial.

He can even borrow on top of borrowing, that is, borrowing to pay past interest. Brazil does exactly this with the IMF and Chase Manhattan *et al* every year. Although Brazil's debt is still kept on the books as current (since the formalities of interest payments are being observed), everybody knows the principal will *never* be repaid. We, too, can play this game.

the necessity of foreign entities

You must learn to think internationally. It will be the only way to survive financially in this century.

domestic entities

own little or nothing, but generate high expenses to their foreign counterparts, thus resulting in little or no taxable income. They operate as hollow "front men" in the hostile environment of taxation, regulation, lawsuits, etc. — offering little to tax, attach, or seize (no assets).

foreign entities

own nearly everything. They lease and lend *to* their domestic counterparts at high rates which creates high U.S.A. expenses and thus low accounting profit. (Remember, the revenue of one firm is an expense for the other.) Properly structured, these foreign entities can reap most of an operation's overall profit, in tax-free form.

the overall structure

Let's say that I wanted to restructure a personally-held factory into a network of foreign and domestic trusts. The main goal is that no entity deriving taxable income should own property. That way, if the IRS has a bone with one of your income entities, it's got no assets to seize — everything is *leased*. Here's a rough example; international entities are underlined.

Example International

owns your personal domicile, furnishings, paintings, antiques, jewelry, clothing, etc. **EI** has utterly no business presence or activity within the U.S. and is in no way connected with any business operation of the empire. **EI** merely owns your personal tangibles and doesn't risk your personal wealth by entangling it with business ventures (which are subject to taxes and lawsuits). Unless **EI** actually sells some asset for a capital gain, it derives no income and pays no state/federal income tax.

Example Investments International

owns all patents, copyrights and business investments (stock, bonds, gold, silver, collectibles, etc.). **EII** has no business presence or activity within the U.S. Regarding U.S. income,

EII makes only *passive* income (i.e., nonactive: interest, capital gain royalties). **Foreign passive income from U.S. sources can be *nontaxable*.**

EII is also your investment banker. It receives all empire venture capital and subsequently lends out (with surcharge) the necessary capital to the other **Example** entities. This creates a greater tax write-off interest expense for domestic **Example** firms, and **EII**'s interest revenue (which naturally includes a profit for brokering these loans) is passive income.

Since maintaining large cash balances in U.S. banks is extremely risky (bank failures, IRS assessments, etc.) and offers no financial privacy in exchange for anemic service, the bulk of your business cash should be kept *outside* the rapacious grasp of the Federal Government — meaning in offshore banks. The U.S. accounts of domestic entities should maintain balances just sufficient to cover routine disbursement, *and no more*. As soon as excess funds arrive, they are expatriated offshore in the form of business expenses (interest, leasing and consulting fees, etc.). If a cash crunch occurs, **EII** will naturally be only too happy to lend the needed funds — at a stiff rate, of course.

Example Properties International

owns all business land and buildings (foreign and domestic), and leases all domestic properties *in toto* (in totality) to **Example Properties U.S.A.** under one lease. To my understanding, a mere single lease does not constitute *"effective trade or commerce"* within the U.S. and would be nontaxable.

Example Properties U.S.A.

leases your domestic properties *from* **EPI** and subleases them to your domestic firms. **EPU** would make income.

Example Leasing International

owns all shop/office equipment, business vehicles, etc. and leases such *in toto* to its domestic counterpart **ELU**. (Notice the identical relationship between **EPI/EPU** and **ELI/ELU**.)

Example Leasing U.S.A.

leases all above equipment *from* **ELI** and subleases it to your domestic firms, independent contractors, etc.

Example Manufacturing U.S.A.

leases property from **EPU** and equipment from **ELU**. It then buys raw materials, contracts out any necessary operations, manufactures its products and wholesales to your domestic and international distributors.

Example Sales U.S.A.

neither owns property/equipment, nor manufactures products, but merely purchases product from **EMU** and serves as origin of all sales inside the U.S.A. **ESU** markets and sells in America, and contracts out certain sales, administrative and clerical responsibilities.

Example Sales International

operates as the origin for all sales *outside* the U.S.A. **ESI** has no business presence or activity within the U.S.A., but may have a conduit "information office" (and officers) to liaise with domestic firms. **ESI**'s revenue must come solely from *foreign* sources, or else it could be subject to U.S. income tax.

ESI purchases its product from **ESU** at just over cost, thus reducing the domestic (taxable) profit of **ESU**.

overview of the empire

To summarize, there are nine firms: four domestic and five foreign. It is no mere coincidence that none of the four domestic firms (**EPU, ELU, EMU, ESU**) own any assets beyond the "shirt on their backs" (if that!). Remember, these domestic firms serve as frontline troops in a hostile legal and regulatory environment. If they are successfully breached by government or lawyers, *there exists no spoils for the "victor."* As empty, replaceable vessels, they could be savaged by the IRS or a court judgment *with no appreciable detriment to the empire's overall net worth or operations.* Clone the destroyed company and get back up on line in a day!

The five foreign firms own everything, without being *"effectively connected with the conduct of a trade or business within the United States"* — therefore tax-proof and lawsuit-proof. Merely owning domestic property or maintaining an "information office" does *not* constitute business activity, according to the IRS.

growth is *encouraged*, not hampered

Such a structure will not hamstring your journey and works *with* you, not against you. Once set up, you'll never have to revamp the thing as you grow. Just add on the necessary modules.

Under this arrangement, responsibilities are clearly defined and separated. Moreover, instead of these duties being under one corporate roof, they operate under their own respective autonomy. This allows every uniquely talented individual to work with little interference.

By the modular separation of ownership and control, capital and risk, expense and revenue, profit and taxes, these items may be strategically placed. This in turn offers unparalleled flexibility, efficiency, versatility, impregnability and maneuverability. Operating similarly to the human body, this empire is organically synergistic. The normal cycles of internal growth and atrophy are smoothly handled occasions.

its many advantages:

☞ Unmatched tax benefits
☞ Defensible contractor status (avoiding "employer" status)
☞ Compartmentalization of liability
☞ Separation of assets from lawsuit-vulnerable firms
☞ Superior vehicle for financial growth and retention
☞ Unbeatable privacy from outsiders (gov't., competitors, etc.)
☞ Minimized overlapping of personnel
☞ Reduced risk/effect of embezzlement and industrial espionage
☞ Smooth incorporation of new investors and partners
☞ Streamlined administrative automation
☞ Bottlenecks within/between modules quickly identified/opened
☞ Allows parallel modules (factory and sales) of intercompetition
☞ Organic/Synergistic

what are the risks?

As this structure is quite judgment-proof, the more likely threat I see to all this is from the IRS. Even though tax-avoidance through trusts *is* legal, the IRS doesn't like it. The IRS might have these areas of contention:

utter absence of employees and total use of contractors

Successfully classifying your independent contractors as employees for tax purposes would clearly mean the most money (and future control) for the IRS. I don't see an IRS victory on this because: independent DBA (doing business as) craftsmen would be renting tools/equipment from **ELU** by the day, working unsupervised to the order specifications of **ESU**, while selling their finished components to **EMU** by lot. Therefore, they meet the IRS criteria for independent contractors:

They have a regular place of business *outside* your office, with phone, bank accounts, multiple customers, etc.

They work on their *own* time.

They bill by the *job,* not by the hour/week/month. If they don't meet the contracted quality/quantity, they aren't paid.

They don't use *your* tools or equipment, as **ESU** and **EMU** own none and **ELU** is not involved in manufacture or sales.

They do *not* work under the direct supervision of **EMU**.

intentionally meager profitability of U.S.A. firms through offshore cost structuring

The huge multinational corporation are experts at the pricing game. Just learn their techniques. There is probably a *de facto* minimum markup which the domestic firm needs to charge to avoid alerting the IRS.

mere existence and use of the offshore trusts themselves

Properly formed and maintained, foreign trusts are nearly unassailable. Strict formalities must be observed, of course, but trusts are amazing flexible devices. Thousands of firms are operating along similar lines to my example; these are *not* uncharted waters.

It is important to create the structure *first,* so that the new companies are the *original* contractors and equipment purchasers. If the foreign trust network is created *after* the company has substantial assets and revenue, the IRS has been known to apply a punitive 35% excise tax on the value of assets *transferred* into foreign entities, or even disallow the new structure. Avoid any subsequent transfer of assets and income by having the empire in operation from Day 1. If the empire has *always* owned the assets from the beginning, then no transfer ever took place, therefore no transfer tax can apply.

the LLC (Limited Liability Company)

Many of the states (*e.g.,* Wyoming, New Mexico) offer LLCs which are more simple than corporations yet act similar to trusts. Useful, inexpensive, easy to create and maintain.

in summary

I realize that forming and running many entities seems complex and perhaps daunting, but this example was for a factory. Most people, however, are likely to need only three trusts. Admittedly, the initial cost of this empire will be higher and will demand more time and paperwork to maintain. However, once set up, it will practically run itself. And, your extra effort and expense will be munificently rewarded by an infrastructure proven remarkably effective in supporting growth and defending your net worth.

If you continue under a sole-proprietorship or partnership form of operation, not only will you *not* be able to grow painlessly, but you will remain defenseless to those ever circling buzzards of envy — government, lawyers and the masses. Right now, a single malicious lawsuit or punitive tax assessment could wipe you out.

With your children's' future at stake, the family's net worth must be protected in these perilous times of rampaging envy. By erecting a network of protective trusts, you not only safeguard your own retirement, but the rightful inheritance to your children. They will immeasurably benefit, not only by their inheritance, but by the *education* in the crucial knowledge of capital protection through common-law trusts. This priceless knowledge will be worth more to them than even their inheritance itself. Without this knowledge (and its practiced application) the next generation can neither hope to *achieve* any personal fortune, nor expect to *retain* it.

Only the courageously wise will prosper during the coming years. The timid I.Q. 100s will, at best, merely exist day by day in Neanderthal boredom with the approximate dignity and freedom of yoked oxen.

become your *own* expert

There are many charlatans out there, so you'll have to gain your *own* knowledge to protect yourself. The primary question you should always ask yourself is, *"Can I trust the Trustee?"* A larcenous trustee will make worthless any trust's fine paperwork and clean out your assets.

Avoid anybody skittish about fully showing and explaining their paperwork. If they won't show you a sample indenture, it's probably because they copied somebody else's and retypeset it as their own. **Finally, *never* sign what you don't *clearly* understand.** Good luck.

www.BulletproofFirearmsBusiness.com

Attorneys Bennet and Angela Langlotz are very knowledgeable about estate planning and LLCs. They wrote a great book about doing just that. www.langlotz.com

PRIVACY'S FUTURE

The problem is, ironically, not with the government and its demand for power, control, and surveillance. Governments have always had insatiable appetite. The problem is not with the government, but the citizenry at large. And I'm not speaking even so much of their ignorance or apathy or approval, but rather their inherent *vulnerability* to being surveilled and controlled. Americans in the early 21st Century live under a system of great and increasing leverage against them. Rather, our modern lifestyle is vast leverage against meaningful freedom of action. It almost wouldn't even matter if people *were* pro-freedom.

> *Indeed nations, in general, are not apt to think until they feel; and therefore nations in general have lost their liberty: For as violations of the rights of the governed, are commonly . . . but small at the beginning, they spread over the multitude in such a manner, as to touch individuals but slightly. Thus they are disregarded . . . They regularly increase the first injuries, till at length the inattentive people are compelled to perceive the heaviness of their burdens. **They begin to complain and inquire — but too late.** They find their oppressors so strengthened by success, and themselves so entangled in examples of express authority on the part of their rulers, and of tacit recognition on their own part, that they are quite confounded.*
> — John Dickenson

Rather, Americans by and large no longer have the temporal possibility of freeing themselves, even assuming an intervening philosophical awakening and emancipation. The quest of

government supremacists over the past four decades has been to make — through technology — actual dissent practically impossible. One has only to research the military's increasing obsession with less-than-lethal weaponry, such as the USMC's Active Denial "Pain Ray" (a focused microwave beam causing unbearable pain from out to 750 meters), using sound as a weapon (*e.g.*, "Brown Note" which causes instant and uncontrollable defecation), and the Pentagon's desire for a teams of robots that can search for, detect, and track *"non-cooperative"* humans in *"pursuit / evasion scenarios"*).
      www.freedomsphoenix.com/Find-Freedom.htm?At=040113 (This reminds me of the "spiders" from the sci-fi thriller *The Minority Report*.)

What all this new technology has in common is rendering people physically helpless and/or compliant, but without killing them. The target of all this can only be our civilian population, and not enemy soldiers (who can be killed as they always have been). **The U.S. military's focus over the coming years will be domestic crowd control.** Quelling mass demonstrations before they can kick off an actual civil war. (There is a window of time during which a sensible and courageous American public could fight and win a civil war to slough off its globalist rulers, and our globalists know it. Thus their panicked rush to box us in before we wake up, pissed off.)

21st century dissenters
The public dissenter of 2020 will likely find himself sufficiently well-known in advance, communicationally challenged (a fully compliant and government-integrated phone and internet), mobility impaired (TSA airport watchlists, highway checkpoints, automated license plate readers, real-time automobile tracking), commercially squeezed out (cashless and digitized payments without any anonymity), readily identifiable through technological means (biometric scans of face, eyes, voice, and fingerprint), and sought after through pervasive media and citizen cooperation ("*Track The Terrorist*" TV shows, 1-800 fink lines with instant reward schemes). The dissenter of the near future will be geographically and socially isolated, with a likely short lifespan. Even if he does manage to hide out in the mountains somewhere, he will have to live the life of Jeremiah Johnson but with the paranoia of Winston Smith. But, will it go *that* far?

TWO KINDS OF PEOPLE

The war against personal privacy is not merely some phenomenon of increasing bureaucracy and regulations. No, it goes much deeper than that, and stems from the clash between two inherently and profoundly different types of people. It is the collision of two distinct and mutually antagonistic cultures. When you understand that, then the privacy war will make sense (for both sides).

There are generally the Masses and the Remnant.

the Masses

While the Masses are usually made up of the poor, poverty does not automatically relegate one there. Some poor people are Remnant people. Conversely, wealth does not assure one's higher status. Many upper class people are actually part of the Masses, though they would be loath to understand that.

This is all a bit difficult to explain, so I will employ some expert assistance. I've read with great profit a 1930 work by the Spanish philosopher Ortega y Gasset titled *The Revolt of the Masses*. Gasset articulated many points that Wyoming Governor Preston in *Molôn Labé!* tried to make regarding the necessary ingredients of a healthy, sustainable society, not usually found in the age of the common man. I am pleased to treat you to some lengthy quotes of Gasset, who thoroughly understood the issue.

> . . . *the direction of society has been taken over by a type of man who is not interested in the principles of civilization. Not of this or that civilization but — from what we can judge today — of any civilization. Of course, he is interested in anesthetics, motorcars, and a few other things. But this fact merely confirms his fundamental lack of interest in civilization. For those things are merely its products, and the fervour with which he greets them only brings into stronger relief his indifference to the principles from which they spring.* (p. 81)
> **Civilization is not "just there," it is not self-supporting. It is artificial and requires the artist or the artisan.** *If you want to make use of the advantages of civilization, but are not prepared to concern yourself with the upholding of civilization — you are done. In a trice you find yourself left without civilization. Just a slip, and when you*

look around everything has vanished into air. The primitive forest appears in its native state, just as if curtains covering pure Nature had been drawn back. The jungle is always primitive and, vice versa, everything primitive is mere jungle. (p. 88)

The mass-man believes that the civilization into which he was born and which he makes use of, is as spontaneous and self-producing as Nature, and ipso facto he is changed into primitive man. For him, civilization is the forest. (p. 89)

Civilization becomes more complex and difficult in proportion as it advances. The problems which it sets before us today (in 1930!) *are of the most intricate. The number of people whose minds are equal to these problems becomes increasingly smaller. . . .* **By reason of the fertility and certainty of its formative principles, its production increases in quantity and subtlety, so as to exceed the powers of normal man. I do not think that this has ever happened in the past.**

. . . In Greece and Rome it was not man that failed, but principles. The Roman Empire came to an end for lack of technique [after it reached a high level of population, which it could not sustain]. (p. 90)

But today it is man who is the failure, because he is unable to keep pace with the progress of his own civilization. *It is painful to hear relatively cultured people speak concerning the elementary problems of the day. They seem like rough farmhands trying with thick, clumsy fingers to pick up a needle lying on a table. Political and social subjects, for example, are handled with the same rude instruments of thought which served two hundred years since to tackle situations in effect two hundred times less complex.* (p. 91)

The concept of "Renaissance Man" meant a man who had the totality of knowledge and expertise to recreate the building blocks of society. He could do anything and everything, from farming to engineering to architecture to cooking. He was a philosopher, a sailor, and a wagon-master. He was always a scientist, tinkering about. He spoke several languages. He was an accomplished musician.

Thomas Jefferson was the classic example of a Renaissance Man. He was a complete fractal of 18th Century

American society as a whole. Robert Heinlein touched on this with his famous quote:

> *A human being should be able to change a diaper, plan an invasion, butcher a hog, conn a ship, design a building, write a sonnet, balance accounts, build a wall, set a bone, comfort the dying, take orders, give orders, cooperate, act alone, solve equations, analyze a new problem, pitch manure, program a computer, cook a tasty meal, fight efficiently, die gallantly. Specialization is for insects.*
>
> — Lazarus Long, *Time Enough For Love*

Today, life has become far too complex to be capably embraced in its totality by any one person. To a large extent, we must all specialize. While specialization has garnered us tremendous scientific and technological gains, it has been at a hidden cost: the age of the Common Man — the Masses. The trouble with the Common Man, the Mass Man, is that he does not realize his own limitations yet feels (because of his own particular localized expertise) capable and worthy of governing others.

> *The* [intellectually hermetic] *finds himself already with a stock of ideas. He decides to content himself with them and to consider himself intellectually complete.* **As he feels the lack of nothing outside himself, he settles down definitely amid his mental furniture.** *Such is the mechanism of self-obliteration. . . . The innate hermetism of his soul is an obstacle to the necessary condition for his discovery of his insufficiency, namely, a comparison of himself with other beings. To compare himself would mean to go out of himself for a moment and to transfer himself to his neighbor. But the mediocre soul is incapable of transmigrations — the supreme form of sport.*
>
> *We find ourselves, then, met with the same difference that eternally exists between the fool and the man of sense. The latter is constantly catching himself within an inch of being a fool; hence he makes an effort to escape from the imminent folly.* **The fool, on the other hand, does not suspect himself; . . . he is a fool for life.** (p. 69)
>
> *The "ideas" of the average man are not genuine ideas, nor is their possession culture.* **An idea is a putting truth in checkmate. Whoever wishes to have ideas must first prepare himself to desire truth and to accept the rules of the game imposed by it.** *It is no use speaking of ideas*

when there is no acceptance of a higher authority [of logic] *to regulate them, a series of standards to which it is possible to appeal a discussion.*

. . . The average man finds himself with "ideas" in his head, but he lacks the faculty of ideation. He has no conception even of the rare atmosphere in which ideas live. He wishes to have opinions, but is unwilling to accept the conditions and presuppositions that underlie all opinion. Hence his ideas are in effect nothing more than appetites in words, something like musical romanzas. (pp. 71-73)

The Earth is degenerating today.   Bribery and corruption abound.   Children no longer obey their parents, every man wants to write a book, and it is evident that the end of the world is fast approaching.
— Assyrian tablet, c. 2800 BC

Since he feels himself complete in every way, nothing outside him need exist. To posit otherwise confounds him. What makes the Mass Man especially dangerous is his insistence on steamrolling over everything that is not "mass" or common.

In his essay, The Empire of the Ugly, the great Belgian Sinologist and literary essayist Simon Leys recounts the story of how, writing one day in a café, a small incident gave him an insight into the real nature of philistinism.

A radio was playing in the background, a mixture of banal and miscellaneous chatter and equally banal popular music. No one in the café paid any attention to this stream of tepid drivel until suddenly, unexpectedly and inexplicably, the first bars of Mozart's clarinet quintet were played.

"Mozart," Leys says, "took possession of our little space with a serene authority, transforming the café into an antechamber of Paradise."

The other people in the café, who until then were chatting, playing cards, or reading the newspaper, were not deaf to the radio after all. The music silenced them, they looked at each other, disconcerted. "Their disarray lasted only a few seconds: to the relief of all, one of them stood up, changed the radio station and re-established the flow of noise that was more familiar and comforting, which everyone could then properly ignore."

*At that moment, I was struck by an obvious fact that has never left me since: that the real philistines are not those people incapable of recognizing beauty — they recognize it only too well, with a flair as infallible as that of the subtlest aesthete, **but only to pounce on it, and smother it before it can take root in their universal empire of ugliness.***
— www.newcriterion.com/articles.cfm/at-the-forests-edge-3780

One of the strange things about our world is that people who take positions that are inconsistent and arbitrary are considered normal while people who act according to logical principles are considered extremists. *Were it the other way around, there'd be no reason for surprise, no tension. Some people always do and believe weird things. Strangeness in individuals is easily ignored and doesn't cause much trouble. When these odd ticks and delusions are institutionalized in the state, it's a different story.*

For those predisposed to thinking carefully, the logic of liberty is inescapable. From the principle of self-ownership springs forth a self-consistent system of ethics, one that most people intuitively understand. In practice, liberty seems to have a short life. Wherever liberty has once flourished, it has evolved into soft totalitarianism. Iceland, England, and America quickly come to mind.

Many libertarians believe the problem is with education. They suppose that if more people learned the logic, a libertarian society would inevitably emerge. I disagree. The conditions that give rise to liberty are simple: begin with a low population density of people who demand to be left alone. No theory required.

America was a one-chance-only experiment in that light. Here, you had self-selected misfits from Europe who didn't trust authority and didn't accept anyone's fooling around in their business. Incidentally, they were mostly dirt farmers who didn't produce enough to support a big government, so they had a small one instead.

It worked for a while, but sure enough, the people had big families, so did their kids, and in a few generations the conditions for liberty were lost. The country didn't have a low population density anymore, nor did it have the same independent go-it-alone streak.

> *It was bound to happen just as a reversion to the mean. Being a libertarian isn't so much a choice as it is a low-rate inborn personality type.*
> — Will Groves, "Eagerly Awaiting Creative Destruction"
>   www.strike-the-root.com/82/groves/groves1.html

the Remnant

As the word masses is commonly used, it suggests agglomerations of poor and underprivileged people, labouring people, proletarians, and it means nothing like that; it means simply the majority. The mass-man is one who has neither the force of intellect to apprehend the principles issuing in what we know as the humane life, nor the force of character to adhere to those principles steadily and strictly as laws of conduct; and because such people make up the great and overwhelming majority of mankind, they are called collectively the masses. **The line of differentiation between the masses and the Remnant is set invariably by quality, not by circumstance.** *The Remnant are those who by force of intellect are able to apprehend these principles, and by force of character are able, at least measurably, to cleave to them.* **The masses are those who are unable to do either.**

> — Albert Jay Nock, "Isaiah's Job" (1936)
>   www.lewrockwell.com/tucker/tucker23.html

. . . the select man, the excellent man is urged, by interior necessity, to appeal from himself to some standard beyond himself, superior to himself, whose service he freely accepts. Let us recall that at the start we distinguished the excellent man from the common man by saying that the former is the one who makes great demands on himself, and the latter the one who makes no demands on himself, but contents himself with what he is, and is delighted with himself. Contrary to what is usually thought, it is the man of excellence, and not the common man who lives in essential servitude. Life has no savior for him unless he makes it consist in service to something transcendental. Hence he does not look upon the necessity of serving as an oppression.

When, by chance, such necessity is lacking, he grows restless and invents some new standard, more difficult, more exigent, with which to coerce himself. **This is life lived as a discipline — the noble life. Nobility is defined by the demands it makes on us — by obligations, not by rights.**

"To live as one likes is plebeian; the noble man aspires to order and law" (Goethe). The privileges of nobility are not in their origin concessions or favours; on the contrary, they are conquests. And their maintenance supposes, in principle, that the [self-]privileged individual is capable of reconquering them, at any moment, if it were necessary, and anyone were to dispute them. Private rights or privileges are not, then, passive [or hereditary] possession and mere enjoyment, but they represent the standard attained by personal effort. On the other hand, common rights, such as those "of the man and the citizen," are passive property, pure usufruct and benefit, the generous gift of fate which every man finds before him, and which answers to no effort whatever, unless it be that of breathing and avoiding insanity. I would say, then, that an impersonal right is held, a personal right is upheld. (pp. 63-64)

For me, then, nobility is synonymous with a life of effort, ever set on excelling oneself, in passing beyond what one is to what one sets up as a duty and an obligation. In this way the noble life stands opposed to the common or inert life, which reclines statically upon itself, condemned to perpetual immobility, unless an external force compels it to come out of itself. **Hence we apply the term mass to this kind of man — not so much because of his multitude as because of his inertia.** (p. 65)

. . . it is illusory to imagine that the mass-man of today, however superior his vital life may be compared with that of other [historic] times, will be able to control, by himself, the process of civilization. I say process, and not progress. The simple process of preserving our present [Western] civilization is supremely complex, and demands incalculably subtle powers. Ill-fitted to direct it is this average man who has learned to use much of the machinery of civilization, but who is characterized by root-ignorance of the very principles of that civilization. (Gasset, op cit., p. 67)

I *do* see a revival in all this, however. A few million Americans are ceasing to have done for them, and are beginning to do for themselves — thus enlarging themselves. They are protecting themselves by the daily carrying of arms, they are educating their own children in the homes they built with their own hands, fed by the gardens of their own cultivation. They are even generating their own electricity. Basically, they are taking the reins of their own civilizations and living increasingly noble lives as defined by Ortega y Gasset.

Listen friends, if peasants can deconstruct steel mills, torch singers can revolutionize admissions at high-tech colleges, junior high dropouts get 100 miles to the gallon, beach-bum surfers can map the human genome, tiny women can blast through the male monopoly of big-time auto racing, dyslexic fish peddlers can establish global merchandising empires, and lap dancers can win Oscars for script-writing, some virtually important piece is missing in the conventional way schools treat learning and accomplishment.

— John Taylor Gatto, *Weapons of Mass Instruction*, p. 39

*If a prophet were not too particular about making money out of his mission or getting a dubious sort of notoriety out of it, the foregoing considerations would lead one to say that serving the Remnant looks like a good job. An assignment that you can really put your back into, and do your best without thinking about results, is a real job; whereas serving the masses is at best only half a job, considering the inexorable conditions that the masses impose upon their servants. They ask you to give them what they want, they insist upon it, and will take nothing else; and following their whims, their irrational changes of fancy, their hot and cold fits, is a tedious business, to say nothing of the fact that what they want at any time makes very little call on one's resources of prophesy. The Remnant, on the other hand, want only the best you have, whatever that may be. Give them that, and they are satisfied; you have nothing more to worry about. The prophet of the American masses must aim consciously at the lowest common denominator of intellect, taste and character among [300,000,000] people; and this is a distressing task. The prophet of the Remnant, on the contrary, is in the enviable position of Papa Haydn in the household of Prince Esterhazy. All Haydn had to do was keep forking out the very best music he knew how to produce, **knowing it would be understood and appreciated by those for whom he produced it, and caring not a button what anyone else thought of it; and that makes a good job.***

— Alfred Jay Nock, *Isaiah's Job* (1936)

www.lewrockwell.com/tucker/tucker23.html

COMPARING EXTREMES

"We're so sane, we're insane."

A very good friend made this comment during a discussion of our national predicament. This was one of the most cogent descriptions of the Remnant I've ever heard.

To elaborate, insanity is a functional disassociation with reality. Conversely, sanity means a firm, clear grasp on how things truly are. However, what's really going on is so sneaky and covert, it bears little semblance to what I term the "public reality." To the Masses, the Remnant have little hold on ("public") reality and we are "delusional, paranoid and militant." We're *so* sane that we're *insane*. A liberal democrat reading my books would conclude that I'm quite nuts.

As William Allen White put it, *"There is no insanity so devastating in man's life as utter sanity."* Utter sanity recognizes the utter *insanity* of this world. Our political systems are driven by fear, ignorance, and power lust. But . . .

> We go by the major vote, and if the majority is insane, the sane must go to the hospital.
> — Horace Mann

Clear thinking and hardy personal responsibility will always be outnumbered by the brute beasts of humanity. America had a miraculous window of opportunity for its birth. Those conditions for independence and growth no longer exist.

> One of the best ways to get yourself a reputation as a dangerous citizen these days is to go about repeating the very phrases which our founding fathers used in the great struggle for independence.
> — Charles A. Beard

Thus, the necessity for this book. If the national soil is no longer fertile ground for liberty, dignity and honest success, then we must quietly and quickly create our own "gardens."

> And the rulers knew not whither I went, or what I did . . .
> — Nehemiah 2:16

Although the Remnant:Masses continuum is nearly a dichotomy, I will sharpen the edges as much as possible to illustrate how little they can have in common — at all levels.

the *über*-Remnant

home-birthed children, with
>   no post-partal vaccinations
>   no automatic SSN issued, and
>   raised in the country as they are
>   home- or privately-educated, auto-didactic

dwell in a chemical-free healthy house (straw bale, log home)
create own energy (solar, wind, and micro-hydro)
grow/eat own organic/heirloom seed vegetables
take homeopathic herbs, supplements, and remedies
raise unregistered and hormone-free livestock
hunt own wild game meat without a license
eat for nutrition, not for entertainment
absorb no TV or corporate media
enjoy solitude for thinking and reflection
savor the incomparable joys of reading
have comparatively little interest in professional spectator sports
have a very pronounced individualist streak, not identifying with any herd
own and daily carry unregistered personal firearms
avoid and resist petty bureaucratic intrusions
rarely accept authority at face value — challenge the "givens"
comprehend the message of "The Matrix"
understand the real jurisdiction of "income" tax (www.losthorizons.com)
do not automatically obey grandstanding regulations
operate lucrative small businesses on a cash-basis
barter whenever possible
shop at used book & thrift stores; will wear a $1 shirt without shame
own and trade gold and silver bullion
if internet-capable, they are very sophisticated about privacy measures
use Mac or Linux
locally network with like-minded and prepared families
constantly expanding and deepening their skillsets
are prepared for times of social unrest, famine, disaster, and martial law

Their "fellow Americans", however, seem more like from another country on a distant continent:

the *über*-Masses

born/vaccinated in a hospital laboratory
given their SSN "slave number" at birth
raised in the city, disconnected from the countryside and nature
schooled in the Pavlovian public academies of mass-compliance
incarcerate themselves in chemically-pestilent pre-fab boxes
are completely dependent on a vulnerable power grid
subsist solely on genetically engineered sterile kilo-caloric "food"
run to the nearest pharmacy for their corporate drugs
know absolutely nothing about raising/slaughtering livestock
could not hunt wild game to save their lives
eat for social entertainment, and know nothing of nutrition
spend 20 hours/week in corporate programming and social conditioning
being alone very quickly causes acute anxiety
rarely read, and if so only gossip magazines and fluff novels
are rabidly enthusiastic about "their" sports team from distant cities
are extremely uncomfortable outside a group setting
are frightened by firearms, and the responsibility of self-defense
view bureaucracy as a social good, though mewling about its inefficiency
accept authority without question — "*the law's the law!*"
see *The Matrix* as an excellent action movie — "*What 'message'?*"
devoutly believe in "paying their taxes" and despise those who do not
work as corporate cogs (the notion of entrepreneurship is terrifying)
have no bartering skills, much less desirable products or services
pay full retail because they "deserve the best"
would spend silver quarters at the car wash
care not a whit about internet privacy as they've "nothing to hide"
Windows all the way — "*What's all the Microsoft hate about?*"
don't know their neighbors even two houses down the street
haven't learned anything new since high school or college
have no stocks of food, water, medical supplies, or fuel
totally dependent on FEMA

different people — different roads

The difference of their roads are polar opposites:

Masses	well lit	wide	downhill	popular	balloon payment
Remnant	dim	narrow	uphill	solo	cover charge

The beautifully smooth six-lane Mass highway leads to constrained options, torpor, general dependency (in putative exchange for some vague thing called "security") — and the *pit*.

The Remnant path is tangly, but leads to personal discovery and freedom, lifelong fulfillment — and the *peak*.

The Masses have little critical thinking skills, and are unable to instantly spot and jeer at obvious fallacies, such as:

> women included in SSN database for deadbeat *dads*
> TSA mixing dangerous shampoo, etc. in a *common* trash bin
> TSA watchlist admitting to lack of confidence in airport security

What makes these two roads so interesting is that both can often be seen from each other, by their respective travelers. Some Remnant folk were born misplaced in the Masses (but found their way out), so they can understand the lure of the wide and sunny highway. Remnant folk don't stare at the Masses, and rarely ever wave. They are too focused on negotiating their own way.

The Masses, however, see glimpses of the Remnant path, and it causes them unquenchable anxiety. Why would anybody be on *another* road? Why *is* there another road? Where does it *lead?* Alternate routes disturb the Masses because they are reminded of that incomprehensible Remnant — reminded that some people are *not* Masses. They have a vague envy of the Remnant, but cannot articulate why. Their way already made for them, the Masses have plenty of time to stare (through their bus windows), if not jeer. When an opportunity comes to thwart the Remnant, they will usually exploit it as the Remnant somehow deserve it solely because they are so indescribably different. To be different from the Masses betokens some form of superiority, and this offends their proletarian nature.

While the Remnant only want to be left alone in peace and are happy to "live and let live", the Masses are offended by anything not of themselves. **The Masses will not leave the Remnant in peace.** It is the Masses who bleat the *"if you've nothing to hide"* excuse for every intrusion upon private life. The Masses *have* no private life — the very concept is alien to them. Introspection and dignity are unknown. TV, music, and sports are their "culture". There is no real Self, no solitude. Their lives are all about mutual approval through a relentless and intricate self-regulating paradigm — driven by the eternal question of *"What would the others think?"*

Where can privacy exist in that? All must be known to the herd for the black sheep to be identified and expelled. All must be known to the herd so that the herd is reassured of itself. This is antithetical at its core to the very notion of personal privacy, and it explains why a very large portion of Americans "*have nothing to hide*" and are wary of and antagonistic to anybody who insists on privacy (a mild form of sneakiness).

When the Remnant object to surveillance cameras, interlinked databases, and airport "*Take Shampoo Away*" silliness, the Masses genuinely cannot understand what the fuss is about. For the safety of the herd, the sheepdog must not be tethered! That sheepdogs historically morph into Morlock wolves is lost on the Eloi Masses — as if the "security" they believe they enjoy was worth it, anyway.

> *If we raise kids with no expectation of privacy, then they're going to become adults and voters and people of influence in society with no expectation of privacy. All the expectations of privacy are going to be eroded by the population of adults who grew up with no privacy and don't see the problem with trading away privacy.*
> — Alex Koroknay-Palicz, executive director of the National Youth Rights Association
> http://newstandardnews.net/content/index.cfm/items/3886

Remember those Top Six Reasons why individuals want to preserve their privacy?

- ❻ **high-pressure salesmen and "legal fraud"**
- ❺ **the increasing threat of burglary and violent crime**
- ❹ **divorce, family disputes, and lawsuits**
- ❸ **gossip and false information**
- ❷ **political, religious, and racial persecution**
- ❶ **oppressive government, high taxes, and war**

All of them are examples of people trying to be left alone from the Masses. I say this with certainty because amongst the Remnant you are exceedingly unlikely to find:

> a telemarketer
> a violent criminal
> the litigious
> a maligner of good character
> a bigot persecutor
> a taxman

I discuss all this so that you understand the tectonic force that society uses against personal privacy. The overriding desire of the Masses is to feel "safe". Safe from crime, safe from hunger, safe from unemployment, safe from terrorists, and safe from being expelled from the herd and suddenly required to do their *own* thinking. They will readily sacrifice all privacy (including yours) to achieve that feeling of "safety".

The Matrix is a system, Neo. That system is our enemy. But when you're inside, you look around. What do you see? Businessmen, teachers, lawyers, carpenters. The very minds of the people we are trying to save. But until we do, these people are still a part of that system, and that makes them our enemy. You have to understand, most of these people are not ready to be unplugged. And many of them are so inert, so hopelessly dependent on the system that they will fight to protect it.
  — from *The Matrix*

It would be so easy for an oppressor to dominate a population accustomed to being watched and controlled by RFID tags and readers in their homes, schools, stores, and workplaces. A people docile enough to allow their medicine cabinets, refrigerators, cash registers, retail shelves, food, guns, passports, mail, work uniforms, car tires, roads, taxis, and subways to be tagged and monitored by authorities would be easy pickings for a tyrant. **If a people can't even fight back against snoopy marketers and their own elected representatives, how would they fare against an armed and aggressive enemy?**
  That's the problem with power, and why total government omniscience is a bad idea. No matter how much you trust the government, giving it unchecked ability to observe and control your life is like putting a noose around your neck and hoping the guy on the other end never pulls the rope. (p. 212)
  — Spychips

In case you've been asleep in a salt mine since 1968 — the world has gone *nuts*. While you can't change that, you can at least carve out a peaceful oasis for yourself and your family. I see no compelling reason why *any* individual should have his domicile vulnerable to strangers or officials.

Go private, folks — while you *can*. Yeah, all this sounds "alarmist", but don't scoff at the notion of volcanos just because lava isn't running all over your feet right now. Go *private*. You can always revert if it turns out that I was horribly mistaken. I may be wrong, but I don't think that this force can any longer be fought and won on a national scale. Any inroads made there will evaporate after the next disaster or emergency or attack. Do not confront, but learn to mask yourself and circumvent.

stealth Remnant

What chiefly makes it so, I think, is that in any given society the Remnant are always so largely an unknown quantity. You do not know, and will never know, more than two things about them. You can be sure of those — dead sure, as our phrase is — but you will never be able to make even a respectable guess at anything else. You do not know, and will never know, who the Remnant are, nor what they are doing or will do. Two things you do know, and no more: First, that they exist; second, that they will find you. (Nock, op. cit.)

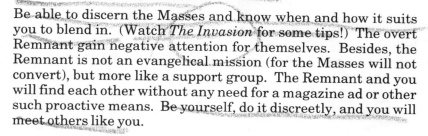

Be able to discern the Masses and know when and how it suits you to blend in. (Watch *The Invasion* for some tips!) The overt Remnant gain negative attention for themselves. Besides, the Remnant is not an evangelical mission (for the Masses will not convert), but more like a support group. The Remnant and you will find each other without any need for a magazine ad or other such proactive means. Be yourself, do it discreetly, and you will meet others like you.

CAN WE EVER BE FREE?

*It will soon be possible to assert almost continuous control over every citizen and to maintain up-to-date files containing even the most personal details about health and personal behavior of every citizen, in addition to the more customary data. These files will be subject to instantaneous retrieval by the authorities. **Power will gravitate into the hands of those who control information.***

— Zbigniew Brzeziński, *Between Two Ages: America's Role in the Technotronic Era* (1970)

Our answer is not to personally and directly confront the Orwellian state. **Rather, you must learn how to *circumvent* it at all levels.** Seek out fellow circumventers.

Don't fight the system: replace it.   www.socialviability.com

The Remnant is all around you. Probably 1:150 these days are Remnant, active or latent. That's about 2,000,000. Remnant Americans must create and energize a parallel system that is not at the mercy and surveillance of the omnipotent State. Two million Remnant Americans are plenty to design and form parallel systems for themselves. (Less than 2,000,000 people populate Montana and Wyoming, if you get my drift.)

Those of you who already own sufficient guns and ammo needn't despair too much about the coming anti-gun measures. This was never totally about guns. It's about being able to live a free and productive life, unbeholden to evil masters. To survive over the long haul, you must envision some other necessities — which will probably point to a change in lifestyle.

The 21st Century will become more computerized, more regulated, and much more draconian. Think about all the leverage that exists over you today. Must you sing a government's or corporation's employment tune, or have you created your own business? Can you be starved or frozen into submission, or can you keep yourself warm and fed regardless of your dissent?

> *Who controls the food supply controls the people; who controls the energy can control whole continents; who controls money can control the world.*
> — Henry Kissinger

Have you a life for yourself which makes what government does practically irrelevant? Do you control your own food, energy, and money? (Home-schoolers with a family business on a rural farm suffer nearly zero leverage. Think about that.)

Self-sufficiency = independence. Not that you *have* to be self-sufficient, but because you *can* be. You have *options*.

> *How to overthrow the system: brew your own beer; kick in your Tee Vee; kill your own beef; build your own cabin and piss off the front porch whenever you bloody well feel like it.*
> — Edward Abbey

Begin now setting things up for yourself, and do it quietly (to avoid future envy from those who didn't prepare).

Unless you plan to grow your own food (or buy from those who reliably self-farm with heirloom seeds), you are vulnerable.

Unless you already generate your own energy, start looking into that now.

Unless you already have several unrelated streams of income (some of them in cash), get cracking, now.

As I said in one of my earlier columns, we are astoundingly vulnerable in this country because we've lost much of the knowledge and skills of our forefathers, the wisdom mankind has honed since the dawn of civilization. We have lost that wisdom in only two or three short generations due to the ease of modern technology. But here's the thing: Technology, if it's gone, doesn't put food on the table. Garden seeds and know-how do.

Girls used to learn cheese making at their mothers' elbows. Boys used to learn carpentry at their fathers' knees. Now we can barely unclog a toilet by ourselves, much less know the proper way to build an outhouse, grow a garden, or butcher a steer.

I'm not saying our culture will backslide to the days where everyone had a cow and an outhouse. I'm saying things are going to be tough economically for a long time, and having food and other necessities stored up is a good thing. I'm saying that blindly putting your trust in a governmental bureaucracy to feed, clothe and house you is stupid. The government cannot do anything with efficiency, certainly not at the individual level. Try asking the government for a tube of toothpaste next time you run out and see what happens.

Your ability to prepare for a depression is clearly dependent on where you live (it's hard to keep a cow in a high-rise apartment) and your income status (it's hard to buy a year's worth of food when you're unemployed). But for cryin' out loud, do something. Anything. If you can't stockpile goods, then stockpile knowledge. Learn a useful, barterable skill such as sewing, carpentry, welding, or canning. Don't become a burden on the rest of us because you're in denial.

Whatever your views on the cause of our current economy, and whatever your views on what is needed to pull us out, remember this: In the end, the only thing you can

depend upon is YOU. You're the only who can tighten your belt, buy seeds, stockpile food, plug those financial leaks — whatever it takes. But don't bury your head in the sand and think that hard times can't hit you personally, because they can. **It's time to stop thinking ideologically and start thinking practically.**   (BTP Note: Hear that, Libertarians?)
      Prepare as best you can so you too don't have to be so depressed when the depression hits.
— Patrice Lewis
      www.worldnetdaily.com/index.php?fa=PAGE.view&pageId=91644

Go through The Capability Checklist Project (*"To be prepared as best as possible, allowing for individual solutions while accomplishing common goals."*). www.alpharubicon.com/~kwll/

Remember, if the Government has ample material leverage over you, does it really *matter* if your politics are libertarian?   What are *laissez-faire* politics if you cannot live apart from and without the oppressive state?   **A right-thinking man — with puppet strings attached — cannot be a right-*doing* man.** Regardless of his thoughts and beliefs, he remains a puppet. It would be kinder if he were ignorant of his status, for nothing is more frustrating than to know what is right but be prohibited from doing it. Resolve yourself not to learn the Truth if you are not committed to acting upon the Truth, whatever the cost.

To desire freedom is an instinct.   To secure it requires intelligence. It must be comprehended and self-asserted. To petition for it is to stultify oneself, for a petitioner is a confessed subject and lacks the spirit of a freeman. To rail and rant against tyranny is to manifest inferiority, for there is no tyranny but ignorance; to be conscious of one's powers is to lose consciousness of tyranny. Self government is not a remote aim. It is an intimate and inescapable fact. To govern oneself is a natural imperative, and all tyranny is the miscarriage of self-government. ***The first requisite of freedom is to accept responsibility for the lack of it.***
— E.C. Riegel, 1949

where are the Remnant in all this?

If my earlier case of the future dissenter seemed too far fetched, then let's instead view a middle case, *i.e.*, that of the

Remnant opt-out. There will be millions of them, initially. They will not readily dissent, but merely wish to be left alone by the modern regulatory police state. They have very little in common with the general population, for virtue of their vastly different beliefs, culture, and lifestyle.

Compared to the urbanite, TV-mesmerized hordes, rural American Remnant opt-outs and hiders are astonishingly healthy, free-thinking, independent-minded, defensive capable, and highly resistant to outside control. They would be the natural backbone of any civil war for liberty. Do you honestly believe that such a potentially fierce class of Americans (however naturally nonaggressive, rural, and isolated) will be left alone in peace?

Absolutely not. By the Government's reckoning, what is not under their control is "out of control." This is paranoia at the systemic level.

How *could* the opt-outs be left alone and in peace to live their own lives?

Their mere existence is a threat to government because not only do they not need government, they are invulnerable to government leverage (unlike the urbanite).

Pavlov made another significant discovery [I am again quoting from The Rape of the Mind by Joost A.M. Meerloo, M.D.: Pavlov was a researcher in Imperial Russia who survived well into Soviet Russia and was used by the gangster hierarchy because of his studies in physiology and psychology, mostly on dogs. It gave them the tools for brainwashing].

"The conditioned reflex could be developed most easily in a quiet laboratory with a minimum of disturbing stimuli. Every trainer of animals knows this from his own experience; isolation and the patient repetition of stimuli are required to tame wild animals. Pavlov formulated his findings into a general rule in which the speed of learning is positively correlated with quiet and isolation. The totalitarians have followed this rule and know that they can condition their political victims most quickly if they are kept in isolation. In the totalitarian technique of thought control, the same isolation applied to the individual is applied also to groups of people. This is the reason the civilian populations of totalitarian

countries are not permitted to travel freely and are kept away from mental and political contamination."

That is the reason, too, for the solitary confinement cell and prison camp; and what of the neighborhoods where people are afraid of each other, where every one is a stool pigeon? Do you think that the 800 numbers about child abuse, elder abuse, environmental abuse, are to protect the public? I propose to you that they are designed to create a state of isolation where no one trusts anyone else. The bounty given to the stool-pigeon in all of these schemes make us all afraid, isolated and, as Meerloo pointed out, better subjects for menticide.

As he states, Pavlovian strategy in the totalitarian sense means imprinting prescribed reflexes on a mind that has been broken down.

— "Dignity", by Dr. Thomas Dorman
www.dormanpub.com/articles/PDFs/FFF_March_2000.pdf

Watch the YouTube 1970s interviews of Yuri Bezmenov, a defected Soviet KGB man who worked to subvert the West.

Speaking of Communists subverting the West, meet Markus Wolfe, the former #2 man of East Germany's *Stasi*.

QUESTION: Do you have anything on the visa situation of Mr. Wolfe, of the former East Germany?

MR. BURNS: You know, I think I do have something on that, George, and I'm glad you raised that question. Yes. We're talking about Markus Wolfe, the former head of Stasi, right? The East German police.

Well, he was refused a visa, as my records show, in 1996. He was deemed to be ineligible for an American visa under Section 212(a)(3)(b) of the Immigration and Nationality Act. This section states that aliens who have engaged in terrorist activities are not eligible for visas to travel to the United States. It covers several types of terrorist activities, including preparing and planning terrorist activities, providing material support to those who have committed or plan to commit terrorist acts.

He was the deputy minister of state security for East Germany. He was the head of the ministry's foreign espionage branch. He actively aided and abetted and fostered international and state-supported terrorism when he was an East German government official.

As the number 2 person in Stasi and the head of the espionage branch, he was absolutely in the decision-making channel. There's no question about that.

By his own admission, he participated in determining the ministry's policy and goals and he's, therefore, ineligible.

We, in the State Department, do not believe it is appropriate to give him a waiver from Section 212(a)(3)(b) because we think it is inadvisable for someone who spent his entire career as an opponent of free German, West Germany, as an opponent of the German people, and someone who is anti-American and trying to bring down our government and sponsor terrorist attacks against us, why would we give him a visa?

So, he is not coming to the United States. He can write his best-selling books, but he won't be able to enjoy the United States throughout the rest of his life if we have anything to do with it.

— Excerpt from the 1997 U.S. Department of State Daily Press Briefing #87, 97-06-09

My point? That Markus Wolfe was hired in 2004 as a consultant to . . . **the Department of Homeland Security.** Can "our" government's intentions be more plain than that? Watch *The Lives of Others* to understand what this betokens. Next, they'll be hiring former KGB generals — *ooops!* — they already did so with Yevgeni Primakov.

The underclass of *über*-self-reliant opt-outs will be pestered by a myriad of regs: local zoning, building codes, truancy, USDA, FDA, National Service, etc. Even the Amish are now being harassed to implant their livestock with an NAIS ID chip. It will continue to be a typical bullies-in-the-playground scenario . . . until Americans have had enough and start punching in some sneering bully faces. Then — and only then — will this disgusting trend of totalitarianism get stopped in its tracks.

Shoot, move, communicate. That is what the government strives to deny us. To shoot unregistered guns. To move in untracked cars. To communicate through foreign proxy tunnels with Zfone-encrypted VoIP.

SOME FINAL ADVICE

establish your own cash-oriented business

This not only directly enhances your privacy, but you will avoid the forthcoming "citizen workers' national I.D. card" to be demanded of all *"employees."* Entrepreneurs will (for a while) escape such a Nazi/Soviet measure. As more and more people use digital gold, a private, parallel economy will emerge. All freedom-loving individuals simply must be a part of it.

stock a self-sufficient RV and set it up in the country

Americans have emasculated themselves because of their wealth — they don't want to "make waves" for fear of losing their stuff. A partial solution: geographically diversify your things. Don't have everything on the line at one public address. Material wealth is a *means*, not an end. Don't let the tail wag the dog. Don't sell your excess items at garage sales for pennies. Put the old TV, kitchen stuff, clothes, etc. in your country RV.

create your escape line far in advance

Think of it as insurance. If you must someday ditch everything, you should have already blazed the trail ahead of you. You'll need cash, gold/silver coins, guns, camping gear, spare ID, clothes, vehicles, safe houses and friends, prearranged meeting points and fall-back plans, and practice drills for the family.

While you might get away with a bit of laziness or carelessness with the *first* layer of privacy — take utterly no chances with the escape line and second layer. Be especially sure not to create any "triggers" with your phone and credit card records. Keep your mouth shut — don't brag or hint around. If they ever come for you, *your house and things are gone already*. You *won't* be able to hold back the focused resources of the U.S. Government.

adopt a more basic and private life in the country

Actually, wealth is more properly measured by that which we can do *without* — not by the things we have. Wealth is in *being* and *knowing* — not in having. Move to the country if you can. The people are better, the environment is healthier and you'll rediscover your family. A VoIP number and mail drop will accomplish the same for you in the country as it does in NYC.

✓ drop your excess "friends" and acquaintances

Write down a list of your "friends" and decide who would risk their lives and property for you. Who would stand by you in some smear campaign or punitive legal action? Who would hide you in their home if you ever became a fugitive from injustice? Who can be trusted to keep their mouth shut? Who is solid and dependable, not flighty or nervous?

✓ Check off your *quality* people and quietly drop the rest. You must quickly lower your social vulnerability.

get your guns, gold and groceries — *now!*

These staples have no substitute. Without them, you must become utterly dependent on and submissive to the Corporate International Socialists for your existence.

✓ have the *training* and the *courage* to defend yourself

Unless you've been to a *quality* defensive shooting school, you really have no idea what you *don't* know about using a gun to protect yourself. There is simply no substitute for having the best training doctrine ingrained in your muscle memory. During a lethal confrontation, you will not be able to *reliably* present your weapon and neutralize the threat — unless you have been *trained* to do so. **If you have not trained, you've in effect trained yourself to do *nothing*.** And *nothing* is exactly what you'll do, even if you've got the best gear and weapons. Get *serious*. Sell some superfluous guns; you can only shoot one at a time, and you need the training more. Such training will be soon restricted as *"terrorist"* or *"paramilitary."* This may be your last year to go. Study *Boston's Gun Bible*.

support freedom-fighting organizations — *today!*

Join the GOA (www.gunowners.org) and CASPIAN to get on their email alert. We may not be able to turn this mess around, but we can certainly slow it down and increase our size.

do you know your neighbors?

This totalitarianism doesn't fly in daily from Washington, D.C. The enforcers are local. They are your neighbors. These tentacles of control live in your town, city, and county. They go to the same supermarket as you do. They get new steel-belted radials at the your tire shop. They golf at the same country club. They eat at your favorite restaurant They probably know of you (the noisy dissenter), but you likely don't know of *them.* They seem just like anybody else. But, they're not like anybody else. They get their paycheck by day controlling and harassing peaceable Americans who just want to live without the crushing burden of taxes and regulations. Then, they go home at night to their families — right down the street from you — and never lose a wink's sleep over their careers. As Pogo said:

We have met the enemy, and the enemy is us.

Why do good Americans allow these brazen slobs of tyranny to materialize from *Nacht und Nebel* like omnipotent ghosts? Why don't you know as much about them as they know about you? They go to work at an office building just like you — why has nobody followed them home? Why has nobody compiled photo dossiers of their own local enforcers? Why are you more worried about them than they are worried about you?

throw an utter *fit* over any biometric national I.D. plan

This scheme is *the* prerequisite to the final tyranny. We must defeat this "on the beaches" and not allow a bridgehead for the following invasion. Don't be polite with Congress — get angry! It will be our last chance to fight *politically.* If we lose that, politics will finally become totally irrelevant.

National self-defense against rulers-gone-amok begins with a simple but firm consensus to *not take anymore.* This stage seems near on the horizon. If it arrives, it will be clear to the clear-headed.

AUDACES FORTUNA IUVAT DOMARI NOLO

You cannot conquer a free man — you can only kill him.

In a word, let us be *resolved.*